Reflections on the Rise and Fall
of the Ancient Republicks

Edward Wortley Montagu

THE THOMAS HOLLIS LIBRARY
David Womersley, General Editor

Reflections on the Rise and Fall of the Ancient Republicks

Adapted to the Present State of Great Britain

Edward Wortley Montagu

Edited and with an Introduction
by David Womersley

LIBERTY FUND
Indianapolis

This book is published by Liberty Fund, Inc., a foundation established to encourage study of the ideal of a society of free and responsible individuals.

𒂼𒄄

The cuneiform inscription that serves as our logo and as the design motif for our endpapers is the earliest-known written appearance of the word "freedom" (*amagi*), or "liberty." It is taken from a clay document written about 2300 B.C. in the Sumerian city-state of Lagash.

Introduction, editorial additions, and index
© 2015 by Liberty Fund, Inc.

Frontispiece: Portrait of Edward Wortley Montagu by Matthew William Peters, oil on canvas, 1775. © National Portrait Gallery, London.

Printed in the United States of America

15 16 17 18 19 C 5 4 3 2 1
15 16 17 18 19 P 5 4 3 2 1

Library of Congress Cataloging-in-Publication Data
Montagu, Edward Wortley, 1713–1776.
Reflections on the rise and fall of the ancient republicks: adapted to the present state of Great Britain / Edward Wortley Montagu; edited and with an Introduction by David Womersley.
pages   cm.—(Thomas Hollis Library)
Includes bibliographical references and index.
ISBN 978-0-86597-871-3 (hardcover: alk. paper)—
ISBN 978-0-86597-872-0 (pbk.: alk. paper)
1. Republics.   2. History, Ancient—Philosophy.   I. Title.
JC51.M74 2015
321.8′6—dc23   2014036692

LIBERTY FUND, INC.
8335 Allison Pointe Trail, Suite 300
Indianapolis, Indiana 46250-1684

CONTENTS

THE THOMAS HOLLIS LIBRARY

Thomas Hollis (1720–74) was an eighteenth-century Englishman who devoted his energies, his fortune, and his life to the cause of liberty. Hollis was trained for a business career, but a series of inheritances allowed him to pursue instead a career of public service. He believed that citizenship demanded activity and that it was incumbent on citizens to put themselves in a position, by reflection and reading, in which they could hold their governments to account. To that end for many years Hollis distributed books that he believed explained the nature of liberty and revealed how liberty might best be defended and promoted.

A particular beneficiary of Hollis's generosity was Harvard College. In the years preceding the Declaration of Independence, Hollis was assiduous in sending to America boxes of books, many of which he had had specially printed and bound, to encourage the colonists in their struggle against Great Britain. At the same time he took pains to explain the colonists' grievances and concerns to his fellow Englishmen.

The Thomas Hollis Library makes freshly available a selection of titles that, because of their intellectual power, or the influence they exerted on the public life of their own time, or the distinctiveness of their approach to the topic of liberty, comprise the cream of the books distributed by Hollis. Many of these works have been either out of print since the eighteenth century or available only in very expensive and scarce editions. The highest standards of scholarship and production ensure that these classic texts can be as salutary and influential today as they were two hundred and fifty years ago.

David Womersley

INTRODUCTION

Edward Wortley Montagu (1713–76) was the son of an exceptionally wealthy father and a celebrated and talented mother. Edward Wortley Montagu senior (1678–1761)—Member of Parliament (MP), diplomat, and man of business—eloped on 23 August 1712 with Lady Mary Pierrepoint (1689–1762), later to achieve fame under her married name of Lady Mary Wortley Montagu as at first the friend and then the foe of Alexander Pope, as a pioneer of inoculation for smallpox, and as an Oriental traveler. Almost nine months to the day after the elopement, on 16 May 1713 Lady Mary gave birth to a son.[1]

After an infancy passed in Constantinople, where his father had been posted as British ambassador, a period of troubled schooling at Westminster, and an imprudent early marriage, Edward Wortley Montagu junior's youth was spent in dissipation, travel, and minor criminality (being, for instance, a known associate of several highwaymen). His early years also included spells as a soldier (when he acquitted himself well enough, being mentioned in dispatches after the battle of Fontenoy on 12 May 1745), as a student of Oriental languages at the University of Leiden, as a bibliophile, and as a diplomat; his command of languages apparently proved useful during the peace negotiations at Aix-la-Chapelle which concluded

1. Grundy, *Lady Mary,* pp. 64–65.

the War of the Austrian Succession. From 1747 until 1761 Montagu led a racketty life in Paris and London, acquiring and discarding wives, mistresses, and illegitimate children. He also served as an MP for first Huntingdonshire and then Bossiney, a constituency in Cornwall controlled by his father. He supplemented his parental allowance by operating as a professional gambler, where he seems not to have been above, if not actual cheating, then certainly entrapment and intimidation.

On the death of his father in 1761 his hopes of inheriting the major part of the vast family estate were disappointed, and he contested the will, which had been drawn up to the advantage of his sister, Lady Bute. Very wealthy herself as a result of her marriage, she was prepared to settle. Furnished by the Butes with cash and an estate, and confirmed as MP for Bossiney (thereby acquiring a useful immunity from imprisonment for debt), Montagu shook "the dust of an ungrateful country" from his feet, and retired to the continent.[2] For the remainder of his life he traveled in Italy and the Levant, pursuing both esoteric scholarly enthusiasms and, on occasion, the wives of other men. He affected Turkish costume and professed to be a Muslim. But in March 1776, a broken bone from an ortolan or beccafico on which Montagu was dining lacerated his throat. An abscess developed, leading to a general infection, and he died in Padua on 29 April 1776. In its mingling of luxury and mishap, touched with a dash of absurdity, the manner of Montagu's death was entirely in keeping with the way he had lived his life.

However, in 1759, and in what seems to have been an attempt to secure the favor of his bookish, political father, Montagu had temporarily laid aside his feckless and dandyish ways. In that year he published *Reflections on the Rise and Fall of the Ancient Republicks*, a work of no little scholarship and some political engagement, which he seems to have begun during the summer of 1756, and which was received by the literary world with polite applause.[3] It was revised and expanded for its second edition

2. J. Curling, *Edward Wortley Montague, 1713–1776: The Man in the Iron Wig* (London: A. Melrose, 1954), p. 161.

3. For extracts from the first reviews, see appendix B, below. For reasoned speculation concerning the beginning of composition, see below, p. 210, n. 43.

the following year, and this revised text was reprinted for an English readership in 1769 and again in 1778. Dark suspicions lingered that the book had in fact been written by Montagu's former tutor, the Rev. John Forster.[4] But setting those rumors to one side, why might Montagu have believed that a book which extracted from the histories of five republics of the ancient world political, military, and economic lessons for mid-eighteenth-century Englishmen would improve his standing in the eyes of his father? The answer to that question must be approached by way of a review of the worsening international situation from the late 1740s, and the early phases of the global conflict in which Britain would thereafter be embroiled with France.

The Political and Military Context

The Peace of Aix-la-Chapelle (1747)—in which, as we saw, Montagu had played a minor diplomatic role—proved to be nothing more than an armed truce. In the early 1750s tensions between the French and English in India began once more to rise as the English East India Company resisted French attempts to establish control over the Carnatic and the Deccan. In the West Indies, England and France squabbled over the "neutral" islands. Most gravely, in America the ambitious French strategy to link their settlements in Canada with Louisiana by means of a series of forts along the Ohio and the Mississippi had led to skirmishes with the English colonists, who were themselves now seeking to break out from the eastern seaboard and acquire additional territory west of the Allegheny Mountains.

The British response to these French provocations was muffled and slow—the consequence of hesitation and a lack of consensus among a political class in transition. But eventually, in October 1754, British regiments under the command of General Braddock set sail for the colonies, and measures for raising troops in America were put in motion. The

---

4. John Forster (d. 1787); for his account of his time spent in the West Indies with Montagu, see the *Public Ledger*, 25 October 1777; reprinted in John Nichols, *Literary Anecdotes of the Eighteenth Century*, 9 vols. (London, 1812–15), vol. 4, pp. 626–29.

outcome was, to begin with, disastrous. In July 1755 Braddock led his troops into a French ambush on the Monongahela and suffered dreadful casualties, from which he himself was not excluded.[5] Public sentiment in Britain was further depressed by the apparent fruitlessness of the naval blockade of Brest which from July to December had been entrusted to Hawke, and which had somehow failed to engage the French fleet under the command of de la Motte. The new year brought fresh reasons for alarm in the form of well-founded fears of a French invasion.[6] The resulting public panic over the state of the nation's defenses prompted Pitt and Townshend to propose a Militia Bill which cleared the Commons in May 1756 but was rejected by the Lords. To fill the gap, mercenary troops were imported from Hanover and Hesse (events to which Montagu would make several references in *Reflections*).[7] The final provocation arrived that same month, with news that (as British ministers since February had feared would happen) French forces had landed in Minorca.

A formal declaration of war with France followed, and although this to some degree cleared the air, it did not herald any immediate improvement in British fortunes. In April a squadron of ten ships under the command of Admiral Byng had been sent to relieve Minorca. Byng was slow to reach the theater of operations, and once there failed to engage the enemy with resolution, instead returning to Gibraltar, leaving the Minorcan garrison to struggle on until it finally surrendered, after a gallant defense, on 28 June 1756. British public opinion was outraged, and a scapegoat was required. Byng was the sole and inevitable candidate. After a court-martial in February 1757 he was shot the following month "*pour encourager les autres*" as Voltaire memorably put it.[8]

However, now the tide of war was beginning to turn in Britain's favor, although as is commonly the case the actual moment of reversal from ebb to flow escaped the attention of most onlookers. In the summer of 1756 the

5. Braddock's last words imply a terrible judgement on his competence: "Who would have thought it?" (Rosebery, *Chatham*, p. 398).

6. See Corbett, *Seven Years' War*, vol. 1, pp. 88–95; Rosebery, *Chatham*, p. 442.

7. See below, p. 90, n. 160; p. 258, n. 16; and p. 261.

8. "To put heart in the others" (*Candide*, ch. 23). For Montagu's allusions to the execution of Byng, see below, p. 94, n. 171; p. 239, n. a; and p. 251, n. 1.

collapse of Newcastle's continental diplomacy and his evident inadequacy as a war leader had led him to make overtures to William Pitt, then the most effective speaker in the Commons, and a man whose Patriot platform was proving popular in the country at large and devastating in the House. Eventually, after several months of maneuvering and false starts, by the summer of 1757 Pitt and Newcastle were working in harness, the latter as First Lord of the Treasury, but the former as the dominant figure in both the Cabinet and the Commons.[9]

The change in the direction of policy and the tone of administration was immediate. The Militia Bill was reintroduced, and finally passed the Lords in June 1757. The German mercenaries were sent home, and two new regiments were raised from the same Highland clans that, a mere twelve years before, had seemed to threaten the very existence of the Hanoverian regime.[10] The American colonists were by turns flattered, encouraged, and cajoled into making greater efforts for their own defense, and for the security and extension of the empire. Frederick the Great, Britain's ally on the continent, was generously supported with money and men; considerable French forces, which might otherwise have made a nuisance of themselves in America, were thus tied up in central Europe. In less than three years the strength of the British navy was increased by fifty-five thousand men and seventy ships, and with it the operational reach of British arms was transformed.

Pitt's strategy, which his extraordinary energy and charismatic personality made feasible, was to exploit Britain's financial advantage over France, and to deploy the manpower so raised to seize the initiative on every front of what he realized was a world war.[11] France was to be

9. On the workings of this ministry, see particularly Richard Middleton, *The Bells of Victory: The Pitt-Newcastle Ministry and the Conduct of the Seven Years' War* (Cambridge: Cambridge University Press, 1985).

10. For Montagu's references to these developments, see below, p. 126, n. 28, and p. 260, n. 24.

11. The British national debt rose from £75,000,000 in 1756 to £133,000,000 in 1763 (Marston, *Seven Years' War*, p. 83). For Walpole's strictures on what he saw as Pitt's financial recklessness, see Walpole, *Memoires*, vol. 2, pp. 346–49. As Lucy Sutherland observed, the Seven Years' War was by far "the most expensive that had ever been fought and imposed heavy strains on the immature fiscal system of the country" (quoted in Pearce, *Pitt*, p. 208).

destroyed as an imperial power, not only in America, but all over the globe. As Johnson observed, "Lord Chatham [as Pitt was to become in 1766] was a Dictator; he possessed the power of putting the State in motion."[12] The fruits of such a strategy inevitably took some time to appear, and the second half of 1757 seemed at first like a continuation of the previous trend of calamity, with the defeat of Frederick the Great at Kolin, the duke of Cumberland's signing of the Convention of Kloster-Zeven which crystallized a temporary French advantage in Germany, the fiasco of failed British raids on the French coast, and the loss of Fort William Henry on Lake George to the accomplished and professional French general Montcalm. The following year, however, was more promising. Frederick enjoyed some spectacular successes on the continent;[13] the navy showed itself to be more effective in disrupting French operations; there were victories in America (including the capture of Louisburg and Fort Duquesne); and a series of well-planned lightning raids on the coast of Brittany and on French settlements in West Africa demonstrated in British forces a new proficiency in mounting combined operations.

That positive trend was consummated in 1759, the famous "Year of Victories"—and also, of course, the year in which Montagu's *Reflections* was published, but too early for its text to take account of the sudden upturn in British military fortunes.[14] In May, Guadeloupe was captured; on 1 August, British regiments were conspicuous at Minden in Ferdinand of Brunswick's great victory over a numerically superior French force under Contades; on 13 September, Wolfe took Quebec (accompanied the following year by Canada in its entirety); and finally in November, a French fleet gathered to escort across the Channel the transports of an invading French army mustered on the Brittany

---

12. Boswell, *Life of Johnson*, p. 716. For an interesting account of Pitt's varying fortunes with historians, see Middleton, *Bells*, pp. 219–32. Middleton's own balanced and persuasive assessment of Pitt's strengths and weaknesses is to be found on pp. 211–14.

13. On which, see below, p. 131, n. 44.

14. Montagu's *Reflections* is listed among the newly-published books in the March 1759 issue of *The Gentleman's Magazine*; see appendix B, below, pp. 278–81.

coast[15] was almost entirely destroyed by Hawke in the battle of Quiberon Bay.

However, the death of George II on 25 October 1760 and the accession of his grandson George III inaugurated the endgame of the Seven Years' War. The new king and his closest adviser, Lord Bute (who happened also to be Montagu's brother-in-law), were determined to bring to a close what they regarded as a bloody and expensive conflict. In the spring of 1761 France and Russia began to negotiate for peace, and relations between Pitt on the one hand and George III and Lord Bute on the other, which in the mid-1750s had been cordial, but which had been put under strain in late 1758 by Pitt's high-handedness in office, steadily worsened, until on 5 October 1761 Pitt resigned the seals of office. By the summer of 1762, and with the resignation of Newcastle on 26 May of that year, Bute became First Lord of the Treasury and was thus fully in the ascendant. Peace negotiations moved forward with renewed velocity, and on 3 November 1762 the duke of Bedford signed the preliminary articles of what on 10 February 1763 would become the Treaty of Paris. Pitt rose from his sickbed to denounce the terms of the preliminary articles as unduly lenient toward France and embodying an unforgivable desertion of Britain's heroic Protestant ally, Frederick the Great—but to no avail.

Nevertheless, and notwithstanding the arguable shabbiness of her behavior in sealing the peace, at the conclusion of the Seven Years' War in 1763 Britain was beyond question the dominant world power, with vastly enlarged territories in America, a free hand in India, and no serious rival among the great nations of Europe. The situation was caught in a remark of Johnson's made a few years afterward:

> It being observed to him [Johnson], that a rage for every thing English prevailed much in France after Lord Chatham's glorious war, he said, he did not wonder at it, for that we had drubbed those fellows into

15. See the report in *The Gentleman's Magazine* for 18 May 1759: "Great preparations are making on the coasts of *Upper Normandy* and *Picardy* for an embarkation for *England*, not less than 3000 hands being employed in finishing flat-bottomed boats in those provinces to facilitate a descent. To prevent the fatal consequences of which, all the troops in *England, Scotland,* and *Ireland* will be stationed along the coast" (*The Gentleman's Magazine*, vol. 29 [1759], p. 240; see also p. 288).

a proper reverence for us, and that their national petulance required periodical chastisement.[16]

Yet it was a precarious eminence, as Johnson's likening of Pitt to a "meteor" (as opposed to the "fixed star" of Walpole) perhaps hinted.[17] At least some of the seeds of the two great convulsions of the later eighteenth century—the War of American Independence, and the French Revolution—can be found in the legacy of the Seven Years' War.

With respect to America, the deceptive glory achieved in 1763 encouraged British statesmen to adopt imperious policies toward the North American colonists—policies which, as Fred Anderson observes, actually ran counter to the lessons a more subtle observer would have drawn from the conflict:

> In the Philippine episode [the capture of Manila by Draper in 1762] more than any other of the Seven Years' War, the principles of imperial dominion stood out with unmistakable clarity. Military power—particularly naval power—could gain an empire, but force alone could never control colonial dependencies. Only the voluntary allegiance, or at least the acquiescence, of the colonists could do that. Flags and governors and even garrisons were, in the end, only the empire's symbols. Trade and loyalty were its integuments, and when colonial populations that refused their allegiance also declined to trade, the empire's dominion extended not a yard beyond the range of its cannons.[18]

Pitt had realized that, to achieve victory, he must embrace Britain's North American colonists. Accordingly he treated them as allies, not as auxiliaries, still less as subordinates; and they in turn saw themselves as partners in the project of empire. But victory turned the minds of British politicians away from the comprehensive policies which had been the mother of success and beckoned them instead down the ruinous paths of autocracy. The exertion of control from Whitehall was now the favored mode of administration. The resulting new techniques of imperial administration raised in the minds of the colonists doubts as to whether their interests and those of Great Britain were not only the same but even aligned.

16. Boswell, *Life of Johnson*, p. 326.
17. Boswell, *Life of Johnson*, p. 76.
18. Anderson, *Crucible of War*, p. 517.

The small irony that Washington acquired in the service of Great Britain during the Seven Years' War the military skills which he would later deploy against the mother country points toward the much larger irony that American independence can, without undue distortion, be seen as the unintended consequence of Britain's triumph in securing and extending her North American colonies. Meanwhile in France, the check to imperial ambitions sustained in 1763 had removed if not the solution then at least a possible palliative for the economic and social problems which would in 1789 demand more drastic remedies.

Montagu's *Reflections* was written as an intervention in the first of these crises, and it went on to enjoy an afterlife in the second and third. As we shall see, it is a work of history which is repeatedly wrong-footed by history itself, being uniformly invoked in support of causes against which events were soon to set their face. Yet the facts of its republication and translation suggest that until the end of the century it never entirely lost its power to interest and even to influence.

Reflections and the Seven Years' War

By publishing the *Reflections* in 1759 Montagu was at one level opportunistically following in the footsteps of John "Estimate" Brown, who two years previously had enjoyed meteoric success with his civic humanist chiding of decadent Britain, *Estimate of the Manners and Principles of the Times.* But Montagu's focus on the ancient republics gave a distinctive twist to his contribution to the chorus of voices lamenting Britain's decline. As he explained in the preface:

> The design therefore of these papers is, to warn my countrymen, by the example of others, of the fatal consequences which must inevitably attend our intestine divisions at this critical juncture; and to inculcate the necessity of that national union, upon which the strength, the security, and the duration of a free state must eternally depend. Happy, if my weak endeavours could in the least contribute to an end so salutary, so truly desirable![19]

19. Below, p. 4.

However, although *Reflections* is a work which asks to be placed in the "civic humanist" tradition described by John Pocock, Montagu's unpacking of the warnings for Britain to be gleaned from the fates of the ancient republics is unusually nuanced, in that each of the five states he examines—Sparta, Athens, Thebes, Carthage, and Rome—supplies a separate "lesson" adapted to the needs of Britain in the nadir of its fortunes during the Seven Years' War. Sparta instructs modern Britain to suppress commerce, refinement, and opulence and to bolster the landed interest. Athens warns of the dangerous levity of a democratical form of government, of the disastrous influence the people can exercise over the constitution and policy of a state if they are not checked by a powerful and confident aristocracy, of the proneness of the people to encourage charismatic despotism (illustrated in the person of Alcibiades), and lastly of the folly of foreign entanglements and "empire-building." Thebes, more encouragingly, demonstrates the potency of a "very small number of virtuous patriots" to save a state from corruption.[20] The calamitous Carthaginian experience with mercenaries shows the incomparable superiority of a militia over hired swords. Finally, Rome plays her customary role in moralized history of showing the fatal consequences of luxury:

> But of all the ancient Republicks, Rome in the last period of her freedom was the scene where all the inordinate passions of mankind operated most powerfully and with the greatest latitude. There we see luxury, ambition, faction, pride, revenge, selfishness, a total disregard to the publick good, and an universal dissoluteness of manners, first make them ripe for, and then compleat their destruction.[21]

In the end, it was the Epicurean atheism of the Roman upper classes which gave the *coup de grâce* to the Roman state; an interpretation of Roman decline which paves the way for Montagu's censure of the irreligion of the Britons of his own day—censure which, given his own confessional history, is certainly cheeky, if probably not tongue-in-cheek.[22]

20. Below, p. 103.
21. Below, p. 145.
22. Below, p. 206–10.

Such a summary of the broad outlines of Montagu's argument in the *Reflections* does little, however, to show how carefully its analyses and recommendations are not only "Adapted to the Present State of Great Britain" (as the title page states) but also tailored to the political alliances and enmities of its author's family. Edward Wortley Montagu senior's political career was defined by his opposition to Sir Robert Walpole. In 1716 he had composed an essay "On the State of Affairs when the King Entered," in which he had anatomized English politics in 1714 on the accession of George I in terms of the malign influence of one ambitious and rising man:

> This brief sketch . . . narrows into a single-minded attack on Walpole. Wortley sees him as duping and manipulating men of higher rank than himself, widening the gap between Whig and Tory, damaging the King's popularity by his bad judgement. . . . Wortley regrets King William's days, when Treasury Commissioners were "all men of great figure," not upstarts like Walpole. [Wortley Montagu had been made a Commissioner of the Treasury on 13 October 1714.] He thinks the Treasury is a reliable ladder to greatness, and Walpole ought to be kept off it. He refers indirectly to himself as the only Treasury man who is not Walpole's creature. He is unable to "hinder any of [Walpole's] projects," and can only "inform the King of his affairs." The essay explains the rift between Court Whigs (bad) and Country Whigs (good but unrewarded).[23]

Wortley Montagu senior's opposition to Walpole endured for more than two decades. Only after the eventual fall of the great minister in February 1742 would he exert himself more vigorously in the Commons.[24] In the meantime, although he stood apart from the Patriot Whig circles which coalesced around Viscount Cobham in the 1730s, he must have applauded their pursuit of an implacable vendetta against Walpole.[25] Conspicuous in the ranks of "Cobham's Cubs" was a brilliant young

---

23. Grundy, *Lady Mary*, p. 112.
24. Halsband, *Letters*, vol. 2, pp. 190, n. 1, and 265, n. 1.
25. See Christine Gerrard, *The Patriot Opposition to Walpole: Politics, Poetry, and National Myth, 1725–1742* (Oxford: Clarendon Press, 1994), pp. 35–40.

orator, William Pitt, whom Walpole had driven into opposition and the arms of his uncle Cobham by depriving him of his cornetcy of horse in punishment for his outspokenness in the Commons in the summer of 1736.[26] Although Pitt seems never to have been particularly close to the Montagus, they nevertheless thought well of him, and, as a natural ally, they later saw him as a possible source of patronage for their friends and connections.[27]

Possibly more important, however, than the enmity with Walpole and the potential affinity with Pitt, would be an alliance forged in 1736 when Montagu's sister, Mary, married John Stuart, third earl of Bute. It was a match apparently entered into out of affection, in the teeth of at least paternal indifference if not active opposition, and without ulterior motives of either a financial or a political kind.[28] The early years of the marriage were spent in the isolation and comparative poverty of the Isle of Bute, where the earl resided on his estates and pursued his interests in botany. But in the mid-1740s he and his countess moved to London, where in 1747 he struck up a friendship with Frederick, prince of Wales. Soon Bute became a leading figure at Leicester House (the

26. Pitt was initially aligned with Walpole but turned against him with a vengeance: Pearce, *Pitt*, pp. 22 and 67.

27. Lady Mary wrote to her daughter, Lady Bute, on 9 October 1757 that: "I have a high value for Mr. Pit's probity and understanding, without having the Honor of being acquainted with him; I am persuaded he is able to do whatever is within the bounds of possibility. But there is an Augaean stable to be clean'd and several other labours that I doubt Hercules himselfe would be equal to" (Halsband, *Letters*, vol. 3, p. 137). On 3 August 1759 she asked Lady Bute to employ her "interest . . . with Mr. Pitt" on behalf of a relative of a friend (Halsband, *Letters*, vol. 3, pp. 221–22). On the Wortley Montagus and Pitt, see also Grundy, *Lady Mary*, p. 571.

28. The union produced eleven children. Wortley Montagu senior offered Bute no dowry with his daughter, although he had been prepared to offer a dowry to other suitors. Lady Mary warned her daughter of the comparative poverty that would follow marriage to Bute, since the intransigence of her father was matched by the intransigence of his uncles, and no further settlement of family money or estates was made on Bute when he married. Bute's uncles were at this time ranged in opposition to Wortley Montagu senior's interests. See Grundy, *Lady Mary*, pp. 324–28.

prince's London residence, and a center of opposition politics). After Frederick's death in 1751 Bute remained a trusted adviser to his widow. He was appointed tutor to her son, the future George III, whom he educated in accordance with the principles of the "country" opposition: "a composite, idealistic political creed advocating an isolationist foreign policy, the abolition of party distinctions, the purging of corruption, and the enhancement of monarchial control over policy and patronage."[29] In the mid-1750s Bute and Pitt stood shoulder to shoulder in opposition to Newcastle's policies. But in the later years of the decade their alliance came under pressure as Pitt took up office and came round to supporting and indeed reinforcing Newcastle's policy of continental engagement.

Montagu trimmed the text of *Reflections* with some skill in deference to the various imperatives of these family alliances and antagonisms. To echo his father's hatred of Walpole was easy. Montagu sowed the text of *Reflections* with disparaging references to "late power-engrossing ministers" and "corrupt and ambitious statesmen" whose misuse of public funds, rather than "superior abilities," allowed them to "reduce corruption into system"—language easily interpretable by the book's first readers as attacks on the memory of Walpole.[30] In a particularly felicitous moment, a glance at Walpole's fall allowed Montagu in one breath to rejoice in the punishment of a villain and to commiserate with his father, one of the "honest men" in the opposition, whose name had been counted in the day of battle, but who had been passed over in the division of the spoils:

> When the leaders of that powerful opposition had carried their point by their popular clamours; when they had pushed the nation into that war [with Spain]; when they had drove an overgrown minister from the helm, and nestled themselves in power, how quickly did they turn their backs upon the honest men of their party, who refused to concur in their measures![31]

29. K. W. Schweizer, "John Stuart, third earl of Bute," *ODNB*.
30. Below, pp. 207, 128, 88.
31. Below, p. 143.

But to pay compliments to both Pitt and Bute, who as the *Reflections* was being written were becoming gradually more estranged, required more careful management.[32]

There seemed to be no call for any perfect even-handedness, however. Although George II's health was not robust, no one could have predicted in 1758 that his death was so imminent; and nothing but the king's death could convert Bute's ascendancy over the heir-apparent into that much more substantial thing, real power at court. Meanwhile, Pitt held the reins of political power as Secretary of State, and was the dominant figure in the administration. Some such calculation seems to lie behind the distribution of Montagu's compliments, which are mainly directed toward Pitt, but which do not preclude some mildly fawning touches designed to gratify Bute, as a kind of insurance policy. The very basis of Montagu's book, in its engagement with ancient history, could be taken as a deferential gesture toward Pitt, who in 1759 would be praised as the English Pericles, whom Horace Walpole had compared to Cicero and Demosthenes, and whose Parliamentary oratory relied heavily on allusions to ancient history.[33] (Pitt is presumably excluded from Montagu's prefatory strictures on those who have "misrepresented" historical facts and employed the "chicane of sophistry.")[34] On this foundation of implicit flattery Montagu went on to erect more overt structures of compliment to "the Great Commoner," couching his analyses of ancient history in language associated with Pitt, expressing relief at the calling of

32. As the real interests of the two men diverged, Pitt tried to disguise the fact from Bute by lavish flattery, of which Lady Bute was rightly suspicious (Pearce, *Pitt*, p. 202).

33. Anonymous, *The English Pericles* (1759) and Rosebery, *Chatham*, p. 494 (where the same comparison is drawn by Bishop Newton). For the comparison with Cicero and Demosthenes, see Rosebery, *Chatham*, p. 405. Pitt's reply to the King's Speech on 14 November 1755 had referred to the Carthaginian use of mercenaries and to Hannibal's crossing the Alps (Rosebery, *Chatham*, p. 405); his speech in the House on 15 December of the same year once more made elaborate use of examples drawn from ancient history (Rosebery, *Chatham*, pp. 437–38); and Walpole reports that Pitt ransacked "Greek and Roman story" for parallels when proposing a monument for Wolfe on 21 October 1759 (Walpole, *Memoires*, vol. 2, p. 393).

34. Below, p. 3.

"a truly disinterested patriot to the helm," and offering vigorous support to a policy with which, as we have seen, Pitt was particularly connected, namely the creation of a national militia.[35] But Montagu also had one eye on Bute, and so this lavish praise of Pitt was accompanied by a trace of reservation concerning one aspect of current British policy, namely its commitments on the continent in support of Frederick the Great.[36] Here, Montagu sounded a note of troubled warning, which no doubt he hoped would gratify the isolationist ears of Leicester House. At such moments we glimpse Montagu caught in the ebb and flow of events, and, with some ingenuity but perhaps less dignity, trying to find a posture in which he might at the same time worship both the rising and the setting sun.

The Afterlife of *Reflections:* America and France

Montagu's support for Pitt would by itself have recommended the *Reflections* to Thomas Hollis and his circle—Hollis, who had medals struck to commemorate the great military triumphs of Pitt's administration, who thought of Pitt as one of the "old friends of liberty" and "an assertor of liberty," and whose close friend Richard Baron had presented a copy of his edition of Milton's *Eikonoklastes* to Pitt, with the inscription: "To William Pitt, Esq. Assertor of Liberty, Champion of the People, Scourge of impious Ministers, their Tools and Sycophants, this book is presented by the Editor."[37]

35. For language particularly associated with Pitt, see below, pp. 11–12, 20, 48, 50, and 67; support for a militia, below, pp. 253–63.

36. For Montagu's misgivings about Britain's policy of continental engagement and subsidy, see below, p. 123, n. 24, and p. 260, n. 22. Pitt had initially been opposed to a policy of continental engagement *tout court*. He had then moved to a willingness to supply money, but not men, before finally capitulating altogether in the face of what he apologetically represented to Lord Bute as "fatal necessity" (Pearce, *Pitt*, pp. 73, 113, 129, and 133). In December 1757 he assured the Commons that he would not send "a drop of our blood to the Elbe to be lost in that ocean of Gore"; but on 19 April 1758 he privately realized that the need might arise "for sending troops to Prince Ferdinand [of Brunswick]" (Pearce, *Pitt*, p. 201).

37. Blackburne, *Memoirs*, vol. 1, pp. 80, 89, 122, 123, 125, 186, 223, 284, 286; vol. 2, p. 586.

But, if it is easy to appreciate the congeniality of Montagu's views to
Hollis personally, what at the level of practical politics did Hollis hope to
achieve by sending a copy of the *Reflections* to Harvard? The question of
whether or not—and if so, to what degree and in what manner—the example of classical antiquity conditioned the thinking and guided the actions
of the Founders has long been the subject of dispute between scholars
of the Founding Period. The easy acceptance of early twentieth-century
historians that classical influence had been real and defining was rejected
by, most influentially, Bernard Bailyn, who judged it on the contrary to
be "illustrative, not determinative, of thought."[38] Gordon Wood and Joyce
Appleby accorded a place to classical republicanism in the early stages of
the colonists' struggle with Great Britain, before it yielded to the "modern
republicanism" embodied in *The Federalist*. John Pocock, Lance Banning,
Drew McCoy, and Paul Rahe have more recently tried to tip the balance
of historical judgment further back to the benefit of classical antiquity, to
the point where the most recent student of the subject can conclude:

> It is clear that the classics exerted a formative influence upon the
> founders. Classical ideas provided the basis for their theories of gov-
> ernment form, social responsibility, human nature, and virtue. The
> authors of the classical canon offered the founders companionship,
> solace, and the models and antimodels which gave them a sense of
> identity and purpose. The classics facilitated communication by fur-
> nishing a common set of symbols, knowledge, and ideas, a literature
> select enough to provide common ground, yet rich enough to address
> a wide range of human problems from a variety of perspectives.[39]

Nevertheless, the American republic sooner or later would embrace ideals
and values sharply at variance with those endorsed by Montagu's *Reflections*.
It would place agriculture below commerce and industry; it would abandon aloof self-sufficiency and instead engage with the world in an imperial
manner (albeit without the symbols of imperialism); it would rely more
upon a professional standing army than upon the state militias; it would
prize consumption, not frugality; and it would elevate private pleasure

38. Richard, *Founders*, p. 2.
39. Richard, *Founders*, p. 232.

above public duty. Even so, Montagu's book would enjoy its greatest lon-
gevity in America, an edition appearing in Philadelphia as late as 1806.

The French translation of *Reflections* allowed Montagu to step upon
the stage of world history for a third time.[40] Although published in 1793,
the final chapter added by the translator, André Samuel Michel, applying the lessons of the book to the situation of France, suggests a date
of composition some time in 1792, and certainly before the execution of
Louis XVI on 21 January 1793. Michel's advocacy of a mixed constitution
also perhaps suggests a date of composition before the abolition of the
monarchy on 21 September 1792. However, although it was published in
the midst of a revolution, this is the least revolutionary of texts. Coun-
seling caution, Michel warns against a republic, against a citizen militia, against the de-Christianizing of the country, against any moves to
extend "égalité" too far. The constitutionalism, moderation, and lack of
fervor shown by Michel make his a rare and lonely voice in the tumults of
1793. His temperate observations on the impossibility of re-creating the
moeurs of the classical republics in an affluent monarchy stood no chance
against the stridency of the revolutionary cult of antiquity, which prized
(or affected to prize) the austere totalitarianism of Sparta and the early
Roman republic, and which was most vividly embodied in the paintings
of David and the enthusiasm of Saint-Just for the pitiless severities of
Lycurgus and Lucius Junius Brutus.[41] Once again, Montagu found himself beached by the retreating tides of history.

***

What thoughts are prompted as we finish Montagu's *Reflections?* In
the first place, we cannot avoid the fact that Montagu's political opinions amount to nothing more than a herd of the holiest cows of vulgar

40. See below, appendix A.
41. On the revolutionary cult of antiquity see (still), H. T. Parker, *The Cult of
Antiquity and the French Revolutionaries: A Study in the Development of the Revolu-
tionary Spirit* (Chicago: University of Chicago Press, 1937). For a comparative per-
spective, see Jonathan Sacks, *Rome in the British Imagination, 1789–1832* (Oxford:
Oxford University Press, 2009). For the pre-revolutionary cult of antiquity in
France, see, e.g., this recent study of Mably: J. K. Wright, *A Classical Republican in
Eighteenth Century France* (Stanford: Stanford University Press, 1997).

Whiggism: an absolute justification of the Revolution of 1688; a fondness for drawing contrasts between English "liberty" and French "slavery"; undeviating veneration for the "ancient constitution" of the common law-yers which had been handed down to the English from freedom-loving barbarians residing in the woods of ancient Germany; unreasoning suspi-cion of standing armies; and a tendency to reflect severely on the inveter-ate wickedness of the Stuart kings.[42]

There is nothing especially shameful about this. Very few of Mon-tagu's contemporaries were able to free themselves, even in part and tem-porarily, from the bewitchment of these Whiggish opinions; and none of them—not even David Hume—managed to do so completely and permanently.[43] But, as Duncan Forbes explains, vulgar Whiggism has harmful consequences for historians and what we would now call social scientists, because it inhibits precisely the forms of thought on which those thinkers most rely:

> It was the essence of "vulgar" Whiggism that the difference between free and absolute government was not one of degree, but of kind, an absolute qualitative difference, a chalk and cheese, sheep and goats type of distinction, which made any science of comparative politics or comparative study of institutions impossible. On the one hand was liberty, the government of laws not men, which was a feature of free governments exclusively; on the other, slavery and absolutism.[44]

The numbing effect of this Manichean creed on the comparative and historical areas of the mind explains why Montagu, although a student of republics, has no interest in or even apparently awareness of republi-can*ism,* and also why he is unembarrassed by any troubling doubts as to

---

42. For examples of these opinions in Montagu, see below, pp. 252–63. On "vul-gar Whiggism," see Forbes, *Hume,* pp. 125–92. After the fading of the dynastic question from English politics following the failure of the Jacobite rebellion of 1745 vulgar Whig sentiments were often found on the lips of those who called them-selves Tories (Forbes, *Hume,* pp. 139–40).

43. As late as March 1763 Hume regretted that he was unable thoroughly to weed his mind of the "plaguy Prejudices" of Whiggism (Forbes, *Hume,* pp. 129 and 150–51).

44. Forbes, *Hume,* p. 142.

whether the examples and precepts he harvests from ancient history are applicable to a modern commercial monarchy, such as Great Britain in the mid-eighteenth century.

But, if we have to classify Montagu as mediocre in terms both of the substance of his political and historical opinions and of the intellectual equipment he brought to bear upon those opinions, then we are immediately confronted by the more stubborn and disturbing problem of explaining the durability of his book. After all, *Reflections on the Rise and Fall of the Ancient Republicks* had at least a walk-on part in the three great crises of the later eighteenth century: the Seven Years' War, the War of American Independence, and the French Revolution. Montagu's book illustrates that intriguing truth, that often in human affairs the most important causes are advanced by means of the most ordinary instruments.

David Womersley

FURTHER READING

Biographical

Anon. *Memoirs of the late Edw. W——ly M——tague, esq.,* 2 vols. London, 1779.

Coates, H. *The British Don Juan.* London, 1823.

Curling, J. *Edward Wortley Montague. 1713–1776: The Man in the Iron Wig.* London: A. Melrose, 1954.

Grundy, I. *Lady Mary Wortley Montagu.* Oxford: Oxford University Press, 1999.

Kenealy, E. V. H. *Edward Wortley Montagu, an Autobiography.* 3 vols. London, 1869.

[Lamberg, Maximilien, comte de]. *Mémorial d'un mondain.* Nouvelle édition, 2 vols. London, 1776.

Wortley Montagu, Lady Mary. *The Complete Letters.* Edited by Robert Halsband. 3 vols. Oxford: Clarendon Press, 1965–67.

Historical and Contextual

Anderson, Fred. *Crucible of War: The Seven Years' War and the Fate of Empire in British North America 1754–1766.* London: Faber and Faber, 2000.

Blackburne, Francis. *Memoirs of Thomas Hollis.* 2 vols. London, 1780.

Brown, Peter. *The Chathamites.* London: Macmillan, 1967.

Clark, J. C. D. *The Dynamics of Change: The Crisis of the Mid-1750s.* Cambridge: Cambridge University Press, 1982.

———— (ed.). *The Memoirs and Speeches of James, 2nd Earl Waldegrave, 1742–1763.* Cambridge: Cambridge University Press, 1988.

Corbett, Sir Julian Stafford. *England in the Seven Years' War: A Study in Combined Strategy.* 2 vols. London: Longmans, 1907.

Forbes, Duncan. *Hume's Philosophical Politics.* Cambridge: Cambridge University Press, 1975.

Mackay, R. F. *Admiral Hawke.* Oxford: Clarendon Press, 1965.

Marston, Daniel. *The Seven Years' War.* Oxford: Osprey Publishing, 2001.

McLynn, Frank. *1759: The Year Britain Became Master of the World.* London: Pimlico, 2004.

Middleton, Richard. *The Bells of Victory: The Pitt-Newcastle Ministry and the Conduct of the Seven Years' War, 1757–1762.* Cambridge: Cambridge University Press, 1985.

Pares, Richard. *War and Trade in the West Indies 1739–1763.* Oxford: Clarendon Press, 1936.

Parker, H. T. *The Cult of Antiquity and the French Revolutionaries: A Study in the Development of the Revolutionary Spirit.* Chicago: University of Chicago Press, 1937.

Pearce, Edward. *Pitt the Elder: Man of War.* London: The Bodley Head, 2010.

Peters, Marie. *Pitt and Popularity: The Patriot Minister and London Opinion during the Seven Years' War.* Oxford: Clarendon Press, 1980.

Pocock, J. G. A. *The Machiavellian Moment: Florentine Political Thought and the Atlantic Republican Tradition.* Princeton and London: Princeton University Press, 1975.

Richard, Carl J. *The Founders and the Classics: Greece, Rome, and the American Enlightenment.* Cambridge, Mass., and London: Harvard University Press, 1994.

Rodger, N. A. M. *The Command of the Ocean: A Naval History of Britain 1649–1815.* London: Allen Lane, 2004.

Rosebery, Lord. *Chatham: His Early Life and Connections.* London: Arthur L. Humphreys, 1910.

Sacks, Jonathan. *Rome in the British Imagination, 1789–1832.* Oxford: Oxford University Press, 2009.

Walpole, Horace. *Memoires of the Last Ten Years of George the Second,* 2 vols. London, 1822.

NOTE ON THE TEXT

Montagu's *Reflections on the Rise and Fall of the Ancient Republicks* was first published in 1759; there was a second edition in 1760 "with additions and corrections," a third in 1769, and a fourth in 1778. On the continent, there was an English edition published in Basle in 1793, and an interesting French translation published in Paris in 1793 (concerning which see appendix A below and the introduction, p. xxv above). An American edition was published in Philadelphia in 1806.

The additions and corrections made for the second edition consisted of some slight changes of wording and the inclusion of additional footnotes, some of which responded to the reviews of the first edition (see appendix B below). In all, some eight extra pages of text were added in 1760.

The copy text for this edition is the fourth edition of 1778, which seems to have been more carefully printed than either the second or the third and which incorporates the revisions made in 1760. Page numbers from the 1778 edition have been inserted throughout the text of this edition in square brackets. Montagu's numbered reference marks have been changed to superscript letters and moved from the beginning of his references to the end of the sentences or clauses; his two symboled notes remain as they were. Michel's numbered footnote has been changed to a symboled note. All numbered notes in this edition are editorial.

ABBREVIATIONS

Anderson, *Crucible of War* Fred Anderson, *Crucible of War: The Seven Years' War and the Fate of Empire in British North America 1754–1766* (London: Faber and Faber, 2000).

Bacon, *Advancement* Francis Bacon, *The Advancement of Learning and New Atlantis,* ed. Arthur Johnston (Oxford: Clarendon Press, 1974).

Barrell, *Survey* John Barrell, *English Literature in History 1730–80: An Equal, Wide Survey* (London: Hutchinson, 1983).

Bennett, *Tory Crisis* G. V. Bennett, *The Tory Crisis in Church and State 1688–1730: The Career of Francis Atterbury, Bishop of Rochester* (Oxford: Clarendon Press, 1975).

Blackburne, *Memoirs* Francis Blackburnc, *Memoirs of Thomas Hollis,* 2 vols. (London, 1780).

Blackstone, *Commentaries*	Sir William Blackstone, *Commentaries on the Laws of England,* 4 vols. (Oxford: Clarendon Press, 1765–69).
Bolingbroke, *Letters*	Henry St. John, Viscount Bolingbroke, *Letters on the Study and Use of History,* 2 vols. (London, 1752).
Bolingbroke, *Political Writings*	Bolingbroke, *Political Writings,* ed. David Armitage (Cambridge: Cambridge University Press, 1997).
Boswell, *Life of Johnson*	James Boswell, *The Life of Samuel Johnson,* ed. David Womersley (London: Penguin Classics, 2008).
Burnet, *Tracts*	Gilbert Burnet, *A Second Collection of Several Tracts and Discourses* (London, 1689).
Corbett, *Seven Years' War*	Sir Julian Stafford Corbett, *England in the Seven Years' War: A Study in Combined Strategy,* 2 vols. (London: Longmans, 1907).
Dalrymple, *Memoirs*	Sir John Dalrymple, *Memoirs of Great Britain and Ireland,* 2 vols. (London, 1771–73).
Davies, *Poland*	Norman Davies, *God's Playground: A History of Poland,* 2 vols. (Oxford: Clarendon Press, 1981).
Dennis, *Works*	*The Critical Works of John Dennis,* ed. Edward Niles Hooker, 2 vols. (Baltimore: The Johns Hopkins Press, 1939–43).
Forbes, *Hume*	Duncan Forbes, *Hume's Philosophical Politics* (Cambridge: Cambridge University Press, 1975).

Gerrard, *Patriot Opposition*	Christine Gerrard, *The Patriot Opposition to Walpole: Politics, Poetry, and National Myth, 1725–1742* (Oxford: Clarendon Press, 1994).
Gibbon, *Decline and Fall*	Edward Gibbon, *The History of the Decline and Fall of the Roman Empire,* ed. David Womersley (London: Allen Lane, 1994).
Gibbon, *Miscellaneous Works*	Edward Gibbon, *Miscellaneous Works,* ed. Lord Sheffield, 3 vols. (London, 1796–1815).
Grundy, *Lady Mary*	Isobel Grundy, *Lady Mary Wortley Montagu* (Oxford: Oxford University Press, 1999).
Halsband, *Letters*	*The Complete Letters of Lady Mary Wortley Montagu,* ed. Robert Halsband, 3 vols. (Oxford: Clarendon Press, 1965–67).
Hobbes, *Behemoth*	Thomas Hobbes, *Behemoth,* ed. F. Tönnies, intr. S. Holmes (Chicago and London: University of Chicago Press, 1990).
Hogan, *Shakespeare*	C. B. Hogan, *Shakespeare in the Theatre, 1701–1800,* 2 vols. (Oxford: Clarendon Press, 1952–57).
Hume, *Enquiries*	David Hume, *Enquiries Concerning the Human Understanding and Concerning the Principles of Morals,* third edition, ed. P. H. Nidditch (Oxford: Clarendon Press, 1975).
Jenyns, *Objections*	Soame Jenyns, *The Objections to the Taxation of our American Colonies, by*

	the Legislature of Great Britain, Briefly Consider'd (London, 1765).
Locke, *Political Writings*	John Locke, *Political Writings,* ed. David Wootton (London: Penguin Books, 1993).
Locke, *Two Treatises*	John Locke, *Two Treatises on Government,* ed. P. Laslett, Cambridge Texts in the History of Political Thought (Cambridge: Cambridge University Press, 1960).
Mackenzie, *Man of Feeling*	Henry Mackenzie, *The Man of Feeling,* ed. Brian Vickers (Oxford: Oxford University Press, 1987).
Marston, *Seven Years' War*	Daniel Marston, *The Seven Years' War* (Oxford: Osprey Publishing, 2001).
Middleton, *Bells*	Richard Middleton, *The Bells of Victory: The Pitt–Newcastle Ministry and the Conduct of the Seven Years' War* (Cambridge: Cambridge University Press, 1985).
Molesworth, *Denmark*	Robert Molesworth, *An Account of Denmark, As it Was in the Year 1692,* fourth edition (London, 1738).
Montaigne, *Essays*	Michel de Montaigne, *The Complete Essays,* tr. Michael Screech (London: Penguin Books, 1991).
Montesquieu, *Considérations*	Charles-Louis de Secondat, baron de Montesquieu, *Considérations sur les causes de la grandeur des Romains et de leur décadence,* ed. F. Weil, C. Courtney, P. Andrivet, and C. Volpilhac-Auger,

	Œuvres complètes de Montesquieu, vol. 2 (Oxford: Voltaire Foundation, 2000).
More, *Utopia*	Thomas More, *Utopia*, ed. George M. Logan and Robert M. Adams, revised edition, Cambridge Texts in the History of Political Thought (Cambridge: Cambridge University Press, 2002).
ODNB	*The Oxford Dictionary of National Biography*
OED	*The Oxford English Dictionary*
Pascal, *Thoughts*	Blaise Pascal, *Thoughts on Religion* (London, 1704).
Pearce, *Pitt*	Edward Pearce, *Pitt the Elder: Man of War* (London: Bodley Head, 2010).
Pocock, *Virtue*	J. G. A. Pocock, *Virtue, Commerce, and History* (Cambridge: Cambridge University Press, 1985).
Richard, *Founders*	Carl J. Richard, *The Founders and the Classics: Greece, Rome, and the American Enlightenment* (Cambridge, Mass., and London: Harvard University Press, 1994).
Rodger, *Command*	N. A. M. Rodger, *The Command of the Ocean: A Naval History of Britain 1649–1815* (London: Allen Lane, 2004).
Rosebery, *Chatham*	Lord Rosebery, *Chatham: His Early Life and Connections* (London: Arthur L. Humphreys, 1910).

Walpole, *Correspondence*	Horace Walpole, *Correspondence,* ed. W. S. Lewis et al., 48 vols. (New Haven and Oxford: Yale University Press and Oxford University Press, 1937–83).
Walpole, *Memoires*	Horace Walpole, *Memoires of the Last Ten Years of George the Second,* 2 vols. (London, 1822).
Warburton, *Divine Legation*	William Warburton, *The Divine Legation of Moses,* fourth edition, 2 vols. (London, 1755).
Woolley, *Corr.*	*The Correspondence of Jonathan Swift, D.D.,* ed. David Woolley, 4 vols. (Frankfurt am Main: Peter Lang, 1999–2007).

ACKNOWLEDGMENTS

I wish to thank Professor Ran Halévi for his prompt assistance in placing the French translation of Montagu's *Reflections* in the complicated and volatile context of French revolutionary politics.

REFLECTIONS

ON THE

RISE AND FALL

OF THE

ANCIENT REPUBLICKS.

ADAPTED TO THE

PRESENT STATE

OF

GREAT BRITAIN.

Οὐ τί τῷδε, ἢ τῷδε δόξει, λογιζόμενος
Ἀλλὰ τί πέπρακται λέγων.

Lucian. Histor. Scribend.[1]

By Edward Wortley Montagu, Esq.

THE FOURTH EDITION

LONDON:

Printed for J. Rivington and Sons, T. Longman, S. Crowder, T. Cadell, T. Becket, and W. Fox.

M DCC LXXVIII.

Preface

Plutarch takes notice of a very remarkable law of Solon's,

> which declared every man infamous, who, in any sedition or civil dis-
> sention in the state, should continue neuter, and refuse to side with
> either party.[a]

Aulus Gellius, who gives a more circumstantial detail of this uncommon
law, affirms the penalty to be

> no less than confiscation of all the effects, and banishment of the
> delinquent.[b]

Cicero mentions the same law to his friend Atticus, and even makes the
punishment capital, though he resolves at the same time not to conform
to it under his present circumstances, unless his friend should advise him
to the contrary.[c]

---

a. Plut. in Vit. Solon. ἄτιμον.[1]
b. A. Gellii Noct. Attic. lib. 2. c. 12.[2]
c. Epist. ad Attic. lib. 10. epist. 1.[3]
1. Plutarch, "Solon," XX.1. "Deprived of privileges," or "disfranchised."
2. Aulus Gellius, *Noctes Atticae*, II.xii.1.
3. Cicero, *Letters to Atticus*, no. 190, X.i.2.

Which of these relators has given us the real penalty annexed to this law by Solon, [2] is scarce worth our enquiry. But I cannot help observing, that strange as this law may appear at first sight, yet if we reflect upon the reasons of it, as they are assigned by Plutarch and A. Gellius, it will not appear unworthy of that great legislator.

The opinion of Plutarch is, "That Solon intended no citizen, as soon as ever he had provided for the security of his own private affairs, should be so unfeeling with respect to the public welfare as to affect a brutal insensibility,[a] and not sympathize with the distress and calamities of his country: but that he should immediately join the honester and juster party; and rather risque his all in defence of the side he had espoused, than keep aloof from danger till he saw which party proved the stronger."[4]

The reason given by A. Gellius is more striking, and less liable to objections than that of Plutarch. "If (says that writer) all the good men in any state, when they find themselves too weak to stem the torrent of a furious divided populace, and unable to suppress a sedition at its first breaking out, should immediately divide, and throw themselves into the opposite sides, the event in such a [3] case would be, that each party, which they had differently espoused, would naturally begin to cool, and put themselves under their direction, as persons of the greatest weight and authority: thus it would be greatly in the power of such men so circumstanced, to reconcile all differences, and restore peace and union, while they mutually restrained and moderated the fury of their own party, and convinced the opposite side, that they sincerely wished and laboured for their safety, not for their destruction."

What effect this law had in the Athenian state is no where mentioned. However, as it is plainly founded upon that relation which every member bears to the body politick, and that interest which every individual is supposed to have in the good of the whole community; it is still, though not in express terms, yet virtually received in every free country. For those who continue neuter in any civil dissention, under the denomination of moderate men, who keep aloof and wait quietly in order to follow the

a. Μὴ συναλγεῖν, μηδὲ συννοσεῖν.
4. Plutarch, "Solon," XX.1.

fortune of the prevailing side, are generally stigmatized with the oppro-
brious name of *Time-servers*, and consequently neither esteemed, nor
trusted by either party. [4]

As our own country is blessed with the greatest share of liberty, so is it
more subject to civil dissentions than any other nation in Europe. Every
man is a politician, and warmly attached to his respective party; and this
law of Solon's seems to take place as strongly in Britain, as ever it did in
the most factious times at Athens. Freedom of thought, or the liberty
of the mind, arises naturally from the very essence of our constitution;
and the liberty of the press, that peculiar privilege of the British subject,
gives every man a continual opportunity of laying his sentiments before
the Public. Would our political writers pursue the salutary intention of
Solon, as delivered to us by A. Gellius in his explication of that extraordinary law, they might contribute greatly to the establishment of that
harmony and union, which can alone preserve and perpetuate the duration of our constitution. But the opposite views and interests of parties
make the altercation endless; and the victory over an antagonist is generally the aim, whilst the investigation of truth only, ought ever to be the
real end proposed in all controversial inquiries. The points which have
lately exercised so many pens, turn upon the present expediency, or absolute insignificancy, of a *Militia*;[5] or, what principles conduce most to the
power, the happiness, and the [5] duration of a free people. The dispute
has been carried on, not only with warmth, but even with virulence. The
chicane of sophistry has been employed, whilst indecent personal reflections, and the unfair charge of disaffection, have been too often made use
of to supply the defect of argument, and to prejudice the reader, where
they despaired of confuting the writer. Historical facts have been either
misrepresented, or ascribed to wrong principles; the history of ancient

---

5. The question of whether arms could be entrusted to a standing army (namely,
a body of soldiers kept permanently available for the service of the supreme magistrate, and paid for out of public funds), or whether they should rather be reserved
to a citizen militia, is a central theme in the political tradition which descends
from the writings of Machiavelli. It was also an issue of great practical importance
in British politics during the long eighteenth century, and possessed particular
urgency in the 1750s; see below, p. 86, n. 149 and p. 99, n. 182.

nations has been quoted in general terms, without marking the different periods distinguished by some memorable change in the manners or
constitution of the same people, which will ever make a wide difference
in the application.

Anxious after truth, and unsatisfied with so many bold assertions
destitute of all proof but the writer's word, which I daily met with, I
determined coolly and impartially to examine the evidence arising from
ancient history, which both sides so frequently appealed to: for bare
speculative reasoning is no more conclusive in political inquiries than
in physical. Facts and experience alone must decide: and political facts
and experience must alone be learned from history. Determined therefore to judge for myself, I carefully read over the histories of the most [6]
celebrated republics of antiquity in their original languages, unbiassed
either by comments or translations; a part of history of all others the most
instructive, and most interesting to an Englishman.[6]

As instruction was the sole end of my inquiries, I here venture to offer
the result of them to the candor of the Public, since my only motive
for writing was a most ardent concern for the welfare of my country.
The design therefore of these papers is, to warn my countrymen, by the
example of others, of the fatal consequences which must inevitably attend
our intestine divisions at this critical juncture; and to inculcate the necessity of that national union, upon which the strength, the security, and
the duration of a free state must eternally depend. Happy, if my weak
endeavours could in the least contribute to an end so salutary, so truly
desirable!

In the numerous quotations from the Greek and Latin historians,
which are unavoidable in a treatise of this nature, I have endeavoured

---

6. In *Behemoth* (composed c. 1668), Hobbes had traced the origins of the English
Civil War, at least in part, to the fondness for the history of the ancient republics
imbibed by Englishmen while at university: "curious questions in divinity are first
started in the Universities, and so are all those politic questions concerning the
rights of civil and ecclesiastic government; and there they [students at the Universi-
ties] are furnished with arguments for liberty out of the works of Aristotle, Plato,
Cicero, Seneca, and out of the histories of Rome and Greece, for their disputation
against the necessary power of their sovereigns" (Hobbes, *Behemoth*, p. 56).

to give the genuine sense and meaning of the author, to the best of my abilities. But as every reader has an equal right of judging for himself, I have subjoined in the margin, the original words of the [7] author, with the book, page, name, and date of the respective edition I made use of, for the ease as well as the satisfaction of the candid and judicious: for that vague and careless manner, which some writers affect, of quoting an author by name only, without specifying the particular passage referred to in evidence, is neither useful, nor satisfactory to the generality of readers; whilst the unfair method, too often practised, of quoting disjointed scraps, or unconnected sentences, is apt to raise strong suspicions, that the real sentiments and intention of the author are kept out of sight, and that the writer is endeavouring to palm false evidence upon his readers.

I must take the liberty of offering another reason, which, I confess, was of more weight with me, because more personally interesting. As the British state and the ancient free Republicks were founded upon the same principles, and their policy and constitution nearly similar, so, as like causes will ever produce like effects, it is impossible not to perceive an equal resemblance between their and our manners, as they and we equally deviated from those first principles. Unhappily, the resemblance between the manners of our own times, and the manners of those republicks in their most degenerate periods, [8] is, in many respects, so striking, that unless the words in the original were produced as vouchers,[7] any well-meaning reader, unacquainted with those historians, would be apt to treat the descriptions of those periods, which he may frequently meet with, as licentious, undistinguishing satire upon the present age.

The behaviour of some of our political writers makes an apology of this nature in some measure necessary; on the one hand, that I may avoid the imputation of pedantry, or being thought fond of an idle ostentatious parade of learning; on the other, *lest a work calculated to promote domestick peace and union, should be strained, by the perverseness of party construction, into an inflammatory libel.*

---

7. A piece of evidence; a written warrant or attestation (*OED*, 2a and c).

Introduction

I am not at all surprised at those encomiums which the philosophers and poets so lavishly bestow upon the pleasures of a country retirement.[1] The profusion of varying beauties, which attend the returning seasons, furnishes out new and inexhaustible subjects for the entertainment of the studious and contemplative. Even winter carries charms for the philosophic eye, and equally speaks the stupendous power of the great Author of nature. To search out and adore the Creator through his works, is our primary duty, and claims the first place in every rational mind. To promote the public good of the community of which we are born members, in proportion to our situation and abilities, is our secondary duty as men and citizens. I judged therefore a close attention to the study of History the most useful way of employing that time which my country-recess afforded, as it would enable [10] me to fulfil this obligation: and upon this principle I take the liberty of offering these papers as my mite[2] towards the public good.

1. The satisfactions of rural retirement have been a perennial theme of poetry from antiquity; e.g. Virgil, *Georgics* and Horace, *Odes*, I.xvii and *Epode* II. In eighteenth-century England notable examples include John Pomfret's *The Choice* (1700).
2. Modest contribution (*OED*, 1c).

In the course of these researches nothing gave me so much pleasure as the study of ancient history: because it made me so truly sensible of the inestimable value of our own constitution, when I observed the very different maxims and conduct, and the strong contrast between the founders of despotick monarchies, and the legislators of the free states of antiquity. In the former, that absurd and impious doctrine[3] of millions created for the sole use and pleasure of one individual, seems to have been the first position in their politicks, and the general rule of their conduct. The latter fixed the basis of their respective states upon this just and benevolent plan,

> That the safety and happiness of the whole community was the only end of all government.

The former treated mankind as brutes, and lorded it over them by force. The latter received them as their fellow-creatures, and governed them by reason; hence whilst we detest the former as the enemies and destroyers, we cannot help admiring and revering the latter, as the lovers and benefactors of mankind.

The histories which I considered with the greatest attention, gave me the highest en-[11]tertainment, and affected me most, were those of the free states of Greece, Carthage, and Rome. I saw with admiration the profound wisdom and sagacity, the unwearied labour and disinterested spirit of those amiable and generous men, who contributed most towards forming those states, and settling them upon the firmest foundations. I traced with pleasure their gradual progress towards that height of power, to which in process of time they arrived; and I marked the various steps and degrees by which they again declined, and at last sunk gradually

---

3. The absurdity of despotism was an important theme in Montesquieu's *De l'esprit des lois* (1748), where he had summarized its essence as a form of government in an anecdote of barbaric wastefulness: "Quand les sauvages de la Louisiane veulent avoir du fruit, ils coupent l'arbre au pied, et cueillent le fruit. Voilà le gouvernement despotique." (When the savages of Louisiana wish to eat fruit, they cut down the tree at the base, and gather the fruit. There you have despotic government. Montesquieu, *De l'esprit des lois*, book 5, ch. 13). Montagu's indebtedness to Montesquieu emerges very clearly later (see below, pp. 209, 225–29, 251).

into their final dissolution, not without a just mixture of sorrow and indignation.

It would be a labour of more curiosity, than of real use at this time, to give a long detail of the original formation of those states, and the wise laws and institutions by which they were raised to that envied degree of perfection; yet a concise account of the primitive constitution of each state may be so far necessary, as it will render the deviations from that constitution more intelligible, and more fully illustrate the causes of their final subversion. But to point out and expose the principal causes, which contributed gradually to weaken, and at length demolish and level with the ground, those beautiful fabricks raised by the public virtue, and cemented by the blood of so many [12] illustrious patriots, will, in my opinion, be more interesting, and more instructive.

When I consider the constitution of our own country, I cannot but think it the best calculated for promoting the happiness, and preserving the lives, liberty, and property of mankind, of any yet recorded in prophane history. I am persuaded too, that our wise ancestors, who first formed it, adopted whatever they judged most excellent and valuable in those states when in their greatest perfection; and did all that human wisdom could do for rendering it durable, and transmitting it pure and entire to future generations. But as all things under the sun are subject to change, and children are too apt to forget and degenerate from the virtues of their fathers, there seems great reason to fear, that what has happened to those free states may at length prove the melancholy fate of our own country; especially when we reflect, that the same causes, which contributed to their ruin, operate at this time so very strongly amongst us. As I thought therefore that it might be of some use to my country at this dangerous crisis, I have selected the interesting examples of those once free and powerful nations, who by totally deviating from those principles upon which they were originally founded, lost first their liberty, and at last their very existence, so far [13] as to leave no other vestiges remaining of them as a people, but what are to be found in the records of history.

It is an undoubted truth, that our own constitution has at different times suffered very severe shocks, and been reduced more than once to the very point of ruin: but because it has hitherto providentially escaped, we are not to flatter ourselves that opportunities of recovery will always offer. To me therefore the method of proof drawn from example, seemed more striking, as well as more level to every capacity, than all speculative reasoning: for as the same causes will, by the stated laws of sublunary affairs,[4] sooner or later invariably produce the same effects, so whenever we see the same maxims of government prevail, the same measures pursued, and the same coincidences of circumstances happen in our own country, which brought on, and attended the subversion of those states, we may plainly read our own fate in their catastrophe, unless we apply speedy and effectual remedies, before our case is past recovery. It is the best way to learn wisdom in time from the fate of others; and if examples will not instruct and make us wiser, I confess myself utterly at a loss to know what will.

In my reflections, which naturally arose in the course of these researches, truth and [14] impartiality have been my only guides. I have endeavoured to shew the principal causes of that degeneracy of manners, which reduced those once brave and free peoples into the most abject slavery. I have marked the alarming progress which the same evils have already made, and still continue to make amongst us, with that honest freedom which is the birthright of every Englishman. My sole aim is to excite those who have the welfare of their country at heart, to unite their endeavours in opposing the fatal tendency of those evils, whilst they are within the power of remedy. With this view, and this only, I have marked out the remote as well as immediate causes of the ruin of those states, as so many beacons warning us to avoid the same rocks upon which they struck, and at last suffered shipwreck.

Truth will ever be unpalatable to those who are determined not to relinquish error, but can never give offence to the honest and well-meaning amongst my countrymen. For the plain-dealing remonstrances of a friend differ as widely from the rancour of an enemy, as the friendly probe of the physician from the dagger of the assassin.

---

4. Literally, situated beneath the moon; metaphorically, relating to the world and its material; ephemeral affairs (*OED*, 1, 2, and 3). In the Ptolemaic system, everything above the orbit of the moon was eternal and changeless.

CHAPTER I

Of the Republick of Sparta

All the free states of Greece were at first monarchial,[a] and seem to owe their liberty rather to the injudicious oppressions of their respective Kings, than to any natural propensity in the people to alter their form of Government. But as they had smarted so severely under an excess of power lodged in the hands of one man, they were too apt to run into the other extreme, Democracy; a state of government the most subject of all others to disunion and faction.

Of all the Grecian states, that of Sparta seems to have been the most unhappy, before their government was new-modelled by Lycurgus. The authority of their Kings and their laws (as Plutarch informs us) were [16] alike trampled upon and despised. Nothing could restrain the insolence of the headstrong encroaching populace; and the whole government sunk into Anarchy and confusion. From this deplorable situation the wisdom and virtue of one great man raised his country to that height of power, which was the envy and the terror of her neighbours. A convincing proof how far the influence of one great and good man will operate towards reforming

a. Dion. Halicarn. p. 248. edit. Rob. Steph. 1546.[1]
1. Dionysius of Halicarnassus, V.lxxiv.1.

the most bold licentious people, when he has once thoroughly acquired their esteem and confidence! Upon this principle Lycurgus founded his plan of totally altering and new-moulding the constitution of his country. A design, all circumstances considered, the most daring, and the most happily executed, of any yet immortalised in history.[a]

Lycurgus succeeded to the moiety[2] of the crown of Sparta at the death of his elder brother; but his brother's widow declaring herself with child, and that child proving to be a son, he immediately resigned the regal dignity to the new-born infant, and governed as protector and guardian of the young prince during his minority. The generous and disinterested behaviour of Lycurgus upon this occasion endeared him greatly to the people; who had already experienced [17] the happy effect of his wise and equitable administration. But to avoid the malice of the Queen-mother and her faction, who accused him of designs upon the crown, he prudently quitted both the government and his country. In his travels during this voluntary exile, he drew up and thoroughly digested his great scheme of reformation. He visited all those states which at that time were most eminent for the wisdom of their laws, or the form of their constitution. He carefully observed all the different institutions, and the good or bad effects which they respectively produced on the manners of each people. He took care to avoid what he judged to be defects; but selected whatever he found calculated to promote the happiness of a people; and with these materials he formed his so much celebrated plan of legislation, which he very soon had an opportunity of reducing to practice. For the Spartans, thoroughly sensible of the difference between the administration of Lycurgus and that of their Kings, not only earnestly wished for his presence, but sent repeated deputations to intreat him to return, and free them from those numerous disorders under which their country at that time laboured. As the request of the people was unanimous, and the Kings no ways opposed his return, he judged it the critical time for [18] the execution of his scheme. For he found affairs at home in the distracted situation they had been represented, and the whole body of the people in a disposition proper for his purpose.

a. Plutarch relates this affair greatly to the honour of Lycurgus in the beginning of his Life.[3]

2. A half (*OED*, 1a).

3. Plutarch, "Lycurgus," V.

Lycurgus began his reform with a change in the constitution, which at that time consisted of a confused medley of hereditary monarchy divided between two families, and a disorderly Democracy, utterly destitute of the balance of a third intermediate power, a circumstance so essential to the duration of all mixed governments.[4] To remedy this evil, he established a senate with such a degree of power, as might fix them the inexpugnable barrier of the constitution against the encroachments either of Kings or people. The Crown of Sparta had been long divided between two families descended originally from the same ancestor, who jointly enjoyed the succession. But though Lycurgus was sensible that all the mischiefs which had happened to the state, arose from this absurd division of the regal power, yet he made no alteration as to the succession of the two families. Any innovation in so nice a point might have proved an endless source of civil commotions, from the pretensions of that line which should happen to be excluded. He therefore left them the [19] title and the insignia of royalty, but limited their authority, which he confined to the business of war and religion. To the people he gave the privilege of electing the senators, and giving their sanction to those laws which the Kings and senate should approve.

When Lycurgus had regulated the government, he undertook a task more arduous than any of the fabled labours of Hercules.[5] This was to new-mould his countrymen, by extirpating all the destructive passions,

4. Polybius had praised the Roman constitution as incorporating a blend of the three simple forms of monarchy, aristocracy, and democracy (VI.iii.5), and in the eighteenth century that praise was often transferred to England. Voltaire, in his *Lettres écrites de Londres* (Basle, 1734), had admired the "mélange dans le Gouvernement d'Angleterre, ce concert entre les Communes, les Lords, & le Roy" (the mixture in the government of England, this harmony between the commons, the lords, and the king; Letter IX, p. 56).

5. Heracles, having killed his wife Megara and his children in a fit of madness sent to him by Hera, was forced to purify himself by serving Eurystheus, king of Tiryns, for twelve years and performing whatever labors Eurystheus should impose. The twelve labors were: slaying the Nemean lion; slaying the Hydra; catching the Erymanthian boar; catching the hind of Ceryneia; driving off the Stymphalian birds; cleansing the Augean stables; capturing the Cretan bull; taming the horses of Diomedes; seizing the girdle of the Amazon queen, Hippolyte; driving off the cattle of Geryon; stealing the apples of the Hesperides; and, finally, capturing and binding the dog of Hades, Cerberus.

and raising them above every weakness and infirmity of human nature. A scheme which all the great Philosophers had taught in theory, but none except Lycurgus was ever able to reduce to practice.

As he found the two extremes, of great wealth and great indigence, were the source of infinite mischiefs in a free state, he divided the lands of the whole territory into equal lots, proportioned to the number of the inhabitants. He appointed publick tables, at which he enjoined all the citizens to eat together without distinction;[6] and he subjected every man, even the Kings themselves, to a fine,[a] if they should violate this law by [20] eating at their own houses. Their diet was plain, simple, and regulated by the law, and distributed amongst the guests in equal portions. Every member was obliged monthly to contribute his quota for the provision of his respective table. The conversation allowed at these publick repasts turned wholly upon such subjects as tended most to improve the minds of the younger sort in the principles of wisdom and virtue. Hence, as Xenophon observes, they were schools not only for temperance and sobriety, but also for instruction.[7] Thus Lycurgus introduced a perfect equality amongst his countrymen. The highest and the lowest fared alike as to diet, were all lodged and cloathed alike, without the least variation either in fashion or materials.

When by these means he had exterminated every species of luxury, he next removed all temptation to the acquisition of wealth, that fatal source of the innumerable evils which prevailed in every other country. He effected this with his usual policy, by forbidding the currency of gold and silver money, and substituting an iron coinage of great weight and little value, which continued the only current coin through the whole Spartan dominions for several ages. [21]

To bar up the entrance of Wealth, and guard his citizens against the contagion of Corruption, he absolutely prohibited navigation and

---

a. Ἄγιδος γοῦν τοῦ βασιλέως . . . ἐζημίωσαν αὐτόν. Plut. vita Lycur. pag. 46. lit. c. Edit. Xiglandri.[8]

6. Common messing is a recurrent feature in Utopian societies; e.g., More, *Utopia,* pp. 56–57.

7. Xenophon, "Spartan Society," V.

8. "They laid a fine upon King Agis"; Plutarch, "Lycurgus," XII.3.

commerce, though his country contained a large extent of sea-coast, furnished with excellent harbours. He allowed as little intercourse as possible with foreigners, nor suffered any of his countrymen to visit the neighbouring states, unless when the publick business required it, lest they should be infected with their vices. Agriculture, and such mechanick trades as were absolutely necessary for their subsistence, he confined to their slaves the Ilotes;[9] but he banished all those arts which tended either to debase the mind, or enervate the body. Musick he encouraged, and poetry he admitted, but both subject to the inspection of the magistrates.[a] Thus, by the equal partition of the lands, and the abolition of gold and silver money, he at once preserved his country from luxury, avarice, and all those evils which arise from an irregular indulgence of the passions, as well as all contentions about property, with their consequence, vexatious law-suits.

To insure the observance of his laws to the latest posterity, he next formed proper [22] regulations for the education of their children, which he esteemed one of the greatest duties of a legislator. His grand maxim was,

> That children were the property of the state, to whom alone their education was to be intrusted.

In their first infancy, the nurses were instructed to indulge them neither in their diet, nor in those little froward humours which are so peculiar to that age; to inure them to bear cold and fasting; to conquer their first fears by accustoming them to solitude and darkness; and to prepare them for that stricter state of discipline, to which they were soon to be initiated.

When arrived at the age of seven years, they were taken from the nurses, and placed in their proper classes. The diet and cloathing of all were the same, just sufficient to support nature, and defend them from the inclemency of the seasons; and they all lodged alike in the same dormitory on beds of reeds, to which for the sake of warmth they were allowed

---

a. Lycurgus was the first who collected the entire works of Homer;[10] which he brought into Greece out of Asia-Minor.

9. The Ilotes, or Helots, were the slave underclass of Spartan society.

10. Plutarch, "Lycurgus," I.2 and IV.4.

in winter to add the down of thistles. Their sports and exercises were such as contributed to render their limbs supple, and their bodies compact and firm. They were accustomed to run up the steepest rocks barefoot; and swimming, dancing, hunting, boxing, and wrestling, were their constant diversions. Lycurgus was equally solicitous in training up the youth to a habit [23] of passive courage as well as active. They were taught to despise pain no less than danger, and to bear the severest scourgings with the most invincible constancy and resolution. For to flinch under the strokes, or to exhibit the least sign of any sense of pain, was deemed highly infamous.

Nor were the minds of the Spartan youth cultivated with less care. Their learning, as Plutarch informs us, was sufficient for their occasions, for Lycurgus admitted nothing but what was truly useful. They carefully instilled into their tender minds the great duties of religion, and the sacred indispensable obligation of an oath, and trained them up in the best of sciences, the principles of wisdom and virtue. The love of their Country seemed to be almost innate; and this leading maxim,

> That every Spartan was the property of his country, and had no right over himself,

was by the force of education incorporated into their very nature.

When they arrived to manhood they were inrolled in their militia, and allowed to be present in their publick assemblies: Privileges which only subjected them to a different discipline. For the employments and way of living of the citizens of Sparta were fixed, and settled by as strict regulations as in an army upon actual service. When [24] they took the field, indeed, the rigour of their discipline with respect to diet and the ornament of their persons was much softened, so that the Spartans were the only people in the universe, to whom the toils of war afforded ease and relaxation. In fact, Lycurgus's plan of civil government was evidently designed to preserve his country free and independent, and to form the minds of his citizens for the enjoyment of that rational and manly happiness which can find no place in a breast enslaved by the pleasures of the senses, or ruffled by the passions; and the military regulations which he established, were as plainly calculated for the protection of his country from the encroachments of her ambitious neighbours.[a] For he left no alternative to his people but death or victory; and he laid them under a necessity of observing those regulations, by substituting the valour of the inhabitants in the place of walls and fortifications for the defence of their city.

If we reflect that human nature is at all times and in all places the same, it seems to the last degree astonishing, how Lycurgus could be able to introduce such a self-denying plan of discipline amongst a disorderly licentious people: A scheme, which not only [25] levelled at once all distinction, as to property, between the richest and the poorest individual, but compelled the greatest persons in the state to submit to a regimen which allowed only the bare necessaries of life, excluding every thing which in the opinion of mankind seems essential to its comforts and enjoyments. I observed before, that he had secured the esteem and confidence of his countrymen; and there was, besides, at that time a very lucky concurrence of circumstances in his favour. The two Kings were men of little spirit, and less abilities, and the people were glad to exchange their disorderly state for any settled form of government. By his establishment of a Senate, consisting of thirty persons who held their seats for life, and to whom he committed the supreme power in civil affairs, he brought the principal nobility into his scheme, as they naturally expected a share in a government which they plainly saw inclined so much to an Aristocracy. Even the two Kings very readily accepted seats in his senate, to secure some degree of authority. He awed the people into obedience by the sanction he procured for his scheme from the oracle at Delphos,[11] whose decisions were, at that time, revered by all Greece as divine and

a. Plutarch has taken no notice of them. But Xenophon has fully explained them in his treatise on the Spartan republick, p. 542, & seq.[12]

11. The oracular shrine of Apollo in his temple at Delphi was one of the two foremost religious centers of the ancient Greek world (the other being the plain of Olympia). The ecstatic priestess of the god (called the Pythia) would respond to the questions of suppliants in elliptical or enigmatic words which would be interpreted by an attendant priest. The oracle was pre-eminently concerned with questions of religion, in particular how men were to be reconciled with the gods, and evil averted.

12. Xenophon, "Spartan Society," XI–XIII.

infallible. But the greatest difficulty he had to encounter, was, to procure [26] the equal partition of the lands. The very first proposal met with so violent an opposition from the men of fortune, that a fray[13] ensued, in which Lycurgus lost one of his eyes. But the people, struck with the sight of the blood of this admired legislator, seized the offender, one Alcander, a young man of a hot, but not disingenuous disposition, and gave him up to Lycurgus to be punished, at discretion. But the humane and generous behaviour of Lycurgus quickly made a convert of Alcander, and wrought such a change, that from an enemy he became his greatest admirer and advocate with the people.

Plutarch and the rest of the Greek historians leave us greatly in the dark as to the means by which Lycurgus was able to make so bitter a pill, as the division of property, go down with the wealthy part of his country-men. They tell us indeed, that he carried his point by the gentle method of reasoning and persuasion, joined to that religious awe which the divine sanction of the oracle impressed so deeply on the minds of the citizens. But the cause, in my opinion, does not seem equal to the effect. For the furious opposition which the rich made to the very first motion for such a distribution of property, evinces plainly, that they looked upon the responses of the oracle as mere priest-craft, and treated it as the *esprits-forts* have done reli-[27]gion in modern times;[14] I mean, as a state-engine fit only to be played off upon the common people. It seems most prob-able, in my opinion, that as he effected the change in the constitution by the distribution of the supreme power amongst the principal persons, when he formed his senate; so the equal partition of property was the bait thrown out to bring over the body of the people intirely to his interest. I should rather think that he compelled the rich to submit to so grating

13. A fight or scuffle.

14. *Esprits-forts* are freethinkers or *libertins* in matters of religion. For the attack on established religion in England made in the name of Enlightenment from the middle of the seventeenth century, see J. A. I. Champion, *The Pillars of Priestcraft Shaken: The Church of England and Its Enemies, 1660–1730* (Cambridge: Cambridge University Press, 1992); and, for the European context, J. I. Israel, *Radical Enlight-enment: Philosophy and the Making of Modernity 1650–1750* (Oxford: Oxford University Press, 2001). Leslie Stephen's *History of English Thought in the Eighteenth Century* (1876) is still useful on this subject for its clarity of outline.

a measure, by the assistance of the poorer citizens, who were vastly the majority.

As soon as Lycurgus had thoroughly settled his new policy, and by his care and assiduity imprinted his laws so deeply in the minds and manners of his countrymen, that he judged the constitution able to support itself, and stand upon its own bottom, his last scheme was, to fix and perpetuate its duration down to the latest posterity, as far as human prudence and human means could effect it. To bring his scheme to bear, he had again recourse to the same pious artifice which had succeeded so well in the beginning. He told the people in a general assembly, that he could not possibly put the finishing stroke to his new establishment, which was the most essential point, till he had again consulted the oracle. As they all expressed the greatest eagerness for his undertaking the journey, he [28] laid hold of so fair an opportunity to bind the Kings, senate, and people, by the most solemn oaths, to the strict observance of his new form of government, and not to attempt the least alteration in any one particular till his return from Delphos. He had now completed the great design which he had long in view, and bid an eternal adieu to his country. The question he put to the oracle was, "Whether the laws he had already established, were rightly formed to make and preserve his countrymen virtuous and happy?" The answer he received was just as favourable as he desired. It was, "That his laws were excellently well calculated for that purpose; and that Sparta should continue to be the most renowned city in the world, as long as her citizens persisted in the observance of the laws of Lycurgus." He transmitted both the question and the answer home to Sparta in writing, and devoted the remainder of his life to voluntary banishment. The accounts in history of the end of this great man are very uncertain. Plutarch affirms, that as his resolution was never to release his countrymen from the obligation of the oath he had laid them under, he put a voluntary end to his life at Delphos by fasting. Plutarch extols the death of Lycurgus in very pompous terms, as a most unexampled instance of heroic patriotism, since he bequeathed, as he [29] terms it, his death to his country, as the perpetual guardian to that happiness, which he had procured for them during his life-time. Yet the same historian acknowledges another tradition, that Lycurgus ended his days in the island of Crete, and desired, as his last request, that his body should be burnt, and his ashes thrown into the sea;[a] lest, if his remains should at any time be carried back to Sparta, his countrymen might look upon themselves as released from their oath as much as if he had returned alive, and be induced to alter his form of government. I own, I prefer this latter account, as more agreeable to the genius and policy of that wise and truly disinterested legislator.

The Spartans, as Plutarch asserts, held the first rank in Greece for discipline and reputation full five hundred years, by strictly adhering to the laws of Lycurgus; which not one of their Kings ever infringed for fourteen successions quite down to the reign of the first Agis. For he will not allow the creation of those magistrates called the Ephori to be any innovation in the constitution, since he affirms it to have been, "not a relaxation, but an extension, of the civil polity."[b] But notwithstanding the gloss thrown over the institution of the Ephori by this nice distinction [30] of Plutarch's, it certainly induced as fatal a change into the Spartan constitution, as the Tribuneship of the people, which was formed upon that model, did afterwards into the Roman. For instead of enlarging and strengthening the aristocratical power, as Plutarch asserts, they gradually usurped the whole government, and formed themselves into a most tyrannical Oligarchy.

The Ephori (a Greek word signifying inspectors or overseers) were five in number, and elected annually by the people out of their own body. The exact time of the origin of this institution, and of the authority annexed to their office, is quite uncertain. Herodotus ascribes it to Lycurgus; Xenophon to Lycurgus jointly with the principal citizens of Sparta. Aristotle and Plutarch fix it under the reign of Theopompus and Polydorus, and attribute the institution expressly to the former of those princes, about 130 years after the death of Lycurgus.[15] I cannot but subscribe to this opinion as the most probable, because the first political contest we meet with

a. Plut. Vit. Lycurg. ad finem.[16]
b. Plut. ibid. p. 58. A. Ἡ γὰρ τῶν ἐφόρων κατάστασις, &c.[17]
15. Aristotle, *Politics*, V.xi. Plutarch, "Lycurgus," VII.1.
16. Plutarch, "Lycurgus," XXXI.5.
17. Plutarch, "Lycurgus," XXIX.6. "For the institution of the ephors."

at Sparta happened under the reign of those princes, when the people endeavoured to extend their privileges beyond the limits prescribed by Lycurgus. But as the joint opposition of the Kings and senate was equally warm, the creation of this magistracy out of the body of the people, seems to [31] have been the step taken at that time to compromise the affair, and restore the publick tranquillity: A measure which the Roman senate copied afterwards, in the erection of the Tribuneship, when their people mutinied, and made that memorable secession to the *mons sacer.*[18] I am confirmed in this opinion by the relation which Aristotle gives us of a remarkable dispute between Theopompus and his wife upon that occasion.[a] The Queen, much dissatisfied with the institution of the Ephori, reproached her husband greatly for submitting to such a diminution of the regal authority, and asked him if he was not ashamed to transmit the crown to his posterity so much weaker and worse circumstanced, than he received it from his father. His answer, which is recorded amongst the laconic *bons mots,*[19] was,

No, for I transmit it more lasting.[b]

But the event shewed that the lady was a better politician, as well as truer prophet, than her husband. Indeed the nature of their office, the circumstances of their election, and the authority they assumed, are convincing proofs that their office was first extorted, and their power afterwards gradually extended, by the violence of the people, irritated too probably by the oppres-[32]sive behaviour of the Kings and senate. For

a. De Rebuspubl. cap. 11. p. 154. vol. 2. Edit. Basil. 1550.[20]

b. "Οὐ δῆτα" φάναι· "παραδίδωμι γὰρ πολυχρονιωτέραν."[21]

18. A reference to an episode in the prolonged struggle between the privileged (patrician) and unprivileged (plebeian) classes in Republican Rome, when in 494 B.C. the plebeians, dissatisfied with the provisions of the primitive Roman legal code known as the Twelve Tables, seceded to the Aventine hill to extract greater constitutional power from the patricians. See Livy, II.xxxii.2–12.

19. Clever or witty sayings. The pithy remarks of the Spartans were collected by Plutarch, but this of Theopompus is not among them.

20. Aristotle, *Politics,* V.xi.3

21. "Certainly not," he said, "for I hand it on to them in a more durable form" (Aristotle, *Politics,* V.xi.3).

whether their power extended no farther than to decide, when the two Kings differed in opinion, and to over-rule in favour of him whose sentiments should be most conducive to the publick interest, as we are told by Plutarch in the life of Agis;[22] or whether they were at first only select friends, whom the Kings appointed as deputies in their absence, when they were both compelled to take the field together in their long wars with the Messenians, as the same author tells us by the mouth of his hero Cleomenes,[23] is a point, which history does not afford us light enough to determine. This however is certain, from the concurrent voice of all the antient historians, that at last they not only seized upon every branch of the administration, but assumed the power of imprisoning, deposing, and even putting their Kings to death by their own authority. The Kings too, in return, sometimes bribed, sometimes deposed or murdered the Ephori, and employed their whole interest to procure such persons to be elected, as they judged would be most tractable. I look therefore upon the creation of the Ephori as a breach in the Spartan constitution, which proved the first inlet to faction and corruption. For that these evils took rise from the institution of the Ephori, is evident [33] from the testimony of Aristotle, "who thought it extremely impolitick to elect magistrates, vested with the supreme power in the state, out of the body of the people; because it often happened, that men extremely indigent were raised in this manner to the helm, whom their very poverty tempted to become venal. For the Ephori, as he affirms, had not only been frequently guilty of bribery before his time, but, even at the very time he wrote, some of those magistrates, corrupted by money, used their utmost endeavours, at the publick repasts, to accomplish the destruction of the whole city. He adds too, that as their power was so great as to amount to a perfect tyranny, the Kings themselves were necessitated to court their favour by such methods as greatly hurt the constitution, which from an Aristocracy, degenerated into an absolute Democracy. For that magistracy alone had engrossed the whole government."[a]

a. Arist. de Rebuspubl. lib. 2. c. 7. p. 122. lit. 1. vol. 2.[24]
22. Plutarch, "Agis," XII.2.
23. Plutarch, "Cleomenes," X.2.
24. Aristotle, *Politics,* II.ix.

From these remarks of the judicious Aristotle, it is evident that the Ephori had totally destroyed the balance of power established by Lycurgus. From the tyranny therefore of this magistracy proceeded those convulsions which so frequently shook the state of Sparta, and at last gradually brought on its [34] total subversion. But though this fatal alteration in the Spartan constitution must be imputed to the intrigues of the Ephori and their faction, yet it could never, in my opinion, have been effected, without a previous degeneracy in their manners; which must have been the consequence of some deviation from the maxims of Lycurgus.

It appears evidently from the testimony of Polybius and Plutarch, that the great scheme of the Spartan legislator was, to provide for the lasting security of his country against all foreign invasions, and to perpetuate the blessings of liberty and independency to the people. By the generous plan of discipline which he established, he rendered his countrymen invincible at home. By banishing gold and silver, and prohibiting commerce and the use of shipping, he proposed to confine the Spartans within the limits of their own territories; and by taking away the means, to repress all desires of making conquests upon their neighbours. But the same love of glory and of their country which made them so terrible in the field, quickly produced ambition and a lust of domination; and ambition as naturally opened the way for avarice and corruption. For Polybius truly observes, that as long as they extended [35] their views no farther than the dominion over their neighbouring states, the produce of their own country was sufficient for what supplies they had occasion for in such short excursions.[a] But when, in direct violation of the laws of Lycurgus, they began to undertake more distant expeditions both by sea and land, they quickly felt the want of a publick fund to defray their extraordinary expences. For they found by experience, that neither their iron money, nor their method of trucking[25] the annual produce of their own lands for such commodities as they wanted (which was the only traffick allowed by

a. Polyb. lib. 6. p. 685. vol. 1. edit. Isaac. Gronov. 1670.[26]
25. To exchange for profit or barter (*OED*, 2).
26. Polybius, VI.x.1–14.

the laws of Lycurgus) could possibly answer their demands upon those occasions. Hence their ambition, as the same historian remarks, laid them under the scandalous necessity of paying servile court to the Persian monarchs for pecuniary supplies and subsidies, to impose heavy tributes upon the conquered islands, and to exact money from the other Grecian states, as occasions required.

Historians unanimously agree, that wealth, with its attendants luxury and corruption, gained admission at Sparta in the reign of the first Agis. Lysander, like a Hero and a Politician; a man of the greatest abilities and the greatest dishonesty that Sparta ever produced; rapacious after money, which at the same time he despised, and a slave only to [36] ambition, was the author of an innovation so fatal to the manners of his countrymen. After he had enabled his country to give law to all Greece by his conquest of Athens,[27] he sent home that immense mass of wealth, which the plunder of so many states had put into his possession. The most sensible men amongst the Spartans, dreading the fatal consequences of this capital breach of the institutions of their legislator, protested strongly before the Ephori against the introduction of gold and silver, as pests destructive to the publick. The Ephori referred it to the decision of the senate, who, dazzled with the lustre of that money, to which 'till that time they had been utter strangers, decreed, "That gold and silver money might be admitted for the service of the state; but made it death, if any should ever be found in the possession of a private person." This decision Plutarch censures as weak and sophistical.[a] As if Lycurgus was only afraid simply of money, and not of that dangerous love of money which is generally its concomitant; a passion which is so far from being rooted out by the restraint laid upon private persons, that it was rather inflamed by the esteem and value which was set upon money by the publick. Thus, as he justly remarks, whilst [37] they barred up the houses of private citizens against the entrance of Wealth by the

a. Plut. in Vit. Lysand. p. 442. lit. E.[28]

27. Athens surrendered to Sparta in 404 B.C., after Lysander had defeated the Athenians at the battle of Aegospotami (405 B.C.), thereby bringing the Peloponnesian War to a close.

28. Plutarch, "Lysander," II.4 and XVI.

terror and safeguard of the Law, they left their minds more exposed to the love of money and the influence of corruption, by raising an universal admiration and desire of it, as something great and respectable. The truth of this remark appears by the instance given us by Plutarch, of one Thorax, a great friend of Lysander's, who was put to death by the Ephori, upon proof that a quantity of silver had been actually found in his possession.[29]

From that time Sparta became venal, and grew extremely fond of subsidies from foreign powers. Agesilaus, who succeeded Agis, and was one of the greatest of their Kings, behaved in the latter part of his life more like a captain of a band of mercenaries, than a King of Sparta. He received a large subsidy from Tachos, at that time King of Egypt, and entered into his service with a body of troops which he had raised for that purpose. But when Nectanabis, who had rebelled against his uncle Tachos, offered him more advantageous terms, he quitted the unfortunate Monarch and went over to his rebellious nephew, pleading the interest of his country in excuse for so treacherous and infamous an action.[a] So great a change had [38] the introduction of money already made in the manners of the leading Spartans!

Plutarch dates the first origin of corruption, that disease of the body politick, and consequently the decline of Sparta, from that memorable period, when the Spartans having subverted the domination of Athens, glutted themselves (as he terms it) with gold and silver.[b] For when once the love of money had crept into their city, and avarice and the most sordid meanness grew up with the possession, as luxury, effeminacy, and dissipation did with the enjoyment of wealth, Sparta was deprived of many of her ancient glories and advantages, and sunk greatly both in power and reputation, till the reign of Agis and Leonidas.[c] But as

---

a. Plut. in Vit. Agesi. p. 617. lit. C.[30]
b. In Vit. Agid. p. 796. lit. C.[31]
c. Ibid. p. 797. lit. C.[32]
29. Plutarch, "Lysander," XIX.4.
30. Plutarch, "Agesilaus," XXXVII.
31. Plutarch, "Agis," II.6.
32. Plutarch, "Agis," III.1.

the original allotments of land were yet preserved (the number of which Lycurgus had fixed and decreed to be kept up by a particular law) and were transmitted down from father to son by hereditary succession, the same constitutional order and equality still remaining, raised up the state again, however, from other political lapses.

Under the reigns of those two Kings happened the mortal blow, which subverted the very foundation of their constitution. Epi-[39]tadeus, one of the Ephori, upon a quarrel with his son, carried his resentment so far as to procure a law which permitted everyone to alienate their hereditary lands, either by gift or sale, during their life-time, or by will at their decease. This law produced a fatal alteration in the landed property. For as Leonidas, one of their Kings, who had lived a long time at the court of Seleucus, and married a lady of that country, had introduced the pomp and luxury of the East at his return to Sparta, the old institutions of Lycurgus, which had fallen into disuse, were by his example soon treated with contempt.[a] Hence the necessity of the luxurious, and the extortion of the avaricious, threw the whole property into so few hands, that out of seven hundred, the number to which the ancient Spartan families were then reduced, about one hundred only were in possession of their respective hereditary lands allotted by Lycurgus.[b] The rest, as Plutarch observes, lived an idle life in the city, an indigent abject herd, alike destitute of fortune and employment; in their wars abroad, indolent dispirited dastards;[33] at home ever ripe for sedition and insurrections, and greedily catching at every opportunity of embroiling [40] affairs, in hopes of such a change as might enable them to retrieve their fortunes. Evils, which the extremes of wealth and indigence are ever productive of in free countries.

Young Agis, the third of that name, and the most virtuous and accomplished King that ever sat upon the throne of Sparta since the reign of

---

a. In Vit. Agid. p. 797. lit. A.[34]

b. Ibid. lit. E.[35]

33. Those who meanly or basely shrink from danger; mean, base, or despicable cowards (*OED*, 2).

34. Plutarch, "Agis," III.5–6.

35. Plutarch, "Agis," V.1–4.

the great Agesilaus, undertook the reform of the state, and attempted to re-establish the old Lycurgic constitution, as the only means of extricating his country out of her distresses, and raising her to her former dignity and lustre. An enterprize attended not only with the greatest difficulties, but, as the times were so corrupt, with the greatest danger.[a] He began with trying the efficacy of example, and though he had been bred in all the pleasures and delicacy which affluence could procure, or the fondness of his mother and grandmother, who were the wealthiest people in Sparta, could indulge him in, yet he at once changed his way of life as well as his dress, and conformed to the strictest discipline of Lycurgus in every particular. This generous[36] victory over his passions,[b] the most difficult and most glorious of all others, had so great an effect [41] amongst the younger Spartans, that they came into his measures with more alacrity and zeal than he could possibly have hoped for. Encouraged by this success, Agis brought over some of the principal Spartans, amongst whom was his uncle Agesilaus, whose influence he made use of to persuade his mother, who was sister to Agesilaus, to join his party.[c] For her wealth, and the great number of her friends, dependants, and debtors, made her extremely powerful, and gave her great weight in all public transactions.

His mother, terrified at first at her son's rashness, condemned the whole as the visionary scheme of a young man, who was attempting a measure not only prejudicial to the state, but quite impracticable. But when the reasonings of Agesilaus had convinced her that it would not only be of the greatest utility to the publick, but might be effected with great ease and safety, and the King himself intreated her to contribute her wealth and interest to promote an enterprize which would redound so much to

a. Vita Agid. p. 797. lit. B.[37]

b. Ibid. lit. C.[38]

c. Ibid. p. 798. lit. B.[39]

36. Appropriate or natural to one of noble birth or spirit; hence, magnanimous, free from meanness or prejudice (*OED*, 2a).

37. Plutarch, "Agis," VI.1.

38. Plutarch, "Agis," VI.1–2.

39. Plutarch, "Agis," VI.3–4.

his glory and reputation; she and the rest of her fe-[42]male friends at last changed their sentiments.[a] Fired then with the same glorious emulation, and stimulated to virtue, as it were by some divine impulse, they not only voluntarily spurred on Agis, but summoned and encouraged all their friends, and incited the other ladies to engage in so generous an enterprize. For they were conscious (as Plutarch observes) of the great ascendency which the Spartan women had always over their husbands,[b] who gave their wives a much greater share in the publick administration, than their wives allowed them in the management [43] of their domestick affairs. A circumstance which at that time had drawn almost all the wealth of Sparta into the hands of the women, and proved a terrible, and almost unsurmountable obstacle to Agis. For the Ladies had violently opposed a scheme of reformation, which not only tended to deprive them of those pleasures and trifling ornaments, which, from their ignorance of what was truly good and laudable, they absurdly looked upon as their supreme happiness, but to rob them of that respect and authority which

a. Something seems plainly to be wanting in this passage, which is strangely obscure and intricate. It is evident that Agis employed his uncle Agesilaus to persuade his mother, who was Agesilaus's sister: τὴν μητέρα πείθειν, ἀδελφὴν οὖσαν τοῦ Ἀγησιλάου.[40] The king himself intreats his mother to assist him, αὐτὸς δὲ ὁ βασιλεὺς ἐδεῖτο τῆς μητρὸς, &c.[41] And after he has enumerated the advantages which would result from his scheme, Plutarch abruptly adds, οὕτω μετέπεσον ταῖς γνώμαις αἱ γυναῖκες, &c.[42] in the plural number, though he had just before mentioned Agis's mother only, as the woman applied to on this occasion. It is evident therefore, that his grandmother and all their female friends and relations must have been present at that time, though not mentioned, and that they were the only Spartan ladies who came heartily into his scheme. For when Agis afterwards offers his whole fortune to the publick, he assures the people that his mother and grandmother, τὰς μητέρας,[43] and his friends and relations, who were the richest families in Sparta, were ready to do the same. As Agis certainly includes the wives of his friends and relations, and mentions no other women, I have taken that speech for my guide in giving the sense of this whole passage, in which I could get no assistance from any of the commentators.

b. In Vit. Agid. p. 798. lit. D.[44]

40. "To persuade his mother, who was a sister of Agesilaus."

41. "And the king himself besought his mother."

42. "The women were so changed in their purposes."

43. "His female relations."

44. Plutarch, "Agis," VII.2–3.

they derived from their superior wealth. Such of them therefore as were unwilling to give up these advantages, applied to Leonidas, and intreated him, as he was the more respectable man for his age and experience, to check his young hot-headed colleague, and quash whatever attempts he should make to carry his designs into execution. The older Spartans were no less averse to a reformation of that nature. For as they were deeply immersed in corruption, they trembled at the very name of Lycurgus, as much as runaway slaves, when retaken, do at the sight of their masters.

Leonidas was extremely ready to side with and assist the rich, but durst not openly oppose Agis, for fear of the people, who were eager for such a revolution. He attempted [44] therefore to counteract all his attempts underhand, and insinuated to the magistrates, that Agis aimed at setting up a tyranny, by bribing the poor with the fortunes of the rich; and proposed the partition of lands and the abolition of debts as the means of purchasing guards for himself only, not citizens, as he pretended, for Sparta.

Agis however pursued his design, and having procured his friend Lysander to be elected one of the Ephori, immediately laid his scheme before the senate. The chief heads of his plan were:

That all debts should be totally remitted; that the whole land should be divided into a certain number of lots; and that the ancient discipline and customs of Lycurgus should be revived.

Warm debates were occasioned in the senate by this proposal, which at last was rejected by a majority of one only.[a] Lysander in the mean time convoked an assembly of the people, where after he had harangued, Mandroclidas and Agesilaus beseeched them not to suffer the majesty of Sparta to be any longer trampled upon for the sake of a few luxurious overgrown citizens, who imposed upon them at pleasure.[b] They reminded them not only of the responses of ancient [45] oracles, which enjoined them to beware of avarice, as the pest of Sparta, but also of

a. Vit. Agid. p. 800. lit. A.[45]
b. Ibid. 799. lit. A.[46]
45. Plutarch, "Agis," XI.1.
46. Plutarch, "Agis," IX.1.

those so lately given by the oracle at Pasiphae, which, as they assured the people, commanded the Spartans to return to that perfect equality of possessions, which was settled by the law first instituted by Lycurgus.[a] Agis spoke last in this assembly; and, to enforce the whole by example, told them in a very few words,

> That he offered a most ample contribution towards the establishment of that polity, of which he himself was the author. That he now resigned his whole patrimony into the common stock, which consisted not only of rich arable and pasture land, but of 600 talents besides in coined money. He added, that his mother, grandmother, friends and relations, who were the most wealthy of all the citizens of Sparta, were ready to do the same.[47]

The people, struck with the magnanimity and generosity of Agis, received his offer with the loudest applause, and extolled him, as the only King who for three hundred years past had been worthy of the throne of Sparta. This provoked Leonidas to fly out [46] into the most open and violent opposition, from the double motive of avarice and envy. For he was sensible, that if this scheme took place, he should not only be compelled to follow their example, but that the surrender of his estate would then come from him with so ill a grace, that the honour of the whole measure would be attributed solely to his colleague. Lysander, finding Leonidas and his party too powerful in the senate, determined to prosecute and expel him for the breach of a very old law, which forbid[48] any of the royal family to intermarry with foreigners, or to bring up any children which they might have by such marriage, and inflicted the penalty of death upon any one who should leave Sparta to reside in foreign countries.

After Lysander had taken care that Leonidas should be informed of the crime laid to his charge, he with the rest of the Ephori, who were

---

a. This is an oracle mentioned by Plutarch, about which the learned are not agreed: however, it seems to have given its responses in dreams.[49]

47. Plutarch, "Agis," IX.3.

48. A permissible archaism in eighteenth-century English.

49. Plutarch, "Agis," IX.2. In Greek mythology Pasiphaë was the daughter of the Sun and the wife of Minos, King of Crete.

of his party, addressed themselves to the ceremony of observing a sign from heaven.[a] A piece of state-craft most probably introduced formerly by the Ephori [47] to keep the Kings in awe, and perfectly well adapted to the superstition of the people. Lysander affirming that they had seen the usual sign, which declared that Leonidas had sinned against the Gods, summoned him to his trial, and produced evidence sufficient to convict him. At the same time he spirited up Cleombrotus, who had married the daughter of Leonidas, and was of the royal blood, to put in his claim to the succession. Leonidas, terrified at these daring measures, fled, and took sanctuary in the temple of Minerva: he was deposed therefore for non-appearance, and his crown given to his son-in-law Cleombrotus.

But as soon as the term of Lysander's magistracy expired, the new Ephori, who were elected by the prevailing interest of the opposite party, immediately undertook the protection of Leonidas. They summoned Lysander and his friends to answer for their decrees for cancelling debts, and dividing the lands, as contrary to the laws, and treasonable innovations; for so they termed all attempts to restore the ancient constitution [48] of Lycurgus. Alarmed at this, Lysander persuaded the two Kings to join in opposing the Ephori; who, as he plainly proved, assumed an authority which they had not the least right to, as long as the Kings acted together in concert. The Kings, convinced by his reasons, armed a great number of the youth, released all who were prisoners for debt, and thus attended went into the Forum, where they deposed the Ephori, and procured their own friends to be elected into that office, of whom Agesilaus the uncle of Agis was one. By the care and humanity of Agis, no blood was spilt on this memorable occasion. He even protected his antagonist Leonidas against the designs which Agesilaus had formed upon his life, and sent him under a safe convoy to Tegea.

a. The reader may be glad perhaps to find here the ceremony made use of upon this occasion. Vit. Agid. p. 800. lit. B.[50] δι᾽ ἐτῶν ἐννέα λαβόντες οἱ ἔφοροι, &c. Every ninth year the Ephori taking the opportunity of a clear still night, when the moon did not appear, sat silently and observed the sky with great attention; and, if they saw a star shoot, they judged the kings had offended the Gods; and removed them from the government, till an oracle came from Delphos which was favourable to them.

50. Plutarch, "Agis," XI.3; "every ninth year the ephors select."

After this bold stroke, all opposition sunk before them, and every thing succeeded to their wishes; when the single avarice of Agesilaus, that most baneful pest, as Plutarch terms it, which had subverted a constitution the most excellent, and the most worthy of Sparta that had ever yet been established, overset the whole enterprise. By the character which Plutarch gives of Agesilaus,[a] he appears to have been artful and eloquent, but at the same time effemi-[49]nate, corrupt in his manners, avaritious, and so bad a man, that he engaged in this projected revolution with no other view but that of extricating himself from an immense load of debt, which he had most probably contracted to support his luxury. As soon therefore as the two Kings, who were both young men, agreed to proceed upon the abolition of debts, and the partition of lands, Agesilaus artfully persuaded them not to attempt both at once, for fear of exciting some terrible commotion in the city. He assured them farther, that if the rich should once be reconciled to the law for cancelling the debts, the law for dividing the lands would go down with them quietly and without the least obstruction. The Kings assented to his opinion, and Lysander himself was brought over to it, deceived by the same specious, though pernicious reasoning: calling in therefore all the bills, bonds, and pecuniary obligations, they piled them up, and burnt them all publickly in the Forum, to the great mortification of the moneyed men, and the usurers. But Agesilaus in the joy of his heart could not refrain from joking upon the occasion, and told them with a sneer, That whatever they might think of the matter, it was the bright-[50]est and most chearful flame, and the purest bonfire, he had ever beheld in his life-time.[b] Agesilaus had now carried his point, and his conduct proves, that the Spartans had learnt the art of turning publick measures into private jobs,[51] as well as their politer neighbours. For though the people call loudly for the partition of the lands, and the Kings gave orders for it to be done immediately, Agesilaus contrived to throw new obstacles in the way, and protracted the time by

a. Plut. Vit. Agid. p. 798. lit. A.[52]
b. Ibid. p. 801. lit. B.[53]
51. Opportunities for private profit (*OED*, "job" *n.*[2], 2a).
52. Plutarch, "Agis," VI.3–4.
53. Plutarch, "Agis," XIII.3.

various pretences till Agis was obliged to march with the Spartan auxiliaries to assist their allies the Achaeans.[54] For he was in possession of a
most fertile and extensive landed estate at the very time when he owed
more than he was worth; and as he had got rid of all his incumbrances
at once by the first decree, and never intended to part with a single foot
of his land, it was by no means his interest to promote the execution of
the second.

The Spartan troops were mostly indigent young men, who, elate with
their freedom from the bonds of usury, and big with the hopes of a share
in the lands at their return, followed Agis with the greatest vigour and
alacrity, and behaved so well in their march, that they reminded the
admiring Greeks of the excellent discipline and decorum for which the
Spartans were formerly so famous under the most renowned of their [51]
ancient leaders. But whilst Agis was in the field, affairs at home took a
very unhappy turn in his disfavour. The tyrannical behaviour of Agesilaus, who fleeced the people with insupportable exactions, and stuck at
no measure, however infamous or criminal, which would bring in money,
produced another revolution in favour of Leonidas. For the people,
enraged at being tricked out of the promised partition of the lands, which
they imputed to Agis and Cleombrotus, and detesting the rapaciousness
of Agesilaus, readily joined that party which conspired to restore Leonidas. Agis finding affairs in this desperate situation at his return, gave up
all for lost, and took sanctuary in the temple of Minerva, as Cleombrotus
had done in the temple of Neptune.

Though Cleombrotus was the chief object of Leonidas's resentment,
yet he spared his life at the intercession of his daughter Chelonis, the wife
of Cleombrotus; but condemned him to perpetual exile. The generous
Chelonis gave a signal instance, upon this occasion, of that heroic virtue,
for which the Spartan ladies were once so remarkably eminent. When her
father was expelled by the intrigues of Lysander, she followed him into
exile, and refused to share his crown with Cleombrotus. In this calamitous reverse of fortune, she was deaf to [52] all intreaties, and rather chose
to partake of the miseries of banishment with her husband, than all the

---

54. Plutarch, "Agis," XIII.4.

pleasures and grandeur of Sparta with her father. Plutarch pays the ladies a fine compliment upon this occasion, when he says,

> That unless Cleombrotus should have been wholly corrupted by false ambition, he must have deemed himself more truly happy in a state of banishment with such a wife, than he could have been upon a throne without her.[a]

But though Cleombrotus escaped death, yet nothing but the blood of Agis could satisfy the vindictive rage of the ungrateful Leonidas, who, in the former revolution, owed his life to that unfortunate Prince's generosity. After many ineffectual attempts to entice Agis from his asylum, three of his intimate friends in whom he most confided, who used to accompany and guard him to the baths and back again to the temple, betrayed him to his enemies. Amphares, the chief of these, and the contriver of the plot, was one of the new Ephori created after the deposition of Agesilaus. This wretch had lately borrowed a quantity of valuable plate, and a number of magnificent vestments of Agis's mother Agesistrata, and determined to make them his own by the [53] destruction of Agis and his family; at their return therefore in their usual friendly manner from the baths, he first attacked Agis by virtue of his office, whilst Demochares and Arcesilaus, the other two, seized and dragged him to the publick prison. Agis supported all these indignities with the utmost magnanimity: and when the Ephori questioned him, whether Agesilaus and Lysander did not constrain him to do what he had done, and whether he did not repent of the steps he had taken; he undauntedly took the whole upon himself, and told them that he gloried in his scheme, which was the result of his emulation to follow the example of the great Lycurgus. Stung with this answer, the Ephori condemned him to die by their own authority, and ordered the officers to carry him to the place in the prison where the malefactors were strangled. But when the officers and even the mercenary soldiers of Leonidas refused to be concerned in so infamous and unprecedented an action as laying hands upon their King, Demochares threatening and abusing them greatly for their disobedience, seized Agis with his own hands, and

a. Vit. Agid. p. 803. lit. A.[55]
55. Plutarch, "Agis," XVIII.2

dragged him to the execution-room, where he was ordered to be dispatched immediately. Agis submitted to his fate with equal intrepidity and resignation, reproving one of the executioners who deplor-[54]ed his calamities, and declaring himself infinitely happier than his murderers. The unfeeling and treacherous Amphares attended the execution, and as soon as Agis was dead, he admitted his mother and grandmother into the prison, who came to interceed that Agis might be allowed to make his defence before the people. The wretch assured the mother, with an insulting sneer, that her son should suffer no heavier punishment than he had done already; and immediately ordered her mother Archidamia, who was extremely old, to execution. As soon as she was dead, he bid Agesistrata enter the room, where, at the sight of the dead bodies, she could not refrain from kissing her son, and crying out, that his too great lenity and good-nature had been their ruin. The savage Amphares, laying hold of those words, told her, that as she approved of her son's actions she should share his fate. Agesistrata met death with the resolution of an old Spartan Heroine, praying only that this whole affair might not prove prejudicial to her country.

Thus fell the gallant Agis in the cause of liberty and publick virtue, by the perfidy of his mercenary friends, and the violence of a corrupt and most profligate faction. I have given a more particular detail of the catastrophe of this unfortunate Prince as trans-[55]mitted to us by Plutarch, because it furnishes convincing proofs, how greatly the introduction of wealth had corrupted and debased the once upright and generous spirit of the Spartans.

Archidamus, the brother of Agis, eluded the search made for him by Leonidas, and escaped the massacre by flying from Sparta. But Leonidas compelled his wife Agiatis, who was a young lady of the greatest beauty in all Greece, and sole heiress to a vast estate, to marry his own son Cleomenes, though Agiatis had but just lain-in of a son, and the match was entirely contrary to her inclinations. This event however produced a very different effect from what Leonidas intended, and after his death proved the ruin of his party, and revenged the murder of Agis.[a]

a. Plut. Vit. Cleom. p. 805. lit. B.[56]
56. Plutarch, "Cleomenes," I.1–2.

For Cleomenes, who was very young, and extremely fond of his wife, would shed sympathising tears whenever she related the melancholy fate of Agis, and occasionally desire her to explain his intentions, and the nature of his scheme, to which he would listen with the greatest attention. From that time he determined to follow so glorious an example, but kept the resolution secret in his own breast till the means and opportunity should offer. He was sensible [56] that an attempt of that nature would be utterly impracticable whilst his father lived; who, like the rest of the leading citizens, had wholly given himself up to a life of ease and luxury. Warned too by the fate of Agis, he knew how extremely dangerous it was even once to mention the old frugality and simplicity of manners, which depended upon the observance of the discipline and institutions of Lycurgus. But as soon as ever he succeeded to the Crown at the death of his father, and found himself the sole reigning King of Sparta without a colleague, he immediately applied his whole care and study to accomplish that great change which he had before projected. For he observed the manners of the Spartans in general were grown extremely corrupt and dissolute; the rich sacrificing the publick interest to their own private avarice and luxury; the poor, from their extreme indigence, averse to the toils of war, careless and negligent of education and discipline; whilst the Ephori had engrossed the whole royal power, and left him in reality nothing but the empty title: Circumstances greatly mortifying to an aspiring young Monarch, who panted eagerly after glory, and impatiently wished to retrieve the lost reputation of his countrymen. [57]

He began by sounding his most intimate friend, one Xenares, at a distance only, enquiring what sort of man Agis was, and which way, and by whose advice, he was drawn into those unfortunate measures. Xenares, who attributed all his questions to the curiosity natural to a young man, very readily told him the whole story, and explained ingenuously every particular of the affair as it really happened. But when he remarked that Cleomenes often returned to the charge, and every time with greater eagerness, more and more admiring and applauding the scheme and character of Agis, he immediately saw through his design. After reproving him, therefore, severely for talking and behaving thus like a madman, Xenares broke off all friendship and intercourse with him, though he had too much honour to betray his friend's secret. Cleomenes, not in the least discouraged at this repulse, but concluding that he should meet with the same reception from the rest of the wealthy and powerful citizens, determined to trust none of them, but to take upon himself the whole care and management of his scheme.[a] However, as he was sensible that the execution of it would be much more feasible, when his country was involved in war, than in a state [58] of profound peace, he waited for a proper opportunity; which the Achaeans quickly furnished him with. For Aratus, the great projector of the famous Achaean league, into which he had already brought many of the Grecian states, holding Cleomenes extremely cheap, as a raw unexperienced boy, thought this a favourable opportunity of trying how the Spartans stood affected towards that Union. Without the least previous notice, therefore, he suddenly invaded such of the Arcadians as were in alliance with Sparta, and committed great devastations in that part of the country which lay in the neighbourhood of Achaia.

The Ephori, alarmed at this unexpected attack, sent Cleomenes at the head of the Spartan forces to oppose the invasion. The young Hero behaved well, and frequently baffled that old experienced commander. But his countrymen growing weary of the war, and refusing to concur in the measures he proposed for carrying it on, he recalled Archidamus the brother of Agis from banishment, who had a strict hereditary right to the other moiety of the kingdom; imagining that when the throne was properly filled according to law, and the regal power preserved entire by the Union of the two Kings, it would restore the balance of government, and weaken the authority of [59] the Ephori. But the faction which had murdered Agis, justly dreading the resentment of Archidamus for so atrocious a crime, took care privately to assassinate him upon his return.

Cleomenes now more than ever intent upon bringing his great project to bear, bribed the Ephori with large sums to intrust him with the management of the war.[b] His mother Cratesiclea not only supplied him with money upon this occasion, but married one Megistonus, a man of the

a. Plut. Vit. Cleom. p. 809. lit. A.[57]
b. Plut. Vit. Cleom. p. 807. lit. B.[58]
57. Plutarch, "Cleomenes," III.4.
58. Plutarch, "Cleomenes," VI.1.

greatest weight and authority in the city, purposely to bring him over to her son's interest. Cleomenes taking the field, totally defeated the army of Aratus, and killed Lydiadas the Megalopolitan General. This victory, which was entirely owing to the conduct of Cleomenes, not only raised the courage of his soldiers, but gave them so high an opinion of his abilities, that he seems to have been recalled by his enemies, jealous most probably of his growing interest with the army. For Plutarch, who is not very methodical in his relations, informs us, that after this affair, Cleomenes convinced his father-in-law, Megistonus, of the necessity of taking off the Ephori, and reducing[59] the citizens to their [60] ancient equality according to the institutions of Lycurgus, as the only means of restoring Sparta to her former sovereignty over Greece.[a] This scheme therefore must have been privately settled at Sparta. For we are next told, that Cleomenes again took the field, carrying with him such of the citizens as he suspected were most likely to oppose him. He took some cities from the Achaeans that campaign, and made himself master of some important places, but harrassed his troops so much with many marches and countermarches, that most of the Spartans remained behind in Arcadia at their own request, whilst he marched back to Sparta with his mercenary forces, and such of his friends as he could most confide in. He timed his march so well that he entered Sparta whilst the Ephori were at supper, and dispatched Euryclidas before with three or four of his most trusty friends and a few soldiers to perform the execution. For Cleomenes well knew that Agis owed his ruin to his too cautious timidity, and his too great lenity and moderation. Whilst Euryclidas therefore amused the Ephori with a pretended message from Cleomenes, the rest fell upon them sword in hand, and killed four upon the spot, with above ten persons more who came to their assistance. Agesilaus the survivor of them fell, and counterfeiting him-[61]self dead, gained an opportunity of escaping. Next morning as soon as it was light, Cleomenes proscribed and banished fourscore of the most dangerous citizens, and removed all the chairs of

a. Vit. Cleom. p. 808. lit. A.[60]
59. Bringing back, or returning (*OED*, 6a).
60. Plutarch, "Cleomenes," VII.1.

the Ephori out of the Forum, except one, which he reserved for his own seat of judicature. He then convoked an assembly of the people, to whom he apologized for his late actions. He shewed them, in a very artful and elaborate speech, "the nature and just extent of the power of the Ephori, the fatal consequences of the authority they had usurped of governing the state by their own arbitrary will, and of deposing and putting their Kings to death without allowing them a legal hearing in their own defence. He urged the example of Lycurgus himself, who came armed into the Forum when he first proposed his laws, as a proof that it was impossible to root out those pests of the commonwealth, which had been imported from other countries, luxury, the parent of that vain expence which ruins such numbers in debt, usury, and those more ancient evils, wealth and poverty, without violence and bloodshed: That he should have thought himself happy, if like an able physician, he could have radically cured the diseases of his country without pain: but that [62] necessity had compelled him to do what he had already done, in order to procure an equal partition of the lands, and the abolition of their debts, as well as to enable him to fill up the number of the citizens with a select number of the bravest foreigners, that Sparta might be no longer exposed to the depredations of her enemies for want of hands to defend her."[a]

To convince the people of the sincerity of his intentions, he first gave up his whole fortune to the publick stock; Megistonus, his father-in-law, with his other friends, and all the rest of the citizens, followed his example. In the division of the lands, he generously set apart equal portions for all those citizens he had banished, and promised to recall them as soon as the publick tranquillity was restored. He next revived the ancient method of education, the gymnastick exercises, publick meals, and all other institutions of Lycurgus; and lest the people, unaccustomed to the denomination of a single King, should suspect that he aimed at establishing a tyranny, he associated his brother Euclidas with him in the kingdom. By training up the youth in the old military discipline, and arming them in a new and better manner, he once more recovered the

a. Vit. Cleom. p. 809. lit. A.[61]
61. Plutarch, "Cleomenes," X.1.

reputation of the Spartan militia, and raised his country to so [63] great a height of power, that Greece in a very short time saw Sparta giving law to all Peloponnesus.[a]

The Achaeans, humbled by repeated defeats, and begging peace of Cleomenes upon his own terms, the generous victor desired only to be appointed general of their famous league, and offered upon that condition to restore all the cities and prisoners he had taken. The Achaeans gladly consenting to such easy terms, Cleomenes released and sent home all the persons of rank amongst his prisoners, but was obliged by sickness to defer the day appointed for the convention, 'till his return from Sparta. This unhappy delay was fatal to Greece.[b] For Aratus, who had enjoyed that honour thirty-three years, could not bear the thought of having it wrested from him by so young a Prince, whose glory he envied as much as he dreaded his valour. Finding therefore all other methods ineffectual, he had recourse to the desperate remedy of calling in the Macedonians to his assistance, and sacrificed the liberty of his own country, as well as that of Greece, to his own private pique and jealousy. Thus the most publick-spirited assertor of liberty, and the most implacable [64] enemy to all tyrants in general, brought back those very people into the heart of Greece, whom he had driven out formerly purely from his hatred to tyranny, and sullied a glorious life with a blot never to be erased, from the detestable motives of envy and revenge. A melancholy proof, as Plutarch moralizes upon the occasion, of the weakness of human nature, which with an assemblage of the most excellent qualities is unable to exhibit the model of a virtue completely perfect. A circumstance which ought to excite our compassion towards those blemishes, which we unavoidably meet with in the most exalted characters.

Cleomenes supported this unequal war against the Achaeans and the whole power of Macedon with the greatest vigour, and by his success gave many convincing proofs of his abilities; but venturing a decisive battle at Sallasia, he was totally defeated by the superior number of his enemies,

---

a. Parallel. inter Agid. & Cleom. & T. & C. Gracch. p. 844. lit. D.[62]
b. Vit. Cleom. p. 811. lit. C.[63]
62. Plutarch, "Agis, Cleomenes and Gracchi," II.4.
63. Plutarch, "Cleomenes," XV.1–2.

and the treachery of Damoteles, an officer in whom he greatly confided, who was bribed to betray him by Antigonus. Out of six thousand Spartans, two hundred only escaped, the rest with their king Euclidas were left dead on the field of battle.[64] Cleomenes retired to Sparta, and from thence passed over to Ptolemy Euergetes king of Egypt, with whom he [65] was then in alliance, to claim the assistance he had formerly promised. But the death of that Monarch, which followed soon after, deprived him of all hopes of succour from that quarter. The Spartan manners were as odious to his successor Ptolemy Philopator, a weak and dissolute prince, as the Spartan virtue was terrible to his debauched effeminate courtiers. Whenever Cleomenes appeared at court, the general whisper ran, that he came as a lion in the midst of sheep; a light in which a brave man must necessarily appear to a herd of such servile dastards. Confined at last by the jealousy of Ptolemy, who was kept in a perpetual alarm by the insinuations of his iniquitous minister Sosybius, he with about twelve more of his generous Spartan friends broke out of prison, determined upon death or liberty. In their progress through the streets, they first slew one Ptolemy, a great favourite of the King's, who had been their secret enemy; and meeting the governor of the city, who came at the first noise of the tumult, they routed his guards and attendants, dragged him out of his chariot, and killed him. After this they ranged uncontrouled through the whole city of Alexandria, the inhabitants flying every where before them, and not a man daring either to assist or oppose them. Such terror could thirteen brave men only strike into one of the [66] most populous cities in the universe, where the citizens were bred up in luxury, and strangers to the use of arms! Cleomenes, despairing of assistance from the citizens, whom he had in vain summoned to assert their liberty, declared such abject cowards fit only to be governed by women. Scorning therefore to fall by the hands of the despicable Egyptians, he with the rest of the Spartans fell desperately by their own swords, according to the heroism of those ages.[a]

a. Plut. Vit. Cleom. p. 822. lit. E.[65]
64. Plutarch, "Cleomenes," XXVII.4 and "Philopoemen," VI.1. The battle of Sellasia (as it is more commonly written today) took place in 222 B.C.
65. Plutarch, "Cleomenes," XXXVII.6–7.

The liberty and happiness of Sparta expired with Cleomenes.[a] For the remains of the Spartan history furnish us with very little after his death, besides the calamities and miseries of that unhappy state, arising from their intestine divisions. Machanidas, by the aid of one of the factions which at that time rent that miserable republick, usurped the throne, and established an absolute tyranny. One Nabis, a tyrant, compared to whom even Nero himself may be termed merciful, succeeded at the death of Machanidas, who fell in battle by the hand of the great Philopaemen. The Aetolians treacherously murdered Nabis, and endeavoured to seize the dominion of Sparta; but they were prevented by Philopaemen, who partly by [67] force, partly by persuasion, brought the Spartans into the Achaean league, and afterwards totally abolished the institutions of Lycurgus.[b] A most inhuman and most iniquitous action, as Plutarch terms it, which must brand the character of that hero with eternal infamy. As if he was sensible that as long as the discipline of Lycurgus subsisted, the minds of the Spartan youth could never be thoroughly tamed, or effectually broke to the yoke of foreign government. Wearied out at last by repeated oppressions, the Spartans applied to the Romans for redress of all their grievances; and their complaints produced that war which ended in the dissolution of the Achaean league, and the subjection of Greece to the Roman domination.

I have entered into a more minute detail of the Spartan constitution, as settled by Lycurgus, than I at first proposed; because the maxims of that celebrated lawgiver are so directly opposite to those which our modern politicians lay down as the basis of the strength and power of a nation.

Lycurgus found his country in the most terrible of all situations, a state of anarchy and confusion. The rich, insolent and oppressive; the poor groaning under a load of debt, mutinous from despair, and ready to [68] cut the throats of their usurious oppressors. To remedy these evils, did this wise politician encourage navigation, strike out new branches

a. Polyb. lib. 4. p. 479.[66]
b. Plut. Vit. Philopaem. p. 365. lit. E.[67]
66. Polybius, IV.lxxxi.14.
67. Plutarch, "Philopoemen," XVI.2.

of commerce, and make the most of those excellent harbours and other natural advantages which the maritime situation of his country afforded? Did he introduce and promote arts and sciences, that by acquiring and diffusing new wealth amongst his countrymen, he might make his nation, in the language of our political writers, secure, powerful, and happy?[68] Just the reverse. After he had new-modelled the constitution, and settled the just balance between the powers of government, he abolished all debts, divided the whole land amongst his countrymen by equal lots, and put an end to all dissentions about property, by introducing a perfect equality. He extirpated luxury and a lust of wealth, which he looked upon as the pests of every free country, by prohibiting the use of gold and silver; and barred up the entrance against their return by interdicting navigation and commerce, and expelling all arts, but what were immediately necessary to their subsistence. As he was sensible that just and virtuous manners are the best support of the internal peace and happiness of every kingdom, he established a most excellent plan of education for training up his countrymen, from their very infancy, in the strict-[69]est observance of their religion and laws, and the habitual practice of those virtues which can alone secure the blessings of liberty, and perpetuate their duration. To protect his country from external invasions, he formed the whole body of the people, without distinction, into one well armed, well disciplined national militia, whose leading principle was the love of their country, and who esteemed death in its defence, the most exalted height of glory to which a Spartan was capable of attaining. Nor were these elevated sentiments confined solely to the men; the colder breasts of the women caught fire at the glorious flame, and glowed even with superior ardour. For when their troops marched against an enemy, "to bring back their shields, or to be brought home

---

68. Montagu is here writing against those who had recently extolled trade and opulence over virtuous austerity, such as Bernard Mandeville in *The Fable of the Bees* (1714; later enlarged editions in 1723 and 1728–29), and David Hume, in "Of Refinement in the Arts" (originally titled "Of Luxury," 1752). More broadly, Montagu is opposing the trend in British imperial policy to build up an oceanic empire held together by trade rather than military force; on the origins of this ideology, see David Armitage, *The Ideological Origins of the British Empire* (Cambridge: Cambridge University Press, 2000).

upon them,"ᵃ was the last command which the Spartan mothers gave their sons at parting.

Such was the method which Lycurgus took to secure the independency and happiness of his country; and the event shewed, that his institutions were founded upon maxims of the truest and justest policy. For I [70] cannot help observing upon the occasion, that from the time of Lycurgus to the introduction of wealth by Lysander in the reign of the first Agis, a space of five hundred years, we meet with no mutiny amongst the people, upon account of the severity of his discipline, but on the contrary the most religious reverence for, and the most willing and chearful obedience to, the laws he established. As on the other hand, the wisdom of his military institutions is evident from this consideration; That the national militia alone of Sparta, a small insignificant country as to extent, situated in a nook only of the Morea,⁶⁹ not only gave laws to Greece, but made the Persian monarchs tremble at their very name, though absolute masters of the richest and most extensive empire the world then knew.

I observe farther, that the introduction of wealth by Lysander, after the conquest of Athens, brought back all those vices and dissentions which the prohibition of the use of money had formerly banished; and that all historians assign that open violation of the laws of Lycurgus, as the period from which the decadence of Sparta is to be properly dated. I observe too, with Plutarch, that though the manners of the Spartans were greatly corrupted by the introduction of wealth, yet that the landed interest (as I may term it) which subsisted as long as the [71] original allotments of land remained unalienable, still preserved their state; notwithstanding the many abuses which had crept into their constitution. But that as soon as ever the landed

a. To bring back their shields implied victory; to be brought home upon them, a glorious death in defence of their country; because the Spartans, if possible, brought back and buried all who fell in battle in their native country.⁷⁰

69. The Morea is another name for that part of Greece which in the classical period was referred to as the Peloponnese, i.e., the peninsula to the west and south of the isthmus of Corinth.

70. The original saying, attributed to an anonymous Spartan mother, is even more laconic: "Another woman, as she was handing her son his shield and giving him some encouragement, said: 'Son, either with this or on this'" (Plutarch, "Sayings of Spartan Women," XVI). In fact the Spartans tended to bury their dead where they fell and repatriated the corpses of only their kings (Plutarch, "Agesilaus," XL).

estates became alienable by law, the moneyed interest prevailed, and at last totally swallowed up the landed, which the historians remark as the death's-wound of their constitution.[71] For the martial virtue of the citizens not only sunk with the loss of their estates, but their number, and consequently the strength of the state, diminished in the same proportion. Aristotle, who wrote about sixty years after the death of Lysander, in his examen of the Spartan Republick, quite condemns that law which permitted the alienation of their lands.[a] For he affirms, that the same quantity of land, which, whilst equally divided, supplied a militia of fifteen hundred horse, and thirty thousand heavy armed foot, could not in his time furnish one thousand; so that the state was utterly ruined for want of men to defend it.[b] In the reign of Agis the third, about a hundred years after the time of Aristotle, the number of the old Spartan families was dwindled (as I remarked before) to seven hundred; out of which about one hundred rich [72] overgrown families had engrossed the whole land of Sparta, which Lycurgus had formerly divided into thirty-nine thousand shares, and assigned for the support of as many families. So true it is, that a landed interest diffused through a whole people is not only the real strength, but the surest bulwark of the liberty and independency, of a free country.

From the tragical fate of the third Agis we learn, that when abuses introduced by corruption are suffered by length of time to take root in the constitution, they will be termed by those whose interest it is to support

a. Aristot. de Rebuspubl. lib. 2. cap. 7. fol. 122. lit. Θ.[72]

b. Ἡ πόλις ἀπόλετο διὰ τὴν ὀλιγανθρωπίαν. Aristot. ibid.[73]

71. A tension between the landed interest (those whose wealth was held predominantly in real property) and the moneyed interest (those whose wealth was held predominantly in the new financial instruments of bonds or shares) had been created in England during the late seventeenth century by the policy of deficit finance, which had paid for England's involvement in the War of the Treaty of Augsburg (1690–97). The suspicion among landed Tories and "Country" Whigs was that the Whig moneyed interest received a high rate on its loans to the government, paid for by a tax on land. As Swift put it: "It was not to be doubted that Money'd Men would be always firm to the Party of those, who advised the Borrowing upon such good Security, and with such exorbitant Praemiums and Interest; and every new Summ that was lent, took away as much Power from the Landed Men, as it added to theirs; so that the deeper the Kingdom was engaged, it was still the better for them" (Swift, *History of the Four Last Years of the Queen*, ed. H. Davis [Oxford: Basil Blackwell, 1951], pp. 69–70).

72. Aristotle, *Politics*, II.ix.

73. "The want of men was the ruin of the city."

them, essential parts of the constitution itself; and all attempts to remove them will ever be clamoured against by such men as attempt to subvert it: As the example of Cleomenes will teach us, that the publick virtue of one great man may not only save his falling country from ruin, but raise her to her former dignity and lustre, by bringing her back to those principles on which her constitution was originally founded. Though the violent remedies made use of by Cleomenes never ought to be applied, unless the disease is grown too desperate to admit of a cure by milder methods.

I shall endeavour to shew in its proper place, that the constitution established by Ly-[73]curgus, which seemed to Polybius to be rather of divine than of human institution,[a] and was so much celebrated by the most eminent philosophers of antiquity, is much inferior to the British constitution as settled at the Revolution.[74] But I cannot quit this subject without recommending that excellent institution of Lycurgus, which provided for the education of the children of the whole community without distinction. An example which under proper regulations would be highly worthy of our imitation, since nothing could give a more effectual check to the reigning vices and follies of the present age, or contribute so much to a reformation of manners, as to form the minds of the rising generation by the principles of religion and virtue. Where the manners of a people are good, very few laws will be wanting; but when their manners are depraved, all the laws in the world will be insufficient to restrain the excesses of the human passions. For as Horace justly observes—

> *Quid leges sine moribus*
> *Vanae proficiunt,*   Ode 24. lib. 3.[75]

---

a. Ὥστε θειοτέραν τὴν ἐπίνοιαν ἢ κατ᾽ ἄνθρωπον αὐτοῦ νομίζειν. Polyb. lib. 6. p. 683.[76]

74. A reference to the constitutional changes introduced in Britain as a consequence of the Glorious Revolution of 1688. These changes were enshrined in the Bill of Rights (1689), which provided for curbs on the exercise of the royal prerogative (including taxation by prerogative), abolition of standing armies in time of peace, freedom to elect members of parliament without royal interference, and the protection of parliamentary proceedings from interference by the crown.

75. "Of what avail are empty laws, if we lack principle?" (Horace, *Odes*, III. xxiv.35–36).

76. "Too divine to be attributed to a man"; Polybius, VI.xlviii.2.

CHAPTER II

Of Athens

The Republick of Athens, once the seat of learning and eloquence, the school of arts and sciences, and the center of wit, gaiety, and politeness, exhibits a strong contrast to that of Sparta, as well in her form of government, as in the genius and manners of her inhabitants.

The government of Athens, after the abolition of Monarchy, was truly democratick, and so much convulsed by those civil dissentions, which are the inevitable consequences of that kind of government, that of all the Grecian states, the Athenian may be the most strictly termed the seat of faction. I observe that the history of this celebrated Republick is neither very clear nor interesting till the time of Solon. The laws of Draco (the first legislator of the Athenians who gave his laws in writing) affixed death as the common punishment of the most capital crimes, or the most trivial offences; a circumstance which implies either the most cruel austerity in the temper of the lawgiver, or such an abandoned profligacy in the manners of the people, as laid him under a necessity of applying such violent remedies. As the historians have not [75] clearly decided which of these was the case, I shall only remark, that the humanity of the people, so natural to the human species, was interested upon the occasion, and the excessive rigour of the laws obstructed the very means of their being carried into execution. A plain proof that a multiplicity of rigorous penal laws are not only incompatible with the liberty of a free state, but even repugnant to human nature. For the natural equity of mankind can easily distinguish between the nature and degree of crimes; and the sentiments of humanity will naturally be excited when the punishment seems to be too rigorous in proportion to the demerits of the offender. The chief reason, in my opinion, why so many offenders in our nation escape with impunity for want of prosecution, is because our laws make no distinction, as to the punishment, between the most trifling robbery on the highway, and the most atrocious of all crimes, premeditated murder.[1]

The remedy which Draco proposed by his laws, proving worse than the disease, the whole body of the people applied to Solon, as the only person equal to the difficult task of regulating their government. The supreme power of the state was at that time vested in nine magistrates, termed Archons or governors, elected annually by the people out of the body of the nobility. But the [76] community in general was split into three factions, each contending for such a form of government as was most agreeable to their different interests. The most sensible among the Athenians, dreading the consequence of these divisions, were willing, as Plutarch informs us, to invest Solon with absolute power;[a] but our disinterested philosopher was a stranger to that kind of ambition, and preferred the freedom and happiness of his countrymen to the splendor of a Crown. He continued the Archons in their office as usual, but limited their authority by instituting a senate of four hundred persons elected by the people, by way of ballot, out

a. Vita Solon, p. 85. lit. D.[2]

1. In early eighteenth-century England the number of capital crimes had increased alarmingly. For instance, the notorious Black Act of May 1723 had, at a stroke, created some fifty new capital offences. Eventually, mid-century unease at this proliferation would find expression in the troubled reflections of Blackstone: "though the end of punishment is to deter men from offending, it never can follow from thence, that it is lawful to deter them at any rate and by any means; . . . Where the evil to be prevented is not adequate to the violence of the preventive, a sovereign that thinks seriously can never justify such a law to the dictates of conscience and humanity" (Blackstone, *Commentaries*, IV.10–11).

2. Plutarch, "Solon," XIV.3–6.

of the four tribes into which the community was at that time divided. He revived and improved the senate and court of Areopagus, the most sacred and most respectable tribunal, not only of Greece, but of all which we ever read of in history.[a] The integrity [77] and equity of this celebrated court was so remarkable, that not only the Greeks, but the Romans, sometimes submitted such causes to their determination which they found too intricate and difficult for their own decision. To prevent all suspicion of partiality either to plaintiff or defendant, this venerable court heard all causes and passed their definitive sentence in the dark, and the pleaders on either side were strictly confined to a bare representation of the plain truth of the fact, without either aggravation or embellishment. For all the ornament of fine language, and those powers of rhetorick which tended to bias the judgment by interesting the passions of the judges, were absolutely prohibited. Happy if the pleaders were restricted to this righteous method in our own courts of judicature, where great eloquence and great abilities are too often employed to confound truth and support injustice![3]

a. The time of the first institution of this court (so denominated from Ἄρειος πάγος, i.e. Hill of Mars, an eminence where they always assembled) is quite uncertain; nor are the historians at all agreed about the number of the members of which it was composed. However, this was the supreme court, which had cognizance of wilful murders, and all matters which were of the greatest consequence to the Republick. Suidas. They had also cognizance of all matters of religion, as we find by the instance of St. Paul.[4]

3. Satire on the perversion of natural justice by the art of lawyers is perennial; hence the exclusion of lawyers from utopian societies (e.g., More, *Utopia*, p. 82). John Locke proscribed professional legal advocacy in the constitution he drew up for Carolina: "It shall be a base and vile thing to plead for money or reward; nor shall anyone . . . be permitted to plead another man's case, till before the judge, in open court, he hath taken an oath that he doth not plead for money or reward" (Locke, *Political Writings*, p. 224). In eighteenth-century English literature, see Jonathan Swift, *Gulliver's Travels* (1726; ed. H. Davis [Oxford: Basil Blackwell, 1941]), part 4, chapter five and Henry Fielding, *Joseph Andrews* (1742), book 4, chapter five.

4. Cf. Acts 17:19. "Suidas" was the conjectured author of a tenth-century Byzantine encyclopedia or lexicon known as the *Souidas* or the *Suda Lexicon*. However, the title of this multi-authored and extremely valuable work on Greek literature and history is now known to derive from the Byzantine Greek word for a fortress. The article on the Areopagus in the Lexicon is barely longer than Montagu's note, which omits only some mythological details concerning the foundation of the court (*Suidae Lexicon*, ed. Ludolphus Kusterus, 3 vols. [Cambridge, 1705], vol. 3, p. 318).

It is evident from history that Solon at first proposed the institutions of Lycurgus as the model of his new establishment. But the difficulty which he met with in the abolition of all debts, the first part of his scheme, convinced him of the utter impracticability of introducing the Laconic equality, and deterred him from all farther attempts of that nature. The laws of Athens gave the creditor so absolute a power over his insolvent [78] debtor, that he could not only oblige the unhappy wretch to do all his servile drudgery, but could sell him and his children for slaves in default of payment. The creditors had made so oppressive an use of their power, that many of the citizens were actually obliged to sell their children to make good their payments; and such numbers had fled their country to avoid the effects of their detestable inhumanity, that, as Plutarch observes, the city was almost unpeopled by the extortion of the usurers.[a] Solon, apprehensive of an insurrection amongst the poorer citizens, who openly threatened to alter the government, and make an equal partition of the lands, thought no method so effectual to obviate this terrible evil, as to cancel all debts, as Lycurgus had done formerly at Sparta. But some of his friends, to whom he had privately communicated his scheme, with an assurance that he did not propose to meddle with the lands, were too well versed in the art of jobbing[5] to neglect so fair an opportunity of making a fortune. For they stretched their credit to the utmost in loans of large sums from the moneyed men, which they immediately laid out in the purchase of landed estates. A precedent which the treacherous Agesilaus copied too successfully after-[79]wards at Sparta. The cheat appeared as soon as the edict for abolishing all debts was made publick: but the odium of so flagitious[6] a piece of roguery was thrown wholly upon Solon; as the censure of the publick for all frauds and exactions committed by officers in the inferior departments will naturally fall upon the minister at the helm, however disinterested and upright.

This edict was equally disagreeable to the rich and to the poor. For the rich were violently deprived of all that part of their property which consisted

---

a. Plut. p. 85. lit. A.[7]

5. Dealing corruptly or unscrupulously for personal gain or political advantage (*OED*, 3a).

6. Extremely wicked or criminal: heinous, villainous (*OED*, 2).

7. Plutarch, "Solon," XIII.2–3.

in their loans, and the poor were disappointed of that share of the lands which they so greedily expected. How Solon drew himself out of this difficulty, historians have no where informed us. All we can learn from them is, that the decree was at last received and submitted to, and that Solon was still continued in his office with the same authority as before.

This experiment gave Solon a thorough insight into the temper of his countrymen, and most probably induced him to accommodate his subsequent regulations to the humour and prejudices of the people. For as he wanted the authority which naturally arises from royal birth, as well as that which is founded on the unlimited confidence of the people, advantages which Lycurgus possessed in so eminent a degree, he was obliged [80] to consult rather what was practicable, than what was strictly right; and endeavour, as far as he was able, to please all parties. That he acknowledged this, seems evident from his answer to one who asked him

"Whether the laws he had given the Athenians were the best he could possibly have made?" "They are the best, replied Solon, which the Athenians are capable of receiving."[a]

Thus whilst he confined the Magistracies and the executive part of the Government solely to the rich, he lodged the supreme power in the hands of the poorer citizens. For though every freeman whose fortune did not amount to a particular census or estimate, was excluded from all state offices by the laws of Solon; yet he had a legal right of giving his opinion and suffrage in the Εκκλησια[8] or assembly of the people, which was wholly composed of this inferior class of citizens. But as all elections, and all causes of appeal from the superior courts, were determined by the voices of this assembly; as no law could pass without their approbation, and the highest officers in the Republick were subject to their censure, this assembly became the *dernier resort*[9] in all causes, and this mob government, as it may be justly termed, was [81] the great leading cause of the ruin of their Republick. Anacharsis the Scythian Philosopher, who at

a. Plut. in Vit. Solon, p. 86. lit. C.[10]
8. An assembly of citizens or a legislative assembly.
9. Court of final appeal (*OED*, "dernier," b).
10. Plutarch, "Solon," XV.2.

that time resided with Solon, justly ridiculed this excess of power which he had lodged in the people.[a] For when he had heard some points debated first in the Senate, and afterwards decided in the assembly of the people, he humourously told Solon, that at Athens

Wise men debated, but fools decided.

Solon was as sensible of this capital defect as Anacharsis; but he was too well acquainted with the licentiousness and natural levity of the people, to divest them of a power, which he knew they would resume by violence at the first opportunity. The utmost therefore he could do was to fix his two senates as the moorings of the constitution:[b] That of four hundred,[c] to secure the state against the fluctuating temper and tumultuous fury of the people; that of the Areopagus,[d] to restrain the dangerous encroachments of the great and wealthy. He repealed all the laws of Draco, those against murder alone excepted; rightly judging, as Plutarch remarks, that it was not only most iniquitous, but most absurd, to inflict the same punishment upon a man for being [82] idle, or stealing a cabbage or an apple out of a garden, as for committing murder or sacrilege.[e] But as the account handed down to us of the laws which Solon established is extremely lame and imperfect, I shall only mention the sarcasm of Anacharsis upon that occasion, as a proof of their insufficiency to answer that end for which Solon designed them. For that Philosopher comparing the corrupt manners of the Athenians with the coercive power of Solon's laws, resembled the latter to cobwebs, which would entangle only the poor and feeble, but were easily broke through by the rich and powerful.[f] Solon is said to have replied,

a. Plut. in Vit. Solon, p. 81. lit. B.[11]
b. Ibid. p. 88. lit. D.[12]
c. The new Senate, which he had instituted.
d. Which he had revived. Vide Note p. 49.[13]
e. Ibid. p. 87. lit. E.[14]
f. Ibid. p. 81. lit. A.[15]
11. Plutarch, "Solon," V.3.
12. Plutarch, "Solon," XIX.2.
13. Plutarch, "Solon," XIX.2.
14. Plutarch, "Solon," XVII.1–2.
15. Plutarch, "Solon," V.2.

That men would readily stand to those mutual compacts, which it was the interest of neither party to violate; and that he had so rightly adapted his laws to the reason of his countrymen, as to convince them how much more advantageous it was to adhere to what was just, than to be guilty of injustice.[a]

The event, as Plutarch truly observes, proved more correspondent to the opinion of Anacharsis, than to the hopes of Solon. For Pisistratus, a near relation of Solon's, having artfully formed a strong party among the poorer citizens by distributing bribes under the specious pretence of [83] relieving their necessities, procured a guard of fifty men armed with clubs only for the safety of his person,[b] by the help of which he seized the citadel, abolished the Democracy, and established a single tyranny in spite of all the efforts of Solon.

This usurpation proved the source of endless faction, and brought innumerable calamities upon the republick. Pisistratus was expelled more than once by the opposite party, and as often brought back in triumph either by the fraud or force of his prevailing faction. At his death he left the kingdom to his two sons Hipparchus and Hippias. The former of these was assassinated by Harmodius and Aristogiton for a personal injury they had received;[c] Hippias was soon after driven out of Athens by the Spartans, at the instigation of some of his discontented countrymen. Despairing of recovering his former sovereignty by any other means, he fled to Darius for assistance, and was the cause of the first invasion of Greece by the Persians, in which he died fighting against his country in the ever memorable battle of Marathon.[16] But the most fatal evil which resulted from the usurpation of Pisistratus, [84] was, that perpetual fear of

a. Ibid. p. 81.[17]

b. Solon in his letter to Epimenides, says 400, which seems most probable. Diog. Laert.[18]

c. Thucyd.[19]

16. In 490 B.C. the Athenian general Miltiades defeated an invading Persian army on the plain of Marathon, some twenty miles northeast of Athens.

17. Plutarch, "Solon," V.3.

18. Diogenes Laertius, I.lxvi.

19. Thucydides, I.xx.2.

seeing the supreme power again lodged in the hands of a single person.[a] For this fear kept the jealousy of the people in a constant alarm, and threw them at last into the hands of the factious Demagogues. Hence superior merit was frequently represented as an unpardonable crime, and a kind of high treason against the Republick.[b] And the real patriots were rendered suspected to the people, just as the Demagogues were influenced by envy or private pique, or even bribed by ambitious or designing men, who aspired at the very thing of which the others were unjustly accused. The history of Athens abounds with instances of the levity and inconstancy of that unsteady people. For how frequently do we find their best and ablest citizens imprisoned or sentenced to banishment by the ostracism,[20] in honour of whom the same people had just before erected statues:[c] nay not unfrequently raising statues to the memory of those illustrious and innocent men, whom they had illegally doomed to death in the wantonness of their power;[d] [85] at once the monuments of their injustice and too late repentance! This evil was the natural consequence of that capital error in Solon's polity, when he entrusted the supreme power to the giddy and fluctuating populace. A defect which (as I observed before) was the great leading cause of the loss of that liberty which they had so licentiously abused. For as the removal of all the honest citizens either by death or banishment, paved an easy way for usurpation and tyranny; so it was a measure invariably pursued, in the Democratick governments of Greece, by all those ambitious men who aimed at subverting the liberties of their country. This truth is so clearly explained, and so incontestibly proved, by the great Thucydides, that whilst I peruse the annals of that admirable

a. Thucyd. lib. 6. p. 415. sect. 60.[21]

b. Xenoph. de Republ. Athen. p. 55. Edit. Luvenel. Bas. 1572.[22]

c. Miltiades, Themistocles, Aristides, Cimon, Thucydides the historian, &c.

d. Socrates, Phocion, &c.

20. In Athens and other ancient Greek cities, the custom or practice whereby a citizen whose power or influence was considered dangerous to the state was sent into exile for ten or five years (*OED*, 1). In Athens, where the practice was introduced by Cleisthenes, the founder of Athenian democracy, it was intended to prevent any attempt to subvert the constitution.

21. Thucydides, VI.lx.1–5.

22. Xenophon, "The Constitution of the Athenians," I.xiv.

historian, I cannot help grieving over the tragick pages stained with the blood of so many patriot citizens, who fell a sacrifice to the dire ambition and avarice of faction. What a striking detail does he give us of the most calamitous situation of all the Grecian Republicks during the Peloponnesian war![23] How does he labour for expression in his pathetick[24] enumeration of the horrible consequences of faction, after his description of the destructive sedition at Corcyra![25] A contempt of all religion, the open violation of the most sacred ties and [86] compacts; devastations, massacres, assassinations, and all the savage horrors of civil discord inflamed even to madness, are the perpetual subjects of his instructive history. Calamities of which he himself was at once an eye-witness and a most faithful recorder.

Thucydides[a] truly ascribes this destructive war to the mutual jealousy which then subsisted between the Spartans and Athenians.[b] The most stale frivolous pretences were trumped up by the Spartans, and as strongly retorted by the Athenians. Both states made the interests or grievances of their allies the constant pretext for their mutual altercations, whilst the real cause was that ambitious scheme which each state had formed, of reducing all Greece under its respective dominion. But an event which both states seemed to have waited for quickly blew up the latent sparks of jealousy into the most violent flame.[c] The Thebans privately entered

---

a. Thucyd. edit. Duker. lib. 1. p. 58. sect. 88.[26]

b. Thucyd. lib. 1. p. 82. sect. 127, 128.[27]

c. Thucyd. lib. 2. p. 98. sect. 2, 3, 4, et sequent.[28]

23. A protracted struggle from 431 to 404 B.C. between Athens and the Delian confederacy on the one hand, and on the other most of the states of the Peloponnese, led by Sparta. It forms the subject matter of the history of Thucydides.

24. Moving, stirring, affecting (*OED*, 1b).

25. Corcyra (modern-day Corfu) is an island in the Ionian sea, straddling the coasts of northern Greece to the south and southern Albania to the north. The advantages for trade of its position between Greece and western Europe made it a valuable prize over which Corinth and Athens contended. For Thucydides' account of the sedition at Corcyra, see III.lxx–xlviii. For his "pathetick enumeration" of the consequences of the sedition, see III.lxxxii–lxxxiv.

26. Thucydides, I.lxxxviii.

27. Thucydides, I.cxxvii–cxxviii.

28. Thucydides, II.ii–iv.

the city of Platea in the night (a small state at that time allied to Athens) which had been betrayed to them by a treacherous faction, who were enemies to the Athenians. But the honester part of the [87] Plataeans recovering from their surprize, and taking notice of the small number of the Thebans, quickly regained possession of their city by the slaughter of most of the invaders. The Plataeans immediately applied to the Athenians for assistance;[a] the Thebans to the Spartans. Both states entered eagerly into the quarrel between their respective allies, and engaged as principals in that destructive war which at last involved all Greece in the common calamity. Where-ever the fortune of the Spartan prevailed, an oligarchical Aristocracy was established, and the friends to a popular government destroyed or banished. Where the Athenians were victors, Democracy was settled or restored, and the people glutted their revenge with the blood of the nobility. Alternate revolts, truces violated as soon as made, massacres, proscriptions, and confiscations, were the perpetual consequences, in all the petty republicks, of the alternate good or bad success of these two contending rivals. In a word, all Greece seems to have been seized with an epidemick madness; and the polite, the humane Grecians, treated one another, during the whole course of this unnatural war, with a ferocity unknown even to the most savage barbarians. The real cause, assigned by Thu-[88]cydides, of all these atrocious evils, was, "The lust of domination arising from avarice and ambition":[b] for the leading men in every state, whether of the Democratick or Aristocratick party, affected outwardly the greatest concern for the welfare of the Republick, which in reality was made the prize for which they all contended. Thus, whilst each endeavoured by every possible method to get the better of his antagonist, the most audacious villanies, and the most flagrant acts of injustice, were equally perpetrated by both sides: Whilst the moderate men amongst the citizens, who refused to join with either side, were alike

a. Thucid. lib. 2. p. 101, &c. sect. 6.[29]

b. Thucyd. Πάντων δ' αὐτῶν αἴτιον ἀρχὴ ἡ διὰ πλεονεξίαν καὶ φιλοτιμίαν. lib. 3. p. 218. sect. 82.[30]

29. Thucydides, II.vi.

30. "The cause of all these evils was the desire to rule which greed and ambition inspire"; Thucydides, III.lxxxii.8.

the objects of their resentment or envy, and equally destroyed without mercy by either faction.[a]

Historians unanimously agree, that the Athenians were instigated to this fatal war by the celebrated Pericles. Thucydides, who was not only cotemporary with Pericles, but actually bore a command in that war, does real honour to that great man's character; for he assigns his desire of humbling the Spartans, and his zeal for the glory and [89] interest of his country, as the real motives of his conduct upon that occasion.[b] But, as a detail of this tedious and ruinous war is wholly foreign to my purpose, I shall only remark, that if ever union and harmony are necessary to the preservation of a state, they are more essentially so when that state is engaged in a dubious war with a powerful enemy.[31] For not only the continuation, but the event, of that long war, so fatal to the Athenians, must (humanly speaking) be wholly attributed to the disunion of their councils, and the perpetual fluctuation in their measures, occasioned by the influence of the ambitious and factious Demagogues. Not the calamities of war, nor the most dreadful plague,[c] ever yet recorded in history, were able to fix the volatile temper of that unsteady people. Elate beyond measure with any good success, they were deaf to the most reasonable overtures of peace from their enemies, and their views were unbounded. Equally dejected with any defeat, they thought the enemy just at their doors, and threw the whole blame upon their commanders, who were always treated as unpardonably criminal when unsuccessful. The Demagogues, who watched every turn of temper in that variable people, took

a. Τὰ δὲ μέσα τῶν πολιτῶν ὑπ᾽ ἀμφοτέρων ἢ ὅτι οὐ ξυνηγωνίζοντο ἢ φθόνῳ τοῦ περιεῖναι διεφθείροντο. Thucyd. p. 219.[32]

b. Thucyd. lib. 1. p. 91. sect. 140.[33]

c. Thucyd. lib. 2. p. 127. sect. 47. et seq.[34]

31. Here Montagu glances at Britain's own situation in the early years of the Seven Years' War.

32. "And citizens who belonged to neither party were continually destroyed by both, either because they would not make common cause with them, or through mere jealousy that they should survive"; Thucydides, III.lxxxii.8.

33. Thucydides, I.cxl.4.

34. For the onset of the plague in Athens and its symptoms, see Thucydides, II.xlvii–liii.

care to adapt [90] every circumstance that offered to their own ambitious views, either of gaining or supporting an ascendancy in the state, which kept up a perpetual spirit of faction in that unhappy Republick. Thus, in the beginning of the Peloponnesian war, Cleon, a noisy seditious Demagogue, declaimed violently against Pericles, and was the constant opposer of all his measures:[a] but the firmness and superior abilities of that great man enabled him to baffle all his antagonists. When Pericles was carried off by that fatal pestilence which almost depopulated Athens, the nobility, jealous of that sway which Cleon had acquired over the people, set up Nicias in opposition. Nicias[b] was honest, and a real lover of his country, but a man of no great abilities; and though an experienced officer, yet cautious and diffident even to timidity. In his temper he was mild, humane, and averse to bloodshed, and laboured to put an end to a war which spread such general destruction; but all his measures were opposed by the turbulent Cleon; for when the Spartans proposed an accommodation, Cleon persuaded the Athenians to insist upon such high terms that the treaty broke off, and war was again renewed with the same in-[91]veterate fury: but the incendiary Cleon, the chief obstacle of all pacifick measures, falling in battle in the tenth year of that war, negociations were again set on foot, and a peace for fifty years concluded between the Athenians and the Spartans by the unwearied endeavours of Nicias.[c] But whilst Nicias was intent upon the enjoyment of that repose which he had procured, a new and infinitely more formidable rival started up, and again involved his country and all Greece in the same calamities by his restless and insatiable ambition.

Alcibiades now appeared upon the stage; a man composed of a motley[35] mixture of virtues and vices, of good and bad qualities; one who could

---

a. Plut. in Vit. Pericl. p. 171. lit. E.[36]

b. Plut. in Vit. Nic. p. 524. lit. B.[37]

c. Hence, as Plutarch informs us, it was termed the Nician peace, lib. 5.[38]

35. Composed of elements of diverse or varied character, form, appearance, with the implication of poor design or organization (*OED*, 2a).

36. Plutarch, "Pericles," XXXIII.6–7; XXXIV.1.

37. Plutarch, "Nicias," II.2.

38. Plutarch, "Alcibiades," XIV.2.

assume even the most opposite characters; and with more ease than a chamaeleon can change its colours, appear a very contrast to himself, just as his interest or ambition required.[a] This State-Proteus[39] was strongly piqued at the growing power and reputation of Nicias. His lust of power was too great to bear either a superior or an equal;[b] and he determined at all events to supplant him, alike regardless either of the [92] equity of the means, or of the consequences of it to his country. The Athenians were not a little displeased with the Spartans, who had not been very punctual[40] in fulfilling the conditions of the treaty.[c] Alcibiades finding his countrymen in a humour very proper for his purpose, inflamed them violently against Nicias, whom he publickly accused as a secret friend and well-wisher to that people. Nicias endeavoured to ward off the blow, and prevent his countrymen from coming to an open rupture; but the intrigues of Alcibiades prevailed, who procured himself to be elected General,[d] and fresh hostilities to be commenced against the allies of Sparta.

The 17th year of this memorable war is remarkable for that fatal expedition against Sicily, which gave a mortal blow to the Athenian grandeur, and affords a signal instance of the terrible consequences of faction. The Egestians, a small state in Sicily, applied to the Athenians for assistance against the oppressions of the Syracusans. Alcibiades, looking upon it as an object worthy of his ambition, undertook the cause of these suppliants, and knew so well how to flatter the vanity of his countrymen, that a large [93] armament was decreed by the people for that purpose,[e] and Nicias, Alcibiades, and Lamachus, a daring but able officer, were elected generals.

a. Plut. in Vit. Alcib. p. 200. lit. B.[41]
b. Plut. Vit. Alcib. p. 197. lit. C.[42]
c. Thucyd. lib. 5. p. 339. sect. 35, 42.[43]
d. Thucyd. lib. 5. p. 350. sect. 52.[44]
e. Thucyd. lib. 6. p. 383. sect. 8.[45]

39. A person who can assume various forms, aspects, or characters; hence changeable, variable, or inconstant (*OED*, 1b).
40. Strict, particular, punctilious, scrupulous (*OED*, 5a).
41. Plutarch, "Alcibiades," XXIII.4–6.
42. Plutarch, "Alcibiades," XIV.1.
43. Thucydides, V.xxxv.3–6 and V.xlii.1–2.
44. Thucydides, V.lii.2.
45. Thucydides, VI.viii.1–3.

Nicias was the only person who had the honesty or courage to oppose a measure which he judged not only rash, but to the last degree impolitick; but the Athenians were deaf to all his remonstrances. The relief of the Egestians was only the pretext; for the entire dominion of Sicily, as Thucydides assures us,[a] was the real object they had in view when they gave orders for that powerful armament. Alcibiades had promised them an easy conquest of that island, which he looked upon only as a prelude to much greater enterprizes; and the besotted people had already swallowed up Italy, Carthage, and Africa, in their idle imaginations.[b] Both factions concurred in the vigorous prosecution of this measure, though from very different motives: the friends of Alcibiades, from the view of aggrandizing their chief by that vast accession of wealth and glory which they hoped for from this expedition: his enemies,[c] from the hopes of supplanting him in his absence, and gaining [94] the lead in the administration. Thus the true interest of the state was equally sacrificed to the selfish and private views of each party! But, in the midst of these vast preparations, an odd accident threw the whole city into confusion, and at once alarmed the superstition and jealousy of the people. The Terms,[d] or statues of Mercury were all defaced in one and the same night by some unknown persons; nor could the Athenians ever discover the real authors of this reputed sacrilege. Proclamations were issued with a free pardon, and reward for any of the accomplices who could make a discovery, and the information of strangers and slaves was allowed as legal evidence; but no information could be procured as to the true authors of that particular fact; a circumstance which to me does not appear at all surprizing: for it was evidently, in my opinion, a piece of party-craft played off against Alcibiades by the

a. Thucyd. lib. 6. p. 381. sect. 6.[46]

b. Plut. in Vita Alcibid. Item Thucyd. in orat. Alcib. ad Lacedaem. lib. 6. p. 436. sect. 90.[47]

c. Thucyd. lib. 6. p. 395, 396. sect. 28, 29.[48]

d. Thucyd. The Terms were statues of Mercury, placed at the doors of their houses, made of square stones of a cubical form.[49]

46. Thucydides, VI.vi.1.

47. Plutarch, "Alcibiades," XVII.2–3. Thucydides, VI.xc.2–4.

48. Thucydides, VI.xxviii.2 and xxix.3.

49. Thucydides, VI.xxvii.1.

opposite faction, who knew that to attack the established religion, was to touch the master-spring of the passions of their countrymen.[a] Some slaves indeed, and other low [95] persons (suborned, as Plutarch asserts,[b] by Androcles, one of the Demagogues) deposed, that long before that, some statues had been mutilated, and the most sacred mysteries of their religion ridiculed, in a drunken frolick by some young wild fellows, and that Alcibiades was of the party.[c] This information, which, according to Plutarch, was a palpable contrivance of his enemies, enabled them to fix the odium of the last action upon Alcibiades.[d] The Demagogues of the opposite faction greatly exaggerated the whole affair to the people. They accused him of a treasonable design against the popular government, and produced his contemptuous ridicule of the sacred mysteries, and the mutilation of Mercury's statues, in support of their charge; as they urged his well-known libertinism, and licentious life as a proof that he must be the author of those insults upon their religion. Alcibiades not only denied the charge, but insisted upon being brought immediately to a legal trial; declaring himself ready to undergo the punishment inflicted by the laws, if he should be found guilty.[e] He beseeched the people not to re-[96]ceive any informations against him in his absence, but rather to put him to death upon the spot if they judged him to be the offender. He urged too, how impolitick it would be to send him with the command of so great an army, whilst he lay under the imputation of a crime of that nature, before they had taken thorough cognizance of the affair: but his accusers dreading the effect which his interest with the army, and his well-known influence over

a. A similar measure was taken in the latter end of Queen Anne's reign.[50]

b. Plut. in Vit. Alcib. p. 200. lit. D.[51]

c. Thucyd. lib. 6. p. 395. sect. 28.[52]

d. Thucyd. ibid.[53]

e. Thucyd. ibid. sect. 29. passim.[54]

50. An allusion to the maneuvers in late April 1713 by Bolingbroke, Harcourt, and Atterbury to cast doubt on the sincerity of Lord Treasurer Oxford's churchmanship, in order to make him docile to their own schemes for a more thoroughly Tory program; see Bennett, *Tory Crisis*, pp. 161–82.

51. Plutarch, "Alcibiades," XIX.1–2.

52. Thucydides, VI.xxviii.1–2.

53. Thucydides, VI.xxviii.2

54. Thucydides, VI.xxix.1–3.

the allied troops, which had engaged in the expedition from their personal attachment to him, might have upon the people, if he should be brought to immediate trial, procured other Demagogues of their party to dissuade the people from a measure which they judged would disconcert their scheme. These men pleaded the dangerous delay which such a proceeding might occasion, and urged the necessity of dispatch in an enterprize of such vast importance. They proposed therefore that the fleet should sail immediately, but that Alcibiades should return when a day was appointed for his trial.[a] For their intention was, as Thucydides remarks, to recall and bring him to his trial when the popular prejudice run strong against him, which they knew they could easily spirit up in his ab-[97]sence. It was decreed therefore that Alcibiades should depart immediately upon the expedition.

This mighty armament, which carried the flower of the Athenian forces, was the most splendid, the best fitted out, and the most expensive, that had ever sailed from any of the Grecian ports to that very time.[b] But the first thing we meet with in this expedition, was (what might naturally be expected) a disagreement between the three Generals as to the manner of beginning their operations.[c] Alcibiades indeed brought them both over to his opinion; but whilst he was disputing with his colleagues in Sicily, his enemies at Athens were by no means idle. The affair of the statues, and the pollution of the sacred mysteries, were again brought upon the carpet.[55] The people, naturally suspicious, never enquired into the character of the informers, or the validity of the evidence, but admitted all that offered without distinction; and, giving easy credit to the most abandoned wretches, apprehended several of the most eminent citizens, and committed them to prison.[d] One of these per-[98]suaded another of his fellow-prisoners, who was most liable to suspicion, to take the crime upon himself, and to impeach

a. Thucyd. lib. 6. p. 395. sect. 23. ad finem.[56]
b. Thucyd. lib. 6. p. 396. sect. 31.[57]
c. Thucyd. lib. 6. p. 408. sect. 47, 48, 49.[58]
d. Thucyd. lib. 6. p. 411. sect. 53.[59]
55. Under consideration (*OED*, "carpet," 1a), the carpet being the covering of a council table.
56. Thucydides, VI.xxiii.3–4.
57. Thucydides, VI.xxxi.1–2.
58. Thucydides, VI.xlvii–xlix.
59. Thucydides, VI.liii.2–3.

some others as his accomplices:[a] urging this as a reason, that whether what he confessed should be true or false, he would at least secure his own pardon, and calm the present suspicions of the people. Andocides, for that was the name of this person according to Plutarch,[b] though it is omitted by Thucydides, was prevailed upon by this kind of reasoning to acknowledge himself guilty of defacing the statues, and to inform against some others as accomplices in the same act of impiety. Upon this declaration the informer received his pardon, and all those who were not mentioned in his information, their liberty:[c] but processes were made out against as many as he had named; and all who were apprehended were tried, condemned, and executed upon his single evidence. Those who escaped by flight were sentenced to die, and a price set upon their heads by a publick proclamation. Whether the persons condemned were guilty or innocent was not at all clear, according to Thucydides. Plutarch tells us, that the friends and acquaintance of Alcibiades, [99] who fell into the hands of the people, were severely handled on this occasion.[d] It is certain therefore that the information was chiefly levelled at him by the artifice of the opposite faction: for Thucydides informs us almost in the very next sentence, that the people received the information against Alcibiades with all the fury of prejudice, at the instigation of such of his enemies as had accused him before he sailed upon the expedition.[e] And since they now had not the least doubt of his being concerned in the affair of defacing the statues, they were more than ever convinced that he was equally guilty of the pollution of the mysteries, and that both those crimes were committed by him and his associates with the same design of subverting the popular government. For a body of Spartan troops happened to make an excursion, in that very juncture, as far as the Isthmus,[60]

---

a. Ibid. p. 415. sect. 60.[61]
b. Plut. in Vit. Alcib. p. 202.[62]
c. Thucyd. p. 416. sect. 60.[63]
d. Plut. in Vit. Alcib. p. 201. lit. C.[64]
e. Thucyd. lib. 6. p. 416. sect. 61.[65]
60. The narrow neck of land connecting the Peloponnese to northern Greece.
61. Thucydides, VI.lx.2–3.
62. Plutarch, "Alcibiades," XXI.1–4.
63. Thucydides, VI.lx.4–5.
64. Plutarch, "Alcibiades," XX.3–4.
65. Thucydides, VI.lxi.1.

upon some design or other against the Boeotians. This unlucky incident confirmed the people in their suspicions that this was a scheme concerted before-hand with Alcibiades, covered with the specious pretext of attacking the Boeotians;[a] and that if the plot had not been happily discovered [100] in time, and the execution of it prevented by the death of the conspirators, their city would most inevitably have been betrayed to the Spartans.[b] Thus on every side suspicions fell strongly upon Alcibiades, and the people determining to put him to death, sent a private express to Sicily to recall him and such of his friends as were named in the information. The officers dispatched in the Salaminian galley,[66] which was sent on that occasion,[c] were ordered to acquaint Alcibiades, that he was desired to return with them to Athens to clear himself of those things which were objected to him before the people; but they received a strict charge not to offer to take him or his friends into custody; not only from the dread of some mutiny amongst their own soldiers upon his account, but for fear the allied troops, whom his influence had engaged, should desert and abandon the enterprize. Alcibiades obeyed the summons,[d] and taking his friends, who were included in the information, into his own ship, left Sicily in company with the Salaminian galley, seemingly as if returning to Athens; but, whether he only suspected, or, which is more probable, had [101] received intelligence of the measures taken by his enemies in his absence, he, with his friends, went ashore at Thuria, and gave the Athenian officers the slip, not caring to stand the sentence of

a. Ibid.[67]

b. Ibid.[68]

c. This vessel may properly be termed the Athenian State-pacquet boat,[69] and was never sent out but upon very extraordinary occasions. Plut.[70]

d. Thucyd. lib. 6. p. 417. sect. 61.[71]

66. So-called to commemorate the great naval battle of Salamis in 480 B.C. when the Athenians defeated the fleet of the Persian king Xerxes.

67. Thucydides, VI.lxi.2.

68. Thucydides, VI.lxi.2.

69. A boat reserved for official business. In an eighteenth-century English context, the packet-boat was the yacht which carried the "packet" of state letters and dispatches between England and Ireland at frequent and regular intervals.

70. Plutarch, "Alcibiades," XXI.5.

71. Thucydides, VI.lxi.6–7.

the credulous and prejudiced people. The officers, finding all their search after him quite fruitless, returned to Athens without him, and the Athenians passed sentence of death upon him and all those who accompanied him, and confiscated their estates for non-appearance.[a] Thus, instead of uniting their joint efforts to promote the success of an enterprize upon which they had staked their All, the infatuated Athenians were intent upon nothing but the cabals and intrigues of faction; and the folly of the people, managed by their ambitious and selfish Demagogues, deprived the state of the only commander from whom they could rationally hope for success in that hazardous expedition. A measure which occasioned the total ruin both of their fleet and army, and gave a fatal shock to their Republick; for the soldiers were not only greatly dispirited at the loss of a chief, in whose abilities they placed the most entire confidence, but Alcibiades, in revenge for his usage, took refuge amongst the Spartans,[b] and prevailed upon [102] them to send such supplies to the Syracusans as compleated the destruction of the Athenians in that country. Nicias was taken and put to death by the enemy; not a single ship returned, and few of the men escaped either slaughter or captivity.[c] The news of this terrible defeat threw the city into the utmost consternation.[d] They at first gave up all hopes, and imagined they should quickly see the enemies fleet in the Pyraeum[72] whilst they were in this exhausted and defenceless condition. However, the dread of the impending danger had this good effect, that it made the populace extremely tractable, and ready to support their magistrates in whatever measures they judged most conducive to the common

a. Thucyd. ibid.[73]
b. Plut. in Vit. Alcib. p. 202.[74]
c. Thucyd. lib. 7. p. 505. ad finem.[75]
d. Thucyd. lib. 8. p. 506, &c.[76]

72. The principal port of ancient Athens, situated on a peninsula five miles to the southwest of the city itself. It was connected to the city by impressive fortifications (the so-called "Long Walls"), and was itself fortified. At the peak of its development it contained docks for the 372 ships of the Athenian navy and an arsenal for stores and tackle.

73. Thucydides, VI.lxi.7.
74. Plutarch, "Alcibiades," XXIII.1.
75. Thucydides, VII.lxxxvi.1–2.
76. Thucydides, VIII.i.1.

safety.^a Nor could any thing but union and harmony amongst themselves have possibly saved them in the midst of so many enemies, with which they were surrounded. For all the Greeks in general were highly elated, as Thucydides tells us, with the ill success of the Athenians in Sicily.^b Those who had hitherto observed a strict neutrality in this war wanted no solicitations to join in crushing that unhappy people, but rather thought it glorious to have a share in a [103] war which they concluded would be but of short duration. The Spartan allies were more than ever desirous of delivering themselves from the calamities of war which they had so long suffered; whilst those states, which till that time had received laws from the Athenians, exerted themselves above their strength to support the revolt which they were then meditating. They judged of the situation of affairs from the blind impulse of passion, regardless of the dictates of reason, and fancied the next campaign would finish the ruin of the Athenians. The Spartans, promising themselves the certain dominion over all Greece, if the Athenians were once reduced, made vast preparations for the war, to which all their allies contributed their utmost; all got ready for opening the campaign the spring following.^c

The Athenians, now harmony was restored to the state, recovered their spirits, and begun to act with vigour.^d They applied themselves to the re-establishment of their marine, the repairs of their fortifications, and the care of storing their magazines with the greatest diligence and oeconomy, retrenching all such expences as they judged useless or superfluous. The good effects of this un-[104]animity were visible when the campaign opened, for they found themselves in a condition to make head against their numerous enemies, though strengthened by a new alliance with the Persians, and assisted with Persian money; and they even gained

a. Thucyd. ibid. p. 507.[77]
b. Thucyd. ibid. p. 508. sect. 2.[78]
c. Thucyd. ibid. sect. 2–3.[79]
d. Thucyd. ibid. sect. 4.[80]
77. Thucydides, VIII.i.4.
78. Thucydides, VIII.ii.1.
79. Thucydides, VIII.ii–iii.
80. Thucydides, VIII.iv.

some considerable advantages. An event too happened, which greatly disconcerted the measures of their enemies, and raised their state once more to its former power and lustre. Alcibiades, a thorough libertine, who never stuck at the most infamous means of gratifying his passions, debauched Timaea, the wife of Agis, King of Sparta, his great friend and protector.[a] Dreading the resentment of that prince for so shameful a breach of friendship and hospitality, as well as the jealousy of the Peloponnesians, who had sent private orders to Astyochus, the Lacedemonian Admiral, to cut him off, he fled to Tissaphernes, at that time Governor of the provinces in the Lower Asia under the Persian Monarch.[b] Alcibiades, who was a consummate master in the art of address, quickly insinuated himself into his good graces,[c] and explained to him the true interest of the Persians with respect to the Grecian [105] Republicks. He shewed him the bad policy of raising one state to a superiority over all the rest, which would deprive his master of all his allies, and oblige him to contend alone with the whole power of Greece. He advised him to permit every state to enjoy its own separate independent government; and demonstrated, that by keeping them thus divided, his master might set them together by the ears,[81] and, by playing them one against another, crush them all at last without the least danger. He added too, that an alliance with the Athenians would be more advantageous to the Persian interest, and preferable to that which he had made with the Lacedemonians. The crafty Persian was too able a politician not to relish his advice; he paid the Peloponnesians their subsidy so ill, and put off a naval engagement so long, under pretence of waiting for the Phaenician fleet, that he wasted the strength of their navy,[d] which was far superior to the Athenian, and ruined all their measures.

a. Plut. in Vit. Alcib. p. 203.[82]
b. Thucyd. lib. 8. p. 531. sect. 45.[83]
c. Thucyd. ibid. sect. 46.[84]
d. Thucyd. ibid.[85]
81. Put them at variance (*OED*, "ear," 1d).
82. Plutarch, "Alcibiades," XXIII.7.
83. Thucydides, VIII.xlv.1.
84. Thucydides, VIII.xlvi.1–5.
85. Thucydides, VIII.xlvi.5.

Whilst Alcibiades resided with Tissaphernes, and gave the Persians the best instructions he could for regulating their conduct,[a] he at the same time formed a scheme for procuring the repeal of his sentence, and [106] liberty to return once more to his native country. He judged the best way to obtain this favour would be to convince the Athenians of his intimacy with Tissaphernes. To effect this, he wrote to the chief officers of the Athenian forces, which then lay at Samos, directing them to inform all those of the greatest weight and authority how desirous he was of revisiting Athens, if the government should be once lodged in the hands of a small number of the principal citizens; but that he could by no means think of returning whilst the Democracy subsisted, and the State was governed by a parcel of abandoned wretches, who had so scandalously driven him out of his country. Upon that condition he promised to procure the friendship of Tissaphernes, and declared himself ready to accept a share with them in the administration. The event answered his expectations; for the officers and the leading men, both of the sea and land forces, which were at Samos, were eagerly bent upon subverting the Democracy. Thus the treaty was set on foot at Samos, and the scheme laid for altering the government.[b] The principal men were in hopes of a share in the administration, and the inferior people acquiesced from the expectation of large subsidies from the [107] Persians. Phrynicus, one of the Generals, alone opposed it, sensible[86] that Alcibiades cared as little for an Aristocratick government, as for a Democracy, and had no other point in view (which, as Thucydides acknowledges, was the real truth) than to procure such a change in the present administration as might enable his friends to recall him. The terms however, which Alcibiades offered, were agreed to by the rest, and Pisander, one of the leading men, was sent to Athens to manage the affair.[c]

a. Thucyd. ibid. sect. 47.[87]
b. Thucyd. ibid. sect. 48.[88]
c. Thucyd. ibid. sect. 49.[89]
86. Aware (*OED*, 11a).
87. Thucydides, VIII.xlvii.1–2.
88. Thucydides, VIII.xlviii.2.
89. Thucydides, VIII.xlix.

Pisander at first met with violent opposition from the people; and the enemies of Alcibiades in particular clamoured loudly against the violation of the laws, when his return was proposed, which they chiefly dreaded.[a] But Pisander applied so artfully to the fears of the people, and shewed them so plainly that it was the only resource they had left which could possibly save the state, that they at last agreed to it, though with great reluctance.[b] He therefore, with ten others, was appointed to settle the affair with Tissaphernes and Alcibiades, as they should judge most conducive to the interest of the Repub-[108]lick; but Tissaphernes, who dreaded the power of the Peloponnesians, was not so ready to enter into a convention with the Athenians, as they were taught to believe.[c] Alcibiades therefore, to save his credit, and conceal from the Athenians his inability to make good what he had promised, insisted, in the name of Tissaphernes, upon such high terms that the treaty broke off, and the deputies returned to Samos, enraged at the trick which they thought had been put upon them by Alcibiades. Determined however, at all events, to pursue their scheme, Pisander, with some of the deputies, returned to Athens, where their party had already made a considerable progress;[d] for they had privately assassinated such of the leading men as were averse to an Aristocracy; and though they permitted the senate and people to assemble and vote as usual, yet they would not allow any thing to be decreed but what they thought proper: besides, none but those of their own faction durst venture to harangue the people;[e] for if any one attempted to speak in opposition, he was sure to be dispatched the first convenient opportu-[109]nity; nor was any enquiry made after the assassins, or any process issued out against those who were strongly suspected of the murders. The people

a. Thucyd. ibid. sect. 53.[90]
b. Thucyd. ibid. sect. 54.[91]
c. Thucyd. ibid. sect. 56.[92]
d. Thucyd. ibid. 65.[93]
e. Thucyd. ibid. 66.[94]
90. Thucydides, VIII.liii.2.
91. Thucydides, VIII.liv.4–5.
92. Thucydides, VIII.lvi.2–3.
93. Thucydides, VIII.lxv.1–3.
94. Thucydides, VIII.lxvi.2

were so terrified with these bloody executions, that they acquiesced to whatever was proposed, and every man thought himself happy if no violence was offered him, even though he continued quiet and silent. They were deprived even of the power of bewailing the common calamity to each other, in order to concert measures for revenge: for the faction had artfully spread so strong and so universal a diffidence amongst the popular party, that no one durst venture to confide in his neighbour, but each man suspected every other as an accomplice of the crimes which were daily perpetrated.

In this situation Pisander found the city at his arrival, and immediately prepared to finish what his friends had so successfully begun:[a] convoking therefore an assembly of the people, the Aristocratick faction openly declared their resolution to abolish the antient form of government, and to lodge the supreme power in the hands of four hundred of the nobility, who should govern the State in the manner they thought best, with the power of assembling five thousand of the citi-[110]zens to consult with as oft as they thought proper. Pisander was the man who acquainted the people with this definitive resolution; but Antiphon was the person who formed the plan, and was chief manager of the whole affair:[b] a man, according to the testimony of Thucydides, who knew him personally, master of the greatest abilities, and of by far the most nervous[95] eloquence of any of his cotemporaries. Thus the Oligarchy was established, and the Athenians deprived of that liberty which they had enjoyed near an hundred years from the expulsion of Hippias: during which whole space they had been subject to none, but had been accustomed, above half that time, to lord it over others; for as soon as this decree had passed in the assembly without opposition, the chiefs of the conspiracy artfully permitted such citizens as were upon duty, but had not been let into the secret, to go wherever they pleased; but directed their own friends to continue under arms, and disposed them in such a manner

a. Thucyd. ibid. 67.[96]
b. Thucyd. ibid. 68.[97]
95. Vigorous, powerful, forcible; free from insipidity and diffuseness (*OED*, 4a).
96. Thucydides, VIII.lxvii.1–3.
97. Thucydides, VIII.lxviii.1–4.

as might best favour their enterprize: for the Athenians kept at that time a constant guard upon their walls, as the Spartan army was encamped in their neighbourhood.[a] When they had made their disposition, the four [111] hundred Nobles with poignards[98] concealed under their habits, and attended by an hundred and twenty daring young fellows, whom they employed in their assassinations, surrounded the Senators, and paying them what was due upon their salaries, commanded them to depart the court.[b] The Senators tamely submitted, and not the least stir happening amongst the citizens, they proceeded to elect magistrates out of their own body, and performed all the religious ceremonies usually practised upon those occasions.[c] When they had thus got possession of the government, they did not think proper to recall those whom the people had formerly banished, for fear of being obliged to include Alcibiades in the number, whose enterprising genius they dreaded extremely; but they behaved most tyrannically to the citizens, putting some to death, throwing some into prison, and banishing others.

The spirit of liberty however is not so easily extinguished. Pisander had brought mercenary troops with him out of some of the cities which he passed through on his return to Athens, who were of great service to the new Governors in their enterprize:[d] but the forces at Samos consisted of Athenian ci-[112]tizens, jealous even of the least attempt upon the liberty of their country, and declared enemies to every species of tyranny. The first news which these brave fellows received of the usurpation, brought such exaggerated accounts of the cruelty and insolence of the four hundred, that they were with great difficulty restrained from cutting every one to pieces who was in the interest of the Oligarchy. However, they took the command from their former Generals, and cashiered every

a. Thucyd. ibid. 69.[99]
b. Solon's new senate of four hundred.
c. Thucyd. ibid. 70.[100]
d. Thucyd. lib. 8. p. 543. sect. 65.[101]
98. Small, slim daggers (*OED*, 1a).
99. Thucydides, VIII.lxix.1.
100. Thucydides, VIII.lxx.1–2.
101. Thucydides, VIII.lxv.1.

officer they suspected, substituting others in their places; the chief of whom were Thrasybulus and Thrasyllus.[a] Alcibiades was recalled, and unanimously declared their Captain General both by the sea and land forces;[b] which gave such a turn to affairs at Athens, that the four hundred were deposed, in spite of all their efforts to continue in power, and the publick tranquillity once more established.

The people confirmed Alcibiades in the command, and committed the whole management of the war to his conduct.[c] But his soul was too great[102] to receive his recall from banishment,[d] and even his high post as [113] an act of favour. He determined to merit both by some signal service, and not to revisit Athens 'till he could return with glory. His usual success attended him in this war, and he seemed to bring victory with him wherever he appeared; for he gained so many victories both by sea and land, and distressed the Peloponnesians so much by his address and conduct, that he once more retrieved the dominion of the sea, and returned triumphant to Athens.[e] His entry was splendidly magnificent, adorned with the trophies of two hundred ships of war, which he had destroyed or taken, and a vast number of prisoners.[f] His reception was attended with all the honours and applause he had so justly merited. The people, conscious of the late happy change in their affairs under the administration of Alcibiades, lamented with tears their miscarriage in Sicily, and other subsequent calamities; all which they imputed to their own fatal error in not trusting the sole command to so able and successful a commander.

a. Thucyd. lib. 8. p. 551. sect. 76.[103]
b. Thucyd. ibid. p. 553. sect. 81.[104]
c. Thucyd. ibid. p. 567. sect. 97.[105]
d. Plut. in Vit. Alcib. p. 206.[106]
e. Plut. ibid. p. 207, 208.[107]
f. Plut. ibid. p. 209.[108]
102. To be great-souled or magnanimous (in Greek, μεγαλοψυχος) was for Aristotle the cardinal moral virtue (*Nicomachean Ethics*, IV.2).
103. Thucydides, VIII.lxxvi.1–2.
104. Thucydides, VIII.lxxxi.1.
105. Thucydides, VIII.xcvii.3.
106. Plutarch, "Alcibiades," XXVII.1.
107. Plutarch, "Alcibiades," XXVII–XXXI.
108. Plutarch, "Alcibiades," XXXII.1.

The fortune however of this great man was perpetually fluctuating, and seemed to be ever on the extreme; and Plutarch re-[114]marks, that if ever man owed his ruin to his own glory, it must be Alcibiades; for the people were so prepossessed with the opinion of his courage and conduct, that they looked upon him as absolutely invincible.[a] Whenever therefore he failed in any one point, they imputed it entirely to his neglect, or want of will; for they could imagine nothing so difficult, but what they thought him able to surmount, if he applied to it with earnestness and vigour. Thus, in the same campaign, he sailed to the isle of Andros with a powerful fleet, where he defeated the joint forces of the inhabitants and Spartans; but, as he did not take the city, he gave his enemies a fresh handle for renewing their usual accusations; for the people already fancied themselves masters of Chios and the rest of Ionia, and were extremely out of humour because his conquests did not keep pace with their heated imaginations. They made no allowance for the wretched state of their finances, which frequently obliged him to quit his army to go in search of money to pay, and provisions to subsist, his forces, whilst their enemies had a constant resource for all their wants in the treasures of Persia. To one of these excursions, which necessity obliged him to make in order to raise money, he properly owed his ruin: for leaving the command of the fleet to one Antiochus, an able seaman [115] indeed, but rash, and in every other respect unequal to such a charge, he gave him the most positive orders not to fight the enemy upon any account whatsoever during his absence; but the vain Antiochus treated his orders with so much contempt, that he sailed out with a few ships to brave the Spartan admiral Lysander, which brought on a general engagement. The event was, the death of Antiochus, the defeat of the Athenians, who lost many of their ships, and a trophy erected by the Spartans in honour of their victory. Alcibiades, at the first news of this misfortune, returned to Samos with precipitation, and endeavoured to bring Lysander to a decisive action; but the wary Spartan knew too well how different a man he had now to deal with, and would by no means hazard a second engagement.

a. Ibid. p. 211.[109]
109. Plutarch, "Alcibiades," XXXV.2.

In the mean time one Thrasybulus,[a] who bore a mortal enmity to Alcibiades, posted to Athens, and impeached him as the cause of the late defeat, affirming that he committed the care of the fleet to his pot companions,[110] whilst he rambled at pleasure amongst the provinces, raising money, and living in a state of riot and dissipation with wine and women. [116] A violent charge, besides, was brought against him for fortifying a place near Bizanthe,[b] as a retreat upon occasion, which his enemies urged as a proof that he either was not able, or not willing, to reside in his native country.

Jealousy and inconstancy were the characteristicks of the Athenian people. They gave implicit belief to the suggestions of his enemies, and discharged, as Plutarch tells us, the fury of their gall upon the unfortunate Alcibiades, whom they deprived immediately of the command.

Thucydides, speaking of the behaviour of his countrymen to Alcibiades upon the impeachment brought against him for defacing the statues, imputes their ruin to that jealousy which they constantly harboured both of his ambition and abilities.[c] For though he had done the State many great and signal services, yet his way of life made him so odious to every individual, that the command was taken from him, and given to others, which not long after drew on the destruction of the Republick.

For Tydeus, Menander, and Adimantus, the new Generals, who lay with the Athenian fleet in the river Aegos,[d] were so [117] weak as to sail out every morning at day-break to defy Lysander, who kept his station at Lampsacus; and, at their return from this idle bravado, spent the rest of the day without order or discipline, or keeping any lookout, from an affected contempt of the enemy. Alcibiades, who was at that time in the neighbourhood, and thoroughly sensible of their danger, came and

---

a. The son of Thrason; the other of that name is called by Thucydides, the son of Lycus. Thucyd. lib. 8. p. 549. sect. 75.[111]

b. A city in Thrace.

c. Thucyd. lib. 6. p. 387. sect. 15.[112]

d. Plut. in Vit. Alcib. p. 211, 212.[113]

110. Drinking companions, drunkards (*OED*).

111. Thucydides, VIII.lxxv.2.

112. Thucydides, VI.xv.4.

113. Plutarch, "Alcibiades," XXXVI.4.

informed them of the inconveniences of the place where their fleet then lay, and the absurdity of suffering their men to go ashore and ramble about the country. He assured them too, that Lysander was an experienced and vigilant enemy, who knew how to make the most of every advantage: but they, vain of their new power, despised his advice, and treated him with the utmost rudeness. Tydeus, in particular, ordered him to be gone; and told him insolently, that not he, but they were now commanders, and knew best what to do. The event happened as Alcibiades had foreseen. Lysander attacked them unexpectedly whilst they lay in their usual disorder, and gained so compleat a victory, that of all their fleet eight vessels alone escaped, which fled at the first onset. The able Spartan, who knew as well how to make use of, as to gain, a victory,[114] soon after compelled Athens itself to surrender at discretion. As soon as he was [118] master of the city, he burnt all their shipping, placed a garrison in their citadel, and demolished the rest of their fortifications.[a] When he had thus reduced them to a state of absolute subjection, he abolished their constitution, and left them to the mercy of thirty governors of his own chusing, well known in history by the appellation of the Thirty Tyrants.

This tyranny, though of very short duration, was to the last degree inhuman. The tyrants sacrificed all whom they suspected to their fear, and all who were rich to their avarice. The carnage was so great, that, according to Xenophon, the Thirty put more Athenians to death in eight months only, than had fallen in battle, against the whole force of the Peloponnesians, during ten years of the war.[b] But the publick virtue of Thrasybulus[c] could not bear to see his country enslaved by such inhuman monsters: collecting therefore about seventy determined citizens,

a. Plut. in Vit. Lysand. p. 441.[115]

b. Τριάκοντα πλήους ἀπεκτόνασιν Ἀθηναίων εν οκτω μησὶν, ἤ πάντες Πελοπόννησιοι δέκα ἔτη πολεμοῦντες. Xenoph. Hellenic. lib. 2. p. 370. Edit. Lewencl. Basil.[116]

c. Most probably the son of Lycus, mentioned by Thucydides, who had so great a share in deposing the Four Hundred, and restoring the ancient constitution.

114. An inverted allusion to the reproach made by Maharbal to Hannibal after the Carthaginian victory at Cannae; see below, p. 236, n. 43.

115. Plutarch, "Lysander," XV.1–5.

116. "The Thirty who have killed in eight months more Athenians almost than all the Peloponnesians in ten years of war," Xenophon, *Hellenica*, II.iv.21.

who, like him, had fled to Thebes for refuge, he first seized upon Phyle,[a] a [119] strong fort near Athens; and, strengthened by the accession of fresh numbers, which flocked in to him from every side, he got possession[b] of the Pyraeum.[117] The Thirty Tyrants endeavoured to retake it, but were repulsed, and Critias and Hippomachus,[c] two of their number, slain in the attempt. The people now, weary of the Tyrants,[d] drove them out of the city, and chose ten magistrates, one out of each tribe, to supply their places. The Tyrants applied to their friend Lysander, who sailed and invested the Pyraeum, and reduced Thrasybulus, and his party, to an extreme want of necessaries; for they were yet confined to the Pyraeum, as the people, though they had deposed the Tyrants, yet refused to receive them into the city; but Pausanias,[e] one of the Kings of Sparta, who commanded the land forces in this expedition, jealous of the reputation which that great man had acquired, gained over two of the Ephori, who accompanied him, and granted peace to the Athenians, notwithstanding all the opposition of Lysander. Pausanias returned to Sparta with his army, and the Tyrants,[f] despairing of assist-[120]ance, began to hire foreign troops, and were determined to re-establish themselves by force in that power of which they had been so lately deprived. But Thrasybulus, informed of their design, marched out with all his forces, and, drawing them to a parley, punished them with that death their crimes so justly merited. After the execution of the Tyrants, Thrasybulus proclaimed a general act of indemnity and oblivion, and by that salutary measure restored peace and liberty to his country without farther bloodshed.

a. Xenoph. ibid. p. 367.[118]
b. Xenoph. ibid. p. 368.[119]
c. Xenoph. ibid. 370.[120]
d. Xenoph. ibid. 371.[121]
e. Xenoph. ibid. 372–373.[122]
f. Xenoph. ibid. p. 375.[123]
117. See above, p. 65, n. 72.
118. Xenophon, *Hellenica*, II.iv.2.
119. Xenophon, *Hellenica*, II.iv.1.
120. Xenophon, *Hellenica*, II.iv.19.
121. Xenophon, *Hellenica*, II.iv.23.
122. Xenophon, *Hellenica*, II.iv.29–38.
123. Xenophon, *Hellenica*, II.iv.39–43.

The conclusion of the Peloponnesian war may properly be termed the period of the Athenian grandeur; for though, by the assistance of the Persians, they made some figure after that time, yet it was but of short duration. The manners of the people were greatly degenerated, and the extreme scarcity of virtuous characters, so visible in their subsequent history, marks at once the progress and the degree of their degeneracy. Conon, who escaped with eight ships only when they were so totally defeated by Lysander, had convinced the Persian Monarch how much his interest was concerned in supporting the Athenians, and obtained the command of a powerful armament in their favour: whilst the artful Tithraustes,[a] general of [121] the Persian forces in Asia, raised a strong confederacy against the Spartans, by properly distributing large sums amongst the leading men of the Grecian Republicks. Conon totally defeated the Spartan fleet commanded by Pisander,[b] and, by the help of the Persian money, rebuilt the strong walls and other fortifications of Athens, which Lysander had demolished.[c] The Spartans, jealous of the rising power of the Athenians, who seemed to aspire at recovering their former grandeur, made such advantageous offers to the Persians by their Admiral Antalcidas, that they once more drew them over to their party.[d] Conon was recalled and imprisoned upon the suggestions of Antalcidas, that he had embezzled the money allotted for the re-establishment of Athens, and was no friend to the Persian interest.[e] The Athenians now sent Thrasybulus, their great deliverer, with a fleet of forty sail to annoy the Spartans: he reduced several cities which had revolted to the enemy, but was slain by the Rhodians in an unsuccessful attempt upon their island. Conon, according to Justin, was executed at

a. Xenoph. lib. 3. p. 392.[124]
b. Xenoph. lib. 4. p. 404.[125]
c. Ibid. p. 420.[126]
d. Ibid.[127]
e. Ibid. 421.[128]
124. Xenophon, *Hellenica*, III.iv.25–26.
125. Xenophon, *Hellenica*, IV.iii.10–12.
126. Xenophon, *Hellenica*, IV.viii.9–12.
127. Xenophon, *Hellenica*, IV.viii.12–14.
128. Xenophon, *Hellenica*, IV.viii.16.

Susa by the Persians.[a] Xenophon, who [122] lived at the same time, is silent
as to his death; but, whatever might be his fate, it is certain he is no more
mentioned in history. After the death of these two great men, we meet with
none but Chabrias, Iphicrates, and Timotheus, the son of Conon, whose
characters are worthy of our notice, 'till the time of Demosthenes and Phocion. The martial spirit of the Athenians subsided in proportion as luxury
and corruption gained ground amongst them. The love of ease, and a most
insatiable fondness for diversions, now took place of those generous sentiments which before knew no other object but the liberty and glory of their
country. If we trace the rise of publick virtue up to its first source, and shew
the different effects arising from the prevailing influence of the different
ruling passions, we may justly account for the fatal and amazing change in
that once glorious Republick. A short digression therefore, on that subject,
may perhaps be neither unuseful nor unentertaining.

Of all the human passions ambition may prove the most useful, or the
most destructive to a people. The—

—Digito monstrari et dicier hic est;[b]

the fondness for admiration and applause [123] seems co-eval with man,
and accompanies us from the cradle to the grave. Every man pants after
distinction, and even in this world affects a kind of immortality. When
this love of admiration and applause is the only end proposed by ambition,
it then becomes a primary passion;[129] all the other passions are compelled

---

a. Justin. in Vit. Conon.[130]

b. Persius, sat. 1.[131]

129. The primary (sometimes, "ruling" or "predominant") passion was a term of
art in popular eighteenth-century English psychology, referring to the prime consideration supposed to govern an individual's actions. For its most salient expressions
in eighteenth-century English literature, see Pope, *An Essay on Man* (1734), II.133–60
and Edward Young, *The Universal Passion* (1725). The full-blown theory is foreshad-
owed by incidental comments in a variety of earlier authors, e.g., Montaigne, *Essays*,
I.38 "How We Weep and Laugh at the Same Thing" (Montaigne, *Essays*, p. 263);
Francis Bacon, *Advancement of Learning*, II.xxiii.21 (Bacon, *Advancement*, p. 184);
Pascal (Pascal, *Thoughts*, p. 348); and Roscommon (*An Essay on Translated Verse*,
London [1685], p. 7).

130. Justin, *Epitoma*, VI.v.8.

131. "To be pointed at, and to hear people say 'That's the man!'" (Persius, I.28).

to be subservient, and will be wholly employed on the means conducive to that end. But whether this passion for fame, this eagerness after that imaginary life, which exists only in the breath of other people, be laudable or criminal, useful or frivolous, must be determined by the means employed, which will always be directed to whatever happens to be the reigning object of applause. Upon this principle, however the means may differ, the end will be still the same; from the hero down to the boxer in the bear-garden;[132] from the legislator who new-models a state, down to the humbler genius who strikes out the newest cut for a coat-sleeve. For it was the same principle directing to the same end, which impelled Erostratus to set fire to the temple of Diana, and Alexander to set the world in a flame so quickly after.

There is no mark which so surely indicates the reigning manners of a people at different periods, as that quality or turn of mind, which happens to be the reigning object of publick applause. For as the reigning ob [124] ject of applause will necessarily constitute the leading-fashion, and as the leading-fashion always takes rise among the great or leading people; if the object of applause be praise-worthy, the example of the Great will have a due influence upon the inferior classes; if frivolous or vicious, the whole body of the people will take the same cast, and be quickly infected by the contagion. There cannot therefore be a more certain criterion, by which we may form our judgment of the national virtue or national degeneracy of any people, in any period of their existence, than from those characters, which are the most distinguished in every period of their respective histories. To analyze these remarkable characters; to investigate the end proposed by all their actions, which opens to us all their secret springs; and to develope the means employed for the acquisition of that end, is not only the most entertaining, but, in my opinion, by much the most useful, part of history. For as the reigning object of applause arises from the prevailing manners of a people, it will necessarily be the reigning object of desire, and continue to influence the manners of succeeding generations,

132. A place originally set apart for the baiting of bears, and used for the exhibition of other rough sports, fig. a scene of strife and tumult (*OED*, "bear," 10). In eighteenth-century English usage, a place of low entertainment and coarse manners.

till it is opposed, and gradually gives way to some new object. Consequently the prevailing manners of any [125] people may be investigated without much difficulty, in my opinion, if we attend to the increase or decrease of good or bad characters, as recorded in any period of their history; because the greater number will generally endeavour to distinguish themselves by whatever happens at that time to be the reigning object of applause. Hence too we may observe the progressive order, in which the manners of any people prepared the way for every remarkable mutation in their government. For no essential mutation can ever be effected in any government (unless by the violence of external force) till the prevailing manners of the people are ripe for such a change. Consequently, as like causes will ever produce like effects;[133] when we observe the same similarity of manners prevailing amongst our own people, with that which preceded the last fatal mutation of government in any other free nation; we may, at such a time, give a shrewd guess at the approaching fate of our constitution and country. Thus in the infancy and rise of the Grecian Republicks, when necessity of self-defence had given a manly and warlike turn to the temper of the people, and the continuance of the same necessity had fixed it into a habit, the love of their country soon became the reigning object of pub-[126]lick applause. As this reigning object consequently became the chief object of desire to every one who was ambitious of publick applause, it quickly grew to be the fashion. The whole people in those states glowed with the generous principle of publick virtue to the highest degree of enthusiasm. Wealth had then no charms, and all the bewitching pleasures of luxury were unknown, or despised. And those

133. The assertion of causal regularity operating throughout human affairs is a commonplace in eighteenth-century English historiography. Subtler minds, however, understood that the principle of causal regularity was compatible with a luxuriant variety of consequences. Bolingbroke had advised the student of history to be aware of "the surprising fertility of one single and uniform cause in the producing of a multitude of effects as different, as remote, and seemingly as opposite" (Bolingbroke, *Letters*, vol. 1, p. 65). In "A Dialogue," Hume illustrated how causal regularity might produce diverse effects by means of an example drawn from geography: "The Rhine flows north, the Rhone south; yet both spring from the *same* mountain, and are also actuated, in their opposite directions, by the *same* principle of gravity" (Hume, *Enquiries*, p. 333).

brave people courted and embraced toils, danger, and even death itself, with the greatest ardour, in pursuit of this darling object of their universal wishes. Every man planned, toiled, and bled, not for himself, but for his country. Hence the produce of those ages was a race of patriot Statesmen and real Heroes. This generous principle gave rise to those seminaries of manly bravery and heroic emulation, the Olympick, Isthmian, and other publick games. To obtain the victory at those scenes of publick glory was esteemed the utmost summit of human felicity. A wreath of wild olive, laurel or parsley (the victor's prize), that *palma nobilis,* as Horace terms it, which

Terrarum dominos evehit ad Deos,[134]

was infinitely more the object of emulation in those generous times, than Coronets and Garters[135] are of modern ambition. Let me add too, that as the former were invariably [127] the reward of merit only, they reflected a very different lustre upon the wearer. The honours acquired at these games quickly became the darling themes of the poets, and the charms of musick were called in to give additional graces to poetry. Panegyrick swelled with the most nervous strokes of eloquence, and decked up with all the flowers of rhetorick, was joined to the fidelity and dignity of History; whilst the canvass glowing with mimick life, and the animated marble, contributed all the powers of art to perpetuate the memory of the victors. These were the noble incentives which fired the Grecian youth with the glorious emulation of treading in the steps of those publick-spirited Heroes, who were the first institutors of these celebrated games. Hence that refined taste for arts and sciences arose in Greece, and produced

134. Montagu refers to the opening lines of Horace's ode to Maecenas, in which Horace rejects various common forms of human pleasure, including the pleasure taken by the victors of chariot races whom "the glorious palm exalts to the level of gods and masters of the earth" (Horace, *Odes,* I.i.5–6).

135. It may be that Montagu here has in mind the celebrated *Examiner* 16 (23 November 1710) in which Swift famously contrasted the frugality of a Roman triumph with the prodigious riches which had been lavished on the Duke of Marlborough following his victories over the French during the War of the Spanish Succession.

those master-pieces of every kind, the inimitable remains of which not only charm, but raise the justest admiration of the present times.

This taste raised a new object of applause, and at last supplanted the parents which gave it birth. Poetry, Eloquence, and Musick became equally the subjects of emulation at the publick games, were allotted their respective crowns, and opened a new road to fame and immortality. Fame was the end proposed and hoped for by all; and those [128] who despaired of attaining it by the rugged and dangerous paths of honour, struck into the new and flowery road, which was quickly crowded with the servile herd of imitators.[a] Monarchs turned poets,[b] and great men, fidlers; and money was employed to biass the judges at the publick games to crown wretched verses and bungling performers with the wreaths appropriated only to superior merit. This taste prevailed more or less in every state of Greece (Sparta alone excepted) according to the different turn of genius of each people; but it obtained the most ready admission at Athens, which quickly became the chief seat of the Muses and Graces.

Thus a new object of applause introducing a new taste, produced that fatal alteration in the manners of the Athenians, which became a concurrent cause of the ruin of their Republick. For though the manners of the Athenians grew more polite, yet they grew more corrupt, and publick virtue ceased gradually to be the object of publick applause and publick emulation. As dramatick poetry affected most the taste of the Athenians; the ambition of excelling in that species of poetry was so violent, that [129] Aeschylus died with grief, because in a publick contention with Sophocles the prize was adjudged to his antagonist.[c] But though we owe the finest pieces of that kind now extant to that prevailing taste, yet it introduced such a rage for theatrical entertainments as fatally contributed to the ruin of the Republick.

a. Lucian, p. 328. Edit. Bourdel. 1615.[136]
b. Dionysius the tyrant of Syracuse.
    Diodor. Sicul. lib. 14. p. 318, 319.[137]

c. Plut. in Vit. Cim. p. 483.[138]
136. Lucian, *Herodotus, or Aëtion,* II–III.
137. Diodorus Siculus, XV.vi.1.
138. Plutarch, "Cimon," VIII.8.

Justin informs us that the publick virtue of Athens declined immediately after the death of Epaminondas.[a] No longer awed by the virtue of that great man, which had been a perpetual spur to their ambition, they sunk into a lethargy of effeminate indolence. The publick revenues appropriated for the service of the fleet and army were squandered in publick festivals and publick entertainments. The stage was the chief object of the publick concern, and the theatres were crowded whilst the camp was a desart. Who trod the stage with the greatest dignity, or who excelled most in the conduct of the Drama; not who was the ablest General, or most experienced Admiral, was the object of the publick research and publick applause. Military virtue and the science of war were held cheap, and poets and players engrossed those honours due only to [130] the patriot and the hero; whilst the hard-earned pay of the soldier and the sailor was employed in corrupting the indolent pleasure-taking citizen. The fatal consequence of this degeneracy of manners, as Justin assures, was this: That the able Philip, taking advantage of the indolence and effeminacy of the Athenians, who before took the lead in defence of the liberty of Greece, drew his beggarly kingdom of Macedon out of its primitive obscurity, and at last reduced all Greece under the yoke of servitude. Plutarch, in his inquiry whether the Athenians were more eminent in the arts of war or in the arts of peace, severely censures their insatiable fondness for diversions.[b] He asserts, that the money idly thrown away upon the representation of the tragedies of Sophocles and Euripides alone, amounted to a much greater sum than had been expended in all their wars against the Persians, in defence of their liberty and common safety. That judicious philosopher and historian, to the eternal infamy of the Athenians, records a severe but sensible reflection of a Lacedemonian who happened to be present at these diversions. The generous Spartan, trained up in a state where publick virtue still continued to be the object of publick [131] applause, could not behold the ridiculous assiduity of the Choragi, or magistrates who

a. Justin. p. 67. Edit. Elziv.[139]
b. Plut. de Glor. Athen. p. 349. Vol. 2.[140]
139. Justin, *Epitoma*, VI.ix.1–5.
140. Plutarch, "On the Fame of the Athenians," V.

presided at the publick shews, and the immense sums which they lavished in the decorations of a new tragedy, without indignation.

He therefore frankly told the Athenians, that they were highly criminal in wasting so much time, and giving that serious attention to trifles, which ought to be dedicated to the affairs of the publick. That it was still more criminal to throw away upon such baubles as the decorations of a theatre, that money which ought to be applied to the equipment of their fleet, or the support of their army. That diversions ought to be treated merely as diversions, and might serve to relax the mind at our idle hours,[a] or when over a bottle; if any kind of utility could arise from such trifling pleasures. But to see the Athenians make the duty they owed to their country give way to their passion for the entertainments of the theatre, and to waste unprofitably that time and money upon such frivolous diversions, which ought to be appropriated to the affairs and the necessities of the [132] state, appeared to him to be the height of infatuation.[b]

Could we raise the venerable Philosopher from the grave to take a short survey of the present manners of our own countrymen, would he not find them an amazingly exact copy of those of the Athenians, in the times immediately preceding their subjection to Macedon? Would he not see the same series of daily and nightly diversions, adapted to the taste of every class of people, from the publick breakfasting (that bane to the time and industry of the tradesman) up to our modern Orgyes, the midnight-revels of the Masquerade?[141] If he censured the Athenians for

a. Ευπότω καὶ ἀνέσει.[142]

b. Plut. Symposiac. p. 710.[143]

141. Masquerades frequently featured in the menu of urban entertainments in England from the 1720s onward. They were regularly denounced as incitements to corruption and depravity which had been imported into English life from the continent, particularly Venice. Writing to Horace Mann on 25 February 1742, Horace Walpole deplored the intrusive power of the masquerade: "But you will wish for politics now, more than for histories of masquerades, though this last has taken up people's thoughts full as much" (Walpole, Correspondence, vol. 17, p. 343). For commentary, see Terry Castle, Masquerade and Civilization: The Carnivalesque in Eighteenth-Century English Culture and Fiction (London: Methuen, 1986).

142. "Hours of ease."

143. Plutarch, Table Talk, VII.7. A very loose translation, which in particular introduces the notion that military expenditure was a better use for the money spent by the Athenians on the theater.

throwing away so much time and attention upon the chaste and manly scenes of Sophocles and Euripides, what must he have thought of that strange *Shakespearomania* (as I may term it) which prevailed so lately, and so universally amongst all ranks and all ages?[144] Had he enquired of those multitudes who so long crowded both theatres at the representation of Romeo and Juliet,[145] what were the striking beauties which so strongly and so repeatedly engaged their attention, could a tenth part of the affected admirers of that pathetick[146] poet, have given him a more satisfactory answer than, "That it was the fashion?" Would he not be convinced that fashion was the only motive, [133] when he saw the same people thronging with the same eagerness, and swallowing the ribaldry of modern farce, and the buffoonery of pantomime with the same fury of applause?[147] Must he not have pronounced, that they as much exceeded the Athenians in thoughtless levity and folly, as they sunk beneath them in taste and judgment? For Plutarch does not find fault with the fine taste of the Athenians for the noble compositions of those incomparable poets; but for that excess of passion for the theatre, which, by setting up a new object of applause, had almost extinguished that publick virtue, for

144. The elevation of Shakespeare as the pre-eminent English author and symbol of English identity began in the 1730s with agitation to erect a monument to him in Westminster Abbey (finally unveiled in 1741), and would come to a climax with the Jubilee organized by Garrick at Stratford-on-Avon in 1769; see Michael Dobson, *The Making of the National Poet: Shakespeare, Adaptation and Authorship, 1660–1769* (Oxford: Clarendon Press, 1992), and Jonathan Bate, *Shakespearean Constitutions: Politics, Theatre, Criticism 1730–1830* (Oxford: Clarendon Press, 1989).

145. In 1748 David Garrick revived *Romeo and Juliet* at Drury Lane, and it was his acting version of the play which held the stage for the rest of the century, being performed more than 450 times by 1800. Between 1750 and 1800 *Romeo and Juliet* was the most popular of all Shakespeare's plays on the London stage (Hogan, *Shakespeare*, vol. 2, pp. 716–17).

146. Moving, stirring, affecting (*OED*, 1b).

147. The pernicious influence on public morals exerted by Italianate theatrical forms, such as opera and pantomime, had been severely censured by critics such as John Dennis, who in *The Causes of the Decay and Defects of Dramatick Poetry, and of the Degeneracy of the Publick Tast* (1725) had deplored "our Pantomimes," where one might see "a Hundred Blockheads with long Bibs and longer perrukes laughing and clapping at the Delicious Diversion of Jack pudding" (Dennis, *Works*, vol. 2, p. 290).

which they had been so greatly eminent; and made them more sollicitous about the fate of a new tragedy, or the decision of the pretensions of two rival players, than about the fate of their country. But what idea must he have of the higher class of our people, when he saw those who should be foremost in a time of distress and danger, to animate the drooping spirit of their countrymen by the lustre of their example, attentive only to the unmanning trills of an Opera; a degree of effeminacy which would have disgraced even the women of Greece, in times of greatest degeneracy. If he was informed that this species of diversion was so little natural to the rougher genius, as well as climate of Britain, that we were obliged to purchase [134] and fetch over the worst performers of Italy[148] at the expence of vast sums; what opinion must he form of our understanding? But if he was to see the insolence of these hirelings, and the servile prostration of their pay-masters to these idols of their own making, how must such egregious folly excite his contempt and indignation! In the midst of these scenes of dissipation, this varying round of unceasing diversions, how must he be astonished at the complaint of poverty, taxes, the decay of trade, and the great difficulty of raising the necessary supplies for the publick service, which would strike his ear from every quarter! Would not his censure upon our inconsistent conduct be just the same which the honest Spartan passed upon the infatuated Athenians? When a national Militia of 60,000 men only was asked for,[149] would he not have blushed for those who opposed a measure (once the support and glory of every free state in Greece) and whittled it down to half the number from a pretended principle of oeconomy? But could his philosophick gravity refrain a smile,

148. In the earlier eighteenth century the popularity of Italian opera among the royal family had made it a convenient proxy for anti-Hanoverian sentiment; see Pope, *Dunciad* (1748), III.255–56. It was also more generally condemned as an effeminate, foreign, debased, and incomprehensible form of drama; see *The Spectator*, nos. 22 and 29 and John Dennis, *An Essay on Opera's after the Italian Manner* (1706); in (Dennis, *Works*, vol. 1, pp. 382–93).

149. In May 1756 William Pitt and George Townshend had got a bill for establishing a national militia passed in the commons, but it had been voted down in the lords. As a result, the British government had been reduced to the humiliating expedient of hiring German mercenaries from Hesse and Hanover to guard the homeland.

when he saw the same people lavishing their thousands in subscriptions to balls, concerts, operas, and a long train of expensive et caetera's, yet so wondrous frugal in pounds, shillings, and pence, in a measure so essential to the very safety of the nation? [135] If therefore he saw a people bending under an accumulating load of debt,[150] almost to bankruptcy, yet sinking more and more into a luxury, known in his time only to the effeminate Persians, and which required the wealth of Persia to support it: Involved in a war,[151] unsuccessful 'till measures were changed with ministers; yet indulging in all the pleasures of pomp and triumph, in the midst of national losses and national dishonour: Contracting daily fresh debts of millions, to carry on that war, yet idly consuming more wealth in the useless pageantry of equipage, dress, table, and the almost innumerable articles of expensive luxury, than would support their fleets and armies; he could not help pronouncing such a people mad past the cure of Hellebore,[152] and self-devoted to destruction.

This strange degeneracy of the Athenian manners, which Plutarch so severely censures, was first introduced (as that great man informs us) by Pericles.[a] That ambitious man determined to supplant his rival Cimon, who, by the *éclât*[153] of his victories, and the services he had done the publick, was considered as the first man in Athens, and supported his popularity by the distribution of a large fortune. Pericles, greatly inferior

---

a. Plut. in Vit. Pericl. p. 156.[154]

150. The British national debt had been created to fund the continental campaigns of William III. It was a subject of popular anxiety in the earlier eighteenth century, and it had been increased alarmingly by the War of the Austrian Succession. In 1739 (the last year of peace) it had stood at £46 million. In 1749, following the conclusion of that war with the signing of the Treaty of Aix-la-Chapelle in 1748, it stood at £77 million. In 1763, at the conclusion of the Seven Years' War, it would be £133 million. See E. L. Hargreaves, *The National Debt* (London: Edward Arnold, 1930) and P. G. M. Dickson, *The Financial Revolution in England: A study in the development of public credit, 1688–1756* (London: Macmillan, 1967).

151. That is, the Seven Years' War (1756–63).

152. A preparation made from the root or other part of a plant of either of the genera *Veratrum* and *Helleborus*, formerly used medicinally as a purgative and as a treatment for mental illness (*OED*, 3).

153. Brilliance.

154. Plutarch, "Pericles," IX.1–4.

in [136] point of fortune, and no way able to contend with him in liberality and magnificence, struck out a new method of gaining over the people to his party. He procured a law, by which every citizen was intitled to a gratuity out of the publick money, not only for attending at the courts of judicature, and assemblies of the states; but even at the entertainments of the theatre, and the publick games and sacrifices on their numerous days of festivity. Thus Pericles bought the people with their own money; a precedent which has been so successfully followed by corrupt and ambitious statesmen in all succeeding ages. To this piece of state-craft, not to superior abilities, late ministers owed their long reigns, which enabled them to reduce corruption into system.[155]

The consequence of this corruption, as we may gather from the writings of Demosthenes, was, that in a few years time the Athenians were no more the same people. The annual fund appropriated to the publick service for the army and navy, was wholly diverted to the support of the theatre. Their officers regarding nothing but their rank and pay, instead of patriots, were degenerated into meer mercenaries.[a] The emu-[137]lation, of who should serve their country best, no longer subsisted amongst them; but of who should obtain the most lucrative command. The people tasting the sweets of corruption, and enervated by the luxury of a city, which was one perpetual scene of festivals and diversions, grew averse to the toils and dangers of war, which now seemed an insupportable slavery, and beneath the dignity of free citizens. The defence of the state was committed to mercenary hirelings, who behaved so ill that their affairs were in the utmost disorder. Of all their leading men, Demosthenes and Phocion were alone proof against the gold of Macedon; the

---

a. Plut. in Vit. Phocion, p. 744. Item Demost. Olynth. 2. p. 25. Edit. Wolf. 1604.[156]

155. A reference to the policies and career of Sir Robert Walpole (1676–1745), the dominant English politician of the earlier eighteenth century. From the early 1720s he had acted as George I's chief minister, and had been retained by George II in the same role until his downfall in 1742. Walpole's mastery of the House of Commons, and hence his long tenure of office, was popularly attributed to his use of secret service funds to buy votes.

156. Plutarch, "Phocion," VII.3; Demosthenes, *Second Olynthiac*, XXIV–XXVII.

rest were Philip's known and avowed pensioners.[157] Demosthenes, at this alarming juncture, laid before the people the ambitious views of Philip, and the distressed situation of their country, with the utmost freedom. He employed all the energy and Pathos of eloquence to rouse them out of that lethargy of indolence and inattention to the publick safety, into which their own luxury, and the flatteries of their corrupt Demagogues, had thrown them.

He demonstrated to them,[a] that the glorious principle, which had so long preserved the liberty of Greece, and had enabled them [138] to triumph over the whole force and opulence of the mighty power of Persia, was that common hatred, that general detestation of corruption, which prevailed so universally amongst their generous fore-fathers. That, in those times of publick virtue, to receive presents from any foreign power was deemed a capital crime. That if any man should be found so shamefully profligate, as to sell himself to any one who had designs upon the liberty of Greece; or should endeavour to introduce corruption into his own country; death without mercy would have been his punishment here, and his memory branded with indelible and eternal infamy hereafter. That the Statesmen and Generals of those happier times, were absolute strangers to that most criminal and infamous kind of traffick; which was grown so common and so universal, that honour, fame, character, the liberty and welfare of their country were all set to sale, and sold publickly by auction to the best bidder.[b] He then made use of his utmost art, backed with the greatest strength of reasoning, to persuade the people, to give

a. Demost. Orat. in Philip. 3. p. 86, 92.[158]

b. Demost. ibid.[159]

157. Possibly a glance at recent English history. The secret Treaty of Dover (22 May 1670) stipulated that Charles II would receive £200,000 from Louis XIV in return for converting to Roman Catholicism and £800,000 per annum for as long as he waged war against the Dutch, although the documents confirming this were not published until 1773 (Dalrymple, *Memoirs*, vol. 2, pp. 45–56). The same cache of documents revealed that the Whig martyr Algernon Sidney had also accepted money for services rendered from Barillon, the French ambassador, having been "d'une grande utilité en bien des occasions" (ibid., vol. 2, p. 257).

158. Demosthenes, *Third Philippic*, XXXVI–XXXVIII; XLI–XLV.

159. Demosthenes, *Third Philippic*, XLI–XLV.

up that fund to the support of the army and navy (the service to which it had been originally appropriated) which from the time of Pericles [139] had been applied solely to defray the expences of the theatre. He shewed next, the folly and danger of confiding the defence of the state to mercenary forces;[160] who had already served them so ill. He informed them, that their allies the Olynthians earnestly insisted, that the troops sent to their assistance might no longer be composed of venal hirelings as before, but of native Athenians, animated with a zeal for the glory of their country, and warm in the interest of the common cause. Both these motions were opposed by the corrupt party who adhered to Philip. The people were unwilling to give up that fund, even to the most pressing exigencies of the state, which enabled them to gratify their favourite passion; thus the opposition of the people quashed the former of these motions. But though the urgent, and repeated remonstrances of Demosthenes prevailed in favour of the latter, yet the Demagogues, who omitted no opportunity of convincing Philip, how well he employed his money, took care to reduce the promised succours to a very small number, and to procure Chares, a creature of their own,[a] to be placed at the head of the expedition. Small as those succours were, yet they did the Olynthians essential service. But as all [140] the eloquence of Demosthenes could not prevail upon his countrymen to make more vigorous efforts, the city of Olynthus fell the year following into the hands of Philip by the treachery of Euthycrates[b] and Lasthenes, two of the leading citizens. Philip still continued his encroachments upon the allies of Athens; sometimes cajoling,[161] sometimes bullying the Athenians; just as he found either method most conducive to his purpose, in which he was punctually seconded by the

a. Plut. in Vit. Phocion, p. 747.[162]

b. Diodor. Sicul. lib. 16. p. 450.[163]

160. Most immediately a satiric reference to the recent British use of mercenary forces from Hesse and Hanover (see above, p. 86, n. 149); but also invoking the long-running dispute in English political life between the merits of, respectively, a militia and professional troops.

161. Prevailing upon or getting one's way by delusive flattery, specious promises, or any false means of persuasion (OED, 1).

162. Plutarch, "Phocion," XIV.2.

163. Diodorus Siculus, XVI.liii.2.

corrupt Demagogues. But at last the joint attack which he made upon the cities of Perynthus and Byzantium, from whose territories the Athenians drew their chief supplies of corn, at once opened their eyes, and rouzed them from their indolence. They equipped a very large armament with great expedition; but the Philippick faction had still influence enough with the people, to obtain the command of it for their friend Chares. The conduct of this general was exactly answerable to the opinion and hopes of his friends, who had procured him that employment. Chares, voluptuous, yet sordidly avaritious; vain and assuming, yet without either courage or capacity; rapacious, and intent only upon enriching himself at the expence either of friend or foe, [141] was refused admittance by the inhabitants of Byzantium; who from experience were too well acquainted with his character. Enraged at such an unexpected affront, this doughty general employed his time in parading along the coasts, detested by his allies whom he plundered, and despised by his enemies whom he had not the courage to face. The Athenians, sensible of their folly, displaced Chares, and gave the command to Phocion. The able and honest Phocion was received with open arms by the Byzantines, and quickly convinced his countrymen, that he was more than a match for Philip. He not only drove that ambitious monarch out of the territories of the allies; but compelled him to retire with great loss and precipitation into his own dominions, where Phocion made several glorious and successful incursions. Philip now throwing off the masque, marched his army towards Athens, with a resolution to humble that people, who were the chief obstacle to his ambitious views. Demosthenes alone took the lead upon this occasion, and persuaded his countrymen to join the Thebans with all the force they could raise, and make head against the invader. Philip finding his measures quite disconcerted by this confederacy, sent an embassy to Athens to propose terms of peace, and to profess his desire of living in amity with the [142] Athenians. Phocion, anxious about the success of a war, which he knew his countrymen had not virtue enough to support, and where the loss of a single battle must be fatal to the state, pleaded strongly for pacifick measures. But the flaming zeal of Demosthenes prevailed. Phocion was not only insulted, but excluded from all share in the command of the army by the infatuated people. Chares, so notorious for his cowardice and incapacity, who (as Diodorus Siculus informs us[a]) knew no more the duty of a general than the meanest private soldier in the army, and one Lysicles, a man of daring courage, but rash and ignorant, were appointed commanders in chief. As Demosthenes had pushed on the people to this war, and was at that time at the head of affairs, this fatal step must be entirely attributed to his private pique at Phocion for opposing his measures. Phocion had more than once beaten Philip with much inferior forces, and was indisputably the ablest general of the age, and the only man whom Philip was afraid of. The conduct therefore of Demosthenes was so rash and weak in the management of this war,[b] that Plutarch resolves the whole into a certain di-[143]vine fatality; which, in the circumvolution of mundane affairs, had limited the freedom of Greece to that particular point of time. The battle of Chaeronea, which ensued quickly after, gave the Athenians a too fatal proof of the superior foresight and sagacity of Phocion, and their own superlative folly in the choice of their generals. The battle was fought with equal bravery and obstinacy on both sides, and the confederates behaved as well as men could do upon the occasion; but their defeat was owing entirely to the incapacity of the Athenian commanders. This was so apparent, that Philip observing a capital blunder[c] committed by Lysicles[d] in the heat of the action, turned about coolly, and remarked to his officers,

That the Athenians knew not how to conquer.

This fault in point of generalship quickly turned the scale in favour of the abler Philip, who knew his trade too well to let slip so material an advantage. The Athenians were totally routed, and that fatal day put a period[164] to the liberty and independency of Greece.[e] [144]

a. Diodor. Sicul. lib. 16. p. 476.[165]
b. Plut. in Vit. Demost. p. 854.[166]
c. Polyaen. Stratagem, lib. 4. c. 3. p. 311.[167]
d. Polyaenus calls this general Stratocles.
e. Hic dies universae Greciae et gloriam dominationis, et vetustissimam libertatem finivit. Justin. lib. 9. p. 79. Edit. Elziv.[168]
164. Ended.
165. Diodorus Siculus, XVI.lxxxv.7.
166. Plutarch, "Demosthenes," XX.2.
167. Polyaenus, *Strategemata*, IV.ii.2.
168. Justin, *Epitoma*, IX.iii.11. "This day put an end to the glorious self-rule and the beautiful freedom of the whole of Greece."

Thus fell the Athenians, and their fall involved the rest of Greece in one common ruin. The decadence of this once glorious and free State was begun by Pericles, who first introduced venality amongst the people for the support of luxury; continued by the venal orators who encouraged that corruption to maintain their influence over the people; but finished by that fatal disunion between the only two men, whose publick virtue and abilities could have saved their country from destruction.

Athens however, by her fall, has left us some instructions highly useful for our present conduct. Warned by her fate we may learn,—that the most effectual method which a bad minister can take, to tame the spirit of a brave and free people, and to melt them down to slavery, is to promote luxury, and encourage and diffuse a taste for publick diversions—That luxury, and a prevailing fondness for publick diversions, are the never-failing fore-runners of universal idleness, effeminacy, and corruption.—That there cannot be a more certain symptom of the approaching ruin of a State than when a firm adherence to party is fixed upon as the only test of merit, and all the qualifications requisite to a right discharge of every employment, are reduced to that single standard.[169]—That these evils take root, and spread by al-[145]most imperceptible degrees in time of peace and national affluence; but, if left to their full and natural effects without controul, they will inevitably undermine and destroy the most flourishing and best founded constitution.—That in times of peace and affluence luxury, and a fondness for diversions, will assume the specious names of politeness, taste, and magnificence. Corruption will put on different masks. In the corruptors it will be termed able management, encouraging the friends of the administration, and cementing a mutual harmony,[a] and mutual dependance between the three different estates of the government. In the corrupted it will be denominated

a. Thus Demades termed the gratuities given to the people out of the publick money, the glue or cement of the different parts of the Republick. Plut. Quest. Platon, p. 1011.[170]

169. An allusion perhaps to the tension between Newcastle and Pitt during the early years of the Seven Years' War which was resolved only in October 1756 when Newcastle was obliged to invite Pitt to join the ministry.

170. Plutarch, "Platonic Questions," X.1011.

loyalty, attachment to the government, and prudence in providing for one's own family. That in such times these evils will gain a fresh accession of strength from their very effects; because corruption will occasion a greater circulation of the publick money; and the dissipations of luxury, by promoting trade, will gild over private vices with the plausible appearance of publick benefits.[a]—That when a State, so circumstanced, is forced into a war with any formi-[146]dable power, then, and not 'till then, these baleful evils will shew themselves in their true colours, and produce their proper effects. The counsels in such a State will be weak and pusillanimous, because the able and honest citizens, who aim solely at the publick welfare, will be excluded from all share in the government from party motives.—Their measures will terminate in poor shifts, and temporary expedients, calculated only to amuse, or divert the attention of the people from prying too closely into their iniquitous conduct. Their fleets and armies will be either employed in useless parade, or will miscarry in action from the incapacity of their commanders, because, as all the chief posts will be filled up with the creatures of the prevailing faction, such officers will be more intent upon enriching themselves than annoying the enemy;[171] and will act as shall be judged most conducive to the private interest of their party, not to the publick service of their country. For they

a. Fable of the bees.[172]

171. On 14 March 1757 Admiral Byng had been executed by firing squad on his own quarterdeck following a court-martial in which it had been found that he had shown culpable reluctance to engage the French fleet then investing the British naval base at Minorca. Voltaire famously remarked in *Candide* (1759) that Byng had been executed "*pour encourager les autres.*" Byng's execution indeed brought to an end a period in which British naval captains had been more than once suspected of diffidence (to put it no more strongly) in the face of the enemy, and initiated a period of exceptional effectiveness in British naval operations; see Rodger, *Command*, pp. 241–326.

172. An allusion to Bernard Mandeville's *Fable of the Bees*, of which the subtitle is "Private Vices, Publick Benefits." First published under the title of *The Grumbling Hive: or, Knaves Turn'd Honest* (1705), this work was reprinted and expanded in 1714, 1723, 1724, 1725, 1728, 1729, and 1732. In its frank admission that economic prosperity need not be coordinated with traditional notions of moral virtue, the *Fable of the Bees* was one of the most provocative, controversial, and influential books of the early eighteenth century.

will naturally imagine, that the same power, which placed them in the command, will have weight enough to screen them from the resentment of an injured people.—Their supplies for the extraordinary expences of the war will be raised with difficulty;—because, as so great a part of the publick money will be absorbed by the number of pensions and lu-[147] crative employments, and diverted to other purposes of corruption, the funds destined for the publick service will be found greatly deficient. If the rich are applied to, in such depraved times, to contribute their superfluous wealth towards the publick expences, their answer will be the same which Scopas the rich Thessalian made to a friend, who asked him for a piece of furniture, which he judged wholly useless to the possessor, because it was quite superfluous.ᵃ "You mistake, my friend; the supreme happiness of our lives consists in those things which you call superfluous, not in those which you call necessaries." The people, accustomed to sell themselves to the best bidder, will look upon the wages of corruption as their birthright, and will necessarily rise in their demands, in proportion as luxury, like other fashions, descends from the higher to the lower classes. Heavy and unequal taxes must consequently be imposed to make up this deficiency; and the operations of the war must either be retarded by the slowness in collecting the produce, or the money must be borrowed at high interest and excessive premiums, and the publick given up a prey to the extortion [148] of usurers. If a venal and luxurious Demadesᵇ should be at the head of the ruling party, such an administration would hardly find credit sufficient to support their measures, as the moneyed men would be averse to trusting their property in such rapacious hands;ᶜ for the chain of

---

a. —Ἀλλὰ μὴν τούτοις ἐσμέν ἡμεῖς εὐδαίμονες καὶ μακάριοι τοῖς περιττοῖς, ἀλλ᾽ οὐκ ἐκείνοις τοῖς ἀναγκαίοις. Plut. de Cupidit. p. 527.[173]

b. Demades, according to Plutarch, by the dissoluteness of his life, and conduct in the administration, shipwrecked the Athenian Republick. Plut. in Vit. Phocion, p. 741.[174]

c. Plut. Apotheg. p. 188.[175]

173. "Why, it is just these articles of superfluity, and not those which are indispensable, that give me the reputation of being enviable and fortunate" (Plutarch, "On Love of Wealth," VIII).

174. Plutarch, "Phocion," I.1.

175. Plutarch, "Sayings of Kings; Phocion the Athenian," XV.

self-interest, which links such a set of men together, will reach from the highest quite down to the lowest officer of the state; because the higher officers, for the mutual support of the whole, must connive at the frauds and rapines of the inferior, or screen them if detected.

If therefore the united voice of a people, exhausted by the oppressions of a weak and iniquitous administration, should call a truly disinterested patriot to the helm,[176] such a man must be exposed to all the malice of detected villany, backed by the whole weight of disappointed faction. Plutarch has handed down to us a striking instance of this truth in the case of Aristides, which is too remarkable to be omitted.

When Aristides was created Quaestor,[a] or high Treasurer of Athens, he fairly laid be-[149]fore the Athenians what immense sums the publick had been robbed of by their former Treasurers, but especially by Themistocles, whom he proved to be more criminal than any of the others. This warm and honest remonstrance produced such a powerful coalition between these publick plunderers, that when Aristides, at the expiration of his office, (which was annual, and elective) came to give up his accompts to the people, Themistocles publickly impeached him of the same crime, and, by the artifice of his corrupt party, procured him to be condemned and fined; but the honester, and more respectable part of the citizens highly resenting such an infamous method of proceeding, not only acquitted Aristides honourably, and remitted his fine, but, to shew their approbation of his conduct, elected him Treasurer for the following year. At his entrance upon his office the second time, he affected to appear sensible of his former error, and, by winking at the frauds of the inferior officers, and neglecting to scrutinize into their accompts, he suffered them to plunder with impunity. These State-leeches, thus gorged

a. Plut. in Vit. Aristid. p. 320.[177]

176. A reference to William Pitt the Elder (1708–78), first earl of Chatham, who in his youth had been associated with the Whig "patriot" opposition to Walpole under his patron Lord Cobham (see Gerrard, *Patriot Opposition*), and who had assumed the dominant position in the British administration as a result of the series of military setbacks in North America and Europe which had blighted Britain's cause in the early years of the Seven Years' War.

177. Plutarch, "Aristides," IV.2–5.

with the publick money, grew so extremely fond of Aristides, that they employed all their interest to persuade the people to elect him a third time to that important office. On the day of election, when the voices of the Athe-[150]nians were unanimous in his favour, this real Patriot stood up with honest indignation, and gave the people this severe, but just reprimand. "When, says he, I discharged my duty in this office the first time, with that zeal and fidelity which every honest man owes to his country, I was vilified, insulted, and condemned. Now I have given full liberty to all these robbers of the publick here present to pilfer, and prey upon your finances at pleasure, I am, it seems, a most upright minister, and a most worthy citizen. Believe me, O Athenians! I am more ashamed of the honour, which you have so unanimously conferred upon me this day, than of that unjust sentence which you passed upon me with so much infamy the year before. But it gives me the utmost concern, upon your account, when I see that it is easier to merit your favour and applause by flattering, and conniving at the rogueries of a pack of villains, than by a frugal and uncorrupt administration of the publick revenues." He then disclosed all the frauds and thefts, which had been committed that year in the treasury, which he had privately minuted down for that purpose. The consequence was, that all those, who just before had been so loud in his praise, were struck dumb with shame and confusion; but he himself received those high encomiums, which he had so justly me-[151]rited, from every honest citizen. It is evident from this whole passage, as related by Plutarch, that Aristides might have made his own fortune, at the expence of the publick, with the same ease, and to as great a degree as any of his predecessors had done before, or any ministers in modern States have done since. For the rest of the officers, who seemed to think their chief duty consisted in making the most of their places, shewed themselves extremely ready to conceal the peculation of their chief, because it gave them a right to claim the same indulgence from him in return. A remark not restricted to the Athenians alone, but equally applicable to every corrupt administration under every government. History, both ancient and modern, will furnish us with numerous instances of this truth, and posterity will probably make the same remark, when the genuine history of some late administrations shall see the light in a future age.

If the Athenians were so corrupt in the time when Aristides lived, ought we to wonder at that amazing height to which that corruption arrived in the time of Demosthenes, when left to its full effects for so long a term of years? Could the State of Athens at that time have been preserved by human means; the indefatigable zeal of Demosthenes, joined to the strict oeconomy, the inflexible integri-[152]ty, and superior abilities of Phocion, might have raised her once more to her ancient lustre. But the event shewed, that luxury, corruption and faction, the causes of her ruin, had taken too deep root in the very vitals of the Republick. The Grecian history indeed affords us ever memorable instances of Republicks bending under the yoke of foreign or domestick oppression, yet freed and restored to their former liberty and dignity by the courage and virtue of some eminent Patriot citizen. But if we reflect upon the means, by which these great events were so successfully conducted, we shall always find, that there yet remained in the people a fund of publick virtue sufficient to support their chiefs in those arduous enterprizes. The spirit of liberty in a free people may be cramped and pressed down by external violence; but can scarce ever be totally extinguished. Oppression will only encrease its elastic force, and when rouzed to action by some daring chief, it will break out, like fired gun-powder, with irresistable impetuosity. We have no occasion to look back to antiquity for convincing proofs of this most important truth. Our own history is but one continued scene of alternate struggles between encroaching princes, aiming at absolute power, and a brave people resolutely determined to vindicate their freedom.[178] The genius of liberty has hither-[153]to rose superior in all those conflicts, and acquired strength from opposition. May it continue to prevail to the end of time! The United Provinces[179] are a striking proof that the spirit of liberty, when animated and conducted by publick virtue, is invincible. Whilst under the dominion of the house of Austria, they were little better than a poor assemblage of fishing-towns and villages. But the virtue of

178. Montagu here adumbrates the "Whig Interpretation" of English history, which compresses and streamlines the English past into a single narrative about the eventual achievement of liberty, and which would receive its fullest expression in the next century with Macaulay's *History of England* (1849–61).

179. Holland.

one great man[180] not only enabled them to throw off that inhuman yoke, but to make a respectable figure amongst the first powers in Europe. All the different States in Europe, founded by our Gothick ancestors,[181] were originally free. Liberty was as truly their birth-right as it is ours; and though they have been wormed out of it by fraud, or robbed of it by violence, yet their inherent right to it still subsists, though the exercise of that right is superseded, and restrained by force. Hence no despotick government can ever subsist without the support of that instrument of tyranny and oppression, a standing army.[182] For all illegal power must ever be supported by the same means by which it was first acquired.[183] France was not broke into the yoke of slavery till the infamous administrations of Richlieu and Mazarin.[184] But though loyalty and zeal for the glory of their Prince seem to form the characteristick of the French nation, yet the [154] late glorious stand against the arbitrary impositions of the crown, which will immortalize the parliament of Paris, proves that

180. Principally a reference to William the Silent (1533–84), but also another allusion to the language surrounding Pitt the Elder, who before his elevation to the peerage was known as the "Great Commoner," a phrase coined as a sarcasm (*The Test*, 1 January and 9 April 1757), but which quickly became an honorific.

181. A reference to the Whiggish belief that English liberty had its roots in the rude freedom enjoyed by the tribes of ancient Germany in the territories north of the Rhine which the Romans had failed to conquer. The credal status of this political doctrine is suggested by Molesworth's definition of a "real Whig" as a supporter of "our old Gothick Constitution." See, most recently, Gerrard, *Patriot Opposition*, pp. 108–49. See below, p. 245, n. 4.

182. A point of contention in English political life since the late seventeenth century. The Bill of Rights (1689) had made it illegal for an English monarch to keep a standing army in England, but William III (in 1697) and George I (in 1715) had both sought to evade this restriction. Advocates for a militia (such as Montagu) tended to be suspicious of standing armies, and of professional military forces more generally.

183. An allusion to a celebrated maxim of Sallust, "Nam imperium facile eis artibus retinetur quibus initio partum est," "for power is easily retained by those arts by which it was first won" (*Bellum Catilinae*, II.4). It is a sentiment not infrequently echoed in English literature; see *King John*, III.iii.135–36 and Marvell, "An Horatian Ode," ll. 119–20.

184. Armand-Jean du Plessis, cardinal and duc de Richelieu (1585–1642); chief minister to Louis XIII from 1624 until 1642. Giulio Raimondo Mazarino, cardinal (1602–1661); chief minister of France following the death of Richelieu. Richelieu was the architect of the system of French royal absolutism which was perfected by Mazarin during the early years of the reign of Louis XIV.

they submit to their chains with reluctance.[185] Luxury is the real bane of publick virtue, and consequently of liberty, which gradually sinks in proportion as the manners of a people are softened and corrupted. Whenever therefore this essential spirit, as I may term it, of a free nation is totally dissipated, the people become a mere *Caput Mortuum,*[186] a dead inert mass, incapable of resuscitation, and ready to receive the deepest impressions of slavery. Thus the publick virtue of Thrasybulus, Pelopidas and Epaminondas, Philopaemen, Aratus, Dion, &c. restored their respective States to freedom and power, because though liberty was suppressed, yet the spirit of it still remained, and acquired new vigour from oppression. Phocion and Demosthenes failed, because corruption had extinguished publick virtue, and luxury had changed the spirit of liberty into licentiousness and servility.

That luxury and corruption, encouraged and propagated by a most abandoned faction, have made an alarming progress in our nation, is a truth too evident to be denied. The effects have been too sensibly felt during the course of the late and present wars, which [155] till the last campaign, were the most expensive, and the least successful of any we ever yet engaged in.[187] But a late signal change must convince our enemies, that we have a fund of publick virtue still remaining, capable of vindicating our just rights, and raising us out of that calamitous situation, into which we were plunged under some late administrations. When the publick imagined the helm in the hands of corruption, pusillanimity and ignorance, they transferred it to a virtuous Citizen,[188] possessed, in their

185. The thirteen *parlements* of France were originally courts of law created by the French crown during the Middle Ages to dispense justice. However, in 1752 a *parlementaire,* Louis-Adrien le Paige, had tried to elevate the constitutional status of the *parlements,* arguing for instance that royal decrees lacked the force of law unless they had been registered with the *parlements.* In the resulting clash with the French crown, the parlements became centers of resistance to the enlargement of monarchical power.

186. A worthless residue (*OED,* 3).

187. Before the "Year of Victories" of 1759, British forces in the Seven Years' War had suffered an unbroken run of defeats; see the introduction, above, pp. xi–xiv.

188. Another glance at Pitt the Elder, who had strong connections in the city of London.

opinion, of the zeal and eloquence of Demosthenes, joined to the publick oeconomy, incorrupt honesty, and immoveable fortitude of Aristides and Phocion. The numerous disinterested marks of approbation, so lately given from every part of this kingdom, demonstrate the resolution and ability of the publick to support that minister, as long as he pursues his upright plan of conduct with undeviating firmness.

From the time of Phocion, the Athenian history affords little more than a detail of scandalous decrees,[a] and despicable instances of the levity and servile adu-[156]lation of that abject people. Reduced at last to a province of the Romans, Athens contributed her taste for arts and sciences towards polishing, and her passion for theatrical performances towards corrupting the manners of that warlike people.

a. Plut. in Vit. Demet. p. 893–94–900.[189]
189. Plutarch, "Demetrius," XII–XXVI.

CHAPTER III

Of Thebes

The accounts of the earlier ages of this ancient Republick are so enveloped in fable, that we must rather apply for them to the poets than the historians. Pausanias gives us a list of sixteen Kings of this country,[a] down from Cadmus inclusive, who evidently belong to the fabulous times of the Heroes. He seems indeed to acknowledge as much, since he confesses, that as he could find no better account of their origin, he was obliged to take up with fable.[b] After the death of Xanthus, the last of those Kings, the Thebans, as the same author relates, disgusted at Monarchy, changed the form of their government into a Republick.[c] But it is in vain to search for the cause, or manner how this revolution was effected, either in Pausanias, or any other historian. All we can learn of

a. Pausan. Grec. Descrip. lib. 9. c. 5. p. 718. Edit. Kechnii.[1]

b. Οὐ γάρ τι ἠδυνάμην ἐς αὐτοὺς παρευρεῖν—ἕπομαι τῷ μύθῳ. Id. ibid.[2]

c. Ibid. p. 723.[3]

1. Pausanias, IX.v.

2. "I adopt the story that makes their name result from the way in which they came into being"; Pausanias, IX.v.3.

3. Pausanias, IX.v.16.

the Thebans or Boeotians[a] from history, is, that they were remarkable for [158] their dullness and stupidity, even to a proverb:[b] that, 'till the time of Pelopidas and Epaminondas, they made as poor a figure in the art of war as in the sciences: that their form of government was Democratick; and that, as usually happens in that kind of government, they were divided into factions.

After the famous peace of Antalcidas, by which the honour and true interest of Greece was sacrificed to the ambition of the Spartans, whatever State refused to come into their measures, was condemned to feel the effects of their resentment. They had compelled the Thebans to accede to that treaty, though it deprived them of the dominion over Boeotia; and afterwards, by the perfidy of the Aristocratick faction, got possession of their citadel, and reduced them to a state of absolute subjection. This was the wretched state of the Thebans 'till they were delivered both from foreign and domestick slavery, and raised to a height of power superior to every other State of Greece by the virtue of Pelopidas and Epaminondas. I have selected therefore this revolution as the most interesting, and most worthy of our attention; because it exhibits a convincing proof, that [159] a brave and warlike people are not the produce of any particular spot, but are the growth of every place and country, where the natives are trained up in a true sense of shame at mean and base actions, and inspired with that manly courage which arises from the emulation after what is just and honourable.[c] And that those who are taught to dread infamy more than the greatest dangers, prove the most invincible, and most formidable to an enemy. It instructs us too, that the most depressed, and most abject State may be extricated from the calamities of oppression, and raised to superior dignity and lustre by a very small number of virtuous patriots, whilst the spirit of

a. Thebes was the capital of Boeotia.
b. Boeotûm in crasso jurares aëre natum. Hor. epis. 1. lib. 2. lin. 244.[4]
c. Plut. in Vit. Pelopid. p. 287.[5]
4. "You'd swear he'd been born in Boeotia's heavy air" (Horace, *Epistles*, II.i.244). The Boeotians were proverbially stupid, in contrast to the acuity of the Athenians.
5. Plutarch, "Pelopidas," IV.3 and XVII.6.

liberty yet remains, and the people second the efforts of their leaders with unanimity and vigour.

The Thebans, by a fatal error in politicks, had chosen Ismenias and Leontidas, who were at that time heads of two opposite parties, their supreme annual magistrates. Ismenias was a steady assertor of the liberty and just rights of the people, and laboured to preserve a due balance in the powers of the constitution. Leontidas wanted to engross[6] the whole power into his own hands, and to govern by a small, but select number of his own creatures. It was impossible for union and harmony to subsist between two men, who had views so diametrically opposite. [160] Leontidas therefore, who found his party the weakest, bargained by a private convention with Phaebidas, the Spartan General, to deliver up his country to the Lacedemonians, upon condition that the government should be lodged in himself, and such as he should think proper to intrust. The agreement was made, and Leontidas conveyed Phaebidas with a strong body of troops into the citadel, at a time when the poor Thebans, wholly unapprehensive of any danger from the Spartans, with whom they had lately concluded a peace, were celebrating a publick religious festival. Leontidas, now sole governor, gave an immediate loose to his passions. He seized his colleague Ismenias, and, by the assistance of the Spartans, procured him to be tried, condemned, and executed, for caballing against the State. A pretence however stale, yet constantly urged by every iniquitous administration against all who have the resolution to oppose their measures. The party of Ismenias, upon the first news of the imprisonment of their chief, fled the city, and were afterwards banished by a publick decree. A strong proof of the fatal lengths a faction will run, which is composed of those profligate wretches whose sole aim is their own private emolument! Yet such a faction, in all free States, when once luxury and corruption[7] are introduced, is generally the most nu-[161]merous, and most prevalent. Athens, not long before, had been betrayed to the Spartans in the same manner, and on the same infamous terms by a detestable faction, composed of the most abandoned of her citizens, and groaned

6. To monopolize (*OED*, 4).

7. In a civic-humanist perspective, luxury was the solvent of virtue; see Pocock, *Virtue*, pp. 37–50.

under the same species of tyranny, 'till she was freed by the great Thra-sybulus. And, I believe, we have not yet forgot the strong apprehensions we were lately under, that a certain free State, upon the continent, was on the point of being sold to a powerful neighbour by a similar faction, and by a like iniquitous contract.[8] We must remember too, after what manner that scheme was defeated by the glorious efforts of patriotism and publick spirit. I shall make no apology for this digression, because I thought the remark too apposite to be omitted.

The honest citizens, who had fled to Athens, enraged to see their country thus tricked out of her liberty, and groaning under the most igno-minious servitude, determined to set her free, or perish in so glorious an attempt. The scheme was well concerted, and as boldly executed by Pelopidas, who entering the city with a small number of the most resolute of his party in disguise, destroyed Leontidas, and his colleague Archias, with the most dangerous of his faction; and, by [162] the assistance of Epaminondas and his friends,[a] with the additional aid of a large body of Athenians, recovered the citadel. The Spartans, at the first news of this surprizing event, entered the Theban territories with a powerful army to take vengeance of the authors of this rebellion, as they termed it, and to reduce Thebes to its former subjection.[b] The Athenians, conscious of their own weakness, and the mighty power of Sparta, which they were by no means able to cope with, not only renounced all friendship with the Thebans, but proceeded with the utmost severity against such of their citizens as favoured that people. Thus the Thebans, deserted by their allies, and destitute of friends, appeared to the rest of Greece as devoted to inevitable destruction. In this desperate situation of affairs, the virtue and abilities of those two great men shone forth with greater lustre. They

---

a. Diodor. Sicul. lib. 15. p. 470.[9]

b. Plut. in Vit. Pelop. p. 284. et sequent.[10]

8. A reference to the political disturbances in the Netherlands following the end of the War of the Austrian Succession (1740–48), and the growth of the Patriot movement in that country during the 1750s.

9. Diodorus Siculus, XV.xxviii.1–3 (where however Pelopidas is not named among those who achieved this celebrated feat; but see XV.lxxxi.1).

10. Plutarch, "Pelopidas," XIV ff.

begun by training their countrymen to the use of arms as well as the shortness of the time would permit, and inspiring them with a hatred of servitude, and the generous resolution of dying in defence of the liberty, and glory of their country. As they judged it imprudent to hazard a decisive battle against the best troops in the [163] world, with their new-raised militia, they harassed the Spartans with daily skirmishes to instruct their men in military discipline, and the trade of war. By this method they animated the minds of their people with the love of glory, and inured their bodies to the fatigues of war by exercise and labour, whilst they acquired experience and courage by those frequent encounters. Thus, as Plutarch remarks, when these able generals, by never engaging rashly, but watching every favourable opportunity, had fleshed the Thebans, like young staghounds, upon their enemies, and rendered them staunch[11] by tasting the sweets of victory, and bringing them off in safety, they made them fond of the sport, and eager after the most arduous enterprizes. By this able management they defeated the Spartans at Platea and Thespia,[a] where they killed Phaebidas, who had before so treacherously surprized their citadel, and again routed them at Tenagra, the Spartan general himself falling by the hand of Pelopidas. Flushed with this success, the Thebans feared no enemy, however superior in number; and the battle of Tegyra[b] soon after raised the reputation of their arms to a degree unknown before. In this action the brave Pelopidas, [164] with a small body of horse, and no more than three hundred foot, broke through, and dispersed a body of Spartans, consisting of above three times that number, made a terrible slaughter of the enemy, killed both their generals upon the spot, took the spoils of the dead, raised a trophy on the field of battle, and brought his little army home in triumph. Here the astonished Greeks first saw the Spartans defeated by a much inferior number, and by an enemy too whom they had always held in the greatest contempt. They had never, 'till that

a. Plut. in Vit. Pelop. p. 285.[12]

b. Id. p. 286, 287.[13]

11. Unwavering (*OED*, 6b; and see *OED*, 5 for the application of the term to dogs). For the passage in Plutarch, see "Pelopidas," XV.1.

12. Plutarch, "Pelopidas," XV.4.

13. Plutarch, "Pelopidas," XVI–XVII.

time, been beaten by equal, and rarely by much superior numbers, and, 'till that fatal day, were justly reputed invincible. But this action was only the prelude to that decisive stroke at Leuctra, which gave a fatal turn to the Spartan affairs, and stripped them of that dominion which they had so long exercised over the rest of Greece. For this series of success, though it greatly elated the Thebans, yet rather enraged than discouraged the Spartans. The Athenians, jealous of the growing power of Thebes, struck up a peace with their ancient rivals, in which all the Grecian States were included, except the Thebans, who were given up a sacrifice to the Spartan vengeance. Cleombrotus, joint King with Agesilaus, entered Boeotia with the largest and finest army the Spartans had ever sent into the field. The [165] great Epaminondas engaged them at Leuctra with a body of six thousand Thebans, which scarce equalled a third part of their enemies; but the admirable disposition he made, joined to the skill and dexterity of Pelopidas, and the bravery of their troops supplied the defect of numbers. Cleombrotus was slain on the spot, his army totally routed, and the greatest slaughter made of the native Spartans that had ever happened 'till that day, with the loss only of three hundred Thebans. Diodorus Siculus gives a concise account of this action in these remarkable words,

> That Epaminondas, being reduced to the necessity of engaging the whole confederate force of the Lacedemonians, and their allies, with only a handful of his city militia, gained so compleat a victory over those hitherto invincible warriors, that he slew their King Cleombrotus, and cut off the Spartan division, which was opposed to him, almost to a man.[a]

This victory gave so happy a turn to the affairs of the Thebans, that their alliance was now as much courted as before it had been despised and shunned. The Arcadians applied to them for succours against the Spartans. Epaminondas and Pelopidas were sent [166] with a powerful army to their assistance. At the head of the joint forces these two great

a. Διὸ καὶ συναναγκαθεὶς ὀλίγοις πολιτικοῖς, &c. Diodor. Sicul. lib. 15. p. 477. Edit. Henr. Stephani.[14]

14. "Hence even when compelled with a very few citizens" (Diodorus Siculus, XV.xxxix.2).

men entered Laconia, and appeared with a hostile army at the gates of Sparta; the first sight of that kind ever seen by that haughty people. The masterly conduct of Agesilaus, and the desperate valour of the Spartans saved the city, but could not prevent the ravage of their territories by the two Theban generals, who restored the Messenians to their kingdom, of which the Spartans had deprived them near three hundred years before, defeated the Athenians, who came to the assistance of the Spartans, and returned home with glory.

The Theban arms were now so terrible, and their power grown so formidable, that whilst some States applied to them for protection, and others for assistance, the Macedonians referred the disputes about the succession to that crown to their decision, and gave hostages as a security that they would abide by their determination. The chief of these hostages was the famous Philip, father of Alexander the Great, who employed his time so well, under those two able masters in the art of war, that from them he acquired that military knowledge which proved afterwards so fatal to all Greece in general.[15] Thus the publick virtue of two private citizens not only restored Thebes to her former li-[167]berty, but raised her to a much more respectable rank than she had ever held before amongst the Grecian Republicks.

But this eminent, and newly acquired degree of power was but of short duration. Pelopidas had freed the Thessalians from the insults of Alexander the Pherean; but going to him afterwards, accompanied only by Ismenias, to compose some differences, he was not only unjustly made prisoner, but treated with the most spiteful cruelty by that perfidious tyrant. The Thebans, enraged at this treacherous act, sent an army against the tyrant, under the command of two new generals, who returned with loss and dishonour. The command was again committed to Epaminondas, who, by the terror of his name alone, brought the tyrant to reason, and procured the release of his friend Pelopidas and Ismenias. But the tyrant soon after

15. A reference to the battle of Chaeronea in 338 B.C., at which Philip of Macedon achieved domination over the whole of Greece by defeating the joint armies of Thebes and Athens. In his sonnet "To the Lady Margaret Ley" Milton epitomized Chaeronea as "fatal to liberty." Isocrates is said to have expired with grief on learning of the Athenian defeat at Chaeronea.

renewing his usual depredations upon the Thessalians, Pelopidas was once more sent with forces to their assistance. The two armies came soon to action, when Pelopidas, blinded by resentment, and eager after revenge, rushed into the right wing, where the tyrant commanded in person, and fell, covered with wounds, in the midst of his surrounding enemies. His death however was not unrevenged; for his troops, quite furious at the loss of a general they so much revered and [168] loved, routed the enemy, and sacrificed three thousand of them to his manes.[16]

Though the death of this truly great man was an irretrievable loss to Thebes, yet Epaminondas still survived, and whilst he lived, the good fortune and power of his country remained unaltered. But new disturbances breaking out not long after, Epaminondas, at the head of his Thebans, broke again into Peloponnesus, eluded the vigilance of Agesilaus, and advanced into the very suburbs of Sparta. But as they had just before received intelligence of his approach by a messenger from Agesilaus, they were so well prepared for his reception, that he judged proper to retire, and, in his return, fell unexpectedly upon the Spartans and their allies at Mantinea. The disposition of his forces upon this occasion is esteemed a master-piece of generalship; nor was his valour inferior to his conduct. He routed and made a terrible slaughter of the Spartans; but, pushing on too eagerly to compleat his victory, he received a mortal wound in his breast, and was carried to his tent. As soon as he recovered his speech, and was satisfied that his shield was safe, and the Thebans were victors, he ordered the broken part of the weapon to be drawn out of his wound, and died rejoicing at the good fortune of his country. Thus fell the incomparable Epaminondas, who, [169] as Polybius observes, overcame his enemies, but was overcome by fortune.[a] The same judicious historian, in his remarks on the different constitutions of the ancient Republicks, observes,

> That the flourishing State of the Thebans was but of short duration, nor was their decay gradual, because their sudden rise was not founded on right principles. He affirms that the Thebans took the opportunity

---

a. Polyb. Comparat. Epaminond. et Hannib. lib. 9. p. 762.[17]
16. The Latin term for the deified souls of dead ancestors (*OED*, 1).
17. Polybius, IX.viii.13.

of attacking the Spartans when the imprudence and haughtiness of that people had made them quite odious to their allies; and that they acquired amongst the Greeks their high reputation for valour by the virtue and abilities of one or two great men, who knew how to make the best use of those unexpected incidents, which so fortunately offered. He adds, that the sudden change in their affairs made it quickly appear to all, that their remarkable success was not owing to the system of their government, but to the publick virtue of those who were at the head of the administration. For that the power and grandeur of the Thebans arose, flourished, and fell with Epaminondas and Pelopidas is too evident, he says, to be denied. [170] Whence he concludes, that the splendid figure the Thebans at that time made in the world, must not be ascribed to their civil polity, but to those two great men only.[a]

I have hitherto considered them only in the light of virtuous citizens, and able generals; perhaps a short sketch of their characters as Patriot-Statesmen may not be unacceptable nor uninstructing.

Pelopidas and Epaminondas were both descended from ancient and worthy families. Pelopidas inherited a large fortune, which he enjoyed with honour to himself and utility to his friends; and by avoiding the two extremes of avarice and dissipation, shewed that he was the master of, not the slave to, riches. The patrimony of Epaminondas on the contrary was extremely small, yet equal to his utmost wants or desires. Devoted wholly to the sciences and the study of history and philosophy, which mend[18] the heart, whilst they instruct the head, he preferred the sweets of retirement and study to a life of pleasure and ostentation. He avoided all lucrative employments and state honours with as much assiduity as they were courted and intrigued for by others: nor did he accept of the highest office in the state, 'till he was called to it by the united cry of the people, and the exigencies of the publick. When [171] dragged out of his retirement, and placed by force, as it were, at the head of affairs, he convinced his countrymen, as Justin informs us, that he was fully equal to the task, and seemed rather to give lustre to, than receive any from the dignity of

a. Id. lib. 6. p. 678–79.[19]
18. Improve (*OED*, 7a).
19. Polybius, VI.xliii.2–7.

his employment.[a] He excelled in the art of speaking, and was the most consummate orator of his time; persuasion hung upon his tongue,[20] and he was the master of the passions of his auditors by his eloquence, and of his own by philosophy. With this truly great man Pelopidas was joined as colleague, who, when he could not prevail upon his friend Epaminondas to share the enjoyment of his own fortune with him, copied him in the humbler virtues of private life. Thus both became the admiration of their countrymen for their temperance and moderation, as well as their plainness in dress, and frugality at their table. But the most striking part of their character, was that unexampled union and perfect harmony which subsisted between these two great men, and ended only with their lives. They filled at one and the same time the two highest posts in the state. The whole management of publick affairs was intrusted to their conduct, and all busi-[172] ness passed through their hands. Yet during all that time, no latent spark of envy, jealousy or ambition, no private or selfish views or difference of sentiments (the fatal, but too general sources of disunion amongst statesmen) could in the least affect their friendship, or ever make any impression upon an union, which was founded upon the immoveable basis of publick virtue. Animated, as Plutarch observes, and directing all their actions by this principle only, they had no other interest in view but that of the publick; and instead of enriching or aggrandizing their own families, the only emulation between them was, which should contribute most to the advancement of the dignity and happiness of his country. To crown all, they both died gloriously in defence of that independency which they had acquired and preserved to the state, and left the Thebans free, great and flourishing.

It is natural to think, that men of such superior merit, and so eminently disinterested, could never possibly be the objects of party-resentment. Yet we are assured in history, that they were frequently persecuted by a virulent faction composed of the selfish;[b] those leeches whom these

a. Justin. lib. 6. p. 74.[21]

b. Plutarch, Justin, Corn. Nepos.[22]

20. See Joseph Addison, "An Ode upon St. Cecilia's Day": "Such were the tuneful Notes that hung | On bright *Cecilia's* charming Tongue."

21. Justin, *Epitoma*, VI.viii.9.

22. Plutarch, "Pelopidas," XXV; Justin, *Epitoma*, VI; Cornelius Nepos, "Epaminondas," VII.i and "Pelopidas," V.i.

two virtuous men [173] prevented from fattening upon the blood of the publick; and of the envious, from that strong antipathy which bad men naturally bear to the good. For envy, that passion of low uncultivated minds, has a greater share in party opposition than we are apt to imagine. A truth of which we have strong proof in that celebrated passage, recorded by Plutarch, between Aristides and the Athenian countryman.[a] Though the virtue of these great men triumphed over all the malicious efforts of these domestick enemies; yet they had power enough at one time to impeach and bring them both to a publick trial for a breach of formality relative to their office,[b] though that very act had enabled them to render the most signal services to their country. They were tried however, but honourably acquitted. At another time, [174] whilst Pelopidas was detained prisoner by Alexander the Pherean, this malignant faction had weight enough to exclude Epaminondas from the office of Polemarch or General, and to procure for two of their friends, the command of that army which was sent to punish the tyrant for his treachery. But the new Generals made such wretched work of it, when they came to face the enemy, that the whole army was quickly thrown into the utmost confusion, and compelled for their own preservation, to put Epaminondas at their head, who was present at the action only as a volunteer: for the malice of his enemies had excluded him from the least shadow of trust or power. This able man, by a manoeuvre peculiar to himself, extricated the Theban troops out of those difficulties in which the ignorance and incapacity of their generals had involved them, repulsed the enemy, and

a. When Aristides had acquired the sirname of Just, he became the object of the Athenian envy, and the Ostracism was demanded against him. Whilst the people were preparing their shells,[23] a country voter, who could neither read nor write, brought his shell to Aristides, and desired him to write the name of Aristides upon it. Aristides, not a little surprized at his request, asked him what injury that Aristides had done him. "Me! none, replied the fellow, for I don't so much as know the man by sight; but it galls me to the soul to hear him every where called the Just."—Plut. in Vit. Aristid. p. 322, 323.[24]

b. They kept the field and attacked Sparta, when the time of their office was near expired, by which means they were in office more than the regular time.

23. Shells or fragments of pottery were used as ballots by the Athenians in the process of ostracism (see above, p. 54, n. 20).

24. Plutarch, "Aristides," VII.5–6.

by a fine retreat brought the army safe to Thebes. His countrymen, now sensible of their error, and how greatly they had been imposed upon by the faction, immediately recalled him to the highest offices in the state, which he continued to execute 'till his death, with the greatest honour to himself, and emolument as well as glory to his country. As the management of publick affairs, after the death of these two illustrious patriots, fell [175] by the intrigues of faction into the hands of men of a quite different character, we need not wonder that the Thebans sunk alike in power and reputation, 'till Thebes itself was totally destroyed by Alexander the Great; and their country, with the rest of Greece, swallowed up at last by the insatiable ambition of the Romans.

CHAPTER IV

Of Carthage

Of all the free states whose memory is preserved to us in history, Carthage bears the nearest resemblance to Britain, both in her commerce, opulence, sovereignty of the sea, and her method of carrying on her land wars by foreign mercenaries. If to these we add the vicinity of the Carthaginians to the Romans, the most formidable and most rapacious people at that time in Europe, and the specifick difference, as I may term it, of the respective military force of each nation, the situation of Carthage with respect to Rome, seems greatly analogous to that of Britain with respect to France, at least for this last century.[1] Consequently, the dreadful fate of that Republick, once the most flourishing state in the universe, and the most formidable rival Rome ever had to cope with, must merit our highest attention at this juncture: both as the greatness of her power arose from, and was supported by commerce, and as she owed her ruin more to her own intestine divisions, than to the arms of the Romans. [177]

1. During the reign of Louis XIV France was suspected of aspiring to universal monarchy. More recently the Seven Years' War had been provoked by French attempts to extend their sphere of influence in America, to the west of the line of British colonies which occupied the eastern seaboard.

We know very little of this opulent and powerful people 'till the time of the first Punick war. For as not one of their own historians has reached our times, we have no accounts of them but what are transmitted to us by their enemies. Such writers consequently deserve little credit, as well from their ignorance of the Carthaginian constitution, as their inveterate prejudice against that great people. Hence it is that we know so little of their laws, and have but an imperfect idea of their constitutional form of government.

The government of Carthage, if we may credit the judicious Aristotle, seems to have been founded on the wisest maxims of policy. For he affirms, the different branches of their legislature were so exactly balanced, that for the space of five hundred years, from the commencement of the Republick down to his time, the repose of Carthage had never been disturbed by any considerable sedition, or her liberty invaded by any single Tyrant: the two fatal evils to which every Republican government is daily liable, from the very nature of their constitution.[a] An additional proof too may be drawn from this consideration, that Carthage was able to support herself upwards of seven hun-[178]dred years in opulence and splendor in the midst of so many powerful enemies, and during the greater part of that time, was the center of commerce of the known world, and enjoyed the uninterrupted sovereignty of the sea without a rival.

The genius of the Carthaginians was warlike as well as commercial, and affords undeniable proof, that those qualities are by no means incompatible to the same people.[2] It is almost impossible indeed to discover the real character of this great people. The Roman historians, their implacable enemies, constantly paint them in the blackest colours, to palliate the perfidious and merciless behaviour of their own countrymen towards that unfortunate Republick. A fact so notorious, that neither Livy nor any other of their writers, with all their art, were able to conceal it. The Greek historians, whose countrymen had suffered so greatly by the Carthaginian arms in Sicily and all the other islands in the Mediterranean, betray as strong a prejudice against them as the Roman. Even the respectable Polybius, the only author amongst

a. Arist. de Republ. lib. 2. cap. 9. lit. 4.[3]

2. An element in the civic-humanist mistrust of material prosperity was that it would undermine the warlike capacity of a people; see above, p. 104, n. 7.

3. Aristotle, *Politics*, II.xi.

them who deserves any degree of credit, is plainly partial, when he speaks of the Carthaginian manners. The Romans continually charge them with the want of publick faith, and have handed down the *Punica Fides*[4] as a proverb. I shall [179] take notice of this scandalous charge in another place, where I shall shew how much more justly it may be retorted upon the Romans.

As the desire of gain is the chief spur to commerce, and as the greatest men in Carthage never thought it beneath them to engage in that lucrative employment, all the historians have represented the whole body of the people as so insatiably fond of amassing wealth, that they esteemed even the lowest and dirtiest means lawful, that tended to the acquisition of their darling object. "Amongst the Carthaginians," says Polybius, when he compares the manners of that people with those of the Romans, "nothing was infamous that was attended with gain.[a] Amongst the Romans nothing so infamous as bribery, and to enrich themselves by unwarrantable means."[b] He adds, in proof of his assertion, that, "at Carthage all the dignities and highest employments in the State were openly sold. A practice, he affirms, which at Rome was a capital crime."[c] Yet but a few pages before, where he inveighs bitterly against the sordid love of money, and rapacious ava-[180] rice of the Cretans, he remarks, that "they were the only people in the world to whom no kind of gain appeared either infamous or unlawful."[d] In another place where he censures the Greeks for aspersing Titus Flaminius the Roman General,[e] as if he had not been proof against the gold of Macedon, he affirms, "that whilst the Romans preserved the virtuous manners of their fore-fathers, and had not yet carried their arms into foreign countries, not a single man of them would have been guilty of a crime

a. Polyb. lib. 6. p. 692.[5]

b. Id. ibid.[6]

c. Ibid.[7]

d. Polyb. lib. 6. p. 681.[8]

e. Excerpt. ex Polyb. de virtutibus et vitiis, p. 1426.[9]

4. Literally, Punic or Carthaginian faith; by extension, perfidiousness or faithlessness (*OED*, "punic," B 1b).

5. Polybius, VI.lvi.2.

6. Polybius, VI.lvi.2.

7. Polybius, VI.lvi.4.

8. Polybius, VI.xlvi.3.

9. Polybius, XVIII.xxxv.1–2. This consul is more correctly referred to as Titus Quinctius Flamininus.

of that nature." But though he can boldly assert, as he says, "that in his time many of the Romans, if taken man by man, were able to preserve the trust reposed in them inviolable as to that point, yet he owns he durst not venture to say the same of all." Though he speaks as modestly as he can to avoid giving offence, yet this hint is sufficient to convince us, that corruption was neither new nor uncommon at that time amongst the Romans. But as I shall resume this subject in a more proper place, I shall only observe from Polybius's own detail of the history of the Carthaginians, That, unless when the intrigues of faction prevailed, all their great posts were [181] generally filled by men of the most distinguished merit.

The charge of cruelty is brought against them with a very ill grace by the Romans, who treated even Monarchs themselves, if they were so unhappy as to become their prisoners of war, with the utmost inhumanity, and threw them to perish in dungeons, after they had exposed them in triumph to the insults of their own populace.[a]

The story indeed of Regulus has afforded a noble subject for Horace, which he has embellished with some of the most beautiful strokes of poetry; and that fine ode has propagated and confirmed the belief of it, more perhaps than the writings of all their historians.[10] But as neither Polybius nor Diodorus Siculus make the least mention of such an event (though the Greeks bore an equal aversion to the Carthaginians), and as the Roman writers from whom we received it, differ greatly in their accounts of it, I cannot help joining in opinion with many learned men, that it was a Roman forgery.

The Greek writers accuse them of barbarism and a total ignorance of the Belles Lettres,[11] the study of which was the reigning taste of

---

a. Perseus, &c.[12]

10. Marcus Atilius Regulus, consul in 267 and 256 B.C., had been one of Rome's generals during the First Punic War (264–241 B.C.). Captured by the Carthaginians, he was sent with an embassy to Rome to propose terms of peace, and sworn to return to Carthage should the negotiations fail. However, Regulus urged the Roman senators to persevere with war. He then kept his word, returned to Carthage, and suffered a cruel death. Horace versified the story of Regulus's courage in *Odes*, III.v.

11. Polite literature (*OED*).

12. Perseus (c. 213–12 B.C.–c. 165 B.C.) was the last king of Macedonia. His defeat in 168 B.C. at the battle of Pydna by the Roman consul Lucius Aemilius Paullus led to the annexation of the region by the Romans. He and his children were among the captives led in triumph by Aemilius Paullus, and he died in captivity.

Greece. Rollin contemptuously [182] affirms, that their education in general amounted to no more than writing and the knowledge of merchants accounts; that a Carthaginian Philosopher would have been a prodigy amongst the learned; and then asks, "What would they have thought of a Geometrician or Astronomer of that nation?"[13] Rollin seems to have put this question too hastily, since it is unanimously confessed, that they were the best ship-builders, the ablest navigators, and the most skilful mechanicks at that time in the world: that they raised abundance of magnificent structures, and very well understood the art of fortification; all which (especially as the use of the compass was then unknown[14]) must of necessity imply a more than common knowledge of Astronomy, Geometry, and every other branch of mathematicks. Let me add too, that their knowledge in Agriculture was so eminent, that the works of Mago the Carthaginian upon that subject were ordered to be translated by a decree of the Senate, for the use of the Romans and their colonies.[a]

That the education of their youth was not confined to the mercantile part only, must be evident from that number of great men, who make such a figure in their history; particularly Hannibal, perhaps the greatest [183] Captain which any age has ever yet produced, and at the same time the most consummate Statesman, and disinterested Patriot. Painting, Sculpture, and Poetry, they seem to have left to their more idle and more luxurious neighbours the Greeks, and applied their wealth to the infinitely nobler uses of supporting their

a. Varro.[15]

13. Charles Rollin (1661–1741), French scholar and historian. The quotation comes from his *The Ancient History of the Egyptians, Carthaginians, Assyrians, Babylonians, Medes and Persians, Macedonians, and Greeks*, 13 vols. (London, 1734–39), vol. 1, p. 140.

14. The magnetic compass seems to have been discovered by mariners at some point in the twelfth century. Records indicate that the Chinese were using rudimentary magnetic compasses around 1100, western Europeans by 1187, Arabs by 1220, and Scandinavians by 1300. Without a compass it is impossible safely to navigate out of sight of land, so the discovery of the compass was crucial for any voyage more ambitious than a cruise around the coastline.

15. Varro, *Res Rusticae*, I.i.10.

marine, enlarging and protecting their commerce and colonies. What opinion even the wiser part of the Romans had of these specious arts, and how unworthy they judged them of the close attention of a brave and free people, we may learn from the advice which Virgil gives his countrymen by the mouth of his Hero's father Anchises.[a] I have endeavoured here to clear the much injured character of this great people from the aspersions and gross misrepresentations of historians, by proofs drawn from the concessions and self-contradictions of the historians themselves.

The State of Carthage bears so near a resemblance to that of our own nation, both in their constitution (as far as we are able to judge of it) maritime power, commerce, [184] party divisions, and long as well as bloody war which they carried on with the most powerful nation in the universe, that their history, I again repeat it, affords us, in my judgment, more useful rules for our present conduct than that of any other ancient Republick. As we are engaged in a war (which was till very lately unsuccessful[16]) with an enemy, less powerful indeed, but equally rapacious as the Romans, and acting upon the same principles, we ought most carefully to beware of those false steps both in war and policy, which brought on the ruin of the Carthaginians. For should we be so unhappy as to be compelled to receive law from that haughty nation, we must expect to be reduced to the same wretched situation in which the Romans left Carthage at the conclusion

a. Excudent alii spirantia mollius aera:
 Credo equidem, vivos ducent de marmore vultus.
　　　　　　　Virg. Aeneid. lib. 6.

 Tu regere imperio populos, Romane, memento
 (Hae tibi erunt artes) pacique imponere morem
 Parcere subjectis, &c.
　　　　　　　　　Ibid.[17]

16. Until the "Year of Victories" of 1759, British forces in the Seven Years' War had suffered an unbroken run of defeats; see the introduction, above, pp. xi–xiv.

17. "Others, I doubt not, shall cast the breathing bronze more delicately, others draw forth living faces from marble . . . But as for you, Roman, it is your task to rule nations. These will be your arts: to crown peace with law, to spare the suppliant and to tame the proud through force of arms!" (Virgil, *Aeneid*, VI.847–48 and 851–53). These are the famous lines in which Aeneas's father, Anchises, whom Aeneas has visited in the underworld, predicts Rome's imperial destiny.

of the second Punick war.[18] This island has been hitherto the inexpugnable barrier of the liberties of Europe, and is as much the object of the jealousy and hatred of the French, as ever Carthage was of the Romans. As they are sensible that nothing but the destruction of this country can open them a way to their grand project of universal monarchy,[19] we may be certain that *Delenda est Britannia* will be as much the popular maxim at Paris, as *Delenda est Carthago* was at Rome.[20] But I shall wave these reflections at present, and point out the [185] real causes of the total ruin of that powerful Republick.

Carthage took its rise from a handful of distressed Tyrians who settled in that country, by permission of the natives, like our colonies in America, and actually paid a kind of rent, under the name of tribute, for the very ground on which their city was founded. As they brought with them the commercial genius of their mother-country, they soon arrived at such a state of opulence by their frugality and indefatigable industry, as occasioned the envy of their poorer neighbours. Thus jealousy on the one hand, and pride naturally arising from great wealth on the other, quickly involved them in a war. The natives justly feared the growing power of the Carthaginians, and the latter feeling their own strength, wanted to throw off the yoke of tribute, which they looked upon as dishonourable, and even galling to a free people. The contest was by no means equal. The neighbouring princes were poor, and divided by separate interests; the Carthaginians were rich, and united

18. The second Punic war ended with Scipio's defeat of Hannibal at the battle of Zama in 202 B.C. Carthage was obliged by Rome to renounce her overseas conquests, to pay an annual tribute, and to limit her armed forces. As a result, Carthage lost her status as a major Mediterranean power, and gradually dwindled into a Roman province.

19. Since the reign of Louis XIV, it had been a British fear that the French policy aimed at dominance in Europe was a prelude to universal monarchy. However, the Seven Years' War would end with France stripped of her possessions in North America, and with her ambitions for an empire in India in ruins.

20. "Carthage must be destroyed": the injunction with which the elder Cato (234–149 B.C.) is supposed to have ended every speech he made in the Roman Senate, on no matter what subject, so convinced was he of the danger Carthage posed to the Roman state.

in one common cause. Their commerce made them masters of the sea, and their wealth enabled them to bribe one part of their neighbours to fight against the other; and thus by playing one against the other alternately, they reduced all at last to be their [186] tributaries, and extended their dominions near two thousand miles upon that continent. It may be objected that the conduct of the Carthaginians in this case was highly criminal. I grant it: but if we view all those master-strokes of policy, and all those splendid conquests which shine so much in history, in their true colours, they will appear to be nothing more than fraud and robbery,[21] gilded over with those pompous appellations. Did not every nation that makes a figure in history rise to Empire upon the ruin of their neighbours? Did not France acquire her present formidable power, and is she not at this time endeavouring to worm us out of our American settlements by the very same means?[22] But though the motives are not to be justified, yet the conduct of the Carthaginians upon these occasions, will afford us some very useful and instructive lessons in our present situation.

It is evident that the mighty power of these people was founded in and supported by commerce, and that they owed their vast acquisitions, which extended down both sides of the Mediterranean quite into the main ocean, to a right application of the publick money, and a proper exertion of their naval force. Had they bounded their views to this single point, viz. the support of their [187] commerce and colonies, they either would not have given such terrible umbrage to the Romans, who, as Polybius observes, could brook no equal, or might safely have bid defiance to their utmost efforts. For the immense sums which they squandered away in subsidies to so many foreign Princes, and to support such numerous armies of foreign mercenaries, which they constantly kept in

21. Compare to the similar, celebrated remark of Gibbon, that history was "little more than the register of the crimes, follies, and misfortunes of mankind" (Gibbon, *Decline and Fall*, vol. 1, p. 102).

22. An allusion to French military maneuvers west of the Alleghenies and in the Ohio valley which had precipitated the Seven Years' War; see above, p. 114, n. 1, and below, p. 227, n. 35.

pay, to compleat the reduction of Spain and Sicily, would have enabled them to cover their coasts with such a fleet as would have secured them from any apprehension of foreign invasions. Besides, the Roman genius was so little turned for maritime affairs, that at the time of their first breach with Carthage, they were not masters of one single ship of war, and were such absolute strangers to the mechanism of a ship, that a Carthaginian galley driven by accident on their coasts gave them the first notion of a model. But the ambition of Carthage grew as her wealth encreased; and how difficult a task is it to set bounds to that restless passion! Thus by grasping at too much, she lost all. It is not probable therefore that the Romans would ever have attempted to disturb any of the Carthaginian settlements, when the whole coast of Italy lay open to the insults and depredations of so formidable a maritime [188] power. The Romans felt this so sensibly in the beginning of the first Punick war, that they never rested till they had acquired the superiority at sea. It is evident too, that the Romans always maintained that superiority: For if Hannibal could possibly have passed by sea into Italy, so able a general would never have harrassed his troops by that long and seemingly impossible march over the Alps, which cost him above half his army; an expedition which has been, and ever will be the wonder of all succeeding ages.[23] Nor could Scipio have landed without opposition so very near the city of Carthage itself, if the maritime force of that people had not been at the very lowest ebb.

The Carthaginians were certainly greatly weakened by the long continuance of their first war with the Romans, and that savage and destructive war with their own mercenaries, which followed immediately after. They ought therefore in true policy, to have turned their whole attention, during the interval between the first and second Punick wars, to the re-establishment of their marine; but the conquest of Spain was their favourite object, and their finances were too much reduced to be sufficient

---

23. Hannibal's passage of the Alps in 218 B.C., in which the Carthaginian army together with its baggage train and elephants traversed frozen mountain passes in order to descend on the lightly defended territories of northern Italy, was regarded as one of the foremost military feats of antiquity.

for both. Thus they expended that money in carrying on a continental
war,[24] which would have put their [189] marine on so formidable a footing, as to have enabled them to regain once more the dominion of the sea;
and the fatal event of the second Punick war convinced them of the false
step they had taken, when it was too late to retrieve it.

I have here pointed out one capital error of the Carthaginians as a maritime power, I mean their engaging in too frequent, and too extensive wars
on the continent of Europe, and their neglect of their marine. I shall now
mention another, which more than once brought them to the very brink
of destruction. This was—their constantly employing such a vast number
of foreign mercenary troops, and not trusting the defence of their country,
nay not even Carthage itself wholly, to their own native subjects.

The Carthaginians were so entirely devoted to commerce, that they
seem to have looked upon every native employed in their armies as a member lost to the community; and their wealth enabled them to buy whatever
number of soldiers they pleased from their neighbouring States in Greece
and Africa, who traded (as I may term it) in war as much as the Swiss and
Germans do now,[25] and were equally ready to sell the blood and lives of

24. Montagu here implicitly criticizes the financial and military support Britain was at this time extending to Prussia and Hanover. In February 1757 Pitt had
obtained Parliamentary approval for the dispatch of troops under the command of
the Duke of Cumberland to guard the banks of the Weser, and thus to secure the
flank of Frederick the Great against French attacks. This strategy was unpopular both within Parliament and without; and Pitt himself had in the past spoken
against such measures. Nevertheless, in retrospect it is clear that this strategy was
essential to Britain's eventual victory. On 13 November 1761 in the House of Commons Pitt would claim, hyperbolically but not inaccurately, that "America had
been conquered in Germany."

25. The willingness of the Swiss and Germans to serve as mercenaries was a
topic of satire in eighteenth-century Britain, when it could serve as a proxy for
anti-Hanoverian sentiment. In chapter 5 of Part IV of *Gulliver's Travels*, Gulliver
explains to his Houyhnhnm master that there is "a Kind of beggarly Princes in
Europe, not able to make War by themselves, who hire out their Troops to richer
Nations for so much a Day to each Man; of which they keep three Fourths to
themselves, and it is the best Part of their Maintenance; such are those in many
Northern Parts of *Europe*" (Swift, *Gulliver's Travels*, ed. H. Davis [Oxford: Basil
Blackwell, 1941], p. 247; see also More, *Utopia*, p. 88).

their subjects to the best bidder. From hence they drew such inexhaustible [190] supplies of men, both to form and recruit their armies, whilst their own natives were at leisure to follow the more lucrative occupations of navigation, husbandry, and mechanick trades. For the number of native Carthaginians, which we read of, in any of their armies, was so extremely small, as to bear no proportion to that of their foreign mercenaries. This kind of policy, which prevails so generally in all mercantile States, does, I confess, at first sight appear extremely plausible. The Carthaginians, by this method, spared their own people, and purchased all their conquests by the venal blood of foreigners; and, in case of a defeat, they could with great ease and expedition recruit their broken armies with any number of good troops, ready trained up to their hands in military discipline. But, alas! these advantages were greatly over-balanced by very fatal inconveniences. The foreign troops were attached to the Carthaginians by no tye but that of their pay. Upon the least failure of that, or if they were not humoured in all their licentious demands, they were just as ready to turn their arms against the throats of their masters. Strangers to that heart-felt affection, that enthusiastick love of their country, which warms the hearts of free citizens, and fires them with the glorious emulation of fighting to the last drop of blood in [191] defence of their common mother; these sordid hirelings were always ripe for mutiny and sedition, and ever ready to revolt and change sides upon the least prospect of greater advantages.

But a short detail of the calamities which they drew upon themselves by this mistaken policy, will better shew the dangers which attend the admission of foreign mercenaries into any country, where the natives are unaccustomed to the use of arms. A practice which is too apt to prevail in commercial nations.

At the conclusion of the first Punick war the Carthaginians were compelled, by their treaty with the Romans, to evacuate Sicily. Gesco, therefore, who then commanded in that Island, to prevent the disorders which might be committed by such a multitude of desperate fellows, composed of so many different nations, and so long inured to blood and rapine, sent them over gradually in small bodies, that his countrymen might have time to pay off their arrears, and send them home to their respective countries. But either the lowness of their finances, or the ill-timed parsimony of the

Carthaginians totally defeated this salutary measure, though the wisest that, as their affairs were at that time [192] circumstanced, could possibly have been taken.[a] The Carthaginians deferred their payment till the arrival of the whole body, in hopes of obtaining some abatement in their demands, by fairly laying before them the necessities of the publick. But the mercenaries were deaf to every representation and proposal of that nature. They felt their own strength, and saw too plainly the weakness of their masters. As fast as one demand was agreed to, a more unreasonable one was started; and they threatened to do themselves justice by military execution, if their exorbitant demands were not immediately complied with. At last, when they were just at the point of an accommodation with their masters, by the mediation and address of Gesco, two desperate ruffians, named Spendius and Mathos, raised such a flame amongst this unruly multitude, as broke out instantly into the most bloody, and destructive war ever yet recorded in history.[b] The account we have of it from the Greek historians must strike the most callous breast with horror; and though it was at last happily terminated by the superior conduct of Hamilcar Barcas, the father of the great Hannibal, yet it continued near four years, and left the territories around Carthage a most shocking scene of blood and [193] devastation. Such was, and ever will be the consequence, when a large body of mercenary troops is admitted into the heart of a rich and fertile country, where the bulk of the people are denied the use of arms by the mistaken policy of their governors. For this was actually the case with the Carthaginians, where the total disuse of arms amongst the lower class of people, laid that opulent country open, an easy and tempting prey to every invader. This was another capital error, and consequently another cause which contributed to their ruin.

How must any nation but our own, which with respect to the bulk of the people, lies in the same defenceless situation; how, I say, must they censure the mighty State of Carthage, spreading terror, and giving law to

a. Polyb. lib. 1. p. 92–3.[26]
b. Polyb. p. 98–9.[27]
26. Polybius, I.lxvi.1–6.
27. Polybius, I.lxix.4–14. The barbaric circumstances of this war were used by Flaubert as the raw material for his novel *Salammbô* (1863).

the most distant nations by her powerful fleets, when they see her at the same time trembling, and giving herself up for lost at the landing of any invader in her own territories?

The conduct of that petty prince Agathocles, affords us a striking instance of the defenceless state of the territories of Carthage. The Carthaginians were at that very time masters of all Sicily, except the single city of Syracuse, in which they had cooped up that tyrant both by land and sea. Aga-[194]thocles, reduced to the last extremity, struck perhaps the boldest stroke ever yet met with in history.[a] He was perfectly well acquainted with the weak side of Carthage, and knew that he could meet with little opposition from a people who were strangers to the use of arms, and enervated by a life of ease and plenty. On this defect of their policy he founded his hopes; and the event proved that he was not mistaken in his judgment. He embarked with only 13000 men on board the few ships he had remaining, eluded the vigilance of the Carthaginian fleet by stratagem, landed safely in Africa, plundered and ravaged that rich country up to the very gates of Carthage, which he closely blocked up, and reduced nearly to the situation in which he had left his own Syracuse. Nothing could equal the terror into which the city of Carthage was thrown at that time, but the panick which, in the late rebellion, struck the much larger, and more populous city of London, at the approach of a poor handful of Highlanders, as much inferior even to the small army of Agathocles in number, as they were in arms and discipline.[28] The success of that able leader compelled the Carthaginians to recall part of their forces out of Sicily to the immediate defence of Carthage itself; and this occasioned the raising the siege of Syracuse, and ended in the total defeat of their [195] army, and death of their General in that country. Thus Agathocles, by this daring measure, saved his own petty State, and, after a variety of good and ill fortune, concluded a treaty with the Carthaginians, and died

a. Diodor. Sicul. lib. 20. p. 735–36.[29]

28. A reference to the Jacobite rebellion of 1745, in which an army of only some five thousand Scottish highlanders under Prince Charles Edward Stuart reached as far south as Derby, before retiring back north of the border.

29. Diodorus Siculus, XX.xiii.3–4.

at Syracuse at a time when, from a thorough experience of their defence-less state at home, he was preparing for a fresh invasion.

Livy informs us, that this very measure of Agathocles set the precedent which Scipio followed with so much success in the second Punick war, when that able General, by a similar descent in Africa, compelled the Carthaginians to recall Hannibal out of Italy to their immediate assistance, and reduced them to that impotent state, from which they never afterwards were able to recover.[a] How successfully the French played the same game upon us, when they obliged us to recall our forces out of Flanders to crush the Rebellion, which they had spirited up with that very view, is a fact too recent to need any mention of particulars.[30] How lately did they drive us to the expence, and I may say the ignominy, of fetching over a large body of foreign mercenaries[31] for the immediate defence of this nation, which plumes herself so much upon her power and bravery? How [196] greatly did they cramp all our measures, how much did they confine all our military operations to our own immediate self-defence, and prevent us from sending sufficient succours to our colonies by the perpetual alarm of an invasion?[32]

Though we may in part truly ascribe the ruin of Carthage to the two above-mentioned errors in their policy, yet the cause which was productive of the greatest evils, and consequently the more immediate object of our attention at this dangerous juncture, was party disunion; that bane of every free State, from which our own country has equal reason to apprehend the same direful effects, as the Republicks of Greece, Rome, and Carthage experienced formerly.

a. Livy, lib. 28. p. 58–9.[33]

30. Montagu refers to the Jacobite rebellion of 1715.

31. Another reference to the British reliance in 1756 on mercenaries from Hesse and Hanover to guard the homeland.

32. It was indeed part of French strategy during the early years of the Seven Years' War to tie down British troops by threatening a descent on the shores of either Britain or Ireland. But after Hawke's decisive defeat of the French fleet at Quiberon Bay in 1759, French naval power was inadequate even to relieve her own colonies in North America, let alone support any amphibious military operations. Once again, Montagu's timing is unlucky.

33. Livy, XXVIII.xliii.21.

By all the lights, which we receive from history, the State of Carthage was divided into two opposite factions; the Hannonian and the Barcan, so denominated from their respective leaders, who were heads of the two most powerful families in Carthage. The Hannonian family seems to have made the greatest figure in the senate; the Barcan in the field. Both were strongly actuated by ambition, but ambition of a different kind. The Barcan family seems to have had no other object in view but the glory of their country, and were always ready to give up their private animosities, and even their pas-[197]sion for military glory to the publick good. The Hannonian family acted from quite opposite principles, constantly aiming at one point; the supporting themselves in power, and that only. Ever jealous of the glory acquired by the Barcan family, they perpetually thwarted every measure proposed from that quarter, and were equally ready to sacrifice the honour and real interest of their country to that selfish view. In short, the one family seems to have produced a race of Heroes, the other of ambitious Statesmen.

The chiefs of these two jarring families, best known to us in history, were Hanno and Hamilcar Barcas, who was succeeded by his son Hannibal, that terror of the Romans. The opposition between these two parties was so flagrant, that Appian does not scruple to call the party of Hanno, the Roman faction; and that of Barcas, the popular, or the Carthaginian, from the different interests which each party espoused.[a]

The first instance, which we meet with in history, of the enmity subsisting between the heads of these factions, was in that destructive war with the mercenaries, from which I have made this explanatory digression.

Hanno was first sent with a powerful, and well provided army against these mutinous [198] desperado's; but he knew little of his trade, and made perpetual blunders. Polybius, who treats his character, as a soldier, with the utmost contempt, informs us, that he suffered himself to be surprized, a great part of his fine army to be cut to pieces, and his camp taken, with all the military stores, engines, and all the other apparatus of war.[b]

a. Appian, de Bell. Punic. p. 36.[34]
b. Polyb. lib. 1. p. 104–5.[35]
34. Appian, VIII.x.68.
35. Polybius, I.lxxiv.1–14.

The Carthaginians, terrified and distressed by the bad conduct of their General, were now compelled, by the necessity of their affairs, to restore Hamilcar to the chief command of their forces, from which he must have been excluded before by the influence of the Hannonian faction. That able commander with his small army (for his whole force amounted to no more than ten thousand men) quickly changed the face of the war, defeated Spendius in two pitched battles, and pushed every advantage to the utmost, which the incapacity of the rebel Generals threw in his way. Sensible that he was too weak alone to cope with the united forces of the Rebels (which amounted to 70,000 men) he ordered Hanno (who had still influence enough to procure himself to be continued in the command of a separate body) to join him, that they might finish this execrable [199] war by one decisive action.[a] After they were joined, the Carthaginians soon felt the fatal effects of disunion between their Generals. No plan could now be followed, no measure could be agreed on; and the disagreement between these two leading men arose to such a height at last, that they not only let slip every opportunity of annoying the enemy, but gave them many advantages against themselves, which they could not otherwise have hoped for.[b] The Carthaginians, sensible of their error, and knowing the very different abilities of the two Generals, yet willing to avoid the imputation of partiality, empowered the army to decide which of the two they judged most proper for their General, as they were determined to continue only one of them in the command.[c] The decision of the army was, that Hamilcar should take the supreme command, and that Hanno should depart the camp.[d] A convincing proof that they threw the whole blame of that disunion, and the ill-success, which was the consequence of it, entirely upon the envy and jealousy of Hanno. One Hannibal, a man more tractable, and more agreeable to Hamilcar, was sent in his room.

a. Ibid. lib. 1. p. 115.[36]
b. Polyb. lib. 1. p. 115.[37]
c. Id. ibid.[38]
d. Idem ibid. 117.[39]
36. Polybius, I.lxxxii.1.
37. Polybius, I.lxxxii.4.
38. Polybius, I.lxxxii.5.
39. Polybius, I.lxxxii.12.

Union was [200] restored, and the happy effects which attended it were quickly visible. Hamilcar now pushed on the war with his usual vigilance and activity, and soon convinced the Generals of the Rebels how greatly he was their master in the art of war. He harrassed them perpetually, and, like a skilful gamester, (as Polybius terms him[a]) drew them artfully every day into his snares, and obliged them to raise the siege of Carthage. At last he cooped up Spendius with his army in so disadvantageous a place, that he reduced them to such an extremity of famine as to devour one another, and compelled them to surrender at discretion, though they were upwards of 40,000 effective men. The army of Hamilcar, which was much inferior to that of Spendius in number, was composed partly of mercenaries and deserters, partly of the city militia, both horse and foot (troops which the enemies to the militia bill[40] would have called raw and undisciplined,[41] and treated as useless) of which the major part of his army consisted.[b] The rebel army was composed chiefly of brave and experienced veterans, trained up by Hamilcar himself in Sicily during the late war with the Romans, whose courage was heightened [201] by despair. It is worthy our observation therefore, that these very men who, under the conduct of Hamilcar, had been a terror to the Romans, and given them so many blows in Sicily towards the latter end of the first Punick war, should yet be so little able to cope with an army so much inferior in number, and composed in a great measure of city militia only, when commanded by the same General. Polybius, who esteems Hamilcar by far the greatest Captain of that age, observes, that though the Rebels were by no

a. Polyb. Ἀγαθὸς πεττευτής, ibid. p. 119.[42]

b. Id. ibid. Πολιτικοὺς ἱππεῖς καὶ πεζούς, p. 120.[43]

40. At the nadir of British military fortunes in 1756 Pitt had brought forward a Militia Bill which established a 32,000-man territorial force for the purposes of home defense. The historian Edward Gibbon served in the militia for Hampshire, and his characteristically shrewd comments on his service life can be found in his *Memoirs*.

41. Montagu here employs terms drawn from the topical literature surrounding the Militia Bill. For example, the 1757 translation of Joachim Christian's *A Political Discourse upon the Different Kinds of Militia* had pointed out that "a war is very rarely well managed by raw, undisciplined troops" (p. 82), and the anonymous author of *The Nature and Utility of Expeditions to the Coast of France* (1758) had also disparaged the British militia as "raw, undisciplined Troops" (p. 29).

42. "Like a good player of draughts" (Polybius, I.lxxxiv.7).

43. "Militia cavalry and infantry" (Polybius, I.lxxv.2).

means inferior to the Carthaginian troops in resolution and bravery, yet they were frequently beaten by Hamilcar by mere dint of Generalship.[a] Upon this occasion he cannot help remarking the vast superiority which judicious skill and ability of Generalship has over long military practice, where this so essentially necessary skill and judgment is wanting.[b] It might have been thought unpardonable in me, if I had omitted this just remark of Polybius, since it has been so lately verified by his Prussian Majesty in those masterly strokes of Generalship, which are the present admiration of Europe.[44] Hamilcar, after the destruction of Spendius and his army,

a. Polyb. lib. i. p. 119.[45]
b. Id. ibid.[46]

44. Frederick II (known as "the Great") (1712–86), king of Prussia since 1740, was one of Britain's allies in the Seven Years' War. On 29 August 1756 Prussian forces had invaded Saxony, the Saxon army surrendering on 17 October after the Battle of Lobositz (1 October). On 18 February 1757, Pitt had risen in the House to urge full British support for Prussia, a commitment which translated into a yearly subsidy of £700,000, thus bankrolling Frederick's military adventures. In the spring of that year Prussian forces invaded Bohemia, and on 6 May defeated an Austrian army under the walls of Prague. On 18 June, largely as a result of his own tactical blunders, Frederick was heavily defeated by the Austrians at Kolin. It was his first defeat after eighteen straight victories in the field. However, in the later months of the year he exacted full revenge, with a technically superb defeat of superior French and Imperial forces at Rossbach on 5 November (10,000 enemy casualties to only 500 Prussians), the defeat of a numerically superior Austrian army at Leuthen on 5 December, and the capitulation of Breslau on 20 December. It is to these brilliant, rapid victories that Montagu must be referring. Frederick's fortunes in 1758 were more mixed. A narrow victory over a Russian army at Zondorf on 25 August after a close-fought and savage battle was followed by a heavy defeat at the hands of the Austrians at Hochkirch on 14 October. Montagu's text must have been completed before this desperate reversal (it was listed as a recent publication in the March 1759 issue of *The Gentleman's Magazine*). The dismal trend continued in 1759, being for the Prussians a year of bloody losses, exemplified by Frederick's defeat by a joint Austro-Russian army at Kunersdorf, notwithstanding the great personal risks Frederick himself ran in that engagement; only the great allied victory of Minden on 1 August, where Ferdinand of Brunswick defeated a numerically superior French army under Contades, saved him. The year 1760 saw some improvement, with victories over the Austrians at Liegnitz on 15 August and at Torgau on 3 November. However, the provisions of the Treaty of Paris (1763) rewarded Prussia with no additional territory, Frederick being forced to renounce Saxony, and so his military genius was in practical terms fruitless.

45. Polybius, I.lxxxiv.9.
46. Polybius, I.lxxxiv.9.

immediately blocked up Mathos, with the remaining corps of the Rebels, in [202] the city of Tunes. Hannibal, with the forces under his command, took post on that side of the city which looked towards Carthage. Hamilcar prepared to make his attack on the side which was directly opposite; but the conduct of Hannibal, when left to himself, was the direct contrast to that of Hamilcar, and proves undeniably, that the whole merit of their former success was entirely owing to that abler General. Hannibal, who seems to have been little acquainted with the true genius of those daring veterans, lay secure, and careless in his camp, neglected his out-guards, and treated the enemy with contempt, as a people already conquered. But Mathos observing the negligence and security of Hannibal, and well knowing that he had not Hamilcar to deal with, made a sudden and resolute sally, forced Hannibal's entrenchments, put great numbers of his men to the sword, took Hannibal himself, with several other persons of distinction, prisoners, and pillaged his camp.[a] This daring measure was so well concerted, and executed with so much rapidity, that Mathos, who made good use of his time, had done his business before Hamilcar, who lay encamped at some distance, was in the least apprized of his colleague's misfortune. [203] Mathos fastened Hannibal, whilst alive, on the same gibbet to which Hamilcar had lately nailed the body of Spendius: A terrible, but just reward for the shameful carelessness in a commanding officer, who had sacrificed the lives of such a number of his fellow-citizens by his own indolence and presumptuous folly. Mathos also crucified thirty of the first nobility of Carthage, who attended Hannibal in this expedition. A commander who is surprized in the night-time, though guilty of an egregious fault, may yet plead something in excuse; but, in point of discipline, for a General to be surprized by an enemy just under his nose in open day-light, and caught in a state of wanton security, from an overweening presumption on his own strength, is a crime of so capital a nature as to admit neither of alleviation nor pardon. This dreadful and unexpected blow threw Carthage into the utmost consternation, and obliged Hamilcar to draw off his part of the army to a considerable

a. Polyb. id. ibid. p. 121.[47]
47. Polybius, I.lxxxvi.5–9.

distance from Tunes. Hanno had again influence enough to procure the command, which he was compelled before by the army to give up to Hamilcar. But the Carthaginians, sensible of the fatal consequences of disunion between the two Generals, especially at such a desperate crisis, sent thirty [204] of the most respectable amongst the Senators to procure a thorough reconciliation between Hamilcar and Hanno before they proceeded upon any operation; which they effected at last, though not without difficulty.[a] Pleased with this happy event, the Carthaginians (as their last, and utmost effort) sent every man in Carthage, who was able to bear arms, to reinforce Hamilcar, on whose superior abilities they placed their whole dependance.[b] Hamilcar now resumed his operations, and, as he was no longer thwarted by Hanno, soon reduced Mathos to the necessity of putting the whole issue of the war upon one decisive action, in which the Carthaginians were most compleatly victors, by the exquisite disposition and conduct of Hamilcar.

I hope the enemies to a militia will at least allow these new levies, who composed by far the greatest part of Hamilcar's army upon this occasion, to be raw, undisciplined, and ignorant of the use of arms; epithets which they bestow so plentifully upon a militia.[48] Yet that able commander, with an army consisting chiefly of this kind of men, totally destroyed an army of desperate veterans, took their General, and all who escaped the slaughter, prisoners, and put an end to the most [205] ruinous, and most inhuman war ever yet mentioned in history. These new levies had courage (a quality

a. Polyb. lib. 1. p. 122.[49]

b. Τοὺς ὑπολοίπους τῶν ἐν ταῖς ἡλικίαις καθοπλίσαντες (οἷον ἐσχάτην τρέχοντες ταύτην) ἐξαπέστελλον πρὸς τὸν Βάρκαν. Polyb. lib. 1. p. 122.[50]

48. See Dryden's mockery of the professional incompetence of militia troops: "The Country rings around with loud Alarms, | And raw in Fields the rude Militia swarms; | Mouths without Hands; maintain'd at vast Expence, | In Peace a Charge, in War a weak Defence: | Stout once a Month they march a blust'ring Band, | And ever, but in times of Need, at hand: | This was the Morn when issuing on the Guard, | Drawn up in Rank and File they stood prepar'd | Of seeming Arms to make a short essay, | Then hasten to be Drunk, the Business of the Day" (*Cymon and Iphigenia*, ll. 399–408). See also above, p. 130, n. 41.

49. Polybius, I. lxxxvii.3.

50. "All their remaining citizens of military age, whom they had armed as a sort of forlorn hope, they sent to Hamilcar" (Polybius, I.lxxxvii.3).

never yet, I believe, disputed to the British commonalty[51]) and were to fight *pro aris et focis*,[52] for whatever was dear and valuable to a people; and Hamilcar, who well knew how to make the proper use of these dispositions of his countrymen, was master of those abilities which Mathos wanted. Of such infinite advantage is it to an army to have a commander superior to the enemy in the art of Generalship; an advantage which frequently supplies a deficiency even in the goodness of troops, as well as in numbers.

The enmity of Hanno did not expire with Hamilcar, who fell gloriously in the service of his country, in Spain some years after. Hannibal, the eldest son, and a son worthy of so heroic a father, immediately became the object of his jealousy and hatred. For when Asdrubal (son-in-law to Hamilcar) had been appointed to the command of the army in Spain, after the death of that General, he desired that Hannibal, at that time but twenty-two years of age, might be sent to Spain to be trained up under him in the art of war. Hanno opposed this with the utmost virulence in a rancorous speech (made for him by Livy[53]) fraught with the most infamous insinuations against Asdrubal, and a strong charge of ambition against the Barcan fami-[206]ly. But his malice, and the true reason of his opposition, varnished over with a specious concern for the publick welfare, were so easily seen through, that he was not able to carry a point, which he so much wished for.

Asdrubal not long after being assassinated by a Gaul, in revenge for some injury he had received,[a] the army immediately appointed Hannibal to the command; and sending advice to Carthage of what they had done, the Senate was assembled, who unanimously confirmed the election then made by the soldiers.[b] Hannibal in a short time reduced all that part of

a. Polyb. lib. 2. p. 172.[54]

b. Μιᾷ γνώμῃ. Polyb. lib. 3. p. 234.[55]

51. See Samuel Johnson's essay on "The Bravery of the English Common Soldiers" in the *British Magazine* (January 1760), in which he inquired into the causes of what he called the "epidemic bravery" of the English soldiery.

52. Literally, "for their altars and hearths"; hence "for their homes and their religion."

53. Livy, XXI.iii.2–6.

54. Polybius, II.xxxvi.1.

55. "Unanimously" (Polybius, III.xiii.4).

Spain which lay between New Carthage, and the river Iberus, except the city of Saguntum, which was in alliance with the Romans. But as he inherited his father's hatred to the Romans, for their infamous behaviour to his country at the conclusion of the war with the mercenaries, he made great preparations for the siege of Saguntum.[a] The Romans (according to Polybius[b]) receiving intelligence of his design, sent ambassadors to him at New Carthage, who warned him of the consequences of either attacking the Saguntines, or crossing the Iberus, which, by the treaty with Asdrubal, had been made the boundary of the [207] Carthaginian and Roman dominions in that country. Hannibal acknowledged his resolution to proceed against Saguntum; but the reasons he assigned for his conduct were so unsatisfactory to the ambassadors, that they crossed over to Carthage to know the resolution of their Senate upon that subject. Hannibal in the mean time, according to the same author, sent advice to Carthage of this Embassy, and desired instructions how to act, complaining heavily that the Saguntines depending upon their alliance with the Romans, committed frequent depredations upon the Carthaginian subjects.[c]

We may conclude that the ambassadors met with as disagreeable a reception from the Carthaginian Senate as they had done from Hannibal, and that he received orders from Carthage to proceed in his intended expedition. For Polybius, reflecting upon some writers, who pretended to relate what passed in the Roman Senate when the news arrived of the capture of Saguntum, and even inserted the debates which arose when the question was put, whether, or no, war should be declared against Carthage, treats their whole accounts as absurd and fictitious.[d] "For how, says

a. This will be explained in another place.[56]
b. Lib. 3. p. 236.[57]
c. Id. ibid. p. 237.[58]
d. Polyb. lib. 3. p. 243–44.[59]

56. In fact, Montagu never returns to the subject of the origin of Hannibal's inveterate hatred of Rome. For Hannibal's own account of his father's forcing him to swear undying enmity to Rome, as given to Antiochus the Great, king of Syria, see Livy, XXXV.xix.1–4.

57. Polybius, III.xv.4–5.
58. Polybius, III.xv.8.
59. Polybius, III.xx.1–2.

he, with indignation, could it [208] possibly be, that the Romans, who had denounced war the year before at Carthage, if Hannibal should invade the Saguntine territories, should now after that city was taken by storm, assemble to deliberate whether war should be commenced against the Carthaginians or not." Now as this declaration of war was conditional, and not to take place unless Hannibal should attack the Saguntines, it must have been made before that event happened, and consequently must be referred to the Embassy above mentioned. And as Hannibal undertook the siege of Saguntum notwithstanding the Roman menaces, he undoubtedly acted by orders from the Carthaginian Senate.

When the Romans received the news of the destruction of Saguntum, they dispatched another Embassy to Carthage (as Polybius relates[a]) with the utmost expedition; their orders were to insist that Hannibal and all who advised him to commit hostilities against the Saguntines should be delivered up to the Romans, and in case of a refusal, to declare immediate war. The demand was received by the Carthaginian Senate with the utmost indignation, and one of the Senators, who was appointed to speak in the name of the rest, begun in an artful speech [209] to recriminate upon the Romans, and offered to prove, that the Saguntines were not allied to the Romans when the peace was made between the two nations, and consequently could not be included in the treaty. But the Romans cut the affair short, and told them that they did not come there to dispute, but only to insist upon a categorical answer to this plain question: Whether they would give up the authors of the hostilities, which would convince the world that they had no share in the destruction of Saguntum, but that Hannibal had done it without their authority; or, whether by protecting them, they chose to confirm the Romans in the belief, that Hannibal had acted with their approbation? As their demand of Hannibal was refused, war was declared by the Romans, and accepted with equal alacrity and fierceness by the majority of the Carthaginian Senate.[b]

a. Polyb. id. ibid.[60]
b. Polyb. lib. 3. p. 259.[61]
60. Polybius, III.xx.6.
61. Polybius, III.xxxiii.1–4.

Livy affirms that the first Embassy was decreed by the Roman Senate, but not sent 'till Hannibal had actually invested Saguntum, and varies from Polybius in his relation of the particulars.[a] For according to Livy, [210] Hannibal received intelligence of the Roman Embassy, but he sent them word, that he had other business upon his hands at that time than to give audience to ambassadors; and that he wrote at the same time to his friends of the Barcan faction to exert themselves, and prevent the other party from carrying any point in favour of the Romans.[b]

The ambassadors, thus denied admittance by Hannibal, repaired to Carthage, and laid their demands before the Senate. Upon this occasion Livy introduces Hanno inveighing bitterly in a formal harangue against the sending Hannibal into Spain, a measure which he foretels, must terminate in the utter destruction of Carthage.[c] And after testifying his joy for the death of his father Hamilcar, whom he acknowledges he most cordially hated, as he did the whole Barcan family, whom he terms the firebrands of the State, he advises them to give up Hannibal, and make full satisfaction for the injury then done to the Saguntines. When Hanno had done speaking, there was no occasion, as Livy observes, for a reply.[d] For almost all the Senate were so entirely in the interest of Hannibal, that they accused Hanno of declaiming against him with more bitterness [211] and rancour than even the Roman ambassadors, who were dismissed with this short answer, "That not Hannibal, but the Saguntines, were the authors of the war, and that the Romans treated them with great injustice, if they preferred the friendship of the Saguntines before that of their most ancient allies the Carthaginians." Livy's account of the second Embassy, which followed the destruction of Saguntum, differs so very little from that of Polybius, both as to the question put by the Romans, the answer

a. Livy, lib. 21. p. 132.[62]
b. Ib. p. 135.[63]
c. Liv. lib. 21. p. 135, 36.[64]
d. Id. ibid.[65]
62. Livy, XXI.vi.5.
63. Livy, XXI.ix.3.
64. Livy, XXI.x.1–13.
65. Livy, XXI.xi.1–2.

given by the Carthaginian Senate, and the declaration of war which was the consequence, that it is needless to repeat it.[a]

If what Hanno said in the speech above-mentioned, had been his real sentiments from any consciousness of the superior power of the Romans, and the imprudence of engaging in a war of that consequence before his country had recovered her former strength, he would have acted upon principles worthy of an honest and prudent Patriot.[66] For Polybius, after enumerating the superior excellencies of Hannibal as a General, is strongly of opinion, that if he had begun with other nations, and left the Romans for his last enterprize, he would certainly have suc-[212]ceeded in whatever he had attempted against them, but he miscarried by attacking those first, whom he ought to have reserved for his last enterprize.[b] The subsequent behaviour of Hanno, during the whole time that Italy was the seat of war, evidently proves, that his opposition to this war proceeded entirely from party motives, and his personal hatred to the Barcan family, consequently is by no means to be ascribed to any regard for the true interest of his country. Appian informs us, that when Fabius had greatly streightened[67] Hannibal by his cautious conduct, the Carthaginian General sent a pressing message to Carthage for a large supply both of men and money.[c] But, according to that author, he was flatly refused, and could obtain neither, by the influence of his enemies, who were averse to that war, and cavilled perpetually at every enterprize which Hannibal undertook. Livy, in his relation of the account which Hannibal

a. Liv. lib. 3. p. 142–43.[68]
b. Polyb. lib. 11. p. 888–89.[69]
c. Appian. de Bell. Annib. 323. Edit. Hen. Steph.[70]

66. At this time, and in the context of British politics, "patriot" meant not merely a lover of his country, but (more specifically and often pejoratively) a libertarian and anti-clerical opponent of monarchy. Hence the primary meaning given to the term in Johnson's *Dictionary* is "One whose ruling passion is the love of his country," but the secondary meaning is "a factious disturber of the government." In 1759 Pitt was a survivor of the Patriot opposition to Walpole of the 1730s, and the acknowledged leader of the Patriot tendency in British politics.

67. Subjected to privation, hardship, or distress (*OED*, "straiten," 7).

68. Livy, XXI.xviii.1–14.

69. Polybius, XI.xix.1–7.

70. Appian, VII.xvi.

sent to the Carthaginian Senate of his glorious victory at Cannae by his brother Mago, with the demand for a large reinforcement of men as well as money, introduces Hanno (in a speech of his own which he gives us on that occasion) strongly opposing that mo-[213]tion, and persisting still in his former sentiments in respect both to the war and to Hannibal.[a] But the Carthaginians, elate with that victory, which was the greatest blow the Romans ever received in the field since the foundation of their Republick, and thoroughly sensible (as Livy informs us) of the enmity which Hanno and his faction bore to the Barcan family, immediately decreed a supply of 40,000 Numidians, and 24,000 foot and horse to be immediately levied in Spain, besides Elephants, and a very large sum of money. Though Hanno at that time had not weight enough in the Senate to prevent that decree, yet he had influence enough by his intrigues to retard the supply then voted, and not only to get it reduced to 12,000 foot and 2500 horse, but even to procure that small number to be sent to Spain upon a different service. That Hanno was the true cause of this cruel disappointment, and the fatal consequences which attended it, is equally evident from the same historian. For Livy tells us, "that when orders were sent to him by the Carthaginian Senate to quit Italy, and hasten to the immediate defence of his own country, Hannibal inveighed bitterly against the malice of his enemies, who now openly and avowedly recalled him [214] from Italy, out of which they had long before endeavoured to drag him, when they tied up his hands by constantly refusing him any supply either of men or money. That Hannibal affirmed he was not conquered by the Romans, whom he had so often defeated, but by the calumny and envy of the opposite faction in the Senate. That Scipio would not have so much reason to plume himself upon the ignominy of his return, as his enemy Hanno, who was so implacably bent upon the destruction of the Barcan family, that since he was not able to crush it by any other means, he had at last accomplished it, though by the ruin of Carthage itself."[b]

a. Lib. 23. p. 265–66.[71]
b. Liv. lib. 30. p. 135.[72]
71. Livy, XXIII.xii.6–xiii.5.
72. Livy, XXX.xix.12–xx.4.

Had that large supply been sent to Hannibal with the same unanimity and dispatch with which it was voted, it is more than probable, that so consummate a General would have soon been master of Rome, and transferred the Empire of the world to Carthage. For the Romans were so exhausted after the terrible defeat at Cannae, that Livy is of opinion, that Hannibal would have given the finishing blow to that Republick, if he had marched directly to Rome from the field of battle, as he was advised to do by his General of horse Maharbal: that many of the nobility, upon [215] the first news of this fatal event, were in actual consultation about the means of quitting Italy, and looking out for a settlement in some other part of the world; and he affirms, that the safety both of the city and empire of Rome must be attributed (as it was then firmly believed at Rome) to the delay of that single day only, on which Maharbal gave that advice to Hannibal.[a] Appian confirms the distressful situation of the Roman affairs at that juncture, and informs us, that including the slaughter at Cannae, in which the Romans had lost most of their ablest officers, Hannibal had put to the sword 250,000 of their best troops in the space of two years only, from the beginning of the second Punick war inclusive.[b] It is easy therefore to imagine how little able the Roman armies, consisting chiefly of new levies, would have been to face such a commander as Hannibal, when supported by the promised reinforcement of 64,000 fresh men, besides money and elephants in proportion. For Hannibal, though deprived of all supplies from Carthage by the malice of the Hannonian faction, maintained his ground above fourteen years more after his victory at Cannae, in spite of the utmost efforts of the Romans. A truth which Livy himself ac-[216]knowledges with admiration and astonishment at his superior military capacity. From that period therefore after the battle of Cannae, when Hannibal was first disappointed of the promised supplies from Carthage, we ought properly to date the fall of that Republick, which must be wholly imputed to the inveterate malice of the profligate Hanno and his impious faction, who were determined,

a. Lib. 22. p. 240.[73]
b. Appian. de Bell. Hannib. p. 328.[74]
73. Livy, XXII.li.1–4.
74. Appian, VIII.v; see VIII.iv (for the statistics concerning the scale of casualties).

as Hannibal observed before, to ruin the contrary party, though by means which must be inevitably attended with the destruction of their country. Appian insinuates, that Hannibal first engaged in this war more from the importunity of his friends, than even his own passion for military glory and hereditary hatred to the Romans.[a] For Hanno and his faction (as Appian tells us[b]) no longer dreading the power of Hamilcar and Asdrubal his son-in-law, and holding Hannibal extremely cheap upon account of his youth, began to persecute and oppress the Barcan party with so much rage and hatred, that the latter were obliged by letter to implore assistance from Hannibal, and to assure him that his own interest and safety was inseparable from theirs. Hannibal (as Appian adds) was conscious of the truth of [217] this remark, and well knew that the blows which seemed directed at his friends, were levelled in reality at his own head, and judged that a war with the Romans, which would be highly agreeable to the generality of his countrymen, might prove the surest means of counter-working his enemies, and preserving himself and his friends from the fury of a pliant and fickle populace, already inflamed against his party by the intrigues of Hanno. He concluded therefore, according to Appian, that a war with so formidable and dangerous a power, would divert the Carthaginians from all inquiries relative to his friends, and oblige them to attend wholly to an affair, which was of the last importance to their country. Should Appian's account of the cause of this war be admitted as true, it would be a yet stronger proof of the calamitous effects of party disunion; though it would by no means excuse Hannibal. For Hanno and his party would be equally culpable for driving a man of Hannibal's abilities to such a desperate measure, purely to screen himself and his party from their malice and power. But the blame for not supporting Hannibal after the battle of Cannae, when such support would have enabled him to crush that power, which by their means recovered strength sufficient to subvert their [218] own country, must be thrown entirely upon Hanno and his party. It was a crime of the blackest dye, and an act of the highest

a. Iberic. p. 259.[75]
b. Appian. id. ibid.[76]
75. Appian, VI.ii.
76. Appian, VI.ii.

treason against their country, and another terrible proof of the fatal effects of party disunion. Nor was this evil peculiar to Carthage only, but was equally common in the Roman and Grecian Republicks. Nay, could we trace all our publick measures up to their first secret springs of action, I don't doubt (notwithstanding the plausible reasons which might have been given to the publick to palliate such measures) but we should find our own country rashly engaged in wars detrimental to her true interests, or obliged to submit to a disadvantageous peace, just as either was conducive to the private interest of the prevailing party.[77] Will not our own annals furnish us with some memorable instances of the truth of this assertion too recent to be denied? Was not the treatment which the great Duke of Marlborough received from Bolingbroke, the English Hanno, parallel to that which the victorious Hannibal met with from the Carthaginian, after the battle of Cannae?[78] Did not Bolingbroke, from the worst of party motives, displace that ever victorious General, desert our allies, and sacrifice the brave and faithful Catalans, and the city of Barcelona, in at least as shameful a manner [219] as the Romans did their unhappy friends at Saguntum? Did not the same minister by the fatal treaty of Utrecht, rob the nation of all those advantages, which she had reason to hope for from a long and successful war? Did he not by the same treaty, give our mortal enemy France time to retrieve her affairs, and recover from that low state to which the Duke of Marlborough had reduced her, and even to arrive at that power, at present so terrible to us and to all Europe?

77. For the remainder of this paragraph Montagu alludes to the conflict of English political opinion over the War of the Spanish Succession (1702–14). The Tories deplored this war as an adventure which served only the national interests of the Dutch and the private interests of Whig statesmen and soldiers such as the Duke of Marlborough (1650–1722). The Tory administration of Robert Harley (1661–1724) and Henry St. John, later Viscount Bolingbroke (1678–1751), therefore set about extricating Britain from this continental entanglement, a goal they achieved with the Treaty of Utrecht (1713) but the terms of which were denounced by the Whigs as conceding too much to the French.

78. Hannibal's great defeat of a Roman army under the command of the consul Aemilius Paullus, who (together with 50,000 of his soldiers) lost his life on the field of battle in 216 B.C.

To what can we attribute the late ill conducted war with Spain,[79] but to the ambition of party?* How was the nation stunned with the noise of Spanish depredations from the press! how loudly did the same outcry resound in parliament! yet when the leaders of that powerful opposition had carried their point by their popular clamours; when they had pushed the nation into that war; when they had drove an overgrown minister from the helm, and nestled themselves in power, how quickly did they turn their backs upon the honest men of their party, who refused to concur in their measures! How soon did they convince the nation, by screening that very minister who had been so many years the object of their resentment, and by carrying on their own war (as I may [220] term it) with the same or greater lukewarmness than what they had so lately exclaimed against in the same minister; they convinced, I say, the whole nation, that the welfare of the publick, and the protection of our trade, had not the least share in the real motives of their conduct.

But as the Carthaginian history during this period, is intimately blended with the Roman, to avoid repetition, I am obliged to defer my farther remarks upon the conduct of this people, 'till I speak of the difference between the civil and military polity, and manners of both those nations.

---

*The first Edition of this work appeared in 1759.

79. The "War of Jenkins' Ear" had broken out between Britain and Spain in October 1739. In 1738 Capt. Robert Jenkins had appeared before a committee of the House of Commons and displayed what he claimed to be his amputated ear, allegedly cut off by Spanish coast guards in the West Indies in 1731. The resulting public outrage was exploited by the political enemies of Sir Robert Walpole (1676–1745), to whom Montagu alludes in the phrase "an overgrown minister," and whose eventual fall from power on 2 February 1742 was in part owing to the unprosperous course of the war with Spain, into which Walpole had been maneuvered despite his own reluctance and misgivings. The "powerful opposition" to whom Montagu refers were primarily the followers of Lord Carteret, who succeeded Walpole in office, and who vigorously pursued the war, which had now broadened into the War of the Austrian Succession (1740–48), thereby exposing himself to the charge that he put the safety of George II's Hanoverian possessions ahead of the interests of Great Britain. It is toward this allegation that Montagu glances when he says that "the welfare of the publick, and the protection of our trade, had not the least share in the real motives of their conduct."

CHAPTER V

Of Rome

Though there is a concurrence of several causes which bring on the ruin of a state, yet where luxury prevails, that parent of all our fantastick[1] imaginary wants, ever craving and ever unsatisfied, we may justly assign it as the leading cause: since it ever was and ever will be the most baneful to publick virtue. For as luxury is contagious from its very nature, it will gradually descend from the highest to the lowest ranks, 'till it has ultimately infected a whole people. The evils arising from luxury have not been peculiar to this or that nation, but equally fatal to all wherever it was admitted. Political Philosophy lays this down as a fundamental and incontestable maxim,[a] that all the most flourishing states owed their ruin, sooner or later, to the effects of luxury; and all history, from the origin of mankind, confirms this truth by the evidence of facts to the highest degree of demonstration. In the great despotick monarchies it produced avarice, dissipation, rapaciousness, oppres-[222]sion, perpetual factions amongst the great, whilst each endeavoured to engross the favour of the

a. Dionys. Halicarn. cap. 2. p. 137. Edit. Wechel.[2]
1. Devised by extravagant fancy (*OED*, 6).
2. Dionysius of Halicarnassus, I.ii.

Prince wholly to himself; venality, and a contempt of all law and discipline both in the military and civil departments. Whilst the people, following the pernicious example of their superiors, contracted such a dastardly[3] effeminacy, joined to an utter inability to support the fatigues of war, as quickly threw them into the hands of the first resolute invader. Thus the Assyrian empire sunk under the arms of Cyrus with his poor but hardy Persians. The extensive and opulent empire of Persia fell an easy conquest to Alexander and a handful of Macedonians; and the Macedonian Empire, when enervated by the luxury of Asia, was compelled to receive the yoke of the victorious Romans.

Luxury, when introduced into free states, and suffered to be diffused without controul through the body of the people, was ever productive of that degeneracy of manners, which extinguished publick virtue, and put a final period to liberty. For as the incessant demands of luxury quickly induced necessity, that necessity kept human invention perpetually on the rack to find out ways and means to supply the demands of luxury. Hence the lower classes at first sold their suffrages in privacy and with caution; but [223] as luxury increased, and the manners of the people grew daily more corrupt, they openly set them up to sale to the best bidder. Hence too the ambitious amongst the higher centuries, whose superior wealth was frequently their own qualification, first purchased the most lucrative posts in the State by this infamous kind of traffick, and then maintained themselves in power by that additional fund for corruption, which their employments supplied, 'till they had undone those they had first corrupted.

But of all the ancient Republicks, Rome in the last period of her freedom was the scene where all the inordinate passions of mankind operated most powerfully and with the greatest latitude. There we see luxury, ambition, faction, pride, revenge, selfishness, a total disregard to the publick good, and an universal dissoluteness of manners, first make them ripe for, and then compleat their destruction. Consequently that period, by shewing us more striking examples, will afford us more useful lessons than any other part of their history.

---

3. Showing mean or despicable cowardice (*OED*, 2).

Rome, once the mighty mistress of the universe, owed her rise, according to Dionysius of Halicarnassus, the most curious and most exact inquirer into the Roman antiquities, to a small colony of the Albans under the conduct of Romulus, the supposed grand-[224]son of Numitor King of Alba. That the Albans derived their origin from the Greeks seems highly probable from the nature of the Alban and Roman monarchical government, which appears to be plainly copied from Lycurgus.

The government first instituted by Romulus, the founder of this extraordinary Empire, was that perfect sort, as it is termed by Dionysius and Polybius, which consisted of a due admixture of the regal, aristocratick, and democratick powers. As this great man received the Crown as a reward for his superior merit, and held it by the best of all titles, the willing and unanimous choice of a free people;[4] and as he is universally allowed to be the sole institutor of their first form of government, I cannot help ranking him amongst the most celebrated law-givers and heroes of antiquity. Romulus's plan of government, though formed upon the model of Lycurgus, was evidently, in some respects, superior to the Spartan. For the executive power in the Roman Government was lodged in one man only; the number of the Senators was much greater; and though the whole body of the Romans was formed into one regular militia, yet the lowest class of the people were directed to apply themselves to agriculture, grazing, and other lucrative employments; a practice [225] wholly prohibited to the free Spartans. The great employments of the State were solely confined to the Patricians, or Aristocratick part; but the Plebeians, or commonalty, had in return the power of chusing Magistrates, enacting laws, and determining about all wars when proposed by the King. But still their

---

4. Words which evoke the radical Whig doctrine of popular sovereignty, supposedly demonstrated in the Glorious Revolution of 1688 and the subsequent Act of Settlement (1701) which fixed the succession of the Crown in the House of Hanover. In his *Antiquities of the House of Brunswick* (1790) Gibbon described that constitutional transaction in carefully balanced words which echo those of Montagu: "An English subject may be prompted, by a just and liberal curiosity, to investigate the origin and story of the House of Brunswick, which, after an alliance with the daughters of our kings, has been called by the voice of a free people to the legal inheritance of the Crown" (Gibbon, *Miscellaneous Works*, vol. 2, p. 637).

decrees were not final, for the concurrence of the Senate was absolutely necessary to give a sanction to whatever the people had determined.

Whether the Romans would have continued the regal power in their founder's family by hereditary succession, cannot possibly be determined, because, when Romulus was put to death by the Patricians for aiming at more power than was consistent with their limited monarchy, he left no children. This however is certain, that their monarchy continued to be elective, and was attended with those disorders which are the usual effects of that capital error in politicks,[5] 'till the usurpation of Tarquinius Superbus.

5. "Capital" here means fatally grave (*OED*, 4). The theoretical attractions and practical defects of elective monarchy was a topic on which British writers since 1688 repeatedly wrote. In *The Idea of a Patriot King* (comp. 1738; first publ. 1741), Bolingbroke wrote: "Nothing can be more absurd, in pure speculation, than an hereditary right in any mortal to govern other men: and yet, in practice, nothing can be more absurd than to have a king to choose at every vacancy of a throne. . . . But in another respect, the advantage is entirely on the side of hereditary succession; for, in elective monarchies, these elections, whether well or ill made, are often attended with such national calamities, that even the best reigns cannot make amends for them" (Bolingbroke, *Political Writings*, p. 229). In his *Commentaries* Blackstone had warned that "Where the magistrate, upon every succession, is elected by the people, and may by the express provision of the laws be deposed (if not punished) by his subjects, this may sound like the perfection of liberty, and look well enough when delineated on paper; but in practice will be ever productive of tumult, contention, and anarchy" (Blackstone, *Commentaries*, vol. 1, p. 211). And in the following decade Gibbon would endorse this orthodoxy: "Of the various forms of government, which have prevailed in the world, an hereditary monarchy seems to present the fairest scope for ridicule. . . . Satire and declamation may paint these obvious topics in the most dazzling colours, but our more serious thoughts will respect a useful prejudice, that establishes a rule of succession, independent of the passions of mankind; and we shall cheerfully acquiesce in any expedient which deprives the multitude of the dangerous, and indeed the ideal, power of giving themselves a master" (Gibbon, *Decline and Fall*, vol. 1, p. 187). In the same year, however, Thomas Paine would pour scorn on this argument: "The most plausible plea which hath ever been offered in favour of hereditary succession, is, that it preserves a Nation from civil wars; and were this true, it would be weighty; whereas, it is the most barefaced falsity ever imposed upon mankind. The whole history of England disowns the fact. Thirty kings and two minors have reigned in that distracted kingdom since the conquest, in which time there have been (including the Revolution) no less than eight civil wars and nineteen Rebellions. Wherefore instead of making for peace, it makes against it, and destroys the very foundation it seems to stand on" (Thomas Paine, *Common Sense* [Philadelphia, 1776], p. 15).

After the death of Romulus, Numa, a man of a very different genius, was invited to the throne by the unanimous consent of the whole body of the Romans. This worthy prince reclaimed his subjects from their savage fondness for war and plunder, and taught them the arts of peace, and the happiness of civil and social life, by instructing [226] them in the great duties of religion, or piety towards their Gods, and the laws of justice and humanity, which contained their duty towards their fellow-creatures. The long reign of this wise and good prince was the most remarkable and the most happy period of time Rome ever knew from her foundation to her dissolution. For during the whole term of forty-three years, which was the extent of his reign, the harmony of the Roman State was neither interrupted by any civil dissention at home, nor the happiness of the people disturbed by any foreign war or invasion. After the death of Numa, who died universally lamented as the father of the people, Tullus Hostilius, a man of real merit, was legally elected King; but, after a victorious reign of thirty-two years, was destroyed with his whole family by lightning, according to some authors, but, according to others, was murdered by Ancus Marcius, grandson to Numa, by his only daughter, who looked upon his own right to the crown as prior to Tullus, or his family. Ancus Marcius, however, received the crown by a free election of the people, and died a natural death after a reign of twenty-four years, in which he restored such of the religious institutions of his grandfather Numa as had been neglected during the reign of his predecessor. He greatly enlarged the city of Rome itself, [227] and made it a sea-port by fortifying the haven at the mouth of the river Tiber.

Lucius Tarquinius, a man of Greek extraction by his father's side, and admitted to the privilege of a Roman citizen under the reign of Ancus Marcius, was raised to the throne for his uncommon merit, and shewed himself worthy of that high trust, which was reposed in him by the Romans. He encreased the number of the Senators to three hundred, greatly enlarged their territories, and beautified the city; and, after an illustrious reign of thirty-eight years, was assassinated in his palace by the contrivance of the two sons of Ancus Marcius, who hoped after his death to recover the kingdom, which their father had been possessed of. But their scheme was far from succeeding, for Tarquinius was so well beloved by his people, that the persons, who committed the murder, were executed, and the sons of Ancus banished, and their estates confiscated. Tullius Servius, who had married the daughter of Tarquinius, succeeded to the crown by the artful management of his mother-in-law, and by the favour of the people, though without the concurrence either of the Senate or Patricians. Tullius was certainly a man of real merit, and, as I think, superior in point of abilities to all the Roman Kings, Romulus alone excepted. But as he seemed to affect a Democracy, and was chiefly supported by the [228] people, he was always disagreeable to the Patricians, who looked upon his advancement to the crown as an illegal intrusion. But as he did most signal services to his country, during a glorious reign of four and forty years, I cannot help taking notice of some of his institutions, without the knowledge of which it is hardly possible to form a perfect idea of the Roman constitution.

Tullius ordered all the Romans to register their names and ages, with those of their parents, wives and children, and the place of their abode, either in the city or the country. At the same time he enjoined them to give in upon oath a just valuation of their effects, on pain of being whipped and sold for slaves, if they failed in registering all these particulars. From this register he formed his plan for a regular and general militia, which was invariably followed by the Romans, 'till the time of Marius. To effect this he divided the whole body of the citizens into six classes. The first class consisted of those whose possessions amounted to a hundred *Minae*.[a] These he armed in the compleatest manner, and divided into eighty centuries; forty of which, composed of the younger men, were appointed to take the field in time of war; the other forty were assigned for the defence [229] of the city. To these eighty centuries of heavy armed foot he added eighteen centuries of horse, selected out of those who had the largest estates, and were of distinguished birth. Thus the first class contained ninety-eight centuries. The second, third, and fourth classes consisted each of twenty centuries only, and were composed of citizens, whose effects were estimated at seventy-five, fifty, and five and twenty *Minae;* and their arms were lighter according to their respective classes.

a. About three hundred pounds.

To the second class he added two classes of armourers and axmen; to the fourth class two centuries of trumpeters and blowers on the horn, which contained the martial musick of the army. The fifth class consisted of those who were worth twelve *Minae* and a half, which he divided into thirty centuries, armed with darts and slings only, and were properly irregulars. The sixth class, which was by much the most numerous, was comprehended in one century only, and consisted of the poorest citizens, who were exempted from all kinds of taxes, as well as all service in the army.

By this wise disposition the burden of the war fell chiefly upon those who were best able to support it. Thus, for instance, if he wanted to raise twenty thousand men, he divided that number amongst the centuries of [230] the first five classes, and ordered each century to furnish its respective quota. He then calculated the sum necessary for the support of the war, which he divided in the same manner amongst the centuries, and ordered every man to pay in proportion to his possessions. Hence the rich, who were fewer in number, but divided into more centuries, were not only obliged to serve oftener, but to pay greater taxes. For Tullius thought it just, that they who had the greatest property at stake should bear the greatest share of the burden, both in their persons and fortunes: as he judged it equitable, that the poor should be exempted from taxes, because they were in want of the necessaries of life; and from the service, because the Roman soldiers served at that time at their own expence; a custom which continued long after. For the Roman soldiers received no pay, as Livy informs us, 'till the three hundred and forty-eighth year from the foundation of the city.[a] As the rich, by this regulation, were subjected to the greatest share of the expence and danger, Tullius made them an ample recompence by throwing the chief power of the Government into their hands, which he effected by the following scheme, too artful for the penetration of the common people. [231]

By the fundamental constitution of the Romans, the electing Magistrates, both civil and military, the enacting or repealing laws, and the

a. Liv. lib. 4. p. 276.[6]
6. Livy, IV.lix.11.

declaring war, or concluding peace, were all determined by the suffrages of the people. But as the people voted by their curiae,[a] into ten of which every tribe was di-[232]vided, the meanest citizen had an equal vote with the greatest: consequently, as the poor were much more numerous than the rich, they carried every point by a sure majority. Tullius altered this method, assembled the people, and took their votes by centuries, not by curiae. This artful measure turned the scale, and transferred the majority to the rich. For as the votes of the first class were first taken, the votes of that class, which contained ninety-eight centuries, if unanimous, always constituted a majority of three votes, which decided the question without taking the votes of the five succeeding classes, as they were in that case wholly useless.

Tullius had married his two daughters to Tarquinius and Aruns, the grandsons of his predecessor, whose guardianship he had undertaken during their minority. But what tye is strong enough to restrain ambition! His younger daughter Tullia, the most ambitious and most detestable of

a. Romulus had divided the whole People into thirty curiae, ten of which composed a Tribe. At their comitia, or general assemblies, the people divided into their respective curiae, and gave their votes man by man. The majority of votes in each curia passed for the voice of the whole curia, and the majority of the curiae for the general determination of the whole people.

Tullius on the contrary took their votes only by centuries, the whole number of which amounted to 193, into which he had subdivided the six classes. But as the first class alone, which was composed wholly of the rich, contained 98 of these centuries, if the centuries of the first class were unanimous, which, as Dionysius informs us, was generally the case, they carried every point by a sure majority of 3. If they disagreed, Tullius called the centuries of the 2d class, and so on 'till 97 centuries agreed in one opinion, which made a majority of one. If the numbers continued equal, that is, 96 on each side of the question, after the five first classes had voted; Tullius called up the sixth class, which was composed wholly of the poorest people, and contained but one century, and the vote of this century determined the question. But this case, as Dionysius observes, happened so very rarely, that even the votes of the 4th class were seldom called for, and thus the votes of the fifth and sixth were generally useless. Consequently, when the people voted by their curiae, where the vote of every individual was taken, the poor, who were much the more numerous, might always be secure of a great majority. But when the votes were taken by centuries, according to the new method instituted by Tullius, that numerous body of the poor, which composed the single century of the sixth class, and consequently had but one vote, became wholly insignificant.

her sex, unable to prevail upon her husband Aruns to join in deposing her father, applied to her brother-in-law Tarquinius, whose temper [233] was congenial with her own, and offered to be his wife if he would assert his just right, as she termed it, and attempt to supplant her father. The offer was accepted, and the incestuous match agreed upon, which was soon after compleated by the death of her husband and sister, who were privately dispatched, that there might be no obstacle remaining. Tarquinius, now the worthy husband of such a wife, attempted in the senate to procure the deposition of Tullius; but, failing in his design, at the instigation of his impious wife, he procured the old King to be openly assassinated in the street before his palace, and the unnatural Tullia drove her chariot in triumph over the body of her murdered father. By this complicated scene of adultery, murder, and parricide, Tarquin, surnamed the Proud, forced his way to the throne, and to usurpation added the most execrable and avowed tyranny. The Patricians, who had favoured his usurpation, either from their hatred to Tullius and the Plebeians, or from the hopes of sharing in the Government, with which, according to Dionysius, they had been privately allured, were the first who felt the bloody effects of his arbitrary temper.[a] Not only the friends of Tullius, [234] and those whom he suspected as uneasy under his usurpation, but all who were distinguished by their superior wealth, fell a sacrifice to his suspicion or avarice. All such were accused by his profligate emissaries, of many fictitious crimes, but particularly of a conspiracy against his person; the common pretence of all tyrants. As the tyrant himself sat as judge, all defence was useless. Some received sentence of death, some of banishment, and the estates of both were alike confiscated. The greater number of those that were accused, knowing the true motives of the tyrant's conduct, and despairing of safety, voluntarily left the city; but some of the greatest note were privately murdered by his orders, whose bodies could never be found. When he had sufficiently thinned the Senate by the death or banishment of its most valuable members, he filled up the vacant seats with his own creatures. But as he allowed nothing to be proposed or

---

a. Dionys. Halicarn. lib. 4. p. 182. edit. 1546.[7]
7. Dionysius of Halicarnassus, IV.xl.4.

done there, but in conformity to his orders, he reduced it to an empty form, without the least shadow of power. The Plebeians, who beheld with pleasure the sufferings of the Patricians, which they esteemed a just punishment for their behaviour under the reign of Tullius, were quickly treated with much greater severity.[a] For the Tyrant [235] not only abolished all the laws which Tullius had established to secure them against the oppressions of the Patricians, but loaded them with ruinous taxes, and prohibited all their publick religious assemblies, that they might have no opportunity of meeting to form secret conspiracies. Proceeding then upon the constant maxim of all tyrants, that idleness in the people is the parent of all sedition, he exhausted them so much by the slavish drudgery in which he kept them constantly employed at the publick works, that the Patricians rejoiced in their turn at the heavier miseries of the Plebeians, whilst neither of them endeavoured to put a period to their common calamities. After the Romans had groaned five and twenty years under this cruel and ignominious bondage, the rape committed by Sextus, the eldest son of Tarquin, upon Lucretia, the wife of Collatinus, an eminent Patrician, and near relation of the Tarquin family, produced a coalition of both orders, which ended in the expulsion of Tarquin and his sons, and a solemn abjuration of monarchical Government.

The tyranny of Tarquin had made the very name of King so odious to the Romans in general, that the Patricians, who were the chief conductors of this revolution, found it no difficult matter to establish an [236] Aristocracy upon the ruins of Monarchy.[b] Two Magistrates were appointed, termed Consuls, vested with the regal power, whose office was annual and elective. The Senate was filled up out of the most eminent of the Plebeians, after they had first been created Patricians, and the people restored to their right of holding assemblies, of giving their votes, and doing whatever they were intitled to by former customs. But the power of the people was rather nominal than real. For though the Consuls were annually elected by the suffrages of the people, a privilege

a. Dionys. Halicarn. id. ibid.[8]
b. Dionys. Halicarn. lib. 5. p. 205.[9]
8. Dionysius of Halicarnassus, IV.xliii.1.
9. Dionysius of Halicarnassus, V.i.1–2.

which carried the appearance of a Democracy, yet as the votes were taken by centuries, not by tribes, the Patricians were generally masters of the election. It is remarkable that, after the expulsion of Tarquin, Dionysius constantly terms the new Government an Aristocracy. It evidently appears too through the whole remaining part of his history, that there was a selfish and haughty faction amongst the Patricians, who affected a tyrannical Oligarchy, and aimed at reducing the Plebeians to a state of servitude. Valerius, surnamed Poplicola, the most humane patriot of all those who were concerned in banishing the Tarquins, introduced some beneficent laws, which, according to Dionysi-[237]us, gave great relief to the Plebeians. For by one he made it capital for any person to exercise any magistracy over the Romans, unless that office should be received from the people: as he ordered by another, that no Roman should be punished without a legal trial; and that if any Roman should be condemned by any magistrate to be fined, whipped, or put to death, the condemned person might appeal from the sentence of that Magistrate to the people, and should be liable to no punishment 'till his fate had been determined by their suffrages. A plain proof that the Plebeians 'till that time laboured under grievances not very consistent with their pretended liberty. Another proof may be drawn from the wretched state of the Plebeians, under the cruel oppressions arising from the avarice and extortions of the Patricians, which first gave birth to those perpetual seditions, which fill the history of that Republick. For as the Roman soldiers, who were all free citizens, not only paid their proportion of the taxes, but were obliged to serve in the field at their own expence during the whole campaign, this frequently obliged them to borrow money at high interest of the Patricians, who had engrossed by far the greater part of publick wealth. But as the Roman territories were often ravaged by their neighbours in those wars, which Tarquin [238] perpetually incited to procure the recovery of his crown, the loss fell heaviest upon the Plebeians, who were frequently stript of all their effects, and reduced to the utmost poverty. Hence unable to pay the principal of their debts, joined to an accumulated load of usury upon usury, they were surrendered by the judges to the discretion of their creditors. These unfeeling wretches confined their debtors in chains, tortured their bodies with whips, and treated them with such inhumanity, that great numbers of the Romans were in as bad a situation as the poor Athenians when Solon first undertook the administration. The effects of this detestable treatment of people, who had been taught to call themselves free, appeared about twelve years after the erection of their new Government. For when the Tarquins had raised up a confederacy of thirty cities of the Latines against them, the Plebeians peremptorily refused to enlist 'till a vote was passed for the abolition of their debts. As persuasions had no effect, the Senate met upon the occasion. Valerius, the son of the humane Poplicola, pleaded strongly in favour of the people, but was violently opposed by Appius Claudius, a haughty and imperious man, who is termed by Dionysius an abettor of the Oligarchy, and head of that faction, which were enemies to the people. The moderate men amongst the Senators [239] proposed that the debts should be paid out of the publick treasury; a measure which would preserve the poor for the service of the State, and prevent any injustice to the creditors. Salutary as this measure must seem, the opposition was so great that nothing was agreed to, and the result of the debates was, "That no decree should be made at present relating to this affair, but that as soon as the war should be concluded with success, the Consuls should lay it before the Senate, and take their vote upon the occasion. That in the mean time no debt should be sued for, and that the execution of all laws, except those relating to the war, should be suspended." This decree did not wholly quiet the ferment amongst the people. Several of the poorer sort demanded an immediate abolition of their debts, as the condition for their taking a share in the dangers of the war, and looked upon this delay rather as an imposition. The Senate, who, as the event shewed, were determined never to grant their request, and yet were afraid of new commotions, resolved to abolish the Consulship, and all other Magistracies for the present, and to invest a new Magistrate with absolute and unlimited power, and subject to no account for his actions. This new officer was termed the Dictator, and the duration of his office was limited to six months, at the end of which [240] term the Consuls were to resume their former authority. The chief reason, as Dionysius informs us, which induced the Senate to make use of this dangerous expedient, was to evade that law which Poplicola had procured in favour of the Plebeians, which made it death for a Magistrate to punish a Roman without a legal trial, or before he was condemned by the people.[a] The Senate then made a decree for the election of a Dictator; and the Plebeians ignorant, as Dionysius observes, of the importance of that decree, not only confirmed the resolutions of the Senate, but gave up to them the power of chusing the person who should be invested with that dignity. Titus Lartius, one of the Consuls, was nominated by his colleague, according to the form at that time agreed upon in the Senate. When the Dictator appeared in all the pomp and grandeur of his new office, he struck a terror into the most turbulent; and the people, thus tricked out of that law which was their only protection, immediately submitted. Lartius, who seems to have been one of the greatest men of his time, ordered in a general register of all the Romans, and formed his army after that wise method first instituted by Servius Tullius. When he took the field he persuaded the Latines, by his singular address, to disband their forces and conclude a truce, and thus divert-[241]ed the impending storm without fighting. He then returned home, and resigned his office before the time was expired, without having exercised any one act of severity upon a single Roman. A noble instance of moderation and publick virtue!

At the expiration of the truce, which was made for one year only, the Latines took the field with a powerful army. Aulus Posthumius was created Dictator by the Romans, and a decisive battle was fought near the Lake Regillus, in which the Romans were compleatly victors. Sextus Tarquin was killed upon the spot, and old Tarquin the father died soon after. As soon as this war was ended, the Senate, regardless of their promise, ordered all those suits for debt to be determined according to law, which had been suspended during the war. This faithless proceeding raised such violent commotions amongst the people, that a foreign war was judged the best expedient to divert the storm which threatened the Aristocracy. The haughty Appius Claudius, and Publius Servilius, a man of a very different character, were nominated Consuls by Posthumius and his colleague, which seems a manifest invasion of the rights

a. Dionys. Halicarn. lib. 5. p. 247.[10]
10. Dionysius of Halicarnassus, V.lxx.2–3.

of the people.[a] A war was resolved upon against the Volscians, but the [242] Plebeians again refused to obey the summons for inlisting. Servilius adhered to the maxims of Valerius, and advised an immediate decree for the abolition of the debts. But he was furiously opposed by the inexorable Appius,[b] who called him a flatterer of the people, and declared that it would be giving up the Government to the people, when they had it in their power to live under an Aristocracy. After much time was spent in these debates, Servilius, who was a popular man, prevailed upon the Plebeians by his intreaties, and raised an army of volunteers, with which he marched against the enemy. The Volscians, who placed their chief dependance upon the disunion which prevailed amongst the Romans, submitted to whatever terms the Consul should think proper to impose, and delivered three hundred hostages chosen out of their principal families, as a security for their behaviour. But this submission was far from real, and calculated only to amuse the Romans, and gain time for their military preparations. War was once more decreed against the Volscians; but whilst the Senate was deliberating about the number of the forces proper to be employed, a man advanced in years appeared in the Forum, and [243] implored the assistance of the people. Famine sat pictured in his pale and meagre face, and the squalid hue of his dress indicated the extremes of poverty and wretchedness.[c] This man, who was not unknown to the people, and, according to report, had borne a command in the army, first shewed several honourable scars in his breast, remains of the wounds he had received in the service of his country, and then informed them:

That he had been present in eight and twenty battles, and frequently received rewards bestowed only upon superior bravery: that in the

a. Dionys. Halicarn. lib. 6. p. 255.[11]
b. Dionys. Halicarn. lib. 6. p. 266.[12]
c. I have chiefly followed Livy in his beautiful relation of this affair, as the description he gives of this unhappy object, is not only much more striking than that of Dionysius, but one of the most pathetick I ever met with in history. Liv. lib. 2. p. 92.[13]

11. Dionysius of Halicarnassus, VI.xxiii.1.
12. Dionysius of Halicarnassus, VI.xxiv.1–3; VI.xxvii.1.
13. Livy, II.xxiii.3–7; cf. Dionysius of Halicarnassus, VI.xxvi.1–2.

Sabine war his cattle were driven off by the enemy, his estate plundered, and his house reduced to ashes: that under these unhappy circumstances he was compelled to borrow money to pay the publick taxes; that this debt, accumulated by usury, reduced him to the sad necessity of selling the estate descended to him from his ancestors, with what little effects he had remaining: but that all this proving insufficient, his devouring debts, like a wasting consumption, had attacked his person, and he, with his two [244] sons, were delivered up as slaves, and led away to the slaughter-house by his creditors.

When he had said this, he threw off his rags, and shewed his back yet bleeding from the scourge of his merciless master. This sight inflamed the people greatly; but the debtors breaking out of their creditors houses, most of whom were loaded with chains and fetters, raised their fury even to madness. If any one desired them to take up arms in defence of their country, the debtors shewed their chains, as the reward they had met with for their past services, and asked with indignation, whether such blessings were worth fighting for?[a] whilst numbers of them openly declared, that it was much more eligible to be slaves to the Volscians than the Patricians. The Senate, quite disconcerted by the violence of the tumult, intreated Servilius to take the management of the people. For an express was just arrived from the Latines, with advice that a numerous army of the enemy had already entered their territories. Servilius remonstrated to the people the consequences of disunion at so critical a juncture, and pacified them by the assurance that the Senate would confirm whatever concessions he should make; he then ordered the crier to [245] proclaim, that no citizen who voluntarily inlisted should be subject to the demands or insults of his creditors whilst the army continued in the field. The people now flocked in with chearfulness, and the levies were soon compleated. Servilius took the field and defeated the Volscians, made himself master of their camp, took several of their cities, and divided the whole plunder amongst his soldiers. At the news of this success the sanguinary Appius ordered all the Volscian hostages to be brought into the Forum, there to be whipped

a. Dionys. Halicarn. lib. 6. p. 268.[14]
14. Dionysius of Halicarnassus, VI.xxvii.3.

and publickly beheaded.[a] And when at his return Servilius demanded a triumph, he loudly opposed it, called him a factious man, and accused him of defrauding the treasury of the booty, and prevailed upon the Senate to deny him that honour. Servilius, enraged at this usage, entered the city in triumph with his army, amidst the acclamations of the people, to the great mortification of the Patricians.

Under the following consulship the Sabines prepared to invade the Romans, and the people again refused to serve unless the debts were first abolished. Lartius, the first dictator, pleaded strongly for the people; but the inflexible Appius proposed the nomination of a Dictator, as the only remedy against the [246] mutiny. His motion was carried in the Senate by a majority of voices, and Manius Valerius, a brother to the great Poplicola, was created Dictator. Valerius, who was a man of great honour, engaged his word to the Plebeians, that if they would serve chearfully upon this occasion, he would undertake the Senate should reward them by quieting the contests relating to their debts, and granting whatever they could reasonably desire; and commanded at the same time that no citizen should be sued for debt during his administration. The people had so often experienced the publick virtue of the Valerian family, and no longer apprehensive of being again imposed upon, offered themselves in such crowds, that ten legions of four thousand men each were levied, the greatest army of natives the Romans had ever brought into the field. The Dictator finished the campaign with glory, was rewarded with a triumph, and discharged the people from farther service. This step was not at all agreeable to the Senate, who feared the people would now claim the performance of the Dictator's promises.[b] Their fears were just; for Valerius kept his word with the people, and moved the Senate that the promise they had made to him might be taken into con-[247]sideration. But the Appian faction opposed it with the utmost virulence, and exclaimed against his family as flatterers of the people, and introducers of pernicious laws.

a. Dionys. Halicarn. lib. 6. p. 270.[15]
b. Dionys. Halicarn. lib. 6. p. 276–77.[16]
15. Dionysius of Halicarnassus, VI.xxx.1–2.
16. Dionysius of Halicarnassus, VI.xxx.3.

Valerius, finding his motion over-ruled, reproached the Senate for their behaviour, and foretold the consequences which would attend it; and quitting the Senate abruptly, called an assembly of the people. After he had thanked them for their fidelity and bravery, he informed them of the usage he had met with in the Senate, and declared how greatly both he and they had been imposed upon; and resigning his office, submitted himself to whatever treatment the people should think proper. The people heard him with equal veneration and compassion, and attended him home from the Forum with repeated acclamations. The Plebeians now kept no measures with the Senate, but assembled openly, and consulted about seceding from the Patricians. To prevent this step, the Senate ordered the Consuls not to dismiss their armies, but to lead them out into the field, under pretence that the Sabines were again preparing for an invasion. The Consuls left the city, and incamped nearly together; but the soldiers, instigated by one Sicinnius Bellutus, seized the arms and ensigns to avoid violating their military oath, seceded from the Consuls, and after they had appointed [248] Sicinnius commander in chief, incamped on a certain eminence near the river Anio, which from that event was always termed the *Mons Sacer,* or the Holy Mountain.

When the news of the secession was brought to Rome, the confusion was so great, that the city had the appearance of a place taken by storm, and the Appian faction were severely reproached as the cause of this desertion. Their enemies at the same time making inroads up to the very gates of Rome, increased the general consternation, as the Patricians were terribly afraid they would be joined by the seceders. But the soldiers behaved with so much decency and moderation, that the Senate after long debates sent deputies to invite them to return, with the promise of a general amnesty. The offer was received with scorn, and the Patricians were charged with dissimulation, in pretending ignorance of the just demands of the Plebeians, and the true cause of their secession. At the return of the deputies, the affair was again debated in the Senate. Agrippa Menenius, a man respectable for his superior wisdom and thorough knowledge of the true principles of government, and who was alike an enemy to tyranny in the aristocracy, and licentiousness in the people, advised healing measures, and proposed to send such persons as the people could confide in [249] with full power to put an end to the sedition in the manner they should judge most proper, without farther application to the Senate. Manius Valerius, the last Dictator, spoke next, and reminded the Senate,

> That his predictions of the evils which would result from their breach of promise were now verified: that he advised a speedy accommodation with the people, lest the same evils, if suffered to make a farther progress, should become incurable: that in his opinion the demands of the people would rise higher than the bare abolition of debts, and that they would insist upon such security as might be the firm guardian of their rights and liberty for the future; because the late institution of the Dictatorship had superseded the Valerian law, which was before the only guardian of their liberty; and the late denial of a triumph to the Consul Servilius, who had deserved that honour more than any man in Rome, evidently proved, that the people were deprived of almost all those privileges they had formerly enjoyed, since a Consul and a Dictator who shewed the least concern for the interests of the people, were treated with abuse and ignominy by the Senate: that he did not impute these arbitrary measures to the most considerable and respectable persons [250] amongst the Patricians, but to a combination of proud and avaritious men, wholly intent upon unwarrantable gain; who by advancing large sums at excessive interest, had enslaved many of their fellow-citizens, and by their cruel and insulting treatment of their unhappy debtors, had alienated the whole body of the Plebeians from the Aristocracy: that these men, by forming themselves into a faction, and placing Appius, a known enemy to the people and abettor of the Oligarchy at their head, had under his patronage, reduced the commonwealth to its present desperate situation.

He concluded by seconding the motion of Menenius for sending ambassadors to put a speedy end to the sedition upon the best terms they should be able to obtain.[17]

17. Livy, II.xxxi.8–11.

Appius, finding himself thus personally attacked, rose up and replied to Valerius in a hot inflammatory speech full of the most virulent invectives. He denied that he was ever guilty of inslaving his debtors:

> He denied too, that those who had acted in that manner could be charged with injustice, since they had done no more than the laws allowed. He affirmed that the imputation of being an enemy to the people, and favouring Oligarchy, arose from his steady adherence to the Aristocracy, [251] and equally affected all those of superior worth, who like him disdained to be governed by their inferiors, or to suffer the form of government which they had inherited from their ancestors[a] to deviate into the worst of all constitutions, a Democracy. He recriminated upon Valerius, and charged him with aiming at Tyranny, by courting the most profligate of the citizens, as the most effectual and shortest way of inslaving his country. He termed the seceders, vile, mean wretches, a thoughtless senseless multitude, whose present arrogance had been first inspired by that old man, as he contemptuously called Valerius. He declared absolutely against sending ambassadors, or making the least concession, and advised rather to arm the slaves, and send for assistance from their allies the Latines, than submit to any thing that might derogate from the power and dignity of the Patricians. He proposed, if the seceders should appear in arms against them, to put their wives and children to death before their faces by the most severe and ignominious tortures. But if they would submit at dis-[252]cretion to the Senate, he advised to treat them with moderation.[18]

This speech produced a violent tumult in the Senate; and the young Patricians who adhered to Appius behaved with so much insolence, that the Consuls threatened to exclude them from the publick councils, by a law which should fix the age for the qualification of every Senator. Nothing was determined at that time, but in a few days, the moderate party, supported by the firmness of the Consuls, prevailed against the still inflexible Appius;

a. It is remarkable that Appius terms the Aristocracy, which, at that very time, was hardly of seventeen years standing, the form of government which they had inherited from their ancestors.

18. Dionysius of Halicarnassus, VI.xxxviii.1–3.

and ten ambassadors, at the head of whom were Menenius and Valerius, were sent with full powers to treat with the seceders. After many debates, Menenius in the name of the Senate promised full redress of all their grievances with respect to the debts, and offered to confirm this promise by the solemn oaths of all the ambassadors. His offer was upon the point of being accepted, when Lucius Junius, who affected the surname of Brutus, a bold and able Plebeian, interposed and insisted upon such a security from the Senate as might protect the Plebeians for the future from the power of their enemies, who might find an opportunity of wreaking their vengeance on the people for the step they had taken. When Menenius desired to know what security he required, Junius demanded leave for the people to chuse an-[253]nually a certain number of magistrates out of their own body, vested with the power of defending their rights and liberties, and protecting their persons from injury and violence. As this new and unexpected demand seemed of too great consequence to be granted by the ambassadors, Valerius with some others were sent to take the opinion of the Senate upon that subject. Valerius laid this demand before the Senate, and gave his opinion that the favour should be granted, and Appius, as usual, opposed it with outrageous fury. But the majority, determined at all events to put a period to the secession, ratified all the promises made by the ambassadors, and granted the desired security. The seceders held their assembly in the camp, and taking the votes by curiae, elected five persons for their annual magistrates, who were termed Tribunes of the people. By a law made immediately after the election, the persons of the Tribunes were rendered sacred; and the people obliged themselves to swear by whatever was held most sacred, that they and their posterity would preserve it inviolably.

The erection of the tribunitial-power, which happened about seventeen years after the expulsion of the Kings, is certainly the aera from which the liberty of the Roman people ought properly to be dated. All the [254] neighbouring States were at that time subject to Aristocracy, where the people had little or no share in the government; and it appears evidently from the Roman historians, that the Romans intended to establish the same form of government at Rome after the abolition of monarchy. For the Senate, as Livy informs us, gave a loose to that unbounded joy which the death of Tarquin inspired, and begun to oppress and injure the people, whom 'till that time they had courted with the utmost assiduity.[a] But Sallust is more full and explicit. For he affirms, "That after the expulsion of the Kings, as long as the fear of Tarquin and the burthensome war with the Etrurians kept the Romans in suspence, the government was administered with equity and moderation. But as soon as ever the dread of those impending dangers was removed, the Senate begun to domineer over the people, and treat them as slaves; inflicting death or scourging after the arbitrary manner of despotick Tyrants; expelling them from their lands, and arrogating the whole power of government to themselves, without communicating the least share of it to the Plebeians."[b] Thus the people, before the creation of this magis-[255]tracy, were amused with the name of Liberty, whilst in fact they had only changed the Tyranny of one, for the more galling yoke of three hundred. But the tribunitial-power proved an invincible obstacle to the arbitrary schemes of the Aristocratick faction, and at last introduced that due admixture of Democracy, which is so essentially necessary to the constitution of a well regulated Republick.

As a minute detail of a history so well known as that of the Romans would be quite superfluous, I shall only observe, That the Democratick power in that Republick did not arrive at its just state of independance, 'till the Plebeians were not only entitled to the highest posts and dignities, equally with the Patricians, but 'till the Plebiscita or decrees made by the people in their assembly by tribes, were confirmed to be [256] equally binding as those made in their assembly by centuries.[c] This law was first

a. Liv. lib. 2. p. 91.[19]

b. Sallust. Fragment. apud Augustin, de civitate Dei, lib. 2. cap. 18, edit. Froben. 1569.[20]

c. In the Comitia Tributa, or assemblies by tribes, the people voted in the same manner as in the Comitia Curiata, or assemblies by curiae. The majority of single votes in every tribe constituted the voice of that tribe, and the majority of the tribes decided the question. But the Patricians conscious of their superiority in the Comitia Centuriata, or assemblies by centuries, constantly refused to obey the Plebiscita or Decrees made by the people in their assemblies by tribes, which they insisted were binding to the Plebeians only. After the abolition of the Decemvirate the people obtained a Law: "That all Laws passed in their assemblies by tribes should have equal force with those made in the assemblies by centuries, and should be equally obligatory to all the Romans without distinction."

19. Livy, II.xxi.5–6.

20. Augustine, *City of God*, II.xviii.

made when the Tyranny of the Decemvirs was abolished by the second secession of the people to the Sacred Mountain, but was perpetually violated by the overbearing power of the Aristocracy. But an event similar to that which occasioned the first secession of the people, to which they properly owed the origin of their liberty, was the cause of the third and last secession, which fully compleated that liberty, and gave the fatal blow to the arbitrary Aristocratick faction. Veturius, the son of Titus Veturius, who had been Consul and died insolvent, borrowed a sum of money of one Plotius to defray the expences of his father's funeral. As the father was greatly indebted to the same Plotius, he demanded of young Veturius the payment of both debts which his father and he himself had contracted. As the unhappy young man was utterly unable to satisfy the demand, Plotius seized his unfortunate debtor, and confined him to the work of a slave, 'till he had discharged both principal and interest. Veturius bore his servitude with patience, and did his utmost to please his creditor. But as he refused to gratify the detestable passion of the infamous Plotius, he treated him with the utmost inhumanity to force him to a compliance. One day he had the good for-[257] tune to escape out of the house of his merciless creditor, and fled to the Forum, where he shewed his back torn with stripes and his body covered with blood, and explained the reason of his shocking treatment. The people, enraged at so dreadful a spectacle, demanded an absolute security against that law, which gave the creditors such a shameful power over their insolvent debtors. For though that law had been abolished near forty years before upon a like occasion, yet the Patricians, by their superior power, had again revived it. The Consuls reported the affair to the Senate, who committed Plotius to prison, and ordered all those who were in custody for debt to be set at liberty. The Plebeians, not satisfied with these trifling concessions, insisted upon the absolute abolition of that inhuman law; but they were opposed with equal animosity by the Patricians. Despairing therefore of gaining their point by intreaties and remonstrances, they retired in a body to the Janiculum, resolutely determined never to enter the city, 'till they had received full satisfaction. The Senate, alarmed at this secession, had recourse to their last resource in all desperate cases, the creation of a Dictator. Q. Hortensius was nominated

Dictator upon this occasion, a man of great temper and prudence, and a real friend to liberty. As he was vested with [258] absolute power by virtue of his office, he totally abolished that law which had given such just cause of uneasiness, and, notwithstanding all the opposition of the Senate, revived and confirmed two laws which had been formerly made, though constantly violated by the Patricians. One was, "that the decrees made by the Plebeians should be equally obligatory to the Patricians;" the other, "that all laws passed in the Senate should be laid before the Comitia, or assemblies of the people, either to be confirmed or rejected." Thus the liberty, which the Plebeians had acquired by the first secession, was confirmed in the plainest and strongest manner by the last, which happened about two hundred and six years after. For the Patricians, from that memorable aera, had scarce any other advantage over the Plebeians, except what arose from their superior wealth, and that respect which is naturally paid by inferiors to men of superior birth.

It is evident, from that sudden change which the Plebeians experienced in the behaviour of the Patricians at the death of Tarquin, that if the Senate could have supported themselves in that arbitrary power, which they so visibly aimed at, the condition of the people would have been just like that of the Polish peasants under their imperious Lords. For in that detestable Aristocracy, the Patri-[259]cians, not content with the wealth of the Republick, which centered chiefly in their own body, used their utmost efforts to engross the entire possession of the lands. The secession of the people, and the creation of the Tribunes, defeated the schemes they had formed for establishing an Aristocratick tyranny. But the frequent attempts to revive the Agrarian law prove undeniably, that the Patricians never lost sight of their ambitious views of aggrandizing their families by an illegal usurpation of the conquered lands. Spurius Cassius, a Patrician, was the first author of this law, about eight years after the secession, with a view of raising himself to the regal power by conciliating the affection and interest of the people. The law itself was certainly just, and founded upon that equality in the distribution of the land, which was a part of the constitution, as settled by their founder Romulus. The plea therefore of Cassius,

That the lands, which had been conquered by the blood and valour of the people, should be taken from the rich and applied to the service of the publick,

was founded upon the strictest equity, as well as the fundamental principles of their constitution. Even Appius, the most inveterate enemy to the people, acknowledged the justice of his proposal, since he moved that commissioners should be ap-[260]pointed by the Senate to fix the boundaries of the land in question, and sell or let it out in farms for the benefit of the publick. This advice was unanimously approved of, and the Senate passed a decree, that ten of the most ancient consular Senators should be appointed commissioners to carry this scheme into execution. This decree at once pacified the people, and ruined Cassius. For as he had proposed to divide two-thirds of the lands between the Latines and the Hernici, whose assistance he at that time courted, the people gave him up to the resentment of the Senate, who condemned him for plotting to introduce a single tyranny, and ordered him to be thrown down the Tarpeian precipice.

This was the first rise of the famous Agrarian law, which occasioned such frequent contests between the Senate and the people, and stirred up the first civil war in Rome, which ended in the murder of both the Gracchi, about three hundred and fifty years after. For the Senate not only evaded the nomination of the commissioners, as they had promised in their decree, but, whenever that affair was brought upon the carpet,[21] they acted with an insincerity and artifice which are highly inconsistent with the so much vaunted probity of the Roman Senate. Unless therefore we attend to the true reasons upon which the Agrarian law was originally [261] founded, we can never form a right judgment of the perpetual dissensions between the Senate and the Tribunes upon that subject. For though the chief blame, in all these contests, is most commonly thrown upon the turbulent and seditious temper of the Tribunes, yet, if the real cause of those dissensions is impartially examined, we shall find that most of them took rise from the avarice and injustice of the Patricians.

21. See above, p. 62, n. 55.

But though the tribunitial power was sometimes made subservient to the interested views of some ambitious Tribunes, yet no argument can justly be drawn from the abuse of that power against its real utility. For how much it was dreaded as the bulwark of the liberty of the people, is evident from this consideration: that it was reduced almost to nothing by Sylla, and afterwards totally absorbed by Augustus and the succeeding Emperors, who never looked upon the people as thoroughly inslaved 'till they had annexed the tribunitial power to the imperatorial dignity.

I remarked before, that when the highest dignities and employments in the Republick were laid open to the Plebeians, and the decrees of the people had the same force, and affected the Patricians in the same manner as those which were issued by the Senate, the Democratick power was raised to an equality with the Aristocratick. But as a third power, [262] or estate (as we term it) was wanting, capable of preserving the requisite aequilibrium between the other two, it was impossible, from the very nature of the Republican constitution, that the equality between the two powers could be long supported. The concessions made by Hortensius quieted indeed the civil dissensions; and it is remarkable too, that after peace was restored to the Republick, the progress of the Roman conquests was so amazingly rapid, that in little more than two hundred years from that period they had subjugated the most opulent empires in the universe. But the same conquests, which raised the Republick to the summit of her grandeur, threw too much weight into the Democratick scale, and, by totally corrupting the Roman manners, brought on the final ruin of their liberty and constitution. For as every conquered Province created successively a new Government, these new dignities immediately became new objects of avarice and ambition. But as the command of the armies, the government of Provinces, and the highest posts in the state, were disposed of by the suffrages of the people; the candidates for those lucrative employments left no means unattempted to secure a majority. Hence, as the poor Plebeians were extremely numerous, the man who was able to distribute the greatest largesses, or divert the [263] mob with the finest shews, was generally the most successful. When the interest of the candidates was nearly equal, force was frequently made use of to decide the contest; and it was not uncommon to see the Forum covered with the slaughtered bodies of the electors.[a] The Generals who were elected fleeced the Provinces to enable themselves to keep up their interest at home with the people, and connived at the rapines of their soldiers to secure their affections. Hence at Rome liberty degenerated into the most outrageous licentiousness, whilst the soldiers gradually wore off that parental love for their country, which was once the characteristick of the Romans, and attached themselves wholly to the fortunes of their Generals. Hence the most successful leaders began to look upon themselves no longer as servants, but as masters of the Republick, and each endeavoured to support his pretensions by force of arms. The factions of Sylla and Marius filled the city alternately with slaughter and rapine, as the fortune of their respective leaders prevailed in the course of that destructive contest; and Rome frequently felt the calamitous effects of war in her own bowels, at a time when her victorious arms abroad were adding new Provinces to [264] her dominions. These factions were far from expiring with their leaders, but broke out again with the same baleful fury under the first and second Triumvirate.[22] Each of these, strictly speaking, were no more than coalitions of the same factions, where three chiefs united their several parties to crush every other. When they had accomplished this, and satiated their ambition, their avarice, and their private resentments, by the most bloody proscriptions, they quarrelled about the division of power, like captains of banditi[23] about the division of booty, with whom they agreed in principle, and differed only in degree. These quarrels occasioned those civil wars, which gave the finishing blow to the Roman Republick. The ablest and most dangerous man, in each Triumvirate, proved at last the conqueror;

a. The place of election.

22. The two triumvirates (that is to say, governments shared among three men) were constitutional expedients arising from the decline of the Roman republic. The first triumvirate was formed in 60 B.C. between Julius Caesar, Pompey, and Crassus, and endured until the defeat and death of Crassus at the hands of the Persians at the battle of Carrhae (53 B.C.). Following the assassination of Caesar (15 March 44 B.C.), the second triumvirate was formed in 43 B.C. by the three leaders of the Caesarian party, Mark Antony, Octavian, and Lepidus, and endured until the defeat of Antony at the battle of Actium (31 B.C.) left Octavian (later Augustus) as the sole master of the Roman world.

23. Gangs of marauders or outlaws (OED).

and Julius Caesar first put those chains upon his country, which Augustus rivetted beyond a possibility of removal.

All the historians, from whom we have received any account of the Roman affairs, agree unanimously in fixing their conquest of Antiochus the Great, as the aera from whence we are to date the rise of luxury and corruption amongst them. Livy assures us, that luxury was first introduced into their city by the army of Manlius at their return from Asia. They, he informs us, were the first [265] who made Rome acquainted with the finely ornamented couches, the rich carpets, the embroidered hangings, and other expensive productions of the looms of Asia, with all those elegant tables of various forms and workmanship, which were esteemed so essential a part of that magnificence which they affected in their furniture. They introduced wenches, who sung and played upon different instruments, with dancers of anticks,[24] to heighten the mirth and indulgence of the table. To shew to what height they carried the expence and luxury of the table, he adds, with indignation, that a cook, who, by their frugal and temperate ancestors, was looked upon, from his very office, as the vilest slave in the houshold, was now esteemed an officer of mighty consequence, and cookery was erected into an art, which before was looked upon as the most servile kind of drudgery. Yet new and strange as these first specimens might seem, Livy assures us, that they were but trifles when compared to their succeeding luxury. Before that fatal aera the Romans were poor, but they were contented and happy, because they knew no imaginary wants; and whilst their manners were virtuous, poverty itself was honourable, and added a new lustre to every other virtue. But when once they had contracted a relish for the luxury of Asia, they quickly found that the wealth of [266] Asia was necessary to support it; and this discovery as quickly produced a total change in their manners. Before that time the love of glory, and a contempt of wealth, was the ruling passion of the Romans. Since that time, money was the only object of their applause and desire. Before, ambition impelled them to war, from a thirst of dominion; now avarice, for the sake of plunder to

24. Grotesque or ludicrous performers (*OED*, "antic," 4).

support the expence of luxury. Before, they seemed a race of Heroes; they were now a gang of insatiable robbers. Formerly, when they had reduced a people to obedience, they received them as their allies; they now made the conquered Nations their slaves. They fleeced the Provinces, and oppressed their friends. As the great offices, which entitled the possessors to the command of armies, and the government of Provinces, were disposed of by the votes of the people, no method was left unattempted to secure a majority of suffrages. The candidates for these employments, not only exhausted their own fortunes, but strained their credit to the utmost, to bribe the people with shews and donatives. To this infamous period we must fix the rise of that torrent of corruption, which so quickly deluged the Roman Republick. The successful candidates set out for their government, like hungry emaciated wolves, to fatten upon the blood of the miserable Provinces. Cicero makes heavy [267] complaints of the rapine and extortion of these rapacious oppressors; and his orations against Verres,[25] when accused by the Sicilians, give us a compleat idea of the behaviour of a Roman Governor in his province. The complaints of the oppressed Provincials were incessant; but every Governor had his friends amongst the leading men, whom he secured by a share of the plunder, and the weight of their whole interest was applied to screen the criminal.[26] Laws indeed were made against this crime of peculation, but they were easily eluded, because the judges, who were chosen out of the body of the people, were as corrupt as the offenders, and were frequently their associates in villany. Thus corruption made its way into the very vitals of the Republick. Every thing was venal, and the venality had made so rapid a progress, even in the time of Jugurtha, which was about eighty years

25. Gaius Verres was the cruel and rapacious propraetor, or governor, of Sicily, from 73 to 71 B.C. The Sicilians retained the services of the young Cicero, who impeached Verres in 70 B.C., and whose first Verrine oration was so devastating that Verres withdrew into voluntary exile. There followed five further Verrine orations, in which Cicero broadened his scope to include an indictment of the corruption of the current Roman system of provincial administration.

26. A phrase with resonance in eighteenth-century British politics. Robert Walpole acquired the nickname of "Screen-master general" because of the suspicion that, in the wake of the South Sea Bubble, he had protected guilty politicians who had profited from the affair. See Pearce, *Pitt*, p. 24.

after the defeat of Antiochus, as to occasion the severe sarcasm of that Prince, recorded by Sallust, which places the corruption of the Romans in a stronger point of view, than the most laboured and pathetick descriptions of their historians.

That Rome had carried her venality to so great a height, as to be ready to sell herself to destruction, if she could but find a purchaser.[27]

When the Romans had beggared the Monarchs, whom they vouchsafed to stile [268] their friends, and drained the Provinces 'till they had scarce any thing left to plunder; the same principle which had induced them to pillage the universe, impelled them now to prey upon one another.[a] Marius and Sylla were the first Romans who set that fatal precedent, and were the first who bridled Rome with a standing army.[28] The civil power was compelled to give way to the military, and from that period we may truly date the ruin of the Roman liberty. The State continued to fluctuate between Despotism and Anarchy, 'till it terminated irretrievably under the Caesars, in the most absolute and most infernal tyranny that any people were ever yet cursed with. Marius opened the bloody scene, and glutted his followers

a. Proscriptiones innoxiorum ob divitias, cruciatus virorum illustrium, vastam urbem fuga et caedibus, bona civium miserorum quasi Cimbricam praedam, venum aut dono datam. Sall. Frag. p. 142.[29]

27. Here Montagu conflates a number of passages in Sallust's *Bellum Jugurthinum*. In the first (VIII.1) the Numidian prince Jugurtha is told that "in Rome all things are for sale" (Romae omnia venalia esse), a judgment Jugurtha later endorses in the same words (XX.1). On leaving Rome, Sallust records that Jugurtha looked over his shoulder and pronounced that Rome was "a city for sale and ripe for destruction, if a buyer can be found!" (Urbem venalem et mature perituram, si emptorem invenerit! XXXV.10). See also XXVIII.1.

28. See above, p. 99, n. 182.

29. An extract from a speech in the Roman Senate attacking Sulla which Sallust places in the mouth of the consul Marcus Aemilius Lepidus, who bitterly asks his fellow senators if they approve of Sulla's conduct in "proscribing innocent men on account of their wealth, the torture of distinguished citizens, the depopulation of the city by exile and murder, and the goods of the miserable citizens sold or given away as if they were booty seized from the Cimbri" (*Oratio Lepidi*, XVII). The Cimbri were a northern Germanic tribe, originating in the region now occupied by Denmark. They invaded Italy, and inflicted a number of severe defeats on the Romans before being decisively defeated by the consul Gaius Marius at Vercellae in 101 B.C.

with the blood and wealth of the friends of Sylla. Sylla repaid the Marian faction in the same coin with usury. Battles were fought in the very streets; and Rome more than once experienced all the horrors of a city taken by storm from her own citizens. Personal resentment and revenge for injuries received, were the pretence on both sides, but plunder and confiscation seem to have been the chief motives. For the rich were equally looked upon as [269] enemies, and equally proscribed by both factions, and they alone were safe who had nothing worth taking.

If we connect the various strokes interspersed through what we have remaining of the writings of Sallust, which he levelled at the vices of his countrymen, we shall be able to form a just idea of the manners of the Romans in the time of that historian. From the picture, thus faithfully exhibited, we must be convinced, that not only those shocking calamities, which the Republick suffered during the contest between Marius and Sylla, but those subsequent and more fatal evils, which brought on the utter extinction of the Roman liberty and constitution, were the natural effects of that foreign luxury, which first introduced venality and corruption. Though the introduction of luxury from Asia preceded the ruin of Carthage in point of time, yet, as Sallust informs us, the dread of that dangerous rival restrained the Romans within the bounds of decency and order.[a] But as soon as ever that obstacle was [270] removed, they gave a full scope to their ungoverned passions.[b] The

---

a. Ante Carthaginem deletam—metus hostilis in bonis artibus civitatem retinebat. Sall. Bell. Jug. p. 80.[30]

b. Postquam remoto metu Punico mores non paulatim ut antea, sed torrentis modo praecipitati. Sall. Frag. p. 139.

—Rapere, consumere, sua parvi pendere, aliena cupere, pudorem, pudicitiam, divina humana promiscua, nihil pensi, neque moderati habere. De Bell. Cat. pag. 8.[31]

30. "Before the destruction of Carthage . . . fear of the enemy preserved the morals of the state" (Bellum Jugurthinum, XLI.2).

31. "Afterwards, once the fear of Carthage had been removed, their manners suffered a headlong decline, rather than their previous gradual descent" (Sallust, Historiae, I.xvi); cf. Augustine, City of God, II.xviii. "They [the Roman youth, once corrupted by luxury] pillaged and squandered; they set little value on their own possessions, but coveted the possessions of others; and, disregarding modesty, chastity, and all things human and divine, they acted in the most thoughtless and exorbitant manner" (Bellum Catilinae, XII.2).

change in their manners was not gradual, and by little and little, as before, but rapid and instantaneous. Religion, justice, modesty, decency, all regard for divine or human laws, were swept away at once by the irresistible torrent of corruption. The nobility strained the privileges annexed to their dignity, and the people their liberty, alike into the most unbounded licentiousness.[a] Every one made the dictates of his own lawless will his only rule of action. Publick virtue, and the love of their country, which had raised the Romans to the empire of the universe, were extinct. Money, which alone could enable them to gratify their darling luxury, was substituted in their place.[b] Power, dominion, honours, and universal respect, were annexed to the possession of money. Contempt, and whatever was most reproachful, was the bitter portion of poverty; and to be poor, grew to be the greatest of all crimes in the estimation of the Romans. Thus wealth and poverty contributed alike [271] to the ruin of the Republick. The rich employed their wealth in the acquisition of power; and their power in every kind of oppression and rapine, for the acquisition of more wealth.[c] The poor, now dissolute and desperate, were ready to engage in every seditious insurrection, which promised them the plunder of the rich, and set up both their

a. Caepere nobilitas dignitatem, populus libertatem in lubidinem vertere. Bell. Jug. p. 80.[32]

b. Postquam divitiae honori esse caeperunt, & eas gloria, imperium, potentia sequebatur hebescere virtus, paupertas probro haberi, innocentia pro malevolentia duci caepit. Bell. Cat. p. 8.[33]

c. Ita cum potentia avaritia sine modo, modestiaque invadere, polluere, & vastare omnia, nihil pensi neque sancti habere. p. 81.

Sibi quisque ducere, trahere rapere. De Bell. Jug. p. 81.[34]

32. "Then the nobles began to abuse their station, and the people their liberty" (*Bellum Jugurthinum*, XLI.5).

33. "After riches began to be held in honor, and gave rise to glory, dominion, and power, virtue began to lose its luster, poverty came to seem disgraceful, and innocence was construed as malevolence" (*Bellum Catilinae*, XII.1).

34. "Thus alongside power arose greed—greed unlimited and unrestrained, which brought about universal violation and devastation, and which respected nothing and held nothing sacred" (*Bellum Jugurthinum*, XLI.9). "Every man for himself robbed, pillaged, and plundered" (*Bellum Jugurthinum*, XLI.5). Montagu omits the final phrase of XLI.9, "quoad semet ipsa praecipitavit" (until it finally brought about its own downfall).

liberty and their country to sale to the best bidder.[a] The Republick, which was the common prey to both, was thus rent to pieces between the contending parties.[b] As an universal selfishness is the genuine effect of universal luxury, so the natural effect of selfishness is to break through every tye, both divine and human, and to stick at no kind of excesses in the pursuit of wealth, its favourite object. Thus the effects of selfishness will naturally appear in irreligion, breach of faith, [272] perjury, a contempt of all the social duties, extortion, frauds in our dealings, pride, cruelty, universal venality and corruption.[c] From selfishness arises that vicious ambition (if I may be allowed the term) which Sallust rightly defines, "The lust of domination:"[d] Ambition, as a passion, precedes avarice; for the seeds of ambition seem almost to be innate. The desire of pre-eminence, the fondness for being distinguished above the rest of our fellow-creatures, attends us from the cradle to the grave. Though as it takes its complection, so it receives its denomination from the different objects it pursues, which in all are but the different means of attaining the same end. But the lust of domination, here mentioned by Sallust,

a. Eos paulatim expulsos agris, inertia atque inopia incertas domos habere subegit: caepere alienas opes petere, libertatem suam cum Republica venalem habere. Sall. Orat. 2. ad Caesarem de Repub. Ordinand. p. 197.[35]

b. Ita omnia in duas partes abstracta sunt: Respublica, quae media fuerat, dilacerata. De Bell. Jug. p. 80.[36]

c. Pecuniae cupido fidem, probitatem caeterasque bonas artes subvertit; pro his superbiam, crudelitatem Deos negligere, omnia venalia habere edocuit. De Bell. Cat. p. 7.[37]

d. Cupido Imperii, id. p. 7.[38]

35. "It happened by degrees that they were gradually driven from their fields, and that poverty and idleness weakened their hold on their homesteads: then they began to covet the wealth of strangers, and to consider their own liberty, as well as the Republic, to be for sale" (Sallust, *Ep. ad Caesarem de re publica 2*, V.iv).

36. "Thus everything was split between two parties, and the commonwealth (which was in between them) was torn to pieces" (*Bellum Jugurthinum*, XLI.5).

37. "The love of money undermined fidelity, honesty, and all other noble qualities. In their place, it taught men to be proud, cruel, neglectful of the gods, and venal in all matters" (*Bellum Catilinae*, X.3–4). Montagu slightly compresses and re-arranges Sallust's Latin, but without distorting his sense.

38. "The lust for power" (*Bellum Catilinae*, X.3).

tho' generally confounded with ambition, is in reality a different passion, and is, strictly speaking, only a different mode of selfishness. For
the chief end which we propose, by the lust of domination, is to draw
every thing to centre in ourselves, which we think will enable us to
gratify every other passion. I confess it may be alledged, that self-love
and selfishness both arise from the general law of self-preservation, and
are but different modes of the same principle. I acknowledge, that if we
examine strictly all those heroick instances of love, friendship, or patriotism, [273] which seem to be carried to the most exalted degree of
disinterestedness, we shall probably find the principle of self-love lurk-
ing at the bottom of many of them.[39] But, if we rightly define these two
principles, we shall find an essential difference between our ideas of
self-love and selfishness. Self-love, within its due bounds, is the practice
of the great duty of self-preservation, regulated by that law which the
great Author of our being has given for that very end. Self-love therefore
is not only compatible with the most rigid practice of the social duties,
but is in fact a great motive and incentive to the practice of all moral
virtue. Whereas selfishness, by reducing every thing to the single point
of private interest, a point which it never loses sight of, banishes all the
social virtues, and is the first spring of action, which impells to all those
disorders, which are so fatal to mixed Government in particular, and to
society in general. From this poisonous source Sallust deduces all those
evils, which spread the pestilence of corruption over the whole face of
the Republick, and changed the mildest and most upright Government
in [274] the universe into the most inhuman, and most insupportable

---

39. The skeptical analysis of apparent altruism into underlying selfishness was
an ethical stance associated in Montagu's day above all with the *Maximes* (1665)
of François, duc de La Rochefoucauld (1613–80). For an example of La Rochefoucauld's psychological hedonism, consider no. 81: "Nous ne pouvons rien aimer que
par rapport à nous, et nous ne faisons que suivre notre goût et notre plaisir quand
nous préférons nos amis à nous-mêmes" (We can love nothing except in relation to
our selves, and we are only consulting our own taste and our pleasure when we put
our friends before our selves).

tyranny.[a] For as the lust of domination can never possibly attain its end without the assistance of others, the man, who is actuated by that destructive passion, must, of necessity, strive to attach to himself a set of men of similar principles, for the subordinate instruments. This is the origin of all those iniquitous combinations, which we call factions. To accomplish this, he must put on as many shapes as Proteus;[40] he must ever wear the mask of dissimulation, and live a perpetual lye.[b] He will court the friendship of every man, who is capable of promoting, and endeavour to crush every man, who is capable of defeating his ambitious views. Thus his friendship and his enmity will be alike unreal, and easily convertible, if the change will serve his interest. As private interest is the only tye which can ever connect a faction, the lust of wealth, which was the cause of the lust of domination, will now become the effect, and must be proportional to the sum total of the demands of the whole faction; and, as the [275] latter know no bounds, so the former will be alike insatiable.[c] For when once a man is inured to bribes in the service of faction, he will expect to be paid as well for acting for, as for

a. Primo pecuniae, dein imperii cupido crevit, ea quasi materies omnium malorum fuere—Post ubi contagio, quasi pestilentia, invasit, civitas immutata, imperium ex justissimo atque optumo, crudele intolerandumque factum. De Bell. Cat. p. 7.[41]

b. Aliud clausum in pectore, aliud promptum in lingua habere, amicitias, inimicitiasq; non ex re, sed ex commodo aestumare, magisq; vultum, quam ingenium bonum habere. Ibid.[42]

c. Malitia praemiis exercetur; ubi ea demferis, nemo omnium gratuitò malus est. P. 200.[43]

40. In Greek mythology Proteus (or "The Old Man of the Sea") is a sea god who knows all things, and who enjoys the power of changing shape in order to evade being questioned; see *Odyssey*, IV.351 ff.

41. "First the love of money, and then the lust for power, increased, and supplied what one might call the nourishment of all evils . . . finally, when the disease had spread like a deadly plague, the state underwent a transformation: the best and most just of governments became cruel and insupportable" (*Bellum Catilinae*, X.3 and 6).

42. "To have one thought locked in the heart, another ready on the tongue; to value friendships and enmities not on their merits but by reference to self-interest, and to prefer a smooth face to a good heart" (*Bellum Catilinae*, X.5).

43. "Villainy was kept active by means of reward; when you take away those inducements, no one whatsoever is bad unless they are paid to be so" (Sallust, *Ep. ad Caesarem de re publica 2*, VIII.iii).

acting against the dictates of his conscience.[a] A truth, which every minister must have experienced, who has been supported by a faction, and which a late great minister[44] (as he frankly confessed) found to be the case with him during his long administration. But how deeply soever a State may be immersed in luxury and corruption, yet the man who aims at being the head of a faction for the end of domination, will at first cloak his real design under an affected zeal for the service of the Government.[b] When he has established himself in power, and formed his party, all who support his measures will be rewarded as the friends, all who oppose him will be treated as enemies to the Government. The honest and uncorrupt citizen will be hunted down as disaffected, [276] and all his remonstrances against mal-administration, will be represented as proceeding from that principle. The cant term, *Disaffection*, will be the watch-word of the faction; and the charge of disaffection, that constant resource of iniquitous ministers, that infallible sign that a cause will not stand the test of a fair enquiry, will be perpetually employed by the tools of power to silence those objections which they want argument to answer. The faction will estimate the worth of their leader, not by his services to his country, for the good of the publick will be looked upon as obsolete and chimerical; but his ability to gratify, or

a. Nam, ubi malos praemia sequuntur, haud facile quisquam gratuitò bonus est. Sall. Orat. Philip. contra Lepid. p. 145.[45]

b. Pauci potentes, quorum in gratia plerique concesserant, sub honesto patrum, aut plebis nomine dominationes affectabant, bonique & mali cives appellati, non ob merita in Rempublicam (omnibus pariter corruptis) sed uti quisque locupletissimus & injuria validior, quia praesentia defendebat, pro bono ducebatur. Frag. p. 139.[46]

44. Presumably another allusion to Sir Robert Walpole, although I have been unable to trace the expression of the sentiment; see above, p. 88, n. 155.

45. "For, when the wicked are rewarded, it is difficult for anyone to be good without payment" (*Oratio Philippi*, IX).

46. "A few powerful men, to whose influential position most people had lent their support, were attempting to win absolute power by pretending to be champions of either the senate or the people; citizens were considered good or bad, not on grounds of public service (for all were equally corrupt); but whoever was exorbitantly rich and reckless in criminality was deemed to be good, because he shored up the *status quo*" (Sallust, *Historiae*, I.xii; cf. Augustine, *City of God*, III.xvii).

screen his friends, and crush his opponents.[a] The leader will fix the
implicit obedience to his will, as the test of merit to his faction: Consequently, all the dignities and lucrative posts will be conferred upon persons of that stamp only, whilst honesty and publick virtue will be
standing marks of political reprobation. Common justice will be denied
to the latter in all controverted elections, whilst the laws will [277] be
strained, or over-ruled in favour of the former. Luxury is the certain
fore-runner of corruption, because it is the certain parent of indigence:
Consequently, a state so circumstanced will always furnish an ample
supply of proper instruments for faction. For as luxury consists in an
inordinate gratification of the sensual passions, the more the passions
are indulged they grow the more importunately craving, 'till the greatest fortune must sink under their insatiable demands.[b] Thus luxury necessarily produces corruption. For as wealth is essentially necessary to
the support of luxury, wealth will be the universal object of desire in

a. Idem illi factiosi regunt, dant, adimunt quae lubet; innocentes circumveniunt:
suos ad honorem extollunt. Non facinus, non probrum, aut flagitium obstat, quo minus
magistratus expetant: quod commodum est, trahunt, rapiunt: postremo tanquam urbe
capta, lubidine ac licentia sua pro legibus utuntur. Sall. Or. 2. ad Caesar, p. 196.[47]

b. Divitiis, quas honeste habere licebat, per turpitudinem abuti properabant.
Lubido strupri, ganeae, caeterique cultus non minor incesserat. Vescendi causa,
terra mariq; omnia exquirere; dormire priusquam somni cupido esset: non famam,
aut sitim, neq; frigus, neq; lassitudinem operiri; sed ea omnia luxu antecapere. Haec
juventutem, ubi familiares opes defecerant, ad facinora incendebant. Animus imbutus
malis artibus haud facile lubidinibus carebat: eò profusius omnibus modis quaestui
atque sumptui deditus erat. Sall. de Bell. Cat. p. 9.[48]

47. "The same faction is in power, who indict and pardon as they wish, who
entrap the innocent, and raise their own creatures to positions of power. Crime,
shame and infamy are powerless to eject them from office. They seize and carry off
whatever suits them. It is like the sack of a captured town: desire and licentiousness
usurp the place of law" (Sallust, *Ep. ad Caesarem de re publica 2*, III.iii–iv).

48. "They hastened to squander in shame those riches which they might have
enjoyed with honor. No less strong was their craving for lewdness, gluttony, and
other vices . . . for the sake of greed they ransacked both land and sea; they slept
before they were drowsy; they did not wait to feel hunger, thirst, cold or tiredness,
but in their luxury they anticipated all these things. These were the weaknesses
which incited young men to crime, once they had run through their family wealth.
A soul accustomed to wrongdoing cannot easily abstain from self-indulgence; and
so it abandons itself all the more recklessly to all means of gain and of extrava-
gance" (*Bellum Catilinae*, XIII.2–5).

every State where luxury prevails: Consequently, all those who have dissipated their private fortunes in the purchase of pleasure, will be ever ready to inlist in the cause of faction for the wages of corruption. A taste for pleasure immoderately indulged, quickly strengthens into habit, eradicates every principle of honour [278] and virtue, and gets possession of the whole man. And the more expensive such a man is in his pleasures, the greater lengths he will run for the acquisition of wealth for the end of profusion. Thus the contagion will become so universal, that nothing but an uncommon share of virtue can preserve the possessor from infection. For when once the idea of respect and homage is annexed to the possession of wealth alone, honour, probity, every virtue, and every amiable quality will be held cheap in comparison, and looked upon as aukward and quite unfashionable.[a] But as the spirit of liberty will yet exist in some degree in a state which retains the name of Freedom, even though the manners of that state should be generally depraved, an opposition will arise from those virtuous citizens, who know the value of their birth-right, *Liberty,* and will never submit tamely to the chains of faction. Force then will be call-[279]ed in to the aid of corruption, and a standing-army will be introduced.[b] A military

a. Ubi divitiae clarae habentur, ibi omnia bona vilia sunt, fides, probitas, pudor, pudicitia. Sall. Orat. 2. ad Caes. p. 199.[49]

b. Itaque omnes concessere jam in paucorum dominationem, qui per militare nomen, aerarium, exercitum, regnum, provincias occupavere, et arcem habent ex spoliis vestris: cum interim more pecudum vos multitudo singulis habendos, fruendosque praebetis, exsuti omnibus, quae majores reliquere: nisi quia vosmet ipsi per suffragia, uti praesides olim, nunc dominos destinatis. Sall. Frag. Orat. Lepid. ad Pleb. p. 160.[50]

49. "When riches are thought to be the basis of a good name, then all noble qualities are held to be vile—all trust, honesty, shame and modesty" (Sallust, *Ep. ad Caesarem de re publica 2,* VII.viii).

50. "And so they [the elected representatives of the people] have now, every one of them, submitted to the despotism of a few men, who, under the pretext of waging war, have seized the treasury, the armies, kingdoms and provinces. They have made a stronghold for themselves out of what they have pillaged from you. In the meantime you, the multitude, submit yourselves like sheep to their individual service and enjoyment. You have been stripped of every privilege which your ancestors bequeathed to you except the right to vote—by which you, who once chose your defenders, now choose your masters" (an extract from the speech of the tribune Macer to the Roman people; Sallust, *Historiae,* III.xlviii.6).

government will be established upon the ruins of the civil, and all commands and employments will be disposed of at the arbitrary will of lawless power. The people will be fleeced to pay for their own fetters, and doomed, like the cattle,[51] to unremitting toil and drudgery for the support of their tyrannical masters. Or, if the outward form of civil government should be permitted to remain, the people will be compelled to give a sanction to Tyranny by their own suffrages, and to elect oppressors instead of protectors.

From this genuine portrait of the Roman manners, it is evident to a demonstration, that the fatal catastrophe of that Republick (of which Sallust himself was an eyewitness) was the natural effect of the corruption of their manners. It is equally as evident from our author, and the rest of the Roman historians, that the corruption of their manners was the natural effect of foreign luxury, introduced and supported by foreign wealth. The fatal tendency of these evils, was too obvious to escape the notice of every sensible Roman, who had any regard for liberty, and their ancient constitution. Many sumptuary laws were made to restrain the various excesses of luxury; but these efforts were too feeble to check the overbearing [280] violence of the torrent. Cato proposed a severe law, inforced by the sanction of an oath, against bribery and corruption at elections; where

---

51. A metaphor with strong connotations in the political language of eighteenth-century Britain. In his *Two Treatises on Government* (1690), Locke had used the image of cattle twice to evoke the miserable conditions of life under despotic monarchs. In the *First Treatise*, section 156, Locke accuses Filmer of characterizing "the Societies of Men . . . as so many Herds of Cattle, only for the Service, Use, and Pleasure of their Prince" (Locke, *Two Treatises*, p. 256). In the *Second Treatise*, section 163, he accuses those who "speak as if the Prince had a distinct and separate Interest from the good of the Community" of implicitly conceiving of the people as "an Herd of inferiour Creatures, under the Dominion of a Master, who keeps them, and works them for his own Pleasure or Profit" (Locke, *Two Treatises*, p. 377). In *The Decline and Fall*, Gibbon would list, among the apparent absurdities of hereditary monarchy, the fact that "on the father's decease, the property of a nation, like that of a drove of oxen, descends to his infant son" (Gibbon, *Decline and Fall*, vol. 1, p. 187).

the scandalous traffick of votes was established by custom as at a publick market. But, as Plutarch observes, he incurred the resentment of both parties by that salutary measure.ᵃ The rich were his enemies, because they found themselves precluded from all pretensions to the highest dignities; as they had no other merit to plead but what arose from their superior wealth. The electors abused, cursed, and even pelted him as the author of a law which deprived them of the wages of corruption, and reduced them to the necessity of subsisting by labour.ᵇ But this law, if it really passed, had as little effect as any of the former; and like the same laws in our own country, upon the same occasion, was either evaded by chicane, or over-ruled by power. Our own septennial scenes of drunkenness,⁵² [281] riot, bribery, and abandoned perjury, may serve to give us an idea

a. Διαφθειρομένου δὲ τοῦ δήμου ταῖς δωροδοκίαις ὑπὸ τῶν φιλαρχούντων καὶ χρωμένων τῷ δεκάζεσθαι καθάπερ ἐργασίᾳ συνήθει τῶν πολλῶν, βουλόμενος ἐκκόψαι παντάπασι τὸ νόσημα τοῦτο τῆς πόλεως, ἔπεισε δόγμα θέσθαι τὴν σύγκλητον ὅπως οἱ κατασταθέντες ἄρχοντες, εἰ μηδένα κατήγορον ἔχοιεν, αὐτοὶ παριόντες ἐξ ἀνάγκης εἰς ἔνορκον δικαστήριον εὐθύνας διδῶσιν. Plut. in Vit. Cat. p. 126.⁵³

b. Ἕωθεν οὖν ἐπὶ τὸ βῆμα τοῦ Κάτωνος προελθόντος ἀθρόοι προσπεσόντες ἐβόων, ἐβλασφήμουν, ἔβαλλον. Plut. ibid.⁵⁴

52. The Septennial Act (1716) had extended the life of Parliament to a maximum of seven years; previously under the Triennial Act (1641) their duration had been only three years. General elections in eighteenth-century Britain were usually accompanied by scenes of public drunkenness, as candidates offered hospitality to the electorate. For more on the unreformed House of Commons in this period, see Frank O'Gorman, *Voters, Patrons, and Parties: The Unreformed Electoral System of Hanoverian England 1734–1832* (Oxford: Clarendon Press, 1989).

53. "However, seeing that the people were corrupted by the gifts which they received from men who were fond of office and plied the bribery of the masses as they would an ordinary business, he wished to eradicate althogether this disease from the state, and therefore persuaded the senate to make a decree that magistrates elect, in case they had no accuser, should be compelled of themselves to come before a sworn court and submit accounts of their election" (Plutarch, "Cato the Younger," XLIV.2).

54. "Early in the morning, therefore, when Cato had gone forth to his tribunal, crowds assailed him with shouts, abuse, and missiles" (Plutarch, "Cato the Younger," XLIV.3).

of the annual elections of the Romans in those abominable times.[a] Corruption was arrived at its last stage, and the depravity was universal. The whole body of the unhappy Republick was infected, and the distemper was utterly incurable. For those excesses which formerly were esteemed the vices of the people, were now, by the force of custom, fixed into habit, become the manners of the people.[b] A most infallible criterion, by which we may ascertain the very point of time, when the ruin of any free state, which labours under these evils, may be naturally expected.

The conspiracies of Cataline and Caesar against the liberty of their country, were but genuine effects of that corruption, which Sallust has marked out to us, as the immediate cause of the destruction of the Republick. The end proposed by each of these bad men, and the means employed for that end, were the same in both. The difference in their success arose only from the difference [282] of address and abilities in the respective leaders. The followers of Cataline, as Sallust informs us, were the most dissolute, the most profligate, and the most abandoned wretches, which could be culled out of the most populous and most corrupt city of the universe.[c] Caesar, upon the same plan, formed his party, as we learn from Plutarch, out of the most infected, and most corrupt members of the very

a. Hinc rapti fasces praetio: sectorque favoris
   Ipse sui populus: lethalisque ambitus urbi
   Annua venali referens certamina campo.
       Lucan. Pharsal. lib. I. Edit. 1506.[55]

b. Mala sua, quod malorum ultimum est, amant—& desinit esse remedio locus, ubi quae fuerant vitia, mores sunt. Senec. Ep. 39. p. 100.[56]

c. In tanta tamque corrupta civitate, Catilina omnium flagitiosorum, atque facinorosorum circum se, tamquam stipatorum catervas habebat. Sall. de Bell. Cat. p. 9.[57]

55. "Hence public office was seized by bribery, and the people auctioned off its own support, while corruption, repeating year by year the venal competition of the Campus, destroyed the city" (Lucan, *Pharsalia*, I.178–80). Elections to public office in Rome were held in the Campus Martius, an open space northwest of the ancient city, which also served as the exercise ground of Rome's first armies.

56. "They love their own ills—which is the greatest ill of all . . . and there is no longer any scope for a remedy, when what were once vices have become habits" (Seneca, *Epistles*, XXXIX.vi).

57. "In a city which was both so large and so corrupt, Catiline was able to surround himself, as a bodyguard, with gangs of criminals and reprobates of all descriptions" (*Bellum Catilinae*, XIV.i).

same State.[a] The vices of the times easily furnished a supply of proper instruments. To pilfer the publick money, and to plunder the provinces by violence, though State-crimes of the most heinous nature, were grown so familiar by custom, that they were looked upon as no more than mere office-perquisites.[b] The younger people, who are ever most ripe for sedition and insurrection, were so corrupted [283] by luxury, that they might be deservedly termed, "an abandoned race, whose dissipation made it impracticable for them to keep their own private fortunes; and whose avarice would not suffer their fellow-citizens to enjoy the quiet possession of theirs."[c]

It is not at all strange that Rome thus circumstanced should fall a victim to the corruption of her own citizens: nor that the Empire of the universe, the toil and labour of ages, to which the Romans had waded through seas of blood, should be destined to feed the detestable vices of a few monsters, who were a disgrace even to human nature. The total change of the Roman constitution, the unlimited Tyranny of the Emperors, and the abject slavery of the people, were all effects of the same cause, extended in degree by a natural progression. The Romans in fact were no more; the name indeed subsisted, but the idea affixed to that name, was as totally changed as their ancient constitution. In the time of Pyrrhus the Roman Senate appeared an assembly of Kings to his ambassador Cyneas. When the East had felt the force of the Roman arms, the most despotick princes received the orders of a Roman Senate, and executed them with as prompt obedience, as a slave would do the commands of his master. A deputy from the Roman Senate made a haughty [284] Monarch tremble at the head of a victorious army,

a. Καισαρος—τὰ νοσοῦντα καὶ διεφθαρμένα τῆς πολιτέιας μέρη ταράττοντος καὶ σύνάγοντος πρὸς αὐτὸν. Plut. in Vit. Cat. Min. p. 241.[58]

b. Peculatus aerarii, & per vim sociis ereptae pecuniae, quae quanquam gravia sunt, tamen consuetudine jam pro nihilo habentur. Sall. de Bell. Jug. p. 73.[59]

c. Adeo juventus luxu atque avaritia corrupta est, uti merito dicatur, genitos esse, qui neque ipsi habere possent res familiares, neque alios pati. Sall. Frag. p. 139.[60]

58. "Caesar . . . was attaching to himself the numerous diseased and corrupted elements in the commonwealth" (Plutarch, "Cato the Younger," XXVI.1).

59. "It is not a matter of plundering the treasury or of extorting money from our allies, which (although serious crimes) are however nowadays considered to be trifles" (*Bellum Jugurthinum*, XXXI.25).

60. "To the same degree as the younger generation were corrupted by greed and debauchery, to just the same degree (it was truly said) they became unable either to keep hold of their own wealth, or to tolerate the wealth of others" (Sallust, *Historiae*, I.xvi).

compelled him to resign all his conquests, and return ingloriously home, by a single motion of his walking-stick.[a]

What an elevated idea must this give us of the Roman manners, whilst that haughty people retained their freedom! Nothing is more grand; nothing more striking. Shift but the scene, and view the manners of the Romans when enslaved. Nothing is so abjectly servile, nothing so despicable. We see the Roman Senate deifying the worst of mankind; wretches, who had sunk even below humanity, and offering the adoration of incense to these idols of their own making, who were more contemptible than the very stone and wooden representatives of their deities. Instead of giving laws to Monarchs, and deciding the fate of nations, we see the august Roman Senate run trembling like slaves at the summons of their master Domitian, to debate in form about the important business of dressing a turbot.[b] The Majesty of the Roman people, which received the tributary homage of the universe, expired together with their liberty. That people, who disposed of the highest offices in the go-[285]vernment, the command of armies, provinces and kingdoms, were sunk into a herd of dispirited slaves. Their total insignificancy screened them from the fatal effects of the caprices of their Tyrants. They dragged on a wretched being in a state of idleness and poverty, in the midst of slavery; and the utmost extent of their wishes amounted to no more, than bread for their daily subsistence, and diversions for their amusement.[c] The Emperors

a. Popilius to Antiochus Epiph. Liv. lib. 45. p. 672.[61]

b. Juv. Sat. 4.[62]

c.   —Ex quo suffragia nulli
    Vendimus, effugit Curas. Nam qui dabat olim
    Imperium, fasces, legiones, omnia, nunc se
    Continet, atque duas tantum res anxius optat
    Panem & Circenses.
             Juv. Sat. 10. lin. 77.[63]

Otium cum servitio.
          Sall. Frag. p. 143.[64]

61. Livy, XLV.xii.4–6.

62. Juvenal, IV.37–149.

63. "Now that nobody buys our votes, we are carefree. Those who once bestowed commands, consulships, legions and all other things, now interfere no more, and long anxiously for only two things—bread and circuses!" (Juvenal, X.77–81).

64. "Ease with servitude" (Sallust, *Historiae*, I.lv.25). See, for similar sentiments, *Paradise Lost,* II.255–57 and *Samson Agonistes,* ll. 268–71.

supplied the one by their frequent largesses of corn, and gratified the other by their numerous publick shews. Hence historians observe, that the most infamous of their Tyrants were as fond of Raree-shews,[65] as the mob themselves; and as they were by much the most profuse of all their Emperors, their deaths were always most regretted by the people. So striking is the contrast between a state when blessed with liberty, and the same state when reduced to slavery by the corruption of its people!

As I have already made some reflections upon that passion for theatrical entertainments, which prevailed at Athens, I cannot [286] help observing, that after the introduction of luxury, the fondness for that kind of diversion amongst the Romans, was at least equal to that of the Athenians. The Romans seem to have been strangers to every kind of stage-plays for the first four hundred years. Their first attempts of that kind were rude and simple, and not unlike the ancient mummery[66] at our country wakes, or Christmas gambols. The regular Drama was imported together with the luxury of Greece, but every species of this kind of entertainment, whether tragedy, comedy, farce, or pantomime, was comprehended under the general denomination of stage-plays,[a] and the different performers alike ranged under the general term of players.[b] The profession itself was reckoned scandalous, and proper only for slaves, and if once a Roman citizen appeared upon the stage, he immediately forfeited his right of voting, and every other privilege of a free man. Upon this account Cicero seems to lament the fate of his friend Roscius, when he tells us, "that he was so superior to all as a player, that he alone seemed worthy of appearing [287] upon the stage: but of so exalted a character, as a

a. Ludi Scenici.[67]

b. Histriones.[68]

65. A set of pictures or a puppet show exhibited in a portable box for public entertainment, or a peep show; hence, by extension, an exhibition, show, or spectacle of any kind, especially one regarded as lurid, vulgar, or populist (*OED*, 1 and 2a).

66. Mummers' plays were performed by traveling troupes of players, usually wearing masks and elaborate costumes. The repertoire was limited and consisted of folkloric or mythical material, particular subjects being associated with certain festivals of the Christian year (although the material of the plays is often of a decidedly pagan nature). They were popular in the eighteenth century. See Thomas Hardy, *The Return of the Native* (1878), Book Second, chapters 4 and 5.

67. Stage-plays.

68. Actors.

man, that of all men he deserved least to be doomed to so scandalous a profession."ᵃ Suetonius, speaking of the licentiousness and insolence of the players, takes notice of an ancient law, which impowered the praetors and aediles to whip those players publickly, who gave the least offence, or did not perform to the satisfaction of the people. Though Augustus, as the same historian informs us, exempted players from the ignominy of that law, yet he took care to restrain them within the bounds of decency, and good manners.ᵇ For he ordered Stephanio, a celebrated comedian, to be whipped publickly through all the three theatres, and afterwards banished him, for presuming privately to keep a Roman matron disguised un-[288]der the habit of his boy. Upon a complaint from the Praetor he made Hylas the pantomime be lashed openly in the court of his own palace, to which place the offender had fled for refuge; and banished Pylades, one of the most eminent players, not only from Rome but even from Italy, for affronting one of the audience who had hissed him upon the stage.ᶜ But these restraints

a. Etenim cum artifex ejusmodi sit; ut solus dignus videatur esse, qui in scena spectetur: tum vir ejusmodi est, ut solus dignus videatur, qui eò non accedat. Orat. pro Rosc. Edit. Glasg. p. 43.⁶⁹

b. Divus Augustus immunes verberum histriones quondam responderat. Tacit. c. 14. p. 42. Edit. Glasg.
Coercitionem in histriones magistratibus in omni tempore et loco lege vetere permissam ademit. Suet. in Vit. Aug. p. 163.⁷⁰

c. Histrionum licentiam adeo compescuit, ut Stephanionem Togatarium, cui in puerilem habitum circumtonsam matronam ministrasse compererat, per tria theatra virgis coesum relegaverit. Hylam pantomimum, querente praetore, in atrio domus suae, nemine excluso, flagellis verberaverit; et Pyladem urbe atque Italia submoverit, quod spectatorem à quo exsibilabatur, demonstrasset digito, conspicuumque fecisset. Ibid.⁷¹

69. "For, just as he is such an artist that he alone seems worthy to be seen on stage; so he is such a man, that he alone seems worthy of never making an entrance upon it" (Cicero, *Pro Publio Quinctio*, XXV).

70. "The deified Augustus had once replied that actors enjoyed immunity from being scourged" (Tacitus, *Annals*, I.77). "He stripped the magistrates of the power granted them by an ancient law of punishing actors at any time and in any place" (Suetonius, "Divus Augustus," XLV.3).

71. "He was so strict in curbing the licentiousness of the actors, that when he learned that Stephanio, an actor of Roman plays, was waited on by a matron with her hair dressed in the manner of a boy, he had him whipped with rods through the three theaters, and then banished. Hylas, a pantomime actor, was publicly scourged in the atrium of his own home when a praetor lodged a complaint against him; and Pylades was exiled from both the city and Italy, because he had pointed with his finger at a spectator who was hissing, and so had made him conspicuous" (Suetonius, "Divus Augustus," XLV.4).

seem to have expired with Augustus. For we find the pride and insolence of
the players carried to so great a height in the reign of his successor Tiberius,
as to occasion their total banishment. The fondness of the populace for
the entertainments of the theatre, and the folly of the degenerate nobility,
were the causes of this alteration. For both Pliny and Seneca assure us, that
persons of the very first rank and fashion were so scandalously mean, as to
pay the most obsequious court to the players, to dangle[72] at their levees, to
attend them openly in the streets like their slaves; and treat them like the
masters, instead of the servants of the publick.[a] Every eminent player had
his party, and these ridiculous factions interested themselves so warmly in
the cause of their respective favourites, that the theatres became a perpetual
scene of [289] riot and disorder. The nobility mingled with the mob in
these absurd conflicts; which always ended in bloodshed, and frequently
in murder.[b] The remonstrances and authority of the magistrates had so
little effect, that they were obliged to have recourse to the Emperor. Bad as
Tiberius was, yet he was too wise to tolerate such shameful licentiousness.
He laid the case before the Senate, and informed them, that the players
were the cause of those scandalous riots which disturbed the repose of the
publick: that they spread lewdness and debauchery through all the chief
families; that they were arrived to such a height of profligacy and insolence, through the protection of their factions, that the authority of the

a. Ostendam nobilissimos juvenes mancipia pantomimorum. Senec. Epist. 47.
p. 118.[73]

b. Variis dehinc et saepius irritis praetorum quaestibus, postremò Caesar de
immodestia histrionum retulit; multa ab iis in publicum seditiose, foeda per domos
tentari—eo flagitiorum & virium venisse, ut auctoritate patrum coercendum sit.
Pulsi tum histriones Italia. Tacit. Annal. 4. p. 134.[74]

72. To hang after or about any one, especially as a loosely attached follower; to
follow in a dallying way, without being a formally recognized attendant (*OED*, 3).

73. "I will show you youths of the noblest birth enslaved to pantomime players!"
(Seneca, *Epistles*, XLVIII.xvii).

74. "Next, after various and usually pointless complaints from the praetors, Caesar at last brought up the matter of the outrageousness of the actors: they were, he
said, frequently the fomenters of sedition in the state and of debauchery in private
houses—the old Oscan farce, the trifling delight of the mob, had attained such a
pitch of indecency and power that it had to be checked by the authority of the senate.
The players were then expelled from Italy" (Tacitus, *Annals*, IV.14).

Senate itself was requisite to restrain them within proper bounds. Upon this remonstrance they were driven out of Italy as a publick nuisance; and Suetonius informs us, that all the frequent and united petitions of the peo-[290]ple could never prevail upon Tiberius to recall them.[a]

Augustus affected an extreme fondness for all kinds of diversions; he invited the most celebrated players of every denomination into Italy, and treated the people, at an immense expence, with every kind of entertainment, which the theatre or circus could furnish. This is remarked as an instance of that refined policy of which he was so thorough a master. For that artful prince was not yet firmly settled in his newly usurped power. He well knew, that if he gave the people time to cool and reflect, they might possibly thwart the execution of his ambitious schemes. He therefore judged that the best expedient to prepare them for the yoke of slavery would be, to keep them constantly intoxicated by one perpetual round of jollity and diversions. That this was the opinion of thinking people, at that time, is evident from that remarkably pertinent answer of Pylades the player to Augustus, transmitted to us by Dion Cassius. Pylades, as I have already observed, had been banished by Augustus for a misdemeanor, but pardoned and recalled to gratify the humour of the people. At his return, when Augustus reproved him with quarrelling with one Bathyllus, a person of the same profession, but protected by his favourite Maecenas; Pylades is report-[291]ed to have made this bold and sensible answer:

> It is your true interest, Caesar, that the people should idle away that time upon us and our affairs, which they might otherwise employ in prying too narrowly into your government.[b]

a. Caede in theatro per discordiam admissa, capita factionum & histriones propter quos dissidebatur, relegavit: nec ut revocaret unquam ullis populi precibus potuit evinci. Suet. in Tib. c. 37.[75]

b. Συμφέρει σοὶ, Καισαρ, περὶ ἡμᾶς τὸν δῆμον ἀποδιατρίβέσθαι. Dion. Cass. lib. 54. p. 533.[76]

75. "When a quarrel in the theatre ended in bloodshed, he banished the leaders of the factions, as well as the actors who were the cause of the disagreement; nor could the entreaties of the people ever induce him to revoke his sentence" (Suetonius, "Tiberius," XXXVII.2).

76. "It is to your advantage, Caesar, that the people should devote their spare time to us" (Dio Cassius, LIV.xvii.5).

I am far from being an enemy to the stage. On the contrary, I think the stage under proper regulations might be rendered highly useful. For of all our publick diversions, the stage, if purged from the obscenity of farce, and the low buffoonery of pantomime, is certainly capable of affording infinitely the most rational, and the most manly entertainment. But when I see the same disorders in our own theatres,[77] which were so loudly complained of in the time of Tiberius; when the ridiculous contests between contending players are judged to be of such mighty importance, as to split the publick into the same kind of factions; when these factions interest themselves so warmly in the support of the supposed merit of their respective favourites, as to proceed to riots, blows, and the most extravagant indecencies; I cannot help wishing for the interposition of the reforming spirit of Augustus. And when I see the same insatiable fond-[292]ness for diversions, the same unmeaning taste (so justly ridiculed by Horace in his countrymen[a]) prevail in our own nation, which mark the

a. Verùm equitis quoque jam migravit ab aure voluptas
Omnis, ad incertos oculos, & gaudia vana.
Hor. Epist. 1. lib. 2. lin. 187.

Tanto cum strepitu ludi spectantur, et artes,
Divitiaeque peregrinae: quibus oblitus actor
Quum stetit in scena, occurrit dextera laevae:
Dixit adhuc aliquid? nil sane. Quid placet ergo?
Lana Tarentino violas imitata veneno.
Ibid. lin. 203.[78]

77. The role of the modern theater in depraving public morals was a frequent theme among the more severe critics of eighteenth-century England. In 1725, in his *The Causes of the Decay and Defects of Dramatick Poetry,* John Dennis had deplored the fact that the theater of his day was "now in Hands of Players, illiterate, unthinking, unjust, ungratefull and sordid, who fancy themselves plac'd there for their extraordinary merits, and for noe other end but to accumulate Pelf, and bring Dishonour upon the Reign of the Best of Kings by sacrifising the British genius to their Insatiable avarice: who reject the Best plays and Receive the worst, if the Blockheads who writt them, are but Sycophants enough to cringe to and fawn upon Half the Town, and by that means engage whole crowds of Fools to aplaud a senselesse Performance" (Dennis, *Works,* vol. 2, p. 277). The following year William Law would denounce the profession of actors as "prophane, wicked, lewd and immodest" (William Law, *The Absolute Unlawfulness of the Stage-Entertainment Fully Demonstrated* [1726], p. 9).

78. "But today all the pleasure even of the *equites* has passed from what is heard to the vain delights of the unfixed eye" (Horace, *Epistles,* II.i.187–88). "Amid such

most degenerate times of Greece and Rome, I cannot but look upon them as a certain indication of the frivolous and effeminate manners of the present age.

---

clamour is the play viewed—the works of art, and the outlandish finery—and when, burdened with this, the actor treads the boards, the right hand strikes the left. 'Has he said anything yet?' 'Not a word.' 'So what is so pleasing?' 'The woollen robe which rivals the violet with its Tarentine dye'" (Horace, *Epistles*, II.i.203–7).

CHAPTER VI

The real CAUSE of the rapid Declension[1] of the ROMAN REPUBLICK

Dionysius of Halicarnassus observes, that Romulus formed his new government in many respects after the model of that of Sparta, which accounts for that great resemblance, we evidently meet with between the Roman and Spartan constitutions.[a] I may add too, that we cannot help observing as great a resemblance for some ages at least between the manners of both those people. For we find the same simplicity in their houses, diet and apparel; the same contempt for wealth, and quite to the last period of their liberty, the same warlike genius. Publick spirit and the love of their country was carried in both states to the highest pitch of enthusiasm; it was deaf to the voice of nature itself, and that amiable virtue wore a kind of savage aspect at Rome and Sparta. But the alteration of their manners, which alike preceded the loss both of the Spartan and Roman liberty, will admit of no kind of comparison either [294] as to degree or progress. Luxury and corruption stole in by very slow degrees, and were never carried

a. Dionys. Halicarn. lib. 2. p. 65.[2]
1. The process of fall or decline. (*OED*, 3).
2. Dionysius of Halicarnassus, II.xiii.4 and xiv.2.

to any remarkable height amongst the Spartans. But, as Sallust beautifully expresses it, the Roman manners were precipitated at once to the depth of corruption, after the manner of a resistless torrent.[a] I observe that the destruction of Carthage is fixed upon by that elegant historian, as the aera from which the rise of this rapid degeneracy is to be dated. He assigns too the removal of the dread occasioned by that dangerous rival, as the cause of this sudden and astonishing change. Because, according to his reasoning, they could then give a full loose to the impetuous fury of their passions, without restraint or fear. But the cause here assigned is by no means equal to the effect. For though it might contribute in some measure to accelerate the progress of luxury, and consequently the corruption of their manners; yet the real cause of their sudden degeneracy was widely different.

The Romans founded their system of policy, at the very origin of their state, upon that best and wisest principle, "The fear of the Gods, a firm belief of a divine [295] superintending Providence, and a future state of rewards and punishments:" Their children were trained up in this belief from tender infancy, which took root and grew up with them by the influence of an excellent education, where they had the benefit of example as well as precept.[b] Hence we read of no heathen nation in the world, where both the publick and private duties of religion were so strictly adhered to, and so scrupulously observed as amongst the Romans. They imputed their good or bad success to their observance of these duties, and they received publick prosperities or publick calamities, as blessings conferred, or punishments inflicted by their Gods. Their historians hardly ever give us an account of any defeat received by that people, which they do not ascribe to the omission, or contempt of some religious ceremony by their Generals.[c] For though the ceremonies there mentioned, justly appear to us instances

a. Mores majorum non paulatim ut antea, sed torrentis modo precipitati. Sallust. Fragment. p. 139.[3]

b. Nulla unquam Respublica sanctior, nec bonis exemplis ditior fuit. Liv. in Praefat.[4]

c. Dionys. Halicarn. lib. 2. p. 61, 62.[5]

3. "Traditional standards of behavior suffered a headlong decline, rather than their previous gradual descent" (Sallust, *Historiae*, I.xvi).

4. "No state was ever more righteous, nor richer in good examples" (Livy, I.Praefatio.11).

5. Dionysius of Halicarnassus, II.vi.1–4.

of the most absurd, and most extravagant superstition, yet as they were esteemed essential acts of religion by the Romans, they must consequently carry all the force of religious principle. We neither exceeded, says [296] Cicero, speaking of his countrymen, the Spaniards in number, nor did we excel the Gauls in strength of body, nor the Carthaginians in craft, nor the Greeks in arts or sciences.[a] But we have indisputably surpassed all the nations in the universe in piety and attachment to religion, and in the only point which can be called true wisdom, a thorough conviction, that all things here below are directed, and governed by Divine Providence.[b] To this principle alone Cicero wisely attributes the grandeur and good fortune of his country. For what man is there, says he, who is convinced of the existence of the Gods, but must be convinced at the same time, that our mighty Empire owes its origin, its increase, and its preservation, to the protecting care of their divine providence.[c] A plain proof that these continued to be the real sentiments of the wiser Romans, even in the corrupt times of Cicero. From this principle proceeded that respect for, and submission to their laws, and that [297] temperance, moderation, and contempt for wealth, which are the best defence against the encroachments of injustice and oppression. Hence too arose that inextinguishable love for their country, which, next to the Gods, they looked upon as the chief object of veneration. This they carried to such a height of Enthusiasm, as to make every human tye of social love, natural affection, and self-preservation, give way

a. —Tamen nec numero Hispanos, nec robore Gallos, nec calliditate Poenos, nec artibus Graecos.[6]

b. Sed pietate ac religione, atque hac unâ sapientiâ, quod deorum immortalium numine omnia regi gubernarique perspeximus, omnes gentes nationesque superavimus. Cic. de Harus. Resp. p. 189.[7]

c. Quis est qui—cum Deos esse intellexerit, non intelligat eorum numine hoc tantum imperium esse natum, et auctum et retentum. Ibid. p. 188.[8]

6. "However, we are neither more populous than the Spanish, stronger than the Gauls, more versatile than the Carthaginians, nor more accomplished as artists than the Greeks" (Cicero, *On the Responses of the Haruspices*, IX.xix).

7. "But in piety, in devotion to religion and in that special wisdom which consists in the recognition of the truth that the world is swayed and directed by divine disposal, we have excelled every race and every nation" (Cicero, *On the Responses of the Haruspices*, IX.xix).

8. "And who is he who . . . once convinced that the gods do exist, can fail at the same time to be convinced that it is by their power that this great empire has been created, extended, and sustained?" (Cicero, *On the Responses of the Haruspices*, IX.xix).

to this duty to their dearer country.[a] Because they not only loved their country as their common mother, but revered it as a place which was dear to their Gods; which they had destined to give laws to the rest of the universe, and consequently favoured with their peculiar care and protection.[b] Hence proceeded that obstinate and undaunted courage, that insuperable contempt of danger, and death itself in defence of their country, which compleat the idea of the Roman character, as it is drawn by historians in the virtuous ages of the Republick. As long as the manners of the Romans were regulated by this first great principle of religion, [298] they were free and invincible. But the Atheistical doctrine of Epicurus,[c] which in-[299] sinuated itself at Rome, under the respectable name of Philosophy, after

a. Cari sunt parentes, cari liberi, propinqui et familiares: sed omnes omnium caritates patriae una complexa est. Cic. de Offic.[9]

b. Pro qua patria, mori, et cui nos totos dedere, et in qua nostra omnia ponere, et quasi consecrare debemus. Cic. de Leg.[10]

9. "Parents are dear; dear, too, are children, relatives and friends: but our native land binds all our attachments into one" (Cicero, *De Officiis*, I.xvii, sect. 57).

10. "It is our duty to die for our homeland; we must dedicate ourselves to her without reserve, and place on her altar, and (as it were) consecrate to her service, all that we possess" (Cicero, *De Legibus*, II.ii, sect. 5).

c. It has been remarked,

> that if I had mentioned Stoicism upon this occasion as the root of Atheism, it might have been more proper; because a true Stoic was a professed Atheist.*

*Critical Review, March, 1759.

That the fundamental principles of the Stoics tended to Atheism, I readily grant: but as the real philosophers of that sect inculcated a thorough contempt for what are called the good things of this life, and were extremely austere in their morals; their Doctrines seem to have had a very different influence upon the manners of the people, wherever they were received, from those of the Epicureans. Brutus and Cato, the inflexible Champions of liberty, and almost the only virtuous characters in that corrupt period, were rigid Stoics. Julius Caesar, who subverted the Constitution of his Country, was a thorough Epicurean, both in principle and practice. His principles we plainly see in Sallust, where he urges the total extinction of our being at death, as an argument for sparing the lives of Cataline's accomplices. For he audaciously affirms to the Senate:

> that death as a punishment was so far from being an evil, that it released us from all our sorrows, when labouring under distress and misery; that it put a final period to all the evils of this life, beyond which there was no longer room either for grief or joy.

their acquaintance with the Greeks, undermined and destroyed this ruling principle. I allow that luxury, by corrupting manners, had weakened this principle, and prepared the Romans for the reception of Atheism, which is the never-failing attendant of luxury. But as long as this principle remained, it controuled manners, and checked the progress of luxury, in proportion to its influence. But when the introduction of Atheism had destroyed this principle, the great bar to corruption was removed, and the passions at once let loose to run their full career without check, or controul. The introduction therefore of the Atheistical tenets attributed to Epicurus,[a] was the real cause of that rapid depravity of the Roman

---

Thus, as the learned Dr. Warburton justly remarks,

> he took occasion, with a licentiousness 'till then unknown to that august assembly, to explain and inforce the *avowed* principles of Epicurus (of whose sect he was) concerning *the Mortality of the Soul.*

Divine Legation, part 2d. pages 111, 112, last edition. That his manners were notoriously infamous, we may learn from the history of his life in Suetonius, where he is termed *the husband of every woman, and the wife of every man:* Omnium Mulierum virum, & omnium Virorum Mulierum. Sueton. in vit. Jul. Caes. c. 52. ad finem.[11]

a. I here mean the tenets of the *Epicurean Atheists*, as they are termed by the very learned Mr. Baxter in his treatise on the Immortality of the Soul; where he has confuted them at large in the first volume of that admirable work.

Enquiry into the Nature of the Human Soul, Vol. 1. p. 355.[12]

11. The remark about Caesar's omnivorous promiscuity is attributed by Suetonius to the elder Curio (Suetonius, "Divus Iulius," LII.3). William Warburton (1698–1779), bishop of Gloucester, was one of the most pugnacious religious controversialists of Hanoverian England. His *Divine Legation of Moses Demonstrated* (1738–41) is an extraordinary assemblage of ill-digested learning and coarse argumentation, in which he undertook to show that Christianity was the only true religion on flamboyantly paradoxical grounds. Because the Mosaic religion had made no promises about a future state of rewards and punishments (so Warburton insisted) this indicated that God had reserved that doctrine until the proper moment for its promulgation.

12. Andrew Baxter (1686/7–1750), natural philosopher and metaphysician, had published the first edition of his *An Enquiry into the Nature of the Human Soul* in 1733. In this work he had argued (against atheists, deists, and materialists such as Lucretius, Hobbes, and Spinoza) that matter was inert, and so needed to be activated by some immaterial principle. The *Enquiry* went into a second edition in two volumes in 1737, and a third edition, again in two volumes, in 1745. Given that the pagination of volume one in both the second and the third editions is the same, it

manners, which has never been satisfactorily accounted for, either by Sallust, or any other historians.

The learned, I know, are not a little divided in their opinions about Epicurus. But [300] a disquisition into what were, or were not the real tenets of that philosopher, would be wholly foreign to my purpose. By the doctrine of the Epicureans, I mean that system which Lucretius has dressed up in his poem[13] with all the beauties of poetry, and all the elegance of diction. This, like the rest of the Atheistick systems, which are attributed to most of the Grecian philosophers, is pregnant with the wildest absurdities that ever entered into the human imagination. Epicurus, if Lucretius has given us his genuine [301] tenets, ascribes the formation of the universe to the fortuitous concourse of senseless atoms of matter.[a]

---

is not clear which of these editions Montagu is using. In both, however, Section V, titled "*The several arguments against the immateriality of the soul, urged by* Lucretius *and others, examined, and shewn fallacious, as applying the equivocal symptoms of a disordered organ in a state of union to the soul itself*" begins on p. 355. The phrase "*Epicurean* Atheists" occurs on p. 362 of this first volume.

13. Lucretius's *De Rerum Natura* had long been recognized as a poeticizing of the doctrines of Epicurus, whom Lucretius had praised in the opening lines of book three as "the glory of the Grecian race" (*Graiae gentis decus;* III.3). For an example of how Lucretius's materialism, mortalism, and atheism could catch between wind and water those who admired his poetic power see Dryden's remarks in the preface to *Sylvae* (1685), where he develops an explicit comparison of Lucretius with Hobbes in respect of both doctrine and manner.

a. It has been remarked, that the Disciples of the ancient Greek philosophers have blended so many of their own opinions with the Doctrine of their masters, that it is often difficult to distinguish the genuine tenets of the latter, from the spurious ones which have been interpolated by their followers. Thus Epicurus taught that the Summum Bonum or Supreme Good consisted in pleasure. His defenders insist, that he placed it in that refined pleasure which is inseparable from the practice of virtue. His enemies affirm, that he meant the grosser pleasure which arises wholly from the sensual passions. His friends reply, that this Notion was first broached by the dissolute part of his disciples, who most injuriously fathered it upon Epicurus, and then alledged his authority as a plea for their debaucheries: they add, that the true Epicureans, who adhered rigidly to the genuine tenets of their master, always treated these spurious disciples as sophists and impostors. But even allowing this to be a true state of the case; yet that the materiality and dissolution of the human soul at death was a genuine tenet of Epicurus, is a truth which the most sanguine of his admirers are not able to deny.

His master, Democritus, from whom he borrowed his system, asserts the same. But Epicurus has exceeded him in absurdity. For Democritus, if we may credit Plutarch, endowed his atoms with a certain living intelligence, which Epicurus scorns to make use of. He boldly deduces life, intelligence, and free-will itself, from the direct, oblique, and other various motions of his inanimate atoms. He admits a sort of insignificant beings, whom he terms Gods; but as he would not allow them to have any hand in the formation of his universe, so neither will he suffer them to have the least share in the conduct of it. He has shewed them plainly, that he could [302] do without them; and, as he has made them so egregiously insignificant as to be able to do neither good nor harm, he has packed them off at a distance, to live an indolent, lazy life, and to divert themselves just as they think proper. Thus he has got rid of the troublesome doctrine of a divine superintending Providence. Sometimes he forgets himself, and seems to deny their very existence. For he tells us in one place, that the whole universe contains nothing but matter and empty space, or what arises from the casual concurrence of these two principles: Consequently, that no third nature, different from these two, can possibly be proved to exist either by the cognizance of our senses, or by the utmost efforts of

---

As this pernicious tenet therefore was equally held, and publickly taught by both these kinds of Epicureans, a very small knowledge of human nature will enable us to decide, which of the two opposite notions of pleasure was most likely to prevail, and gain the greatest number of proselytes amongst a luxurious and corrupt people.

The dissolute manners of the Romans in the last period of their Republick, prove evidently, in my opinion, that the sensual doctrines of the later Epicureans were almost universally received. And if the evidence of Horace in his humourous description of the manners of those philosophers is to be depended upon, they seem to have ingrossed the *name* of the *sect* wholly to themselves.

> Me pinguem et nitidum bene cura tacute vises;
> Cum ridere voles, *Epicuri de Grege porcum.*
> Hor. Epist. 4. lib. 1.[14]

14. "As for me, when you want a laugh, you will find me in the pink, fat and sleek, a hog from the herd of Epicurus" (Horace, *Epistles*, I.iv.15–16). This poem is addressed to the poet Albius Tibullus (c. 60–19 B.C.), a sensitive and shy man whom Horace is attempting to divert and encourage with an invitation to pass some time at his Sabine farm.

our reasoning faculty.[a] He teaches, that the soul is composed of the finest and most subtile atoms, consequently discerpable[15] and mortal. That the identity of man consists in the union of these finer corpuscles with the grosser ones, which compose the body. That, at [303] their disunion by death, the soul evaporates, and is dissipated in the upper regions, from whence it first distilled, and the same man exists no more.[b] Nay, he is so amazingly absurd as to assert, that if the soul, after its separation, should still retain its consciousness, and, after a length of time, by some lucky jumble of his atoms, should happen to animate another body, this new compound would be quite a different man: Consequently, that this new man would be no more interested in the actions of the former, than the former would be responsible for the behaviour of the latter, or for that of any future man, who might happen hereafter to be produced by another casual assemblage of the atoms of the same soul, united to those

a. Omnis, ut est igitur per se natura duabus
   Consistit rebus; nam corpora sunt et inane.
   Ergo praeter inane et corpora tertia per se.
   Nulla potest rerum in numero natura relinqui
   Nec quae sub census cadat ullo tempore nostros
   Nec ratione animi quam quisquam possit apisci.[16]

b. Et nebula ac sumus quoniam discedit in auras;
   Crede animam quoque diffundi, multoque perire
   Ocius, et citius dissolvi corpora prima,
   Cum semel omnibus è membris ablata recessit.[17]

15. Capable of being separated or detached; divisible (*OED,* "discerptible").

16. "The nature of the universe, therefore—as it is in itself—comprises two things: for there are bodies, and there is emptiness. . . . Therefore, besides emptiness and bodies, no third thing can be left existing in the sum of things—nothing that can ever be grasped by either our senses, or our mental reasoning" (Lucretius, *De Rerum Natura,* I.419–20 and 445–48).

17. "Since both mist and smoke disperse in air, hold to the belief that the soul, too, is spread about and passes away much more quickly, and is more swiftly dissolved into its primary bodies, as soon as it has withdrawn and departed from the limbs of a man" (Lucretius, *De Rerum Natura,* III.436–39). Modern texts of Lucretius read "dissolvi in corpora" and "semel ex hominis membris," and I have translated accordingly (the impact of these variants on the mortalist doctrine Lucretius is advancing in these lines is slight).

of another body.[a] This doctrine is plainly stolen from the Pythagorean system of the transmigration of souls;[18] but mutilated, and miserably perverted to the purposes of Atheism. The absurdities in this wild philosophy are so self-evident, that to attempt a refutation of them, would be an affront to common sense. Yet, from [304] this source, these philosophers draw their pretended consolations against the fear of death: "That at death the identity of the man absolutely ceases, and we totally lose our existence."[b] Yet, from these excellent comforters, our modern sceptics have revived their senseless tenet of annihilation to serve the cause of libertinism.[19] The grand *Desideratum*, in libertinism, is, to be able to give

a. Et si jam nostro sentit de corpore, postquam
   Distracta est animi natura, animaeque potestas:
   Nil tamen hoc ad nos; qui caetu conjugioque
   Corporis atque animae consistimus uniter apti.[20]

b. Nil igitur mors est, ad nos neque pertinet hilum,
   Quandoquidem natura animi mortalis habetur:
   —Ubi non erimus: cum corporis, atque animaï
   Discidium fuerit, quibus è sumus uniter apti,
   Scilicet haud nobis quicquam, qui non erimus tum,
   Accidere omnino poterit, sensumque movere.[21]

18. Pythagoras, the Greek philosopher and mathematician born at Samos c. 580 B.C., taught the doctrine of the transmigration of souls (that is to say, the belief that, on death, the soul is incarnated in another body), and claimed to be able to remember his own earlier incarnations. His doctrines were revived during the early years of the Roman principate, when they were combined with those of Orphism.

19. Originally, free-thinking in the matter of religious doctrine (Fr. *libertinisme*); subsequently, by extension, a disregard of moral restraint and the pursuit of a dissolute way of life (Fr. *libertinage*) (*OED*, 1 and 2). The broader meaning would have been available to Montagu in 1759, although the resonance of the word in this context seems to vibrate between that and the more precise meaning relating to religious doctrine.

20. "And even if the nature of the mind and the power of the spirit is able to feel after being sundered from our body, that is nothing to us, who by the yoking and wedding together of body and spirit exist as a single whole" (Lucretius, *De Rerum Natura*, III.843–46).

21. "Therefore death is nothing to us, it is less than nothing, since the nature of the mind is understood to be mortal. . . . when we shall no longer exist, when the parting of body and spirit from which we are compacted into a whole will have happened, then to be sure nothing whatsoever can happen to us (since we will no longer exist), and nothing will be able to make us feel" (Lucretius, *De Rerum Natura*, III.830–31 and 838–41).

an unbounded loose to the sensual passions to their very utmost extent, without any impertinent hints from a certain disagreeable monitor, called Conscience, and the dread of an after-reckoning. Now as both these terrors are removed by this system of annihilation, it is no wonder that libertines, who abound in a corrupt licentious age, should fly eagerly to so comfortable a doctrine, which at once silences those enemies to their pleasures. This is the creed introduced by the sect of Epicurus amongst the Romans, which easily accounts for that sudden, and universal revolution in their manners. For manners can never be so effectually, and so speedily depraved, as by [305] a total extinction of all religious principle, and all religious principle must be necessarily subverted wherever this doctrine of annihilation is received.[a] I allow that Lucretius gives us some excellent maxims from Epicurus, and inveighs in many places against the vices of his countrymen. But the cheat is too gross and palpable, and only proves, that he has gilt over the pill of Atheism to make it go down more smoothly.[b] For how can a superstructure stand when the foundation is taken away; and of what service is the best system of morality when the sanction of future rewards and punishments, the great motive which should enforce the practice, is removed by the denial of a Providence, and the doctrine of annihilation? Cicero informs us, that all the fine things, which Epicurus asserts of the existence of his Gods, and their excellent nature, are mere grimace,[22] and only thrown out to screen him from censure. For he could not be ignorant, that the laws of his country punished every man with the utmost severity, who

a. Epicurus vero ex animis hominum extraxit radicitus religionem, quum Diis immortalibus et opem et gratiam sustulit. Cic. de Nat. Deor. p. 76 & 77.[23]

b. At etiam liber est Epicuri de sanctitate. Ludimur ab homine non tam faceto, quam ad scribendi licentiam libero. Quae enim potest esse sanctitas, si Dii humana non curant? Cic. de Nat. Deor. p. 78.[24]

22. Affectation, pretense, sham (*OED*, 3).

23. "Epicurus, however, in abolishing divine beneficence and divine benevolence, uprooted and exterminated all religion from the human heart" (Cicero, *De Natura Deorum*, I.xliii.121).

24. "But (so you say) Epicurus wrote a book about holiness. I reply that Epicurus is making fun of us, though he is not so much a humorist as a loose and careless writer. For how can holiness exist if the gods take no interest in the affairs of men?" (Cicero, *De Natura Deorum*, I.xliv.123).

struck at that fundamental principle of all religion, the existence of a [306] Deity. Cicero therefore, who had thoroughly examined his tenets, affirms him, by his own principles, to have been a downright Atheist.[a] For in reality, a man who should assert the existence of such idle Gods, as are neither capable of doing good or hurt, must, if he expects to be believed, be a greater fool than the man, "Who says in his heart there is no God at all." Yet this strange system, though fraught with such absurdities and contradictions as could scarce be palmed upon the genius of an Hottentot,[25] has been implicitly swallowed by too many of those gentlemen, who affect to call themselves the *esprit forts*[26] of the present age. These are the Atheistical tenets of Epicurus, preserved by Lucretius in his beautiful poem, which, like poison, conveyed in sweets, please and murder at the same time.[b] [307]

a. Verius est igitur nimirum illud quod familiaris omnium nostrûm Posidonius disseruit in libro quinto de naturâ Deorum, nullos esse Deos Epicuro videri: quaeque is de Diis immortalibus dixerit, invidiae detestandae gratia dixisse, p. 78.[27]

25. Literally, a native of the southern tip of Africa; metaphorically, a person of inferior intellect and culture.

26. Literally, in French, a "strong-minded" or "strong-spirited" person, and so one who claims to be superior to vulgar prejudices, especially in matters of religion (*OED,* "esprit," 2b). On the continent, Spinoza, and in England, Hobbes, had revived aspects of Epicureanism, particularly its atomism and materialism. Later, cruder and more sensational, expressions of these doctrines included the *L'Homme Machine* (1747) of La Mettrie, and Holbach's *Système de la Nature* (1770); both authors would have figured prominently on a list of *esprits forts* of the later eighteenth century. Mozart's *Cosi fan Tutte* (1790) can be viewed as a wry commentary on this theme in eighteenth-century moral philosophy.

27. "It is doubtless therefore closer to the truth to say, as that good friend of us all, Posidonius, argued in Book V of his *On the Nature of the Gods,* that Epicurus does not really believe in the gods at all, and that he said what he did about the immortal gods only for the sake of deprecating unpopularity" (Cicero, *De Natura Deorum,* I.xliv.123).

b. I am much obliged to the Gentlemen who write the Critical Review for the compliments paid to my little performance in their Review for March 1759.[28] Their candid remarks upon these quotations from Cicero have been truly serviceable; as they have induced me to read over his philosophical works with close attention, as well as the writings of some of our ablest moderns upon that subject.

The principles of the New Academy, that doubting sect, which Cicero had espoused, led so directly to Scepticism, that he keeps us in a state of perpetual

The Greeks were early infected with this execrable doctrine, and shew the effect it [308] had upon their manners by their violation of publick faith, and contempt for the most sacred tyes of religion. Trust, says Polybius, [309] but a single talent to a Greek, who has been used to finger the publick money, and though you have the security of ten counterparts,

---

doubt and uncertainty as to his opinions. Mr. Baxter in his Enquiry into the Nature of the Human Soul, Vol. II. p. 70, complaining of Cicero's inconsistencies and self-contradictions, observes, that

> as philosophers, he teaches men to be Sceptics, or to maintain *that truth is not to be perceived.*

And afterwards adds,

> But it is long since it hath been observed of this *great man,* that his *academical writings are at variance* with his other works; and that he may be confuted out of himself, and in his own words.

Dr. Warburton expatiates largely upon the great difficulties there are in getting to Cicero's *real sentiments.* I shall mention only two of them, and in his own words:

> A fourth difficulty arises from Tully's purpose in writing his works of philosophy; which was, not to deliver his own opinion on any point of Ethics or Metaphysics; but to explain to his Countrymen in the most intelligible manner, whatsoever the Greeks had taught concerning them. In the execution of which design, no sect could so well serve his turn as the *New Academy,* whose principle it was, *not to interfere with their own opinions,* &c. But the principal difficulty proceeds from the *several* and *various* characters he *sustained* in his life and writings; which habituated him to feign and dissemble his opinions. Here (though he acted neither a weak nor an unfair part) he becomes perfectly inscrutable. He may be considered as an orator, a statesman, and a philosopher; characters all equally *personated,* and no one more the *real man* than the other; but each of them taken up and laid down, for the occasion. This appears from the numerous inconsistencies we find in him throughout the course of his sustaining them, &c.

And afterwards, p. 171. the Dr. adds,

> We meet with numbers of the like contradictions delivered in his own person, and under his philosophical character;

of which he gives us several instances. In the note upon the word Personated, p. 169, the Dr. observes;

> that as a philosopher, his end and design in writing was not to deliver his own opinion; but to explain the Grecian philosophy; on which account he

drawn up by as many publick notaries, backed by as many seals, and the testimony of twice as many witnesses, yet, with all these precautions, you cannot possibly prevent him from proving a rogue.[a] Whilst the Romans, who, by their various offices, are intrusted with large sums of the publick money, pay so conscientious a regard to the religion of their office-oath,

---

blames those as too curious, who were for having his own sentiments. In pursuance of his design, he brings in Stoics, Epicureans, Platonists, Academics, New and Old, in order to instruct the Romans in their various opinions, and several ways of reasoning. But whether it be himself or others that are brought upon the stage, it is the *Academic* not Cicero; it is the Stoic, the Epicurean, not Balbus, nor Velleius, who deliver their opinions.

See Warburton's Divine Legation, part 2. book 3. last edition, where the character of Cicero, as drawn by that very learned and able writer, p. 165, &c. is the best clue I know of to guide us through his philosophical works.[29] See also, Critical Inquiry into the Opinions and Practice of the ancient philosophers, passim.

28. See appendix B below.

29. For Warburton, see above, p. 196, n. 11. In 1759 the "last edition" of the *Divine Legation* would have been the fourth edition in two volumes of 1755. In the second volume of that work Warburton draws a detailed portrait of Cicero as a thinker, in which he draws attention to the dissimulating character of many of his philosophical writings (for he was "habituated . . . to feign and dissemble his opinions"); and argues that it is only in Cicero's letters that we receive an undistorted image of Cicero's true beliefs ("It is only . . . in his EPISTLES to his friends, where we see the *man* divested of the *Politician*, the *Sophist*, and the *Advocate*")—beliefs which Warburton characterizes as Epicurean ("this is the very language of the Epicureans"; Warburton, *Divine Legation*, vol. 2, pp. 165–78; quotations on pp. 169, 173–74, and 178).

a. Οἱ τὰ κοινὰ χειρίζοντες παρὰ μὲν τοῖς Ἕλλησιν, ἐὰν ταλάντου μόνον πιστευθῶσιν, ἀντιγραφεῖς ἔχοντες δέκα καὶ σφραγῖδας τοσαύτας καὶ μάρτυρας διπλασίους οὐ δύνανται τηρεῖν τὴν πίστιν· παρὰ δὲ Ῥωμαίοις κατά τε τὰς ἀρχὰς καὶ πρεσβείας πολύ τι πλῆθος χρημάτων χειρίζοντες δι᾽ αὐτῆς τῆς κατὰ τὸν ὅρκον πίστεως τηροῦσι τὸ καθῆκον. Polyb. lib. 6. p. 693.

I have called ἀντιγραφεῖς, Notary-publick, because that office answers the idea much better, in my opinion, than *Contrarotulator*, from which may possibly be derived our Comptroller, which, I think, is by no means what is here meant.[30]

30. "The consequence is that among the Greeks members of the government, if they are entrusted with no more than a talent, though they have ten copyists and as many seals and twice as many witnesses, cannot keep their faith; whereas among the Romans those who, as magistrates and legates, are dealing with large sums of money behave correctly just because they have sworn on oath to do so"; "copyists" (Polybius, VI.lvi.13–14).

that they were never known to violate their faith, though restrained only by that single tye. How greatly they deviated from this rectitude of manners, after these infidel tenets had taken root amongst them, we may learn from Cicero, in his orations and epistles. Sallust too will inform us, how extremely common the crime of perjury was grown, in that severe reproach, which Lucius Philippus, a Patrician, makes to Lepidus, the Consul, before the whole Senate, That he neither stood in awe of men or Gods, whom he had so frequently injured, and defied by his villanies and perjuries.[a]

Polybius gives it as his real opinion, that [310] nothing shews the superior excellence of the civil Government of the Romans to that of other people, so much as those religious sentiments with respect to their Gods, which they constantly inculcated and supported.[b] He affirms too his real sentiments to be, that the chief support and preservation of the Roman Republick arose from that awful fear of the Gods, which was so much ridiculed and exploded by the Grecians. I have taken the liberty to render τοῖς ἄλλοις ἀνθρώποις, the Grecians, who are evidently pointed at [311] in this passage.[c] For so just and accurate a writer as Polybius could not be ignorant, that the Grecians were the only people in the world at that time, who had been debauched into Atheism by the pernicious tenets of Epicurus. Polybius firmly believed the existence of a Deity, and the

a. Te neque hominum neque Deorum pudet, quos perfidia & perjurio violâsti. Sall. Fragm. Orat. L. Phil. Cont. Lep. p. 146.[31]

b. Μεγίστην δέ μοι δοκεῖ διαφορὰν ἔχειν τὸ Ῥωμαίων πολίτευμα πρὸς βέλτιον ἐν τῇ περὶ θεῶν διαλήψει, καί μοι δοκεῖ τὸ παρὰ τοῖς ἄλλοις ἀνθρώποις ὀνειδιζόμενον, τοῦτο συνέχειν τὰ Ῥωμαίων πράγματα, λέγω δὲ τὴν δεισιδαιμονίαν· Polyb. lib. 6. p. 692.[32]

31. "Do you not blush before either men or the gods, whom you have insulted with your perfidy and falsehood?" (Sallust, *Oratio Philippi in Senatu*, XV).

32. "But the quality in which the Roman commonwealth is most distinctly superior is in my opinion the nature of their religious convictions. I believe that it is the very thing which among other peoples is an object of reproach, I mean superstition, which maintains the cohesion of the Roman state" (Polybius, VI.lvi.6–7).

c. There is indeed little occasion for an apology for this translation. The judicious critick will easily see, that in this passage there is a plain contrast drawn between the manners of the Grecians and the Romans in the time of Polybius. The cause of that difference this able writer justly ascribes to that δεισιδαιμονία, or awful fear of the Gods, so strongly inculcated amongst the Romans, and so much despised and ridiculed amongst the Grecians, who were at that time greatly tinctured with the Atheism of Epicurus. The instance he selects in proof, drawn from the very different interposition of a divine superintending Providence, though he was an enemy to superstition. Yet when he observed the good effects produced amongst the Romans by their religion, though carried even to the highest possible degree of superstition, and the remarkable influence it had upon their manners in private life, as well as upon their publick councils,[a] he concludes it [312] to be the result of a wise and consummate policy in the ancient Legislators. He therefore very justly censures those as wrong-headed, and wretchedly bungling politicians, who at that time endeavoured to eradicate the fear of an after-reckoning, and the terrors of a hell, out of the minds of a people.[b] Yet how few years ago did we see this

effect of an oath upon the manners of those two people, must convince us beyond a doubt, that by the words τοῖς ἄλλοις ἀνθρώποις ὀνειδιζομενον, he plainly characterises his own countrymen. As by "οἱ νῦν εἰκῇ καὶ ἀλόγως ἐκβάλλειν αὐτά," they who now (that is, in his time) inconsiderately and absurdly reject those great sanctions of religion, he evidently points at such of the leading men amongst the Romans, as in his time had embraced the pernicious tenets of Epicurus. For though he had stigmatized the Carthaginians immediately before for their avarice and lust of gain, yet no man knew better than Polybius, that the Carthaginians rather exceeded the Romans in superstition. That they were sincere too in their belief, is evident from that most horrible method, by which they expressed their δεισιδαιμονία, which was their frequent sacrifices of great numbers of their own children (those of the very first families not excepted) to their God Moloch, who, by the Greeks and Romans, was termed Chronos and Saturn.

I thought this remark might not be unuseful, because as none of the Commentators have taken any notice of it, so neither Casaubon, nor any translator I have yet met with, seems to have given me the true spirit and meaning of this remarkable passage.[33]

a. Ἐπὶ τοσοῦτον γὰρ ἐκτετραγῴδηται καὶ παρεισῆκται τοῦτο τὸ μέρος παρ᾽ αὐτοῖς εἴς τε τοὺς κατ᾽ ἰδίαν βίους καὶ τὰ κοινὰ τῆς πόλεως ὥστε μὴ καταλιπεῖν ὑπερβολήν. Ibid.[34]

b. Διόπερ οἱ παλαιοὶ δοκοῦσί μοι τὰς περὶ θεῶν ἐννοίας καὶ τὰς ὑπὲρ τῶν ἐν ᾅδου διαλήψεις οὐκ εἰκῇ καὶ ὡς ἔτυχεν εἰς τὰ πλήθη παρεισαγαγεῖν, πολὺ δὲ μᾶλλον οἱ νῦν εἰκῇ καὶ ἀλόγως ἐκβάλλειν αὐτά. Lib. 6. p. 693.[35]

33. "Superstition" (Polybius, VI.lvi.7); "[which] among other people is an object of reproach" (Polybius, VI.lvi.7); "the moderns are foolish to banish such beliefs" (Polybius, VI.lvi.12).

34. "These matters are clothed in such pomp and introduced to such an extent into their public and private life that nothing could exceed it, a fact which will surprise many" (Polybius, VI.lvi.8).

35. "For this reason I think, not that the ancients acted rashly and at haphazard in introducing among the people notions concerning the gods and beliefs in the terrors of hell, but that the moderns are most rash and foolish in banishing such beliefs" (Polybius, VI.lvi.12).

miserably mistaken policy prevail in our own country, during the whole administration of some late power-engrossing ministers.[36] Compelled at all events to secure a majority in Parliament to support themselves against the efforts of opposition, they found the greatest obstacle to their schemes arise from those principles of religion, which yet remained amongst the people. For though a great number of the electors were not at all averse to the bribe, yet their consciences were too tender to digest perjury.[37] To remove this troublesome test at elections, which is one of the bulwarks of our constitution, would be impracticable. To weaken or destroy those principles, upon which the oath was founded, and from which it derived its force and obligation, would equally answer the purpose, and de-[313] stroy all publick virtue at the same time. The bloody and deep-felt effects of that hypocrisy which prevailed in the time of Cromwell,[38] had driven great numbers of the sufferers into the contrary extreme. When therefore so great a part of the nation was already prejudiced against whatever carried the appearance of a stricter piety, it is no wonder that shallow superficial reasoners, who have not Logic enough to distinguish between the use and abuse of a thing, should readily embrace those Atheistical tenets, which were imported, and took root in the voluptuous and thoughtless

36. Another censorious reference to the policies of Sir Robert Walpole; see above, p. 88, n. 155.

37. Blackstone gives a detailed account of the measures taken at the time of an election to Parliament to guard against "undue influence" being exerted over the casting of votes, including a liberal recourse to oaths: "the sheriff or other returning officer first taking an oath against bribery, and for the due execution of his office. The candidates likewise, if required, must swear to their qualification; and the electors in counties to theirs; and the electors both in counties and boroughs are also compellable to take the oath of abjuration and that against bribery and corruption. And it might not be amiss, if the members elected were bound to take the latter oath, as well as the former; which in all probability would be much more effectual, than administring it only to the electors" (Blackstone, *Commentaries,* vol. 1, pp. 173–74).

38. Montagu suggests that the triumph of puritanism during the Interregnum (1649–60), which he stigmatizes as "hypocrisy," aroused an antipathy toward overt piety among those of more moderate religious opinions; and that this antipathy created a climate propitious for the flourishing of religious unbelief.

reign of Charles the Second. But that solid learning,[39] which revived after
the Restoration, easily baffled the efforts of open and avowed Atheism,
which from that time has taken shelter under the less obnoxious name
of Deism.[40] For the principles of modern Deism, when stript of that disguise which has been artfully thrown over them, to deceive those who
hate the fatigue of thinking, and are ever ready to admit any conclusion
in argument, which is agreeable to their passions, without examining the
premises, are in reality the same with those of Epicurus, as transmitted
to us by Lucretius. The influence therefore, which they had upon the
manners of the Greeks and Romans, will readily account for those effects
which we experience from them in [314] our own country, where they
so fatally prevail.[41] To patronize and propagate these principles, was the
best expedient which the narrow selfish policy of those ministers could
suggest. For their greatest extent of genius never reached higher, than a
fertility in temporary shifts and expedients, to stave off the evil day of
national account, which they so much dreaded. They were sensible that
the wealth and luxury, which are the general effects of an extensive trade
in a state of profound peace, had already greatly hurt the morals of the
people, and smoothed the way for their grand system of corruption. Far
from checking this licentious spirit of luxury and dissipation, they left it
to its full and natural effects upon the manners, whilst, in order to corrupt
the principles of the people, they retained, at the publick expence, a venal
set of the most shameless miscreants that ever abused the liberty of the

39. On the Church of England during the Restoration, and its scholarly achieve-
ments, see John Spurr, *The Restoration Church of England, 1646–1689* (New Haven
and London: Yale University Press, 1991).

40. Whereas atheism implies a positive disbelief in the existence of any god or
gods, deism implies acceptance of the existence of a supreme being, but denial of
the revelations and supernatural doctrines of Christianity (or indeed of any other
religion).

41. The 1750s were a period of moral crisis in England, with many commentators diagnosing a decline in public morals, most notably John Brown, *An Estimate
of the Manners and Principles of the Times* (1757). Victories in the last four years of the
Seven Years' War (1756–63) went some way toward dissipating these apprehensions
of imminent moral collapse.

press, or insulted the religion of their country. To the administration of such ministers, which may justly be termed the grand aera of corruption, we owe that fatal system of bribery, which has so greatly affected the morals of the electors in almost every borough in the kingdom. To that too we may justly attribute the present contempt and disregard of the sacred obligation of an oath, which is the strongest bond of society, and the best security and support of civil government. [315]

I have now, I hope, satisfactorily accounted for that rapid and unexampled degeneracy of the Romans, which brought on the total subversion of that mighty Republick. The cause of this sudden and violent change of the Roman manners, has been just hinted at by the sagacious Montesquieu,[42] but, to my great surprize, has not been duly attended to by any one historian I have yet met with.[a] I have shewed too, how the same cause

---

a. I have been favoured with the following remark upon this passage.

I have lately met with an obscure book, entitled, Christian Morals, and Christian Prudence, by *John Lawrence*, M. A. rector of *Yelvertoft, Northamptonshire*, printed for *Knapton*, 1717, in which are these words:—But as soon as Epicurus and his followers began to weaken the foundation principles of religion, by calling them in question, all manner of immorality came rolling in like a mighty torrent, and threw down the banks of law and sobriety.

The book indeed I never heard of before, and as I have not the honour to know the gentleman who sent me the remark, I take this opportunity of returning him thanks for his very obliging letter.

42. Charles-Louis de Secondat, baron de Montesquieu (1689–1755), man of letters and political philosopher. In chapter ten of his *Considérations sur les causes de la grandeur des Romains et de leur décadence* (1734), entitled "De la Corruption des Romains," he writes: "Je crois que la Secte d'Epicure qui s'introduisit à Rome sur la fin de la République contribua beaucoup à gâter le coeur & l'esprit des Romains. Les Grecs en avoient été infatués avant eux; aussi avoient-ils été plûtot corrompus. Polybe nous dit que de son tems les sermens ne pouvoient donner de la confiance pour un Grec; au lieu qu'un Romain en étoit, pour ainsi dire, enchainé." (I believe that the sect of Epicurus which was introduced into Rome at the end of the Republic contributed greatly toward spoiling the hearts and minds of the Romans. The Greeks had been infatuated with it before them; so too were they corrupted by it. Polybius tells us that in his day oaths would not make a Greek trustworthy, whereas a Roman was, so to speak, bound by them. Montesquieu, *Considérations*, p. 160.)

has been working the same effects in our own nation, as it invariably will in every country where those fatally destructive principles are admitted. As the real end of all history is instruction, I have held up a just portrait of the Roman manners, in the times immediately preceding the loss of their liberty, to the inspection of my countrymen, that they may guard in time against those calamities, [316] which will be the inevitable consequence of the like degeneracy. The unpromising aspect of our affairs, at the time of the sudden and unexpected alliance between the houses of Bourbon and Austria,[43] gave the first rise to these reflections. But as the interests and situation of this kingdom, with respect to France, are so greatly analogous to those of Carthage with respect to Rome, I shall proceed to compare the different manners, policy, and military conduct of those two rival nations. By thus comparing the different policy of these warlike people, whose views and interests were as diametrically opposite, and as irreconcileable as those of Great Britain and France, we may learn the superior advantages which each enjoyed, and the different disadvantages arising from their different policy, which each people laboured under, during their long and inveterate contests. The result, which I most sincerely wish from this inquiry, is, that we may avoid those egregious blunders on the side of the Romans, which reduced them to the very brink of ruin, and those more capital defects on the part of the Carthaginians, which terminated in the utter destruction of their very being as a people.

43. The House of Bourbon was at this time the royal house of France. In the mid-1750s the customary alliances between the various nations of Europe had been overturned in the so-called *renversement des alliances*. In the aftermath of the War of the Austrian Succession (1740–48), George II had been anxious to secure the safety of Hanover, and this was most easily accomplished by an alliance with Prussia, embodied in the Convention of Westminster of 16 January 1756. The formation of an alliance with Prussia, however, entailed the abandonment of Britain's "Old System" of alliance with the Dutch and the Austrians. The Dutch were by now in serious decline as a major European power, and could be cast off with impunity. However, the much more powerful Austrians entered into an alliance with the French, embodied in the first Treaty of Versailles of 1 May 1756, with which the Russians later associated themselves on 11 January 1757. This casual aside by Montagu serves to date the beginning of composition of his work to the summer of 1756.

CHAPTER VII

Carthaginians and Romans Compared

The origin of both these people seems alike to have been extremely low. Romulus, according to Dionysius of Halicarnassus, could form no more than three thousand foot and three hundred horse out of his whole people, where every individual was obliged to be a soldier. The Tyrians, who accompanied Dido in her flight from her brother Pygmalion,[1] could be but few in number from the very circumstances of their escape from an avaritious and vigilant Tyrant.

Romulus, to supply this defect, not only opened an asylum for all fugitives, whom he admitted as subjects, but in all his conquests over the neighbouring States, annexed the lands to his own small territory, and incorporated the prisoners amongst his own Roman citizens. By this masterly policy, notwithstanding the number of men he must necessarily have lost during a warlike reign of thirty-seven years, he left at his death, according to Dionysius, forty-five thousand foot and a thousand horse. As the

---

1. A reference to the founding myth of Carthage, which the disguised Venus recounts to her son Aeneas when he lands on the coast of North Africa having fled from Troy (Virgil, *Aeneid,* I.335–68).

same [318] policy was pursued under the Republican as under the regal government, the Romans, though involved in continual wars, found themselves not inferior in number even to those nations, who were reputed the most populous. Dionysius, from whom I have taken this account, extols the policy of the Romans in this point as greatly superior to that of the Grecians. The Spartans, says that judicious historian, were obliged to give up their dominion over Greece by their single defeat at Leuctra; as the loss of the battle of Chaeronea reduced the Thebans and Athenians to the sad necessity of yielding up the government of Greece, as well as their liberty, to the Macedonians. These misfortunes Dionysius imputes to the mistaken policy of the Grecians, who were, in general, unwilling to communicate the privileges of their respective States to foreigners. Whereas the Romans, who admitted even their enemies to the rights of citizenship, derived additional strength even from their misfortunes. And he affirms, that after the terrible defeat at Cannae, where out of eighty-six thousand little more than three thousand three hundred and seventy men escaped, the Romans owed the preservation of their State, not to the benevolence of fortune, as some, he says, imagine, but to the number of their disciplined Militia, which [319] enabled them to encounter every danger. I am sensible that the remarks of Dionysius, which have been adopted by many of our modern writers, are extremely just in relation to the Thebans and Athenians. Because as the former of these people endeavoured to extend their dominions by arms, the latter both by arms and commerce, both States ought, like the Romans, to have attracted as many foreigners as possibly they could, to enable them to execute plans which require an inexhaustible supply of people. But the exclusion of foreigners ought not, in my opinion, to be censured as a defect in the Spartan constitution. Because it is evident, from the testimony of Polybius and Plutarch, that the great end which Lycurgus proposed by his laws, was not to increase the wealth and power of his countrymen, but to preserve the purity of their manners: as his military regulations, according to the same authors, were not calculated for making conquests and serving the purposes of ambition, but for the defence and security of his Republick. I observe too, in proof of my opinion, that the Spartans gradually lost their virtue, and afterwards their liberty, only so far as they deviated from the institutions of their legislator—But I return from the digression into which this subject unavoidably led me. [320]

In our researches back into the remote times of antiquity, we must lay hold of whatever helps we are able to meet with. If Justin therefore is to be credited, Dido not only received considerable assistance from a colony of Tyrians which she found settled in Utica, but admitted great numbers of the natives who settled with her in the new city, and consequently became Carthaginians.[a] I may add too, in proof of this account, that unless the Carthaginians had long pursued this wise policy, it is scarce possible, by the course of nature, that the Tyrians alone could have multiplied by propagation to so prodigious a degree, as to be able to furnish men sufficient to raise and carry on that extensive commerce, and plant those numerous colonies which we meet with in the earlier ages of their history.

As to their constitution, Rome and Carthage were both Republicks, both free, and their form of Government nearly similar, as far as we can collect from history. Two Supreme Magistrates, annually elected, the Senate, and the people, formed the body politick in each Republick.[b] The annual elections of their chief magistrates, were a per-[321]manent source of division and faction alike in both; a defect which Lycurgus guarded against in the Spartan government, where the chief magistracy was perpetual and hereditary. The Senate in both nations was composed out of the most respectable and greatest men in each Republick. At Rome the Consuls chose the Senators with the approbation of the people, but at last the Censors arrogated that power to themselves. At Carthage, as Aristotle informs us, the Senators were elected; but as he has no where told us who were the electors, it is most probable, that the right of election was the inherent privilege of the people, since he censures that Republick as too much leaning towards Democracy. At Rome, in the virtuous times of that Republick, birth and merit alone intitled the possessor to a place in the Senate, as well as the chief offices in the State. At Carthage, though birth and merit seem to have been qualifications indispensably necessary, yet even these could not succeed, unless the

a. Justin. lib. 18. c. 5.[2]
b. Termed consuls by the Romans, *Sufetes* by the Carthaginians.
2. Justin, *Epitoma*, XVIII.v.12.

candidate was at the same time master of such a fortune[a] as would enable
him to support his dignity with lus-[322]tre.[b] This Aristotle censures as a
defect. For he looks upon all that merit, which was unsupported by the
proper proportion of wealth, as so much lost to the Carthaginians; and he
lays down that maxim in their Government, as the real cause of that undue
respect for wealth, and that lust of gain, which prevailed so much in that
Republick. But the sentiments of this philosopher, like those of his master
Plato, are, I fear, too ideal to be reduced to practice. For he does not seem to
attend to the different genius of different nations, but aims at adjusting the
balance of power in his Republick by the nice standard of philosophick theory. The genius of nations differs perhaps as much as their climate and situation,[3] which seem (at least in some degree) to be the natural cause of that
difference. The Republicks of Sparta and Rome were both military, and
military glory stamped the primary character of both these people. The
Republick of Carthage, like that of their ancestors, the Tyrians, was commercial. Hence the lust of gain marked their ruling character. Their military
character arose from the necessity of defending that wealth which their
commerce had acquired. Hence military glory was but a secondary passion,
and generally subservient to their lust of gain. Unless we attend to the different ruling passion,[4] which forms the dif-[323]ferent character of each

a. Οὐ γὰρ μόνον ἀριστίνδην ἀλλὰ καὶ πλουτίνδην οἴονται δεῖν αἱρεῖσθαι τοὺς
ἄρχοντας. Arist. de Repub. lib. 2. p. 334. c. 11.[5]

b. Αἱροῦνται γὰρ εἰς δύο ταῦτα βλέποντες, καὶ μάλιστα τὰς μεγίστας, τούς τε
βασιλεῖς καὶ τοὺς στρατηγούς. Ibid. p. 335.[6]

3. A glance toward the, at this time, fashionable doctrine of impersonal causes
in history, such as climate and geography, which had been popularized by Montesquieu in Books 14–18 of De l'esprit des lois (1748).

4. The ruling passion was a theory of vulgar psychology which traced the appar-
ently incoherent or various actions of individuals to the operation of a single, domi-
nant impulse. The most famous statement of the doctrine is to be found in Pope's
Epistle to Cobham (1734), ll. 174–265, which begins: "Search then the Ruling Pas-
sion: There alone, | The Wild are constant, and the Cunning known; | The Fool
consistent, and the False sincere; | Priests, Princes, Women, no dissemblers here. |
This clue once found, unravels all the rest" (ll. 174–78). See also Edward Young,
Love of Fame, the Universal Passion (1728).

5. "They think that the rulers should be chosen not only for their merit but also
for their wealth" (Aristotle, Politics, II.xi.8).

6. "For there [in Carthage] elections are made with an eye to these two qualifications, and especially elections to the most important offices, those of the kings
and of the generals" (Aristotle, Politics, II.xi.9).

Republick, we shall never be able to make such a comparison as will do equal justice to each people. At Sparta and Rome wealth was despised, when put in competition with honour, and poverty joined with merit formed the most estimable of all characters. Quite different maxims prevailed at Carthage. Wealth with them was the chief support of merit, and nothing was so contemptible as poverty. Hence the Carthaginians, who were well acquainted with the power and influence of wealth, required the additional qualification of an ample fortune in all candidates for the senatorial dignity, and publick employments. For they judged that such men would be less exposed to the temptations of corruption, and at the same time more anxious for the welfare of a State in which they were so deeply interested by their private property. That this was the real state of the case, at Carthage, notwithstanding the suggestions of Aristotle and the Greek and Roman historians, may, I think, be fairly proved from the behaviour of their Senate and the choice of their officers, which ought certainly to be admitted as the best evidence. For we constantly find all their publick employments filled up with men of the greatest families, and, unless when the intrigues of faction sometimes prevailed, of the greatest abilities. [324] We find in general the same firm and steady attachment to the service of their country, and the same indefatigable zeal for extending the territories and power of their Republick. Nor does the most partial historian charge any one of them with sacrificing the honour and interest of his country to any foreign power for money: a practice which was shamefully common amongst the Roman Generals in the time of Jugurtha. Hence we may, I think, assign the true reason, why the greatest families in Carthage, as we are informed by historians, thought it no way derogatory to their honour to engage in commerce. For as this is most probably to be understood of the younger sons of their nobility, the true motive seems to arise, not from avarice, as their enemies object, but from a view of raising such a fortune, as might qualify them for admission into the Senate, or any of the great employments. Hence too it is evident, that a regulation which might be highly useful and salutary, in an opulent commercial Republick, would be greatly injurious to such military Republicks as Rome and Sparta, by corrupting their manners. We need no other proof than the fate of those two Republicks, who both owed their ruin to the introduction of that wealth, which was unknown to their virtuous ancestors. The Carthaginian Senate seems to have been much more [325] numerous than the

Roman. For at Carthage there was a select standing committee established, of one hundred and four of the most respectable members, to keep a watchful eye over the great families, and repress any attempts which their ambition might make to subvert the constitution.[a] To this committee all their commanding officers by sea and land, without exception, were obliged to give a strict account of their conduct at the end of every campaign. We may therefore properly term it the Carthaginian court-martial. Out of this venerable body another select committee was formed of five members only, who were most conspicuous for their probity, ability, and experience. These served without fee or salary; as glory, and the love of their country, were esteemed motives sufficient to engage men of their superior rank, and character, to serve the publick with zeal and fidelity.[b] For which reason they were not chosen by lot, but elected by merit. Their power was very [326] extensive. Their office was for life, and they filled up any vacancy in their own body, out of the one hundred and four, and all vacancies in that grand committee, out of the rest of the Senate, by their own authority, and at their own discretion.[c] They were the supreme judges, besides, in all causes whatsoever without appeal. The institution of this grand committee, in my opinion,

a. Ἔχει δὲ παραπλήσια τῇ Λακωνικῇ πολιτείᾳ τὰ μὲν συσσίτια τῶν ἑταιριῶν τοῖς φιδιτίοις, τὴν δὲ τῶν ἑκατὸν καὶ τεττάρων ἀρχὴν τοῖς ἐφόροις (πλὴν οὐ χεῖρον· οἱ μὲν γὰρ ἐκ τῶν τυχόντων εἰσί, ταύτην δ᾽ αἱροῦνται τὴν ἀρχὴν ἀριστίνδην). Ibid. p. 334.[7]

b. Τὸ δ᾽ ἀμίσθους καὶ μὴ κληρωτὰς ἀριστοκρατικὸν θετέον, καὶ εἴ τι τοιοῦτον ἕτερον. Ibid.[8]

c. Τὸ δὲ τὰς πενταρχίας κυρίας οὔσας πολλῶν καὶ μεγάλων ὑφ᾽ αὑτῶν αἱρετὰς εἶναι, καὶ τὴν τῶν ἑκατὸν ταύτας αἱρεῖσθαι τὴν μεγίστην ἀρχήν, ἔτι δὲ ταύτας πλείονα ἄρχειν χρόνον τῶν ἄλλων (καὶ γὰρ ἐξεληλυθότες ἄρχουσι καὶ μέλλοντες) ὀλιγαρχικόν. Ibid.[9]

7. "Points in which the Carthaginian constitution resembles the Spartan are the common mess-tables of its Comradeships corresponding to the Phiditia, and the magistracy of the Hundred and Four corresponding to the Ephors (except one point of superiority—the Ephors are drawn from any class, but the Carthaginians elect this magistracy by merit)" (Aristotle, *Politics*, II.xi.3).

8. "Their receiving no pay and not being chosen by lot and other similar regulations must be set down as aristocratic" (Aristotle, *Politics*, II.xi.7).

9. "The appointment by co-optation of the Boards of Five which control many important matters, and the election by these boards of the supreme magistracy of the Hundred, and also their longer tenure of authority than that of any other officers (for they are in power after they have demitted office and before they have actually entered upon it) are oligarchical features" (Aristotle, *Politics*, II.xi.7).

exceeded every thing in the Roman policy. For it preserved their State from all those violent concussions, which so frequently shook, and at last totally subverted the Roman Republick.[a] But the power of the committee of five was exorbitant, and dangerous to the lives and fortunes of their fellow-citizens. The proof is from fact. For at the conclusion of the second Punick war, they had made so arbitrary an use of their power, and were grown so odious to the people, that the great Hannibal regulated that amongst other abuses, and procured a [327] law, which made that office annual and elective, with a clause forbidding any future alteration. Whether the Carthaginian Senators enjoyed their seats for life, or whether they were liable to be expelled for any misdemeanour, and by whom, are points in which history is quite silent. At Rome, as the censors had the power of promoting to that dignity, so they had equally the power of expelling any member for bad manners, by the single ceremony of leaving out his name when they called over the list of the Senate. I cannot help thinking this a great defect in the Roman polity: since it threw the power of garbling[10] and modelling the Senate into the hands of two men, who were liable to be corrupted to serve the ends of faction. A power which ought never to be lodged in so few hands in a country which enjoys the blessings of liberty. For how serviceable soever it might have been, as a curb to licentiousness in the earlier ages of that Republick; yet Cicero, in his Oration for A. Cluentius, inveighs bitterly against the abuse of the censorial power in his time, and gives several instances where it was made subservient to the ends of faction in modelling the Senate.[11] And he seems to fear that the censors list may bring as many calamities upon the citizens as the late most inhuman proscription; and that the point of the cen-[328]sors pen may prove as terrible as the sword of their late Dictator.

---

a. Σημεῖον δὲ πολιτείας συντεταγμένης τὸ τὸν δῆμον ἔχουσαν διαμένειν ἐν τῇ τάξει τῆς πολιτείας καὶ μήτε στάσιν, ὅ τι καὶ ἄξιον εἰπεῖν, γεγενῆσθαι μήτε τύραννον. Ibid.[12]

10. "Sifting" or "weeding" an army or other body of men, so as to exclude unfit or uncompliant members (OED, 2b).

11. Cicero, Pro Cluentio, XLII–XLVIII.

12. "Proof that its constitution is well-regulated is that the populace willingly remain faithful to the constitutional system, and that neither civil strife has arisen in any degree worth mentioning, nor yet a tyrant" (Aristotle, Politics, II.xi.2).

C. Nepos, in the life of Hamilcar, takes notice of an officer of the same nature amongst the Carthaginians, to whose inspection the greatest men in that Republick seem to have been subject.[13] But it does not appear from history, whether his power extended so far as to expel a Senator. Should a bad prince, or a wicked minister, ever be invested with the power of weeding the house, and modelling a parliament at pleasure, there would be an end of our constitution and liberty.

In the Roman Senate all questions were decided (as in our parliament) by a majority of voices. At Carthage no law could pass, unless the Senate were unanimous, like the Polish diet.[14] One single Veto from any one member, took the question out of the hands of the Senate, and gave up the ultimate decision to the people, who were the *dernier ressort* of all power.[15] This Aristotle censures as inclining more towards Democracy [329] than was consistent with the just rules of a well regulated Republick.[a] Because the magistrates were not only obliged to open all the different opinions and debates of the Senators upon the question, in the hearing of the people, who were the absolute and decisive judges in all these cases of appeal; but any one, even the lowest fellow in the mob, might freely give his opinion in opposition just as he thought proper. A source of endless

a. Τοῦ μὲν γὰρ τὰ μὲν προσάγειν, τὰ δὲ μὴ προσάγειν πρὸς τὸν δῆμον οἱ βασιλεῖς κύριοι μετὰ τῶν γερόντων, ἂν ὁμογνωμονῶσι πάντες· εἰ δὲ μή, καὶ τούτων ὁ δῆμος· ἃ δ᾽ ἂν εἰσφέρωσιν οὗτοι, οὐ διακοῦσαι μόνον ἀποδιδόασι τῷ δήμῳ τὰ δόξαντα τοῖς ἄρχουσιν, ἀλλὰ κύριοι κρίνειν εἰσὶ καὶ τῷ βουλομένῳ τοῖς εἰσφερομένοις ἀντειπεῖν ἔξεστιν, ὅπερ ἐν ταῖς ἑτέραις πολιτείαις οὐκ ἔστιν. Ibid. pag. 334.[16]

13. Cornelius Nepos, "Hamilcar," XXII.iii.

14. In 1652 the Polish *sejm*, or diet, had adopted what was to become the notorious principle of *liberum veto*, under which a single negative vote was sufficient to defeat a proposal. Adopted as a safeguard of liberty, in practice it increasingly condemned the Polish government to impotence; for example, during the reign of Augustus II (1697–1733), ten out of eighteen *sejms* were paralyzed by the use of *liberum veto*.

15. Literally "the last resort"; in this jurisdictional context, a court of final appeal.

16. "The reference of some matters and not of others to the popular assembly rests with the kings in consultation with the elders in case they agree unanimously, but failing that, these matters also rest with the people; and when the kings introduce business in the assembly, they do not merely let the people sit and listen to the decisions that have been taken by their rulers, but the people have the sovereign decision and anybody who wishes may speak against the proposals introduced, a right that does not exist under other constitutions" (Aristotle, *Politics,* II.xi.5–6).

discord, anarchy, and confusion! A kind of polity, as Aristotle observes, unknown in any other form of Republican government.

In this point, I think the Roman polity far preferable to the Carthaginian, except in those abuses of the tribunitial power, which so frequently happened towards the decline of that Republick. But when any one turbulent, seditious tribune, instigated by ambition, or corrupted by a faction (which in those times was generally the case) could by his single Veto, stop all proceedings of the Senate, and haul the case before the people; nay, when he could drag the supreme magistrates, the Consuls themselves, to prison, by his sole authority, and could commit the most outrageous, and most shameful acts of licentiousness with impunity, because their office rendered their persons sacred by law, I esteem the Carthaginian polity infinitely [330] more eligible.[17] For that fear and jealousy of ceding any part of their authority, which is so natural to men in power, would always be a strong motive to union in a Carthaginian Senate; because it would naturally induce any member, rather to give up his private opinion, than suffer an essential part of their power to devolve to the people. But the Roman tribunitial power, which was in constant opposition to the Senatorial, drew at last by much too great a weight into the Democratick scale, and in the last period of their liberty was a principal leading cause of the ruin of that Republick. For as the Senate was unsupported by a third power, so essentially requisite to preserve the balance of government in its due aequipoise, the Tribunes perpetually fomented and kept up those terrible feuds, which brought on Anarchy, and terminated in absolute insupportable Tyranny.

The condition of the Roman populace before the erection of the tribunitial power, seems, in my judgment, to have been little better than that state of vassalage, which the peasants groan under in Poland.[18] The relation

17. Preferable (*OED* 3).

18. In the eighteenth century Polish peasants were serfs, and landowners (who were the absolute masters of both their lands and the people who worked them) were entitled to their unpaid services (the so-called *pańszczyzna*). Serfdom was regularized in Poland at approximately the same time as slavery in America, and "lasted almost as long." The emancipation of the serfs occurred in a piecemeal fashion during the first half of the nineteenth century, full emancipation being achieved only with the *ukaz* of 3 March 1861, in the Russian partition of what had been Poland (Davies, *Poland*, vol. 1, pp. 280 and 350; vol. 2, pp. 185 and 188).

between Patron and Client amongst the Romans, seems to be something analogous to the relation between Lord and Vassal, with this difference, that the Client had the free choice of his patron, which the [331] Vassal has not with respect to the Lord. At least it is certain, if we may credit the Roman historians, that their people were subject to equal, if not greater exactions and oppressions from the Patricians. How heavy these were, we may learn from the numerous mutinies, insurrections, and that great secession, which compelled the Patricians to create the tribunitial office in their favour. This new office occasioned a great revolution in their new government, and produced those perpetual conflicts between the Aristocratick and Democratick powers, which fill the history of that Republick. The Patricians had recourse frequently to their only resource, a Dictator with absolute power, to defend them from the insolence of the Tribunes. But this was only a temporary expedient. The people renewed their attacks, 'till they had abolished the distinct prerogatives arising from birth and family, and laid open all honours, even the Consulship, and Dictatorship, the supreme magistracy of all, to the free admission of their own body. The people were highly elated with these repeated victories, as they imagined them, over their old enemies the Patricians; but they were quickly sensible, that in fact, they were only the dupes of their ambitious leaders. The most opulent and powerful of the Plebeians, by serving the high offices of [332] the State, acquired the title of Nobles, in contradistinction to those, who were descended from the Patrician families, who still retained their ancient appellation. These new Nobles, many of whom had crept into the Senate, sided constantly with the Patricians in all disputes and contests with their former friends, the people, and were generally their greatest enemies. The Patricians, strengthened by this new acquisition of power, were frequently too hard for the Tribunes. In those memorable contests with the two Gracchi,[19] who endeavoured in

19. Tiberius Sempronius Gracchus (d. 133 B.C.) and Gaius Sempronius Gracchus (d. 121 B.C.); two brothers who, notwithstanding the fact that they were themselves patricians, used the office of tribune of the plebs to address long-standing inequities of land distribution which had resulted in, on the one hand, the creation of vast estates, and on the other, the suppression of small-scale agriculture (on which see Sallust, *Bellum Jugurthinum*, XLI.1–10). Both Gracchi lost their lives in the violence stirred up by their far-sighted reforms. Plutarch composed biographies of both men. See also Sallust, *Bellum Jugurthinum*, XLII.1–3.

their Tribuneship to revive the Agrarian law (calculated to divide the conquered lands among the poor citizens) the dispute seems to have lain wholly between the rich and the poor: for the Nobles and rich Plebeians were as unwilling to part with their land, as the Patricians. This strengthened the Patricians so much, that they were able in each of those contests, to quell the efforts of the people by force, and quash the whole affair by the death of both the Gracchi.

It has been a general remark of most writers, both ancient and modern, that the Roman Republick owed its preservation to the firmness and wisdom of the Senate, and the subordinate obedience of the people: and that the Republick of Carthage must ascribe its ruin to that ascendency, which the [333] people had usurped over the authority of the Senate. The reverse of this seems to be the truth. We meet with but one instance in history, where the power of the Carthaginian people over-ruled the authority of their Senate, so far as to compel them to act contrary to their opinion. This was that shameful violation of the law of nations in seizing the transports which were bringing necessaries to Scipio's camp, during the truce he had granted that they might send ambassadors to Rome to negotiate a peace with the Roman Senate. For though they threatened violence to the Senate, if they submitted to those hard terms which were imposed by Scipio after the defeat at Zama; yet they were easily reduced to obedience by Hannibal, and resigned the whole affair to the decision of the Senate. The Roman history, on the contrary, is one continued detail of animosities, and frequently most bloody contests, between the Senate and the people in their perpetual struggles for power. And the frequent elections of that low Plebeian Marius[20] to the consular dignity, in opposition to the Patricians, the malignant effects of the overbearing power of

20. Gaius Marius (157–86 B.C.), who although born into a family which had never before held high office in the Roman state, was tribune of the plebs and thereafter consul on no fewer than seven occasions. A successful military commander, who cut his teeth in the war with Jugurtha, Marius reformed the Roman army from a citizen militia with a property qualification to a professional army of volunteers recruited from all classes. His final years were dominated by a struggle with Sulla, the leader of the aristocratic party in Rome. Plutarch composed a life of Marius. See also Sallust, *Bellum Jugurthinum*, LXIII.1–7.

the people, opened that scene of blood and anarchy, which ended only in the utter subversion of their liberty and constitution. [334]

The judicious Montesquieu observes,

> that the Carthaginians grew rich much sooner than the Romans, and consequently sunk much sooner into corruption.

He adds too;

> that whilst merit alone entitled the possessor to the great employments at Rome, every thing which the public at Carthage had the power of bestowing, was venal.[21]

The former part of this assertion is too general to be admitted without proper restrictions, the latter is a plain transcript from Polybius. The Carthaginians must have been rich several ages before the Romans. For both Herodotus and Thucydides, (who was but thirteen years younger) take notice of them as a very formidable maritime power, a circumstance which could only arise from their naval genius and extensive commerce. Yet we find no instance of their being corrupt, 'till the conclusion of the second Punick war, when Hannibal reformed those shameful abuses, which had crept into the management of the publick revenue, and restrained that power which the committee of five had usurped over the lives and fortunes of their fellow-citizens. As for the quotation out of Polybius, whose country was at that time a province to the Romans, with whom he resided only as a state prisoner; I esteem it as no more than a compliment

---

21. A free and selective translation of a passage from chapter four of Montesquieu's *Considérations sur les causes de la grandeur des Romains et de leur décadence:* "Carthage devenuë riche plûtôt que Rome, avoit aussi été plûtôt corrompuë: ainsi pendant qu'à Rome les emplois publics ne s'obtenoient que par la vertu, & ne donnoient d'utilité que l'honneur, & une préference aux fatigues, tout ce que le public peut donner aux Particuliers se venoit à Carthage, & tout service rendu par les Particuliers y étoit payé par le public" (Carthage, having become wealthy earlier than Rome, was also corrupted earlier: so while at Rome public office was the reward of virtue, and gave no benefit aside from honor and a preference for hard work, in Carthage everything which the state could offer to individuals was for sale, and the state paid for all services rendered to it by individuals. Montesquieu, *Considérations,* p. 110).

to the Roman vanity at [335] the expence of the Carthaginians, whose very name was odious to that people. Or very probably he might bring that charge against the Carthaginians, as a hint to shew the consequences of the same species of corruption, which even in his time, had found entrance amongst the Romans.

As to religion, both nations were equally superstitious. If many of the religious ceremonies amongst the Romans were absurd and childish, it must be owned that the Carthaginian worship, like that of their ancestors the Canaanites,[22] from whom they received it, was truly diabolical.[a] But it is by no means candid to judge of the natural bent and temper of a people, from effects produced in their minds by superstition. For the same superstition which enjoins such horrid rites, will naturally place the chief efficacy of the sacrifice in the zeal and sincerity of the offerer. Consequently, the highest degree of merit in such oblations, will consist in stifling every human affection, and over-ruling nature. Thus in the Carthaginian idolatry, the softer sex, as more susceptible of tenderness for their offspring, [336] were required to attend in person. They were even compelled, upon this dreadful occasion, to affect all the joy and chearfulness of festivity, because, as Plutarch informs us, if a sigh or a tear escaped them, the merit of the offering would be absolutely lost, and themselves liable to a fine.[b] That the Carthaginians were no more void of parental affection than other nations, is evident from that pious fraud they had so long practised, of secretly buying up poor children, whom they substituted as victims to their bloody deity instead of their own.[c] But after a great defeat which they received from Agathocles, they attributed their ill fortune to the resentment of their God for their repeated sacrilege. They sacrificed two hundred children of the first families in

a. The idol to whom the Carthaginians sacrificed their children was the Moloch of the Canaanites, from whom they were lineally descended. This idol was the Chronos of the Greeks, and Saturn of the Latines.

b. Plut. de Superstit. p. 171.[23]

c. Diodor. Sicul. lib. 20. p. 739.[24]

22. See Genesis 9:20–29 and (relating to the ceremonies of Canaanite idol-worship) Psalms 106:38.

23. Plutarch, "Superstition," XIII.

24. Diodorus Siculus, XX.xiv.4.

Carthage, and three hundred other persons offered themselves as voluntary victims to atone for a crime, to which the highest degree of guilt was affixed by their impious religion.[a] The Roman superstition must in general be acquitted of the charge of inhumanity. The only tendency towards it, was in the custom of inhuming alive such of the vestal virgins, [337] as had violated their vow of chastity.[b] But the bloody and frequent shews of the gladiators, which were the delight of the Romans, fix an indelible blot on the character of a brave people.[c] Historians in general brand the Carthaginians with cruelty and inhumanity. If the charge is just, it must be chiefly attributed to that execrable custom of human sacrifices, which always prevailed amongst that people. Nor do I in the least doubt, but that savage ferocity, which the Romans were so guilty of in war, was in a great measure owing to those barbarous spectacles, where wounds, and murder in cold blood, made the most agreeable part of the entertainment.

As to publick virtue or love of their country, the Carthaginians were no way inferior to the Romans. The intrepid behaviour of [338] the Philaeni, two Carthaginian brothers, who consented to be buried alive to inlarge the boundaries of their country, equals the most heroic instance of that

a. Id. ibid.[25]

b. This institution has been adopted since, by the Greek and Latin churches. The only difference in the punishment is, that the ancient vestals were buried alive, the modern vestals are immured between four walls.[26]

c. Polybius informs us, that when the Romans took a city by storm, they not only put all the men to the sword, but even quartered the dogs, and hewed off the limbs of every other living creature they found in the place.

Πολλάκις ἰδεῖν ἐστιν ἐν ταῖς τῶν Ῥωμαίων καταλήψεσι τῶν πόλεων, οὐ μόνους τοὺς ἀνθρώπους πεφονευμένους, ἀλλὰ τοὺς κύνας δεδιχοτομένους, καὶ τῶν ἄλλων ζώων μέλη παρακεκομμένα. Polyb. lib. 10. p. 820.[27]

25. Diodorus Siculus, XX.xiv.5.

26. That is, in nunneries. The presence in the Roman Catholic Church of institutions with apparently pagan origins was frequently noted in enlightened historiography in eighteenth-century England; see in particular Conyers Middleton, *A Letter from Rome: Shewing an Exact Conformity Between Popery and Paganism* (1729), and chapter twenty-eight of Gibbon's *Decline and Fall* (vol. 2, pp. 71–97).

27. "So that when towns are taken by the Romans one may often see not only the corpses of human beings, but dogs cut in half, and the dismembered limbs of other animals" (Polybius, X.xv.5).

kind of enthusiasm, which the Roman story can boast of.[a] The fate of Machaeus, Bomilcar, Hanno, and others, afford undeniable proof, that neither birth, dignity, nor the greatest services, could screen that man from the most ignominious death, who made the least attempt to subvert the liberty of his country. I have before taken notice of the *Punica fides*,[28] or that proverbial want of sincerity, which has been so often objected by the Roman historians: but I cannot help observing with the more impartial Montesquieu,

> That the Romans never made peace with sincerity and good faith, but always took care to insert such conditions as, in the end, proved the ruin of the people with whom they treated: that the peace they granted was no more than a politick suspension of arms, 'till an opportunity offered of compleating their conquests: that it was their invariable maxim to foment divisions among the neighbouring powers, and by siding alternately with either party, as they found it most conducive to their own interest, play one [339] against the other, 'till they had reduced all equally into Provinces: that they frequently employed the subtilty and ambiguity of terms in their own language, to finesse and chicane in their treaties.[b]

Thus they cheated the Aetolians by the ambiguous phrase of yielding themselves up to the faith of the Roman people.[c] The poor Aetolians

a. Sallust. de Bell. Jugurth. p. 226–27.[29]

b. Grandeur des Romains, p. 68, &c.[30]

c. In fidem populi Romani sese dedere. Vide Polyb. Excerpt. Legat. p. 1114, 15.[31]

28. See above, p. 116, n. 4.

29. For the story of the Philaeni brothers, see Sallust, *Bellum Jugurthinum*, LXXIX.1–10.

30. A free translation of parts of, and a compression of the general argument of, chapter six of Montesquieu's *Considérations sur les causes de la grandeur des Romains et de leur décadence*. Two passages of the French are particularly close to Montagu's English: "Comme ils ne faisoient jamais la paix de bonne foi, & que dans le dessein d'envahir tout, leurs Traités n'étoient proprement que des suspensions de guerre, ils y mettoient des conditions qui commençoient toûjours la ruïne de l'Etat qui les acceptoit" and "Quelquefois ils abusoient de la subtilité des termes de leur Langue" (Montesquieu, *Considérations*, pp. 131 and 137).

31. "To entrust themselves to the good faith of the Roman people"; Polybius, XXI.iii.

imagined, that the term implied only alliance. But the Romans soon convinced them, that what they meant by it, was absolute subjection. They destroyed Carthage under sanction of the most vile equivocation, pretending, "that though they promised that deluded people to preserve their State, they did not mean to grant them their city, which word they had purposely omitted."[a] Maxims which the French have steadily and too successfully pursued, and are still pursuing! Montesquieu very judiciously observes, "That the Romans were ambitious from the lust of domination: the Carthaginians from the lust of gain."[32] This accounts for the different reception which commerce met with in the two nations. At Carthage commerce was esteemed the most honourable of all employments. At Rome [340] commerce was held in contempt. It was there looked upon as the proper occupation of slaves only, and disgraceful to a free citizen. Thus the one loved war for the sake of glory and acquiring dominion; the other looked upon war as a means of acquiring wealth, and extending commerce. The Romans plundered the vanquished enemy to make a parade with their wealth in the triumphal procession. The Carthaginians fleeced not only their enemies, but their tributary Provinces, and oppressed their allies, to feed their own private avarice, as well as that of the publick. The oppressions of the Carthaginian Generals in Spain lost them all their allies. The wiser policy of Scipio attached those allies unalterably to the Romans. The exactions of their rapacious Governors in the African Provinces, was the source of perpetual revolts, upon the approach of any invader, from a desire of changing masters. When Scipio landed, he was joined by all those Provinces, who looked upon the Romans as their deliverers. As soon as luxury had introduced avarice and corruption amongst the Romans, their Generals and Governors pursued the same destructive maxims, which was one leading cause of the final ruin of both the Western and Eastern Empires.

There cannot be a stronger proof of a weak or a corrupt administration, than when [341] indigent and necessitous men are appointed to

a. Ibid. p. 1349, 50.[33]

32. "Les Romains étoient ambitieux par orgueil; & les Carthaginois par avarice" (Montesquieu, *Considérations,* chapter 4, p. 112).

33. Polybius, XXXVI.iii–viii.

the government of distant Provinces, from no other motive than party merit, and with no other view than to raise a fortune at the expence of the people.[34] Whether the wretched and defenceless condition in which the French found our colonies at the beginning of this war,[35] ought not to be ascribed chiefly to this cause, is a question I shall wave at present. Because the evils we have already suffered from former misconduct, will, I hope, be now removed, by a total alteration of measures under an able and honest administration.[36]

It is remarkable, that not one of the historians who reproach the Carthaginians with corruption, were ever able to accuse them of luxury and effeminacy. The Carthaginians, to their immortal honour, stand single upon the records of history, "the only people in the universe, upon whom immense wealth was never able to work its usual effects." The Romans, corrupted by wealth, quickly lost all pretensions both to publick and

34. Montagu here perhaps encourages a comparison with the British government of India, which allowed men of very modest backgrounds to amass incredible fortunes in a short space of time, provided that they could endure the climate. For example, Robert Clive, first baron Clive of Plassey (1725–74) was the son of a lawyer and MP. Employed initially as a clerk in the East India Company, he made himself a successful military commander, and after three periods of service in India he retired to England in 1767 with wealth estimated at death of £500,000. Another example from later in the century would be Warren Hastings (1732–1818). Such overnight fortunes attracted the fascinated envy, the indignation (to the extent that they were suspected to derive from extortion and oppression of the native people), and the derision of the public—a cocktail of emotions captured in Samuel Foote's comedy, *The Nabob* (1772). See also Henry Mackenzie, *The Man of Feeling* (1771), "A Fragment: The Man of Feeling Talks of What He Does Not Understand—An Incident" (Mackenzie, *Man of Feeling*, pp. 76–78).

35. The Seven Years' War was precipitated by French attempts to prevent the westward expansion beyond the Allegheny Mountains of English settlements in North America. Accordingly the French sought to construct a series of forts along the Ohio and Mississippi rivers, thus linking French territories in Canada and Louisiana. Initial clashes in the spring of 1754 had culminated in the calamitous defeat of British forces under General Braddock at Monongahela on 6 July 1755. The early years of this conflict had revealed how ill-adapted was British colonial government in America for waging war, and even for providing for self-defense. See above, p. 121, n. 22.

36. A reference to the administration formed on 29 June 1757 which brought together Pitt the Elder (who took charge of the conduct of the war, and of foreign policy) and the Duke of Newcastle (who was First Lord of the Treasury).

private virtue, and from a race of heroes, degenerated into a nation of the most abject slaves. The Carthaginian virtue was so far from degenerating that it shone brighter in the last period of their history, than in any of the former. Even the behaviour of their women in that long and brave defence of [342] their city against the whole Roman power, equalled, or rather exceeded that of the Roman matrons in those times, when they were most celebrated for publick virtue. When the Romans were masters of the city, one small part only excepted, and that part actually in flames, the generous wife of Asdrubal the chief commander, closed the scene by as desperate an act of heroick bravery, as can be met with in history.[a] After she had upbraided her husband as a coward and a traitor for submitting to Scipio, she declared her determined resolution of dying free, and not surviving the fate of her country. She first stabbed both her children, and threw them into the flames; then leaped in after their bodies, and buried herself in the ruins of Carthage.

The sententious Montesquieu[37] remarks,

> That when Carthage made war with her opulence against the Roman poverty, her great disadvantage arose from what she esteemed her greatest strength, and on which she placed her chief dependence. The reason, as he judiciously observes, is evident. Gold and silver may be easily exhausted, but publick virtue, constancy, and firmness of mind, fortitude and poverty, are inexhausti-[343]ble.[b]

The Carthaginians in their wars employed foreign mercenaries. The Roman armies were composed of their own natives. A defeat or two at sea obstructed the Carthaginian commerce, and stopped the spring which

a. Appian. de Bell. Pun. p. 82.[38]

b. Grandeur des Romains, p. 34.

37. "Sententious" here means "abounding in pointed maxims, aphoristic" (*OED*, 3), and does not bear its now more common pejorative sense of being "addicted to pompous moralizing" (*OED*, 4). What follows is a free translation of a passage from chapter four of Montesquieu's *Considérations sur les causes de la grandeur des Romains et de leur décadence:* "Carthage qui faisoit la guerre avec son opulence contre la pauvreté Romaine, avoit par cela même du desavantage; l'or & l'argent s'épuisent, mais la vertu, la constance, la force & la pauvreté ne s'épuisent jamais" (Montesquieu, *Considérations,* p. 112).

38. Appian, VIII.xix.131.

supplied their publick exchequer. The loss of a battle in Africa, where their country was quite open, and destitute of fortresses, and the natives as much strangers to the use of arms as our own country people, reduced them to submit to whatever terms the victors thought proper to impose. Regulus, in the first Punick war, cooped up the Carthaginians in their capital, after he had given them one defeat by sea, and one by land. The Romans, after receiving four successive defeats from Hannibal, the last of which was the fatal battle of Cannae, where they lost most of their best officers, and all their veteran troops, would hearken to no terms of accommodation, and even sent reinforcements to Spain and other places, though Hannibal was at their gates. The reason is plain. The citizens of Carthage consisted chiefly of unarmed, and undisciplined tradesmen. The citizens of Rome, without distinction, composed a regular body of disciplined militia. A short comparison between the Roman and Carthaginian polity, with respect to the military of each people, will easily point out to us the true [344] cause which gave the Romans their manifest superiority.

I have already taken notice of some capital defects of the Carthaginians, both in their marine and military departments. Montesquieu imputes several capital errors to the Romans, but he attributes their preservation after the defeat at Cannae, when they were at the very brink of ruin, to the force of their institution. He seems to place this force in the superior wisdom and firmness of the Roman Senate. A short inquiry into their conduct, during the second Punick war, will shew that the cause of their preservation at that time must be ascribed to a very different principle, and that Montesquieu too hastily adopted that opinion from the Greek and Roman historians,

If we examine the boasted behaviour of the Roman Senate, from the first attack of Saguntum to the memorable battle of Cannae, we shall find it to consist of one continued series of blunders, which carry all the marks of weak, factious, and divided counsels. The Romans had certain intelligence of Hannibal's design of attacking them in Italy. This was no secret in Spain, where every preparation, and every motion of Hannibal's was directed to that point of view. The Romans were certainly jealous of such a design, when they sent ambassadors to Hanni-[345]bal, to inform him, that if he passed the Iberus, and attacked the Saguntines, they should look upon it as a declaration of war. When they had received an evasive answer from Hannibal, they crossed over to Africa, and made the same declaration to the Carthaginian Senate. When Hannibal laid siege to Saguntum, did the Romans act up to their formidable declaration, or did they send a single man to the assistance of those faithful allies? Just the reverse: They wasted nine months, the time the siege lasted, in useless debates, and fruitless embassies. They sacrificed that faithful and heroick people, together with their own interest and character, by their folly and irresolution.[a] For if they had sent a powerful army at first, they might have saved Saguntum, or at least confined the war to Spain, and prevented it from penetrating into their own bowels. After Hannibal had laid Saguntum in ashes, did the boasted wisdom and firmness of the Roman Senate [346] appear in more vigorous or more politick measures? They again employed a whole winter in a wise embassy to Carthage, to just as little purpose as the former, and gave Hannibal all the time he could wish to prepare for his expedition. When Hannibal was on his march for Italy, instead of shutting up the passages of the Alps, which would easily have defeated that daring enterprize, they ordered the Consul Scipio, with his army, to oppose his passage over the Rhone. The Consul came just time enough to learn, that such dilatory measures would never check the progress of so active and vigilant an enemy, who had already passed that river, and was on his march for the Alps.[b] The Consul immediately reimbarked his troops, and hastened to meet him in his descent from those mountains. But Hannibal was already near the banks of the Po, where the Consul attacked him, but was defeated and

---

a. When the Roman ambassadors, soon after the loss of Saguntum, sollicited an alliance with the Volsicani, a people of Spain, that people seemed astonished at the effrontery of the Romans, and bid them go and seek for allies amongst those nations who had never heard of the destruction of Saguntum, which, as they assured them, would be a melancholy, and striking warning to the Spaniards how they ever placed any confidence in the good faith and friendship of the Romans. Liv. lib. 21. c. 19. p. 144.[39]

b. Polyb. lib. 3. p. 270, et seq.[40]

39. Livy, XXI.xix.8–11.

40. Polybius, III.xlix.1–2.

dangerously wounded. The Senate, alarmed at Hannibal's passage over the Alps, which they had taken no precaution to prevent, sent in a great fright for the other Consul Sempronius, with his army, out of Sicily. He arrived, and joined his wounded colleague Scipio, who was an able officer, and having learnt, by experience, how dangerous an enemy they had [347] to cope with, advised caution and prudence in all their operations. But Sempronius, vain, rash, and ignorant, was deaf to all salutary advice, which he ridiculed as the effect of fear. Hannibal, who never inquired into the number of his enemies, but studied only the foibles of their commanders, directed all his operations upon that principle. He applied therefore to the foible of Sempronius, which he was soon master of, drew him into a snare, and cut off almost his whole army. The Senate was dreadfully frighted at this second defeat; but to mend the matter, they suffered Flaminius, a man more vain, more headstrong, and more rash than Sempronius, to be chosen Consul, and sent against Hannibal. Flaminius fared much worse than Sempronius. As he acted upon the same principles, he run headlong into the trap laid for him by his artful enemy, and lost his life together with his whole army. Though this terrible blow threw the Romans into inexpressible consternation, yet it seems to have brought them to their senses. For they at last created the celebrated Fabius Dictator, who was the only Roman commander capable of opposing Hannibal. Yet even here they could not help giving another instance of their folly, by forcing Minucius upon him for his general of horse, a man of the same character with Sempronius or Flaminius. [348] Fabius acted upon a quite different plan. He knew the danger and folly of opposing new raised troops to veterans, flushed with repeated victories, and commanded by so consummate a General. He therefore opposed art to art, watched every motion of his enemy, and cut off his foragers. Hannibal, whose army was composed chiefly of soldiers of fortune out of different nations, connected to him by no other tye than the hopes of plunder, and their esteem for his personal abilities, was sensible, that such a conduct in his enemy would quickly put an end to all his hopes in Italy. He tried therefore every art he was master of to bring Fabius to a battle; but the wary Roman convinced him, that he knew his trade too well to deviate from that plan, which alone could save his country. Though Hannibal did justice to those fine strokes of his antagonist, yet they were too delicate for the eyes of the Romans. They were disgusted at his conduct, because they wanted capacity to understand it, and gave credit to the idle boasts of Minucius, though they had already suffered so severely by trusting men of his genius. Yet, by the most unaccountable folly, they raised Minucius to an equality of power with Fabius; and Rome, for the first time, saw two Dictators vested with unlimited authority. The wiser Fabius, though amazed at the [349] stupidity of his countrymen, adhered steadily to his first plan. He gave up half the army to the command of his new colleague, but was determined to preserve the other moiety at least, upon which so much depended. Hannibal was sensible, that the Romans could not have done him a more essential piece of service, unless they had recalled Fabius. He immediately threw out a bait for Minucius, which that rash, unthinking commander as greedily bit at. He fell into the trap laid for him by the crafty Hannibal; was enveloped by the Carthaginians, and must inevitably have perished, with all the troops under his command, if Fabius had not flown to his assistance, repulsed the enemy, and rescued him from the most imminent danger of death or captivity. Though Fabius had been so ill used by his countrymen in general, and by his colleague Minucius in particular, yet he shewed, by this generous action, a greatness of soul superior to private resentment, and every selfish passion, which he was always ready to sacrifice to the publick welfare. Minucius indeed felt the force of the obligation, as well as of his own incapacity: he nobly acknowledged it in the strongest terms, and returned to his former post and duty to his abler Commander. But this heroick behaviour of Fabius seems to have made no more impression upon his countrymen, than his [350] masterly conduct. Two new Consuls were chosen, to whom he resigned his authority and army, and retired to Rome neglected and unemployed. The new Consuls followed the advice of Fabius, and avoided coming to action, which distressed Hannibal extremely. But the following year exhibits such a masterpiece of folly and stupidity in that Roman Senate, whose firmness and wisdom are so much boasted of by historians, and such infatuation in the body of the Roman people, as would seem incredible, if the facts, as handed down to us by their own historians themselves, did not prove it beyond a possibility of doubt or contradiction. Determined to drive Hannibal out of Italy, and put a speedy end to so ruinous a war, they raised one of the mightiest armies they had ever yet brought into the field, and employed in it every officer of note or distinction at that time in Rome, the great Fabius alone excepted. This was the last stake of the Romans, upon which their all was ventured. But where does the boasted wisdom of the Senate appear in the management of this affair, which was of the last importance? Of the two Consuls, Paulus Aemilius, the one, was a respectable man, and an experienced officer: Terentius Varro, the other, was a fellow of the lowest extraction, who, by noise and impudence had raised himself to [351] the Tribuneship, was afterwards made Praetor, and, by the assistance of one Bebius, his relation, at that time a Tribune of the people, had forced himself into the consular dignity. This wretch, who had but just talents sufficient for a captain of the mob, who had never seen an action (nor perhaps an army) in his life, had the impudence to censure the conduct of Fabius, and to boast in the Senate, that he would immediately drive Hannibal out of Italy. The wise Senate were not only so weak as to believe, but, in opposition to all the remonstrances of Fabius, even to trust such an empty coxcomb with an equal share in the command. They even gave the Consuls orders to fight the enemy without delay, so great was their confidence in the gasconading[41] Varro. Hannibal at that time was so greatly distressed for want of provisions, that his Spanish troops begun to mutiny, and talked openly of revolting to the Romans, and he himself had thoughts of retiring into Gaul for his own personal safety. Aemilius, who endeavoured in every point to follow the advice of Fabius, declined fighting, and was convinced by his intelligence, that Hannibal could not subsist his troops above ten days longer. But Varro was alike deaf to reason or persuasion. Debates at last run so high between the Consuls, that repeated expresses were sent to the [352] Senate by Aemilius for fresh orders. Had the Senate acted with that prudence, which has been so loudly celebrated by historians, they would certainly have created Fabius Dictator at that critical juncture, which would have put an end to the differences and authority of the Consuls. For how could they reasonably hope for success, whilst the army was

41. Given to extravagant boasting (*OED*).

commanded by two Generals, vested with equal power, who differed as widely in opinion as in temper? But their chief view at [353] that time seems to have been to mortify Fabius, and to that favourite point they wil-[354]fully sacrificed the publick honour and safety.[a] Aemilius at last

a. It has been asked—for what reason? I answer, Livy will inform us in the 22d book of his history.[42] "The studied delay of Fabius (who industriously avoided fighting) which, according to that historian, gave such just cause of uneasiness to Hannibal, was treated at Rome with the utmost contempt by the citizens of every rank both military and civil; particularly after the General of the Horse Minucius had gained some slight advantage over Hannibal during his absence."—He adds, "that two unlucky incidents concurred to augment the displeasure of the citizens against the dictator. One was, the artful behaviour of Hannibal; who wasted all the country around with fire and sword, the Estate of Fabius alone excepted, which he carefully preserved, in hopes that such a different treatment might be thought the effect of some clandestine correspondence between the two Commanders."— The other was, his settling an exchange of prisoners with Hannibal by his own proper authority, and by the same cartel which had subsisted between the Roman and Carthaginian Generals in the first Punick war. By that it was agreed: that if any prisoners should remain on either side, after the exchange of man for man was finished, such prisoners should be redeemed at the rate of two pounds and a half of silver for each soldier. When the exchange was made, 247 Roman prisoners remained to be ransomed.—But as the Senate hesitated greatly at passing a decree for the payment of the stipulated sum, because the Dictator had not consulted them upon the occasion; he sold those very lands which Hannibal had left untouched, and discharged the debt due from the publick out of his own private fortune.—Whether these were the only reasons or not, yet they had evidently such an effect upon the Romans, that Fabius seems to have been at that time the object of their resentment, which they never failed to give proofs of upon every occasion.— Thus when Fabius opened the campaign, his cautious conduct was so disagreeable to the officers as well as soldiers, who listened wholly to the idle boasts of Minucius, that if the choice of their commander had depended upon the voices of the military men, Minucius, as Livy affirms, would undoubtedly have been preferred to Fabius. The same historian tells us; that when Fabius returned to Rome to preside as Dictator at their religious ceremonies, the Tribunes of the people inveighed so bitterly against him in their publick harangues, that he refrained from coming to their assemblies.—Even what he spoke in the Senate met with a very indifferent reception, especially when he extolled the conduct and abilities of Hannibal, and enumerated the repeated defeats they had received for the two last years through the rashness and incapacity of their own commanders.—When Fabius returned to the camp, he received a much more mortifying proof of their displeasure. For they raised Minucius to an equality with him in the command, an act for which there had been no precedent since the first erection of the dictatorial office.—Nor did their enmity to Fabius subside 'till after the fatal defeat at Cannae.

returned to Rome, and laid the whole affair before the Senate. But Varro's party proved the majority, and orders were renewed for fighting, but not immediately. Aemilius still declined fighting, and followed the advice of Fabius; but the alternate command of the two Consuls, which took place every day, defeated all his measures. Varro, on the day of his command, marched the army so close to the enemy, that it was impossible to retire without fighting. This imprudent step brought on the famous battle of Cannae, where Hannibal, whose whole force scarce equalled the moiety of the [355] Romans, gave them the most remarkable defeat we ever read of in their history. Polybius, and after him the rest of the historians, impute this defeat to the great superiority of the Carthaginian army in horse, and the ignorance of Varro in pitching upon a plain open country for the field of battle, where Hannibal could employ his cavalry to the best advantage. That the Carthaginian horse was superior to the Roman in goodness, is readily admitted. But if we compute the number of the cavalry of the Romans, and that of their allies, as given us by Polybius himself, we shall find the difference in each army amounted but to four thousand; so small an advantage therefore, in point of number, could never possibly have turned the scale in favour of Hannibal when the Romans had such prodigious odds in the number of their infantry, who shewed themselves no way inferior to Hannibal's foot, either in bravery or intrepidity. The true reason was, the infinite superiority of Hannibal in point of Generalship. That consummate leader, by a most exquisite disposition of his troops, a *manoeuvre* much too fine for the eyes of the

---

For the worthless Varro obtained not only the Consulship, but, what is still more extraordinary, even the confidence of the greater part of the Senate, and almost the whole army by railing at Fabius and Fabian measures, and out-boasting Minucius. I have shewed above from Polybius what trust the majority of the Senate reposed in Varro. But I cannot omit a remarkable instance, which Livy gives us, of the absurd and fatal partiality of the military men to Varro, in opposition to Aemilius, who avowedly followed the advice of Fabius.—In a council of war, says that historian, held a little before the battle of Cannae, when each Consul persisted firmly in his former opinion; Aemilius adhering to Fabius's plan for avoiding fighting, Varro to his resolution of engaging the enemy immediately; Servilius, one of the Consuls of the former year, was the only one who joined Aemilius, the rest declared for Varro.

42. Livy, XXII.xv.1–2; XXII.xxiii.4–6.

Roman Generals, caught their whole infantry fairly in a trap (though in a plain level country) where they were almost to a man cut to pieces, or taken. Aemilius, and all the other general officers, [356] with 70,000 Romans, lay dead upon the field of battle after a brave and obstinate resistance.[a] The infamous Varro, that base-minded fellow, as Polybius terms him, who commanded the cavalry of the allies on the left wing, behaved like a true bully in the face of danger.[b] He fled almost at the first attack, and rather chose to live with infamy than die with honour. When the fatal news reached the city of Rome, both Senate and people gave up all hopes of safety. Fabius alone took the lead, and acted with his usual firmness and calmness upon this occasion. He placed guards at the gates to prevent the desertion of the citizens, who were flying in great numbers to escape the conquerors, whom they expected every moment. He confined the women to their houses, who had filled the city with lamentations. He manned the walls and outworks, and took every other precaution which the shortness of the time would admit of. All resigned themselves implicitly to his conduct, and he acted for the time as sole Governor. Many of the Senators, and principal of the Roman nobility, were in actual consultation about leaving Italy, and retiring elsewhere for safety. But they were prevented, as Livy in-[357]forms us, by the terrible threats of young Scipio, and compelled to stay and share the fate of their country.[c] Hannibal has been greatly censured for not attacking Rome itself immediately after the battle, and is accused of not knowing how to make the proper use of a victory, though he knew so well how to conquer. The candid Montesquieu[43] acquits him of this charge. His reasons are, that

a. Above 80,000, according to Dionysius of Halicarnassus.[44]

b. Polyb. lib. 3. p. 370.[45]

c. Liv. lib. 22, p. 242.[46]

43. The saying that Hannibal's refusal to follow the devastating victory at Cannae with a march on Rome demonstrated that he knew how to conquer but not how to make use of a victory is attributed to Maharbal, the commander of Hannibal's Numidian cavalry at the battle (Livy, XXII.li). Thereafter it became a commonplace, and so was ripe for correction by Montesquieu, who took pleasure in overturning received opinions: "Il y a des choses que tout le monde dit parce qu'elles ont été dites une fois: on croit qu'Annibal fit une faute insigne de n'avoir point été assieger Rome après la bataille de Cannes: il est vrai que d'abord la frayeur y fut extrême: mais il n'en est pas de la consternation d'un Peuple

though Rome at that time was in the highest degree of consternation, yet the effects of fear upon a warlike people, inured to arms like the Romans, and a low undisciplined rabble, who are strangers to the use of arms, are very different. In the former, who are conscious of their own strength, it almost always changes into the most desperate courage. In the latter, who feel their own weakness too sensibly, it dispirits so much as to render them incapable of resistance. Hence he gives it as his real opinion, that Hannibal would have failed of success if he had undertaken the siege of that city. His proof is, because the Romans at that very time were able to send sufficient succours, drawn from their own citizens, to every part where they were then wanted. Thus Rome was saved, not by the wisdom or firmness of the Senate, but the prudence and magnanimity of one old officer, whom they despised and hated, and the intrepidity of a boy of eighteen, joined, as I observed [358] before from Dionysius, to the force of that part of their institution, which formed the whole body of their citizens into a militia, ever ready, and capable of taking the field as soldiers. All the Roman armies which were opposed to Hannibal, were drawn out of this militia. Nor do we meet with one instance of cowardice, or ill-behaviour amongst the men, but rather of intrepidity even to rashness, which used to be the characteristick of the British Nation. Polybius, who was at least as able a judge of the military as any man of that age, and who lived very near the time of the Hannibalick war (as he terms it) is loud in

---

belliqueux qui se tourne en courage, comme de celle d'une vile populace qui ne sent que sa foiblesse: une preuve qu'Annibal n'auroit pas réussi, c'est que les Romains se trouverent encore en état d'envoyer par tout du secours." (There are some things that everybody says because they have been said once: it is believed that Hannibal made a remarkable blunder in not besieging Rome after the battle of Cannae: it's true that at first the panic there was extreme: but the consternation of a warlike people which mutates into courage is far from that of a vile rabble which feels only its own weakness: the fact that the Romans were still in a condition to send out reinforcements in all directions is a proof that Hannibal would not have succeeded. Montesquieu, *Considérations*, p. 118.) Montagu loosely paraphrases Montesquieu's French. Montagu himself applies Maharbal's aphorism in an inverted form to the Spartan general Lysander (above, p. 75).

44. Dionysius of Halicarnassus, II.xvii.4.
45. III.cxvi.13.
46. Livy, XXII.liii.6–13.

his praises of the Roman troops, whose infantry he prefers greatly to the Carthaginian mercenaries.[a] Nor does he once impute any of their defeats to the fault of their men, but invariably to the folly and incapacity of their commanders.

Upon the whole, the great defect in the Carthaginian military institution consisted in the want of a national militia, which, as Polybius observes, was the reason of their employing foreign mercenaries. The capital defects in the Roman lay in that equality of power with which each Consul was vested in the field, and the short duration of their command, as their office was only annual. Every battle which the Romans lost to Han-[359]nibal, except the first, may be fairly ascribed to the former of these causes. The defeats of Trebia and Thrasymene were plainly occasioned by the jealousy of one of the Consuls, lest the other should share with him in the glory of beating Hannibal; as the want of harmony, and difference of opinion between the two Consuls, was the primary cause of the dreadful defeat at Cannae. To the latter cause we may justly attribute the long duration of the Hannibalick war; when that great man, who entered Italy with no more than 20,000 foot and 6000 horse, maintained his ground above sixteen years, without any assistance from Carthage, against the whole united force and efforts of the Romans, by the mere strength of his own extraordinary genius. For as every man, who had interest sufficient to obtain the Consulship, was immediately vested with the command of an army, however qualified or not, so he was obliged to resign his command at the end of the year, before he had well time to be thoroughly acquainted with the true method of dealing with his enemy. Thus every new successive commander amongst the Romans, had the same task to begin afresh at the opening of every campaign. I know that political writers ascribe this mistaken policy to that jealousy, and fear of lodging so much power in so few [360] hands for any length of time, which is so natural to all Republican Governments; and that the office of Dictator was contrived as a remedy against any abuse, or inconveniency, which might at any time arise from the consular power: but the event

a. Polyb. lib. 6. p. 688.[47]
47. Polybius, VI.lii.1–11.

shewed, that the remedy was much worse than the disease. Whilst publick virtue existed, the office of Dictator was frequently useful; but when
luxury had introduced corruption, the *pro tempore*[48] Dictator soon came
to be perpetual, and the perpetual Dictator terminated in a perpetual and
despotick Emperor.

At Carthage their military institution was entirely different. The
power of their Generals in the field was absolute and unlimited, and, if
their conduct was approved of, generally continued to the end of whatever war they were engaged in. They had no occasion for the dangerous
resource of a Dictator. The watchful eye of their standing court-martial,
the committee of 104 of their ablest Senators, was a perpetual and nev-
erfailing check upon the ambition, or ill behaviour of their Generals.[a]

a. Our method of trying delinquents, either in the land or sea-service, by a court
martial composed of their respective officers, has been judged liable to many objections, and has occasioned no little discontent in the Nation.[49] For as their enquiry is
restricted to a particular set of articles in each service, I don't see how a commanding
officer, vested with a discretionary power of acting, can strictly or properly come under
their cognizance, or be ever liable to their censure, unless he is proved guilty of a direct
breach of any one of those articles. But as a commander in chief may easily avoid an
offence of that nature, and yet, upon the whole of his conduct in any expedition, be
highly culpable; a court-martial, thus circumscribed in their power of enquiry, can never
be competent judges in a cause where they are denied a proper power of examining into
the real demerits of the supposed offender. Much has been said about trying offences
of this nature, like other criminal cases, by juries: a scheme which, at the very first sight,
must appear absurd and impracticable to the rational and unprejudiced.

As therefore instruction is the true end and use of all history, I shall take the liberty
of offering a scheme, drawn from that wise and salutary institution of the Carthaginians, which is, "That a select standing committee be appointed, to be composed of
an equal number of members of both houses, chosen annually by balloting, with a
full power of enquiring into the conduct of all commanders in chief, without any
restraint of articles of war; and that, after a proper examination, the committee shall
refer the case, with their opinion upon it, to the decision of his Majesty."

This scheme seems to me the least liable to objections of any I have yet met with.
For if the numbers are chosen by balloting, they will be less liable to the influence
of party. If they are chosen annually, and refer the case to the decision of the crown,
which is the fountain of justice as well as mercy, they will neither encroach upon
the royal prerogative, nor be liable to that signal defect in the Carthaginian committee, which sat for life, and whose sentence was final without appeal.

48. Temporary; elected for a fixed period of time only.

49. Another reference to the court-martial and execution of Admiral Byng on

The Sacred [361] Cohort, amongst the Carthaginians, consisted of a large body of volunteers of the richest [362] and greatest families of the Nation. This wise and noble institution was one of the chief supports of the Carthaginian State; and as it was the constant seminary of their officers and commanders, might very probably be one cause why luxury and effeminacy could never obtain footing in that warlike Republick. For we always find this generous body giving the most signal instances of bravery and conduct, and bearing down all before them.[a] Nor did they ever quit the field of battle, 'till they were deserted by the rest of the army, and even then generally retired in excellent order.

The Romans were gradually trained up, from the very infancy of their Republick, in long and obstinate wars with their Italian neighbours, who were masters of the same arms and discipline, and were no way their inferiors in bravery. Nor did they perfect themselves in the art of war, 'till they learned it by bloody experience from Pyrrhus, the most consummate Captain of that age. The Carthaginians were only exercised in war with the wild undisciplined Africans, or the irregular Spaniards; nor were they able with their numerous fleets and prodigious armies [363] to compleat the reduction of that part of Sicily, which was inhabited by Grecian colonies, who retained their native arms and discipline. Hence arose the great superiority of the Romans, both in soldiers and commanders; though the Barcan family produced some great officers, who at least equalled the ablest Generals Rome could ever boast of.

It is evident from the course of this enquiry, that the ruin of the Roman Republick arose wholly from internal causes. The ruin of Carthage was owing remotely to internal, but immediately to external. The Plebeian faction reduced Rome to the verge of ruin at the battle of Cannae, and a complication of factions compleated the subversion of that Republick

---

14 March 1757; see above, p. 94, n. 171. George II's refusal to commute the sentence was deplored at the time by the governing elite, and provoked widespread public disapproval (hence Montagu's "no little discontent").

a. Diodor. Sicul. lib. 20. p. 739.[50]

50. Diodorus Siculus, XX.xii.3.

under the two Triumvirates. The envy and jealousy of the Hannonian faction deprived Carthage of all the fruits of Hannibal's amazing victories and progress, and paved the way for the utter excision of their very name and nation by the Roman arms. Such are the direful effects of faction, when suffered to run its natural lengths without controul, in the most flourishing and best constituted Government!

CHAPTER VIII

Of Revolutions in Mixed Governments

Polybius remarks, that the best form of Government is that which is composed of a due admixture of monarchy, aristocracy and democracy.[a] He affirms that his assertion may not only be proved from reason, but from the evidence of fact, and cites the Spartan constitution in proof, which was modelled upon that very plan by Lycurgus. He adds too, that to perpetuate the duration of his Government, he united the peculiar excellencies of all the best Governments in one form, that neither of the three parts, by swelling beyond its just bounds, might ever be able to deviate into its original inborn defects: but that whilst each power was mutually drawn back by the opposite attraction of the other two, neither power might ever preponderate, but the balance of Government continue suspended in its true aequipoise.[b]

a. Polyb. Hist. lib. 6. p. 628.[1]
b. Id. ibid. p. 638–9.[2]
1. Polybius, VI.iii.7. Montesquieu had described the British Constitution in terms of a blending of these three pure types of government in book 6, chapter 6 of *De l'esprit des lois* (1748).
2. Polybius, VI.x.6–7.

From the observance of this nice adjustment of the balance of Government, he [365] foretels the duration or fall of all mixed Governments in general. He adds, that as all Government arises originally from the people; so all mutations in Government proceed primarily from the people also. For when once a state has struggled through many and great difficulties, and emerged at last to freedom and wealth, men begin to sink gradually into luxury, and to grow more dissolute in their morals. The seeds of ambition will spring up, and prompt them to be more fond of contending for superiority in the magistracy, and carrying their point, in whatever they had set their hearts upon, than is consistent with the welfare of the community: when once these evils are got to a head in a country so circumstanced, the change must necessarily be for the worse; because the principle of such change will arise from the gratification, or disappointment of the ambition of the chief citizens, with respect to honours and preferments; and from that insolence and luxury arising from wealth, by which the morals of the private people will be totally corrupted. Thus the change in Government will be primarily effected by the people. For when the people are galled by the rapine and oppression of those in power, arising from a principle of avarice; and corrupted, and elated with an undue opinion of their own weight, [366] by the flatteries of the disappointed, which proceed from a principle of ambition, they raise those furious commotions in the State, which unhinge all Government. These commotions first reduce it to a State of anarchy, which at last terminates in absolute monarchy and tyranny.

I have here given the sentiments of Polybius (and almost in his own words) from that excellent dissertation in Government, preserved to us in the sixth book of his history, which I would recommend to the perusal of my countrymen. He there traces Government up to its first origin. He explains the principles, by which different Governments arose to the summit of their power and grandeur, and proves, that they sunk to ruin by a more or less rapid progress, in proportion as they receded more or less from the first principles, on which they were originally founded. He survived the ruin of all the Grecian Republicks, as well as Carthage, and lived (as he more than once tells us) to see the Romans masters of the known world. Blest with parts and learning superior to most men of his time, joined to the most solid judgment, and the experience of eighty-two years; no man better understood the intrinsick nature of Government in general. No man could with more certainty foretel the various mutations, which so frequently [367] happen in different forms of Government, which must be ever in a fluctuating state, from the complicated variety of the human passions. Nor can any man give us better hints, than he has done, for guarding against the effects of those dangerous passions, and preserving the constitution of a free people in its full force and vigour. Of all the legislators, which he knew of, he prefers Lycurgus, whom he looks upon rather as divinely inspired, than as a mere man. He esteems the plan of Government which he established at Sparta, the most perfect, and proposes it is a general model worthy the imitation of every other community; and he remarks, that the Spartans, by adhering to that plan, preserved their liberty longer than any other nation of the known world.

I cannot help observing upon this occasion, that our own constitution, as settled at the Revolution,[3] so nearly coincides with Lycurgus's general plan of Government, as laid down by Polybius, where the monarchy was for life and hereditary, that it seems, at first sight to have been formed by that very model. For our plan of Government intended to fix and preserve so just a proportion of the Monarchick, Aristocratick, and Democratick powers, by their Representatives, King, Lords, and Commons; that any two of those powers might be able joint-[368]ly to give a check to the other, but not to destroy it, as the destruction of any one power must necessarily induce a different form of Government. This is the true basis of the British constitution, the duration of which must absolutely depend upon the just equilibrium preserved between these three powers. This consequently is the unerring test, by which every unbiassed and attentive considerer may judge, whether we are in an improving state, or whether, and by what degrees, we are verging towards ruin. But as I aim at reformation, not satire; as I mean no invidious reflections, but only to give my sentiments with that honest freedom, to which every Briton is intitled by birthright; I shall just state from Polybius, the means by which all mixed Governments

---

3. That is, the Glorious Revolution of 1688. While Montagu is correct to say that the monarchy was confirmed as being tenable for life and hereditary in 1688, it is difficult to see many other respects in which the settlement of 1688 recalls Lycurgan Sparta, since it contained no sumptuary dimension.

have originally deviated from those first principles, which were the basis of their rise and grandeur: how by this deviation they tended towards their decline, and that those means acquiring additional force from that very decline, necessarily produced those evils, which accelerated the destruction of every free people. As the remarks of this most judicious historian, are founded upon long experience, drawn from undeniable facts, to many of which he himself was eye witness, they will [369] not only carry greater weight, but will enable us to form a right judgment of our own situation, as it is at present circumstanced.[a]

Polybius observes, that of all the mixed Governments ever known to him, that of Lycurgus alone was the result of cool reason and long study. The form of the Roman Republick, on the contrary, was the production of necessity. For the Romans came at the knowledge of the most proper remedies for all their political evils, not by dint of reasoning, but by the deep-felt experience of the many and dangerous calamities, with which they had so long and so often struggled. I don't in the least doubt, but that excellent form of Government established by our rude Gothick ancestors,[4] wherever their arms prevailed, arose from the same cause,

a. Polyb. lib. 3. p. 223.[5]

4. The notion that the liberty of European nations is an inheritance from the boisterous independence of the ancient German tribes derives ultimately from Tacitus's *Germania*. The theory had been elaborated by Montesquieu in books 30 and 31 of *De l'esprit des lois* (1748). In seventeenth- and eighteenth-century England the notion of an ancient Gothic constitution became a commonplace of political discourse; see J. G. A. Pocock, *The Ancient Constitution and the Feudal Law: A Study of English Historical Thought in the Seventeenth Century* (Cambridge: Cambridge University Press, 1957). The final chapter of Blackstone's *Commentaries* (book 4, chapter 33) offers an outline of English juridical history which finds that the "most important guardian both of public and private liberty, we owe to our Saxon ancestors" (Blackstone, *Commentaries*, vol. 4, pp. 400–436; quotation on p. 407). At the end of chapter two of *The Decline and Fall* Gibbon dwells on the barbarian contribution to the history of political freedom: "This diminutive stature of mankind, if we pursue the metaphor, was daily sinking below the old standard, and the Roman world was indeed peopled by a race of pygmies; when the fierce giants of the north broke in, and mended the puny breed. They restored a manly spirit of freedom; and after the revolution of ten centuries, freedom became the happy parent of taste and science" (Gibbon, *Decline and Fall*, vol. 1, p. 84).

5. Polybius, III.i.3.

necessity founded upon experience. Every mixed Government therefore, where the three powers are duly balanced, has a *ressource*[6] within itself against all those political evils to which it is liable. By this *ressource*, I mean, that joint coercive force, which any two of these powers are able to exercise over the other. But as nothing but necessity can authorize the exercise of this power, so it must be strictly regulated by those principles, on which the Government was founded. For if by an undue exercise of this power, any one of the three should be diminished, or [370] annihilated, the balance would be destroyed, and the constitution alter proportionally for the worse. Thus in Denmark, where the monarchy was limited and elective, the people, exasperated by the oppressions of the nobility, who had assumed an almost despotick power, out of a principle of revenge threw their whole weight into the regal scale.[7] Frederick the IIId, the then reigning monarch, strengthened by this accession of power and the assistance of the people, compelled the nobility to surrender their power and privileges. In consequence of this fatal step taken by the people, the monarchy, in the year 1660, became absolute and hereditary. Lord Molesworth observes upon this occasion, in his Account of Denmark, that the people of Denmark have since felt by sad experience, that the little finger of an absolute Prince is heavier than the loins of a hundred Nobles.[8]

The late revolution of Government in Sweden, though arising from the same principles, took a very different turn. Charles the XIIth, brave even to enthusiasm, and as insatiably fond of glory as the ambitious Alexander, had quite tired out and exhausted his people, by his destructive expeditions.

6. Resource (with the connotation of "last resort" or "final expedient").

7. Montagu refers to events at a meeting of the three Danish estates at Copenhagen in 1660, where the commons, incensed at the intransigence of the nobles on the point of their customary exemption from taxes, and infuriated by their being branded as slaves, sought an audience with the king and offered him "their Votes and Assistance to be absolute Monarch of the Realm, as also that the Crown should descend by Inheritance to his Family, which hitherto had gone by Election" (Molesworth, *Denmark*, p. 34).

8. "The Commons have since experienced, that the little Finger of an absolute Prince can be heavier than the Loins of many Nobles" (Molesworth, *Denmark*, p. 46).

But when that fortunate shot from the town of Frederickshal[9] gave repose to his own country as well as to a great part of Europe, the [371] States of Sweden, no longer awed by a warlike Monarch, who had usurped a despotick power, and a veteran army, again resumed the exercise of their own inherent powers. Stimulated by a desire of vengeance for the evils they had already suffered, and the fear of smarting again under the same evils, they beheaded Gortz, the minister of their late Monarch's oppression, and left the crown no more than the bare shadow of authority. For though they continued the Monarchy for life and hereditary, yet they imposed such rigid terms upon their succeeding Kings, as reduced them to a state of dependance and impotence nearly equal to a Doge of Genoa or Venice.[10] We see, in both these instances, the revolution in Government effected by the union of two powers of the Government against the third. The catastrophe indeed in both nations was different, because that third power, which was obnoxious to the other two, was different in each nation. In the former of these instances, the people, fired with resentment against the nobility, and instigated by secret emissaries of the crown, blindly gave up their whole power to the King, which enabled him to deprive the nobility (the second estate) of their share of power, and bring the whole to center in the crown. Thus the Government in Denmark was changed into absolute Monarchy. In [372] the latter, the Senate took the lead during the *interregnum,* which followed the death of Charles, and changed the Government into Aristocracy. For though the outward form

9. Charles XII of Sweden (1682–1718) was fatally shot through the head at the siege of Fredrikshald at an early stage of his invasion of Norway. An absolute monarch, he had defended Sweden during the Great Northern War, but had launched a ruinous invasion of Russia (1707–9) which destroyed Sweden's military forces and her status as a great power. Comparisons between Charles XII and Alexander the Great were not uncommon, the most famous being Alexander Pope's contemptuous yoking of the two men in the couplet "Heroes are much the same, the point's agreed, | From Macedonia's madman to the Swede" (*An Essay on Man* [1734], IV.219–20). See also Samuel Johnson's more gravely satirical portrait of Charles in *The Vanity of Human Wishes* (1749), lines 191–222.

10. The Doge was the head of state in the Italian republics of Genoa and Venice, but by the mid-eighteenth century in both republics the growing power of oligarchies had reduced the Doge to a mere figurehead.

of Government indeed is preserved, yet the essence no longer remains. The Monarchy is merely titular, but the whole power is absorbed by the Senate, consequently the Government is strictly Aristocratick. For the people were by no means gainers by the change, but remain in the same state of servitude, which they so much complained of before. Thus in all revolutions in mixed Governments, where the union of the two injured powers is animated by the spirit of Patriotism, and directed by that salutary rule before laid down, which forbids us to destroy, and only enjoins us to reduce the third offending power within its proper bounds, the balance of Government will be restored upon its first principles, and the change will be for the better. Thus when the arbitrary and insupportable encroachments of the crown under James the IId,[11] aimed so visibly at the subversion of our constitution, and the introduction of absolute Monarchy; necessity authorized the Lords and Commons (the other two powers) to have *recourse* to the joint exercise of that restraining power, which is the inherent *ressource* of all mixed Governments. But as the exercise of this power [373] was conducted by Patriotism, and regulated by the above-mentioned rule, the event was the late happy Revolution; by which the power of the crown was restrained within its proper limits, and the Government resettled upon its true basis, as nearly as the genius of the times would admit of. But if the passions prevail, and ambition lurks beneath the masque of Patriotism, the change will inevitably be for the worse. Because the restitution of the balance of Government, which alone can authorize the exercise of the two joint powers against the third, will be only the pretext, whilst the whole weight and fury of the incensed people will be directed solely to the ends of ambition. Thus if the regal power should be enabled to take the lead by gaining over the whole weight of the people, the change will terminate in absolute Monarchy; which so

11. James II had alarmed his subjects during the months leading up to the Glorious Revolution in two respects. His Declaration of Indulgence of April 1687 was seen primarily not as offering relief to Dissenters, but rather as striking at the Church of England and opening the door for a re-introduction of Roman Catholicism. His attempts, in late 1687 and early 1688, to fill public offices and corporations with either Roman Catholics or compliant Dissenters was seen as a high-handed attempt to subvert the constitution.

lately happened in Denmark, as it had happened before in almost all the old Gothick Governments. If the Aristocratick power, actuated by that ambition, which, an extreme few instances excepted, seems inseparable from the regal, should be able to direct the joint force of the people against the Crown, the change will be to an Aristocratick Government, like the present State of Sweden,[12] or the Government of Holland, from the death of William the IIId, to the late [374] revolution in favour of the Stadtholder.[13] If the power of the people impelled to action by any cause, either real or imaginary, should be able to subvert the other two, the consequence will be, that Anarchy, which Polybius terms, the ferine[14] and savage dominion of the people.[a] This will continue 'till some able and daring spirit, whose low birth or fortune precluded him from rising to the chief dignities of the state by any other means, puts himself at the head of the populace enured to live by plunder and rapine, and drawing the whole power to himself, erects a Tyranny upon the ruins of the former Government; or 'till the community, tired out and impatient under their distracted situation, bring back the Government into its own channel. This is what Polybius terms the circumvolution of Governments; or the rotation of Governments within themselves 'till they return to the same point.[b] The fate of the Grecian and Roman Republicks terminated in the former of these events. The distracted state of Government in this

a. Δημοκρατία θηριώδης. Polyb. p. 638.[15]

b. Πολιτειῶν ἀνακύκλωσις. p. 637.[16]

12. On the death of Charles XII in 1718, his sister Ulrika Eleonora had attempted to prolong his regime of absolutism, before abdicating in 1720 in favour of her husband, Frederick of Hessen. During his reign (1720–51) Sweden moved from absolutism to a form of parliamentary government.

13. During the first half of the eighteenth century, from the death of William III in 1702 to the last phase of the War of the Austrian Succession in 1747, Holland was ruled not by the head of state, or Stadtholder, but by an oligarchy of regents. In April 1747 military reversals at the hands of the French led to rioting, and to the election of William IV as Stadtholder; it is to this revolution that Montagu refers. William IV died in 1751, and was succeeded by his son William V, who assumed personal rule in 1759.

14. Wild or savage; bestial (OED, 2).

15. "Savage democracy"; Polybius VI.x.5.

16. "The cycle of political revolution"; Polybius VI.ix.10.

nation from 1648, to the restoration of Charles the IId, ended happily in the latter, though the nation for [375] some years experienced the former of these catastrophes under the Government of Cromwell.[17]

I have here given a short, but plain general analysis of Government, founded upon experience drawn from historical truths, and adapted to the general capacity of my countrymen. But if any one desires to be acquainted with the Philosophy of Government, and to investigate the ratio and series of all these mutations, or revolutions of Governments within themselves, I must, with Polybius, refer him to Plato's Republick.

The plan of a good and happy Government, which Plato lays down, by the mouth of Socrates, in the former part of that work, is wholly ideal, and impossible to be executed, unless mankind could be new moulded. But the various revolutions of government, described above, which he treats of in the latter part, was founded upon facts, facts which he himself had been eye-witness to in the numerous Republicks of Greece and Sicily, and had fatally experienced in his own country Athens. The divine Philosopher, in that part of his admirable treatise, traces all these mutations up to their first source, "The intemperance of the human passions,"[18] and accounts for their various progress, effects and consequences, from the various combinations of the same perpetually [376] conflicting passions. His maxims are founded solely upon the sublimest truths, his allusions beautiful and apposite, and his instructions alike applicable to publick or private life, equally capable of forming the statesman or the man.

17. Oliver Cromwell (1599–1658) was the pre-eminent parliamentary military commander during the Civil Wars, and subsequently became Lord Protector of England, Scotland, and Ireland from 1653 to 1658. Montagu sees Cromwell as a type of the "able and daring spirit" which can erect a "Tyranny upon the ruins of the former Government."

18. See, e.g., Plato, *Republic*, X.xv; but the need to curb the passions is a general theme dissolved throughout that work.

CHAPTER IX

Of the British Constitution

Xenophon observes, that if the Athenians, together with the sovereignty of the seas, had enjoyed the advantageous situation of an island, they might with great ease have given law to their neighbours.[a] For the same fleets which enabled them to ravage the sea-coasts of the continent at discretion, could equally have protected their own country from the insults of their enemies as long as they maintained their naval superiority. One would imagine, says the great Montesquieu, that Xenophon in this passage was speaking of the island of Britain.[b] The judicious and glorious exertion of our naval force[1]

a. Xenophon. de Republ. Athen.[2]

b. Esprit des Loix, vol. 2. p. 3.[3]

1. In the late summer of 1758 British forces had made a series of raids on the French coast at St. Malo and Cherbourg, and on French settlements in West Africa. That naval momentum had been sustained and crowned when in November 1759 Hawke had trapped and devastated the French fleet under Conflans in Quiberon Bay, thus expunging the disgrace of the loss of Minorca (1756), which had been attributed (at least by George II) to the pusillanimous conduct of Admiral Byng.

2. Xenophon, *Constitution of the Athenians,* II.xiv.

3. "Vous diriez que Xénophon a voulu parler de l'Angleterre" (Montesquieu, *De l'esprit des lois,* book 21, ch. 7).

under the present ministry* so strongly confirms Xenophon's remark, that one would imagine their measures were directed, as well as dictated by his consummate genius. We are masters both of those natural and acquired advantages, which Xenophon required to make his countrymen invincible. We daily feel their importance more and more, and must be sensible that [378] our liberty, our happiness, and our very existence as a people, depend upon our naval superiority, supported by our military virtue and publick spirit. Nothing, humanly speaking, but luxury, effeminacy and corruption can ever deprive us of this envied superiority. What an accumulated load of guilt therefore must lye upon any future administration, who, to serve the ends of faction, should ever precipitate Britain from her present height down to the abject state of Athens, by encouraging these evils to blast all publick virtue in their unlimited progress.

As Britain is so confessedly superior to all the maritime powers of the antients by the advantages of situation; so the British constitution, as settled at the Revolution,[4] is demonstrably far preferable to, and better formed for duration, than any of the most celebrated Republicks of antiquity. As the executive power is vested in a single person, who is deemed the first branch in the legislature; and as that power is for life and hereditary; our constitution is neither liable to those frequent convulsions, which attended the annual elections of Consuls, nor to that solecism[5] in politicks, two supreme heads of one body for life, and hereditary, which was the great defect in the Spartan institution. As the House of Commons, elected by, and out of the body of the people, is [379] vested with all the power annexed to the Tribunitial office amongst the Romans; the people enjoy every advantage which ever accrued to the Roman people by that institution, whilst the nation is secure from all those calamitous seditions, in which every factious Tribune could involve his country at pleasure. And as all our questions in parliament are decided by a majority of voices; we can never be subject to that capital defect in the Carthaginian

*The first edition of this Work appeared in 1759.

4. Another reference to the constitutional settlement which followed the Glorious Revolution of 1688 (see above, p. 45, n. 71).

5. Literally, a grammatical error; by extension, an error, incongruity, inconsistency, or impropriety of any kind (*OED*, 1 and 3).

constitution, where the single *Veto* of one discontented senator referred the decision of the most important affair to a wrong-headed, ungovernable populace. The House of Peers is placed in the middle of the balance, to prevent the Regal scale from preponderating to Despotism or Tyranny; or the Democratical to Anarchy and its consequences. The equitable intent of our laws is plainly calculated, like those of Solon, to preserve the liberty and property[6] of every individual in the community; and to restrain alike the richest or the poorest, the greatest or the meanest, from doing or suffering wrong from each other. This is the wise and salutary plan of power established at the Revolution.[7] Would we always adhere steadily to this plan, and preserve the just aequilibrium, as delivered down to us by our great Ancestors, our constitution would [380] remain firm and unshaken to the end of time.

I have already shewed in the course of these papers, that, since that ever memorable aera, we suffered some breaches to be made in the most interesting part of this constitution, not by the hand of open violence, but by the insidious, and consequently more dangerous arts of corruption.

6. "Liberty and Property" was the slogan of that broadly Whiggish political ideology which, although at times cogently and energetically challenged, nevertheless achieved hegemony in British political life between the Glorious Revolution of 1688 and the Great Reform Bill of 1832. As Gilbert Burnet had put it, in his "An Exhortation to Peace and Union": "We are all then Brethren, as we are *Englishmen* and *Freemen,* born under a Government that gives us all possible Securities for both Liberty and Property, the two chief earthly Blessings of human Nature, whose Persons can neither be restrained, nor punished beyond the bounds of Law; who can be charged with no Taxes but by their own Consent; and who can be subject to no Laws but what were prayed by themselves" (Burnet, *Tracts,* p. 8). "Liberty" and "Property," then, denoted not so much two discrete values, as a certain peculiarly English stroke of political good fortune: namely, the possession of liberty construed as the provision of certain safeguards for the tenure of property. By the later eighteenth century, however, the power of the phrase was being called into question, as Soame Jenyns would note when he referred dismissively to "patriotic and favorite words such as Liberty, Property, *Englishmen,* &c., which are apt to make strong Impressions on that more numerous Part of Mankind who have Ears but no Understanding" (Jenyns, *Objections,* p. 4). The notion that political power was naturally associated with the possession of property had been a commonplace in the English political tradition since the publication of James Harrington's *Oceana* in 1656.

7. Again, Montagu refers to the consequences of 1688 (see above, p. 45, n. 71).

The great increase of our commerce after the peace of Utrecht, brought in a vast accession of wealth; and that wealth revived, and gradually diffused that luxury through the whole nation, which had lain dormant during the dangerous reign of James the IId, and the warlike reigns of William and Ann.[8] To this universal luxury, and this only, we must impute that amazing progress of corruption, which seized the very vitals of our constitution. If therefore we impartially compare the present state of our own country with that of Rome and Carthage, we shall find, that we resemble them most when in their declining period.

To the commercial maxims of the Carthaginians, we have added their insatiable lust of gain, without their oeconomy, and contempt of luxury and effeminacy. To the luxury and dissipation of the Romans, we have joined their venality, without their [381] military spirit: and we feel the pernicious effects of the same species of faction, which was the great leading cause to ruin in both those Republicks. The Roman institution was formed to make and to preserve their conquests. Abroad invincible, at home invulnerable, they possessed all the resources requisite for a warlike nation within themselves. The military spirit of their people, where every citizen was a soldier, furnished inexhaustible supplies for their armies abroad, and secured them at home from all attempts of invasion. The Carthaginian was better calculated to acquire than to preserve. They depended upon commerce for the acquisition of wealth, and upon their wealth for the protection of their commerce. They owed their conquests to the venal blood and sinews of other people, and, like their ancestors the Phoenicians, exhibited their money bags as symbols of their power. They trusted too much to the valour of foreigners, and too little to that of their own natives. Thus whilst they were formidable abroad by their fleets and mercenary armies, they were weak and defenceless at home. But the event shewed, how dangerous it is for the greatest commercial nation to rely on

8. James II reigned from 1685 to 1688, William III from 1688 to 1702 (until 1694 jointly with his wife Mary), and Queen Anne from 1702 to 1714. James's reign had been "dangerous" because he had attempted to introduce absolute monarchy on the Continental pattern into England. The subsequent reigns were "warlike" because they saw England involved in two major European conflicts: first the War of the League of Augsburg, sometimes referred to as the War of the Grand Alliance (1690–97), and then the War of the Spanish Succession (1702–13).

this kind of mercantile policy; and that a nation of unarmed undisciplined traders can never be a match, whilst they are so circumstanced, for [382] a nation of soldiers. About two centuries ago a handful (comparatively speaking) of rude irregular Tartars subdued, and still enjoy the dominion of China, the most populous, and the richest commercial Empire in the universe.[9] And a neighbouring mercantile Republick,[10] by adhering too closely to these maxims, is at this time neither respected by her friends, nor feared by her enemies.

The English constitution was originally military, like that of every kingdom founded by our Gothick ancestors. Henry the VIIth gave the first spur to commerce, by diffusing property more equally amongst the commons at the expence of the nobility. From that time, the ancient military spirit of this nation has gradually dwindled to the low ebb, at which we now find it. But the great epocha of our marine, as well as commerce, ought properly to be fixed to the glorious reign of Elizabeth. The colonies settled during the peaceful reign of James the Ist, laid the foundation of our present extensive commerce. The civil wars between Charles the Ist and the parliament revived and diffused the ancient military spirit thro' the whole body of the people; and the able Cromwell made the English name more respectable in Europe,[11] than it ever had been under any of

9. Towards the end of the sixteenth century, the Manchu, who had hitherto lived quietly in eastern Manchuria, began to encroach on central Manchuria, and by 1621 the Manchu warlord Nurhachi controlled the entire northeast section of the Ming empire. Ming resistance endured until 1644, when the Manchu achieved hegemony. They went on to rule China until the Chinese Revolution (1911–12). Montagu's knowledge of Chinese history perhaps derives from the writings of the Jesuit missionary Joseph de Guignes, whose *Histoire Générale des Huns* had been published in Paris between 1756 and 1758.

10. The Netherlands. The golden age of Dutch prosperity had begun in the early years of the seventeenth century, and had lasted until the early years of the eighteenth. Thereafter her trade was eclipsed by that of France and England, and she entered a period of comparative stagnation. Montagu touches on Dutch military reversals during the War of the Austrian Succession (1740–48), when Dutch forces were brushed aside by the armies of France and Prussia.

11. During the Protectorate, Cromwell's foreign policy of concluding the Anglo-Dutch War, of entering into an alliance with France against Spain, and of acting as a mediator in the Baltic, had the effect of elevating England into a European great power.

our Monarchs. Our naval [383] glory seems to have reached its summit under that period; for though our marine is greatly encreased both in the number and strength of our shipping, yet we have by no means surpassed the commanders and seamen of that time either in bravery or ability. The reason is evident. Publick virtue then existed in its full force, and zeal for the national glory was the great spur to action. The commanders sailed in quest of honour, not lucre, and esteemed the glory of the capture as an adequate reward for the most hazardous enterprizes. Luxury was as much unknown to the highest class, as spirituous liquors were to the lowest. Discipline, sobriety, and an awful sense of religion, were strictly kept up amongst the private seamen; whilst the humane usage of the officers taught them to obey from love, and a just sense of their duty, not from the slavish principle of fear only. The immortal Blake[12] esteemed 500 l. for a ring, and the publick thanks of parliament, a glorious recompence for all those illustrious actions, which made Africa and Europe tremble, and raised the English flag to the summit of glory. Inferior merit, in later times, has been rewarded with coronets and great lucrative employments.

Luxury with its fatal effects was imported by Charles the IId at the Restoration. The [384] contagious influence of that bane to publick virtue and liberty, corrupted our manners, enervated our bodies, and debased our minds, whilst our military spirit subsided, in proportion as the love of pleasure increased. Charles the IId, nurtured in the high principles of prerogative,[13] was diffident of a militia composed of the whole body of the people. He obtained a standing force of about 4 or 5000 men under the specious denomination of guards and garrisons; which he increased afterwards to 8000, and suffered the Militia gradually to decay, 'till it became

12. Robert Blake (1598–1657), army and naval officer; along with Sir Francis Drake and Lord Nelson, one of the triumvirate of great English seamen. During the Anglo-Dutch war Blake engaged in the Channel four times with the Dutch admiral von Tromp between May 1652 and June 1653, emerging victorious on three occasions. After the conclusion of peace with the Dutch in 1654, Blake made English seapower felt in the Mediterranean, destroying a Barbary pirate fleet in the Gulf of Tunis in 1655. Finally, in April 1657 he destroyed a Spanish treasure fleet in the Canary Islands without suffering any loss himself.

13. The special right or privilege exercised by a monarch over all other persons, especially in relation to the common law (*OED*, 2a).

almost useless. A policy fatal to liberty, which has been too successfully copied, since that reign, by every iniquitous minister, who supported himself by faction. James the IId, devoted to bigotry, and influenced by the most weak, as well as the most wicked counsels, that ever prevailed in this kingdom, at one stroke disarmed the people, and established a large standing army. As the militia were unwilling to act against Monmouth and his followers,[14] whom they looked upon as the protector of their religion and liberties, James, concealing the true reason, declared to his Parliament, that he had found the Militia useless and unserviceable by experience, and insisted upon such supplies, as would enable him to support those additional troops, which he should find necessary for his security. And he had actually in-[385]creased his army to 30,000 men at the time of the Revolution. The whole reigns of William the Third and Ann are distinguished by war abroad and factions at home.[15] Yet though we entered into both those wars as principals, the military spirit of our people was not much improved; our national troops composed but a small part of the allied armies, and we placed our chief dependance upon foreign mercenaries.

14. James Scott, Duke of Monmouth (1649–85), was the illegitimate son of Charles II and Lucy Walter. As a Protestant, Monmouth was regarded by many as a plausible claimant to the throne, notwithstanding his illegitimacy, because of the absence of any legitimate heir of Charles's body, and because of the Roman Catholicism of the presumptive heir to the throne, the Duke of York (later James II). On the death of his father and the accession of his uncle James II on 6 February 1685, Monmouth, who had been banished to the Netherlands by Charles II for his part in the Rye House Plot, resolved to return to England and attempt a *coup d'état*. With a few followers he landed at Lyme Regis in June and quickly raised an army of 4,000 men. On 6 July 1685 his army, composed largely of West Country peasants, was routed at the battle of Sedgemoor. Monmouth himself was captured, taken to London, and beheaded on 15 July.

15. During the reign of Queen Anne (1702–14) the factional warfare between the two parties generated by the constitutional crises of the late seventeenth century, the Whigs and the Tories, reached alarming heights. As Swift reported to Archbishop King from Leicester on 6 December 1707: "They have been polling these three days, and the number of thousands pretty equall on both sides, the Partyes as usuall, High and Low, and there is not a Chambermaid, Prentice or Schoolboy in this whole Town, but what is warmly engaged on one side or tother" (Woolley, *Corr.*, vol. i, p. 164).

Frequent attempts have been made since that time to revive a national disciplined Militia, which have been as constantly defeated by corruption and the malignity of faction. Our late fears of an invasion, and the introduction of so large a body of foreign troops, a measure highly unpopular and distasteful, procured at last the long wished-for act for a Militia.[16] Mutilated as it was, and clogged with almost insuperable difficulties by the same faction, who durst not openly oppose it at that dangerous juncture, the real well-wishers to their country were glad to accept it. They looked upon it as a foundation laid for a much more useful and extensive Militia; which time and opportunity might enable them to perfect. Much has been said, and many assertions boldly thrown out of the utter impracticability of a national Militia. But this is either the language of corruption or of effeminacy and cowardice. The Ro-[386]mans, in the first Punick war,[17] found themselves unable to contend with the Carthaginians for want of a marine. Yet that magnanimous people, without any other knowledge of the mechanism of a ship, than what they acquired from a galley of their enemies, thrown by accident upon their coasts, without either shipwright or seaman, built, manned, and fitted out a fleet under the Consul Duilius in three months time, which engaged and totally defeated the grand fleet of Carthage, though that Republick had enjoyed the sovereignty of the sea unrivalled for time immemorial. This effort of the Roman magnanimity gives a higher idea of the Roman genius, than any other action recorded in their history. And by this alone we must be convinced, "That nothing is insurmountable to the unconquerable hand of liberty, when backed by publick virtue, and the generous resolution of a brave and willing people."[18]

16. Well-grounded fears of an invasion by France in 1756 had been strong enough to throw the ministry into a panic concerning the weakness of the nation's defences. For their response of an abortive Militia Bill, followed by the importing of foreign mercenaries, see above, p. 86, n. 149.

17. The first Punic war between Rome and Carthage lasted from 264 to 241 B.C. Now for the first time the Romans built a fleet (reportedly by copying a Carthaginian vessel wrecked on the coast of Italy), and won a great naval victory at Mylae, near Messina, in 260 B.C., which paved the way for their invasion of North Africa.

18. Despite appearances, not a quotation from another writer, but rather an instance of Montagu using the convention (slightly archaic in 1759) of using quotation marks to highlight a particularly important or sententious maxim.

The difficulties and obstacles in either case, I mean of making a fleet or establishing a good militia, will admit of no comparison. The Romans may almost be said to have created a fleet out of nothing. We have nothing more to do than to rouze and diffuse that martial spirit through the nation, which the arts of ministerial policy have so long endeavoured to keep dormant. Great indeed has been the outcry of the danger of [387] trusting arms in the dissolute hands of the scum and refuse of the nation in these licentious times. These I consign to the proper severity of the martial discipline of an army; for of this kind of people, the bulk of every army in Europe is at this time composed. I speak to the nobility and gentry, the traders and yeomanry of this kingdom, to all those who are possessed of property, and have something to lose, and, from the interest of their respective shares, are equally concerned in the preservation of the whole. Of such as these the Roman armies were composed who conquered Italy.[19] Every Roman soldier was a citizen possessed of property, and equally interested in the safety of the Republick. The wisdom of the Romans in the choice of their soldiers never appeared in so conspicuous a light as after the defeat at Cannae.[20] Every citizen pressed to take up arms in defence of his country, and not only refused his pay, but generously gave up what gold and silver he was master of, even to the most trifling ornaments, for the publick service. The behaviour of the women too, to their immortal honour, was equally great and disinterested. Such is the spirit, which a truly brave and free people will ever exert in a time of distress and danger. Marius was the first man who broke through that wise maxim, and raised his forces out of the [388] sixth class, which consisted only of the dregs and refuse of the people. Marius too gave the first stab to the constitution of his country. People of property are not only the chief support, but the best and safest defence of a free and opulent country; and their example will always have a proper influence upon their inferiors.[21]

19. For the transformation of the Roman army by the consul Marius from a citizen militia with a property qualification to a professional army of volunteers recruited from all classes, see above, p. 221, n. 20.

20. See above, p. 142, n. 78, and pp. 236–37, n. 43.

21. The notion that men of property enjoyed a natural moral authority was widely diffused in mid-eighteenth-century England. For a discussion of the origins and ramifications of that prejudice, see Barrell, *Survey,* esp. pp. 51–109.

Nothing but an extensive Militia can revive the once martial spirit of this nation, and we had even better once more be a nation of soldiers, like our renowned ancestors, than a nation of abject crouching slaves to the most rapacious, and most insolent people in the universe. Let us not be too much elated, and lulled into a fatal security from some late successes, in which our national forces had no share. Nothing is so common as unexpected vicissitudes in war. Our enemies have many and great resources; our heroick ally,[22] in case of a reverse of fortune, few or none. Our haughty and implacable enemy, unaccustomed to insults in their own territories, will think the blot in their honour indelible, 'till they have returned the affront upon our coasts with redoubled vengeance.[23] Whilst a pretender to this crown exists,[24] France will never want a plausible pretext for invading this kingdom. Their last attempt answered the proposed end so well, that we may be certain, so politick [389] an enemy, instigated by revenge, will omit no opportunity of playing the same successful engine once more against us. The French are now perfectly well acquainted with our weak side. The violent shock our national credit received by the inroad of a few Highlanders[25] only, into the heart of this country, has taught them the infallible method of distressing us in that essential point. Should therefore our measures for annoying that nation be ever so wisely planned, yet we can never hope to execute them with

22. That is, Frederick the Great; see above, p. 131, n. 44.

23. A reference to anticipated French reprisals for the English raids on Cherbourg and St. Malo in the late summer of 1758; see above, p. 251, n. 1.

24. Charles Edward Stuart, the grandson of James II, the leader of the Jacobite rebellion of 1745–46, and the last serious Stuart claimant to the throne of England, lived until 1788 (although after he settled in Italy in 1766 the major Roman Catholic powers no longer pressed his claim).

25. Charles Stuart landed on the west coast of Scotland in July 1745, and raised an army from the Highland clans. In September he took possession of Edinburgh, and defeated the forces under Sir John Cope at the battle of Prestonpans. In November, with an army of some 5,000 men, he crossed the border and began a march on London, reaching Derby and causing panic in the capital before being forced to retreat by the approach of a vastly superior Hanoverian army. His forces were finally defeated at the battle of Culloden (16 April 1746), Charles Stuart himself making his escape to France only after five months of desperately evading capture.

proportionate vigour, whilst we remain defenceless at home. If the bare alarm only of an invasion frightened us so lately into the expence, as well as ignominy, of importing foreign mercenaries for our own defence, the French know by experience, that an actual attempt would compel us to recall our fleets and forces, and again expose our commerce, colonies, and our only ally to their mercy. No man, I believe, is so weak as to imagine, that France will be deterred from such an attempt by the danger which may attend it. For if we reflect upon the number of her troops, the risque of 10 or 20,000 men, can hardly be deemed an object worthy the attention of so formidable a power. For should they all perish in the attempt, yet France would be amply repaid by the advantages she would draw from that [390] confusion, which they would necessarily occasion. The traitor who lately pointed out the proper time,[26] as well as place for an invasion, and the fatal effects it would have upon publick credit, whatever success might attend it, furnishes us with a convincing proof, that France never loses sight of so useful a measure. A consideration which greatly inforces the necessity of national union, and a national Militia. The unequalled abilities of one man[a] (humanly speaking) have given a turn to the affairs of Germany, as happy, as it was amazing; and hope begins to dawn upon

a. The King of Prussia.

26. Montagu refers to spy and traitor Florence Hensey (fl. 1748–60), whose case had attracted much attention in the summer of 1758. Hensey, of Irish Catholic extraction, had been educated at the English College at St. Omer, and subsequently at the University of Leiden, where he had studied medicine. After an itinerant career on the continent as a doctor, in 1756 he had returned to England. *The Gentleman's Magazine* for June 1758 picks up the narrative:

> Soon after the declaration of war in 1756, he [Hensey] became a pensioner to *France*, and agreed, for 100 guineas a year, to give the best intelligence he could of the state of affairs in this kingdom. But a difference afterwards arising about his salary, which he represented as too small, and as an argument in his favour said he belonged to a club in the *Strand* (from which he could gain intelligence) at which they always drank *French* wine at dinner: the correspondence appears to have been some time discontinued; but in *January* 1757, it was agreed, that the Doctor should receive 25 guineas a month, on condition of sending intelligence every post, but to forfeit a guinea for every omission; he received however no more than one monthly payment, and they gave for reason, that his intelligence was nothing but extracts from the news-papers.

our late despairing nation. The wise and vigorous measures of our present Patriot-ministry have conciliated not only the esteem, but the universal confidence of the people. Under the present ministry we laid the foundation of this long wished-for, though long despaired of, Militia. If we support their administration with unanimity and vigour, we may fix this great national object, upon that extensive and useful plan, which was designed and hoped for by every lover of his country. The fate therefore of the Militia depends absolutely upon the present crisis. For if we supinely neglect this auspicious opportunity, future efforts will be just as ineffectual, as the point we [391] have already carried with so much labour and assiduity. For the same faction, which has invariably opposed every attempt for a national Militia, are avowed enemies to the present ministers, from that

---

The plan for carrying on this correspondence was the following: The Dr wrote a common letter with ink, and between each line the secrets of *England* in lemon juice. This was inclosed under three or four different covers, directed to different persons, in the secret, who conveyed them from one hand to another, till the first inclosed came to the principal for whom it was designed. He had a brother who is a Jesuit, and was chaplain and secretary to the *Spanish* ambassador at the *Hague*, from whom our resident at that court gained a knowledge of some secrets relating to *England*, even before he had received any account thereof from his own court. This put him upon enquiry, and he soon learnt that the secretary had a brother, a physician in *London*, from whom possibly he might get his intelligence; suspicion being thus raised, the Dr was watch'd, and 29 of his letters stopt.

From these letters it appeared, that he gave the *French* the first account of Adm. *Boscawen*'s sailing to *North America*, and of the taking the *Alcide* and *Lys*, with every minute circumstance relating to it, and from that time, of the sailing of every fleet, and its destination; and was so minute as to give an account even of the launching of a man of war; he also gave an account of all difficulties relating to raising money; and particularly described the secret expedition in 1757, assuring them, it was intended against *Rochfort* or *Brest*, but gave his opinion for the former. And in one of his letters he particularly advised a descent of the *French* upon our coast, as the most certain method of distressing the government by affecting publick credit; and mentioned the time when, and the place where it would be most proper (*Gentleman's Magazine*, vol. 18 [1758], p. 287).

On 14 June 1758 Hensey was found guilty of treason, and was sentenced to be hanged, drawn, and quartered on 12 July. A series of reprieves followed, and Hensey was eventually released from Newgate on 7 September 1759. On the accession of George III Hensey was pardoned, and went to reside in France.

antipathy, which private interest and the lust of power for selfish ends, will ever bear to Patriotism and publick virtue. Should therefore the evil genius of this nation again prevail, and the same faction once more seize the helm of Government, we must give up all hopes of a Militia as well as every other national measure.

Let us throw but one glance upon the present situation of these once glorious Republicks, and we cannot help reflecting upon the final and direful catastrophe, which will eternally result from the prevalence of ambitious and selfish faction supported by corruption.

Greece, once the nurse of arts and sciences, the fruitful mother of Philosophers, Lawgivers, and Heroes, now lies prostrate under the iron yoke of ignorance and barbarism—Carthage, once the mighty sovereign of the ocean, and the center of universal commerce, which poured the riches of the nations into her lap, now puzzles the inquisitive traveller, in his researches after even the vestiges of her ruins.—And Rome, the mistress of the universe, which once [392] contained whatever was esteemed great or brilliant in human nature, is now sunk into the ignoble seat of whatever is esteemed mean and infamous.

Should faction again predominate and succeed in its destructive views, and the dastardly maxims of luxury and effeminacy universally prevail amongst us—Such too will soon be the fate of Britain.

FINIS

The French Translation of Montagu's
Reflections

In 1793 a French translation of Montagu's work, by "le Citoyen Cantwell" (the usual pseudonym of the translator André Samuel Michel), was published in Paris as *De la Naissance et de la Chute des Anciennes Républiques.*[1] For the most part, Michel made only small changes to Montagu's text. But he also added a final chapter (pp. 373–84), in which he applied the lessons of the work to the situation of the French republic in 1793. For a discussion of what the emphases of this chapter reveal about Michel's political affinities, see the Introduction (above, pp. ix–xxvii).

The French text of this final chapter, followed by a translation, is given below.

CHAPITRE X

Réflexions & conclusion du Traducteur

L'AUTEUR anglois du présent ouvrage ayant eu pour but d'offrir à ses compatriotes des conseils & des réflexions fondés sur des faits & sur une

---

1. Michel, André Samuel (1744–1802); translator as "M. de Cantwel" of Anne Hughes's *Henry and Isabella* (1788) as *Isabella et Henri,* 2 vols. (Paris, 1789) and as "Cantwell" of Mrs. Burton's *Laura, or The Orphan* (1797) as *Laure, ou la grotte du père Philippe,* 2 vols. (Paris, "l'an 7" [1799]).

longue expérience, j'ai cru que ces mêmes réflexions pourroient être de quelque utilité dans les circonstances où la France se trouve aujourd'hui. Tel est le motif qui m'en a fait entreprendre la traduction.

Au moment de fonder, en lui donnant des loix, une république trop vaste peut-être, ce n'est que dans l'étude des différentes constitutions de toutes les républiques de l'antiquité, & dans l'examen suivi du cercle qu'elles ont parcouru depuis leur naissance jusqu'à leur chûte, que nos législateurs pourront puiser de solides instructions.

Ils verront que les plus célèbres législateurs de l'antiquité ont tous donné la préférence aux gouvernemens mixtes, ou composés de différens pouvoirs que se balancent & se maintiennent réciproquement dans les limites fixées par la constitution.

Ils verront que la liberté n'exista jamais dans les états où il n'y avoit qu'un seul pouvoir, parce qu'un pouvoir unique est toujours absolu: ils seront forcés de convenir que les gouvernemens strictement populaires ont toujours été les moins durables, les plus sujets aux factions, les plus voisins de l'anarchie; qu'ils ne peuvent subsister que chez un peuple dont les mœurs sont encore pures, & chez qui les vertus publiques sont encore dans toute leur vigueur: mais qu'un peuple corrompu est toujours esclave sous la plus libre des constitutions; parce qu'il ne sait faire de sa liberté d'autre usage que celui de la vendre.

Toutes les républiques de l'antiquité ont constaté successivement cette vérité douloureuse; & l'histoire ne nous présente qu'un seul exemple d'un peuple dont les mœurs ont été régénérées. C'est au moyen d'un gouvernement mixte que le grand Lycurgue a opéré ce miracle unique.

Les Romains ont inutilement multiplié les loix les plus sages; la dépravation de leurs mœurs a toujours été en croissant jusqu'à la dissolution de leur empire. On m'observera peut-être que ce que Lycurgue a fait, il est encore possible de le faire. Je répondrai que, pour pouvoir l'espérer, il faudroit pouvoir aussi réunir les mêmes circonstances. La corruption n'avoit pas poussé à Sparte des racines très-profondes; les Lacédémoniens étoient un peuple de soldats presque toujours en guerre, qui conservoit toute son énergie & un fonds de vertu publique réelle & non pas simulée. Ils étoient tous rassemblés dans l'enceinte d'une même ville.

Lycurgue abolit les dettes, fit des terres un partage égal & inaliénable, & rendit les Lacédémoniens strictement égaux: mais cette égalité de fait ne pouvoit exister que chez un peuple composé de citoyens qui jouissoient tous sans travailler d'une fortune égale & inaliénable. Toute œuvre servile étoit sévérement défendue à un Lacédémonien. Les Ilotes, leurs esclaves, exerçoient toutes les professions viles ou lucratives. Les Lacédémoniens ne connoissoient point d'autre métier que celui des armes. Leur temps se passoit dans les assemblées publiques ou dans des exercices militaires; ils mangeoient publiquement en commun, & l'emploi de toutes leur heures étoit fixé par la constitution. Lycurgue défendit le commerce, & l'usage des monnoies d'or & d'argent. Les Lacédémoniens obtenoient difficilement la permission de sortir de leur pays; & toute relation avec les étrangers leur étoit interdite. Telles furent les précautions de Lycurgue pour ramener & conserver la pureté des mœurs parmi ses compatriotes. Je ne connois point de peuple chez lequel ces mesures fussent aujourd'hui praticables; & je les crois cependant indispensables pour régénérer des mœurs corrompues, & établir l'égalité dans toute l'étendue de son acception.

J'observerai aussi que Lycurgue & tous les législateurs de l'antiquité dont on admire encore le génie, donnèrent pour base à leur institution une religion & un culte public; que les préceptes religieux firent une partie de l'éducation nationale, & que le moindre manque de respect pour les cérémonies de cette religion étoit puni rigoureusement. Le victorieux Alcibiade, soupçonné d'avoir mutilé les statues de Mercure & profané des mystères religieux, fut condamné par les Athéniens à perdre la vie. Les Romains se distinguèrent long-temps par leur respect inviolable pour leurs Dieux & pour toutes leurs cérémonies religieuses. J'ajouterai que tous ceux qui ont lu l'histoire avec attention, doivent avoir apperçu que chez toutes les nations qui ont successivement disparu de la surface du globe, les vices & la corruption ont pris naissance & fait leurs progrès funestes en proportion du mépris des opinions religieuses. Lorsque les Romains commencèrent à mépriser leurs Dieux & leurs oracles, ils perdirent aussi beaucoup de leur valeur militaire, & ne respectèrent pas long-temps la foi de traités & les conventions des hommes. De toutes les religions connues, celle des chrétiens a sans contredit la morale la plus pure & la plus sublime; mais elles tendent toutes plus ou moins à rendre les hommes justes & bienfaisans. Elles viennent toutes à l'appui de la loi. Combien l'effrayante alternative des peines & des récompenses après la mort n'a-t-elle pas détourné de crimes de ce monde! Combien n'a-t-elle pas soutenu de vertus chancelantes, épouvanté d'hommes pervers, & consolé de vertueux infortunés! Si cette sublime idée étoit une chimère, il faudroit tâcher de la conserver. Quelques philosophes ont aimé & pratiqué, dit-on, la vertu pour elle, sans espoir & sans crainte d'une autre vie. J'ignore si leurs vertus auroient résisté à de fortes épreuves: mais, quoi qu'il en soit, de tels hommes seront toujours très-rares; & c'est d'après le caractère des hommes en général qu'il faut raisonner.

Les legislateurs de l'antiquité ne se sont pas bornés à établir des préceptes religieux, ils y ont joint des cérémonies & ont attaché à leur pratique la même conséquence qu'à celle des préceptes; parce qu'ils sentoient qu'il faut ramener l'homme à la réflexion par ses sens, & que les cérémonies de la religion sont les plus fermes appuis de ses préceptes.

Chez les nations qui habitent aujourd'hui l'Europe, où la masse du peuple forcée de travailler constamment pour vivre, ne peut pas acquérir une grande instruction morale, les préceptes religieux sont indispensables, parce qu'ils contiennent en peu de mots tous les devoirs de l'homme envers son semblable; parce qu'ils ordonnent le respect & l'obéissance à la loi. Otez à ces peuples leur culte public, ils oublieront bientôt les préceptes religieux & ceux de la morale qu'ils contiennent. Leurs passions n'auront plus de frein, & la loi sera toujours insuffisante pour les calmer. Le code de loix le plus sage & le plus complet ne peut pas atteindre toutes les actions condamnables, il n'a de prise ni sur les sentimens ni sur la volonté. La crainte des loix peut empêcher l'homme de commettre publiquement un crime; mais elle ne suffira point pour lui inspirer l'amour de la vertu. La croyance d'un Dieu qui connoît nos plus secrettes pensées tend à épurer l'ame; & si la vertu n'est pas inutile dans ce monde, les principes religieux y sont indispensables.

Des législateurs véritablement amis des hommes & de leur patrie, prendront ces objets en sérieuse considération. Ils s'occuperont d'assurer l'unité de la république françoise & ne se dissimuleront point la difficulté de cette entreprise. Ils sentiront que lorsque l'enthousiasme sera passé avec le danger, lorsque la république n'aura plus d'ennemis à combattre, les efforts cesseront de se porter vers un même but; & que chaque département de cette vaste république commencera à s'occuper des ses avantages locaux ou particuliers. Cet événement peut entraîner des commotions & des déchiremens funestes. Ce n'est qu'au moyen d'un système sage & modéré qu'on pourra peut-être les prévenir. Sous le prétexte de jouir pleinement de leur liberté & de leurs avantages naturels, des villes maritimes essayeront peut-être de se délivrer du poids de la dette & des contributions publiques en se déclarant indépendantes. Cet exemple une fois donné, seroit aveuglément suivi par les autres départemens, sans examiner si cette scission leur seroit à tous également avantageuse.

La milice nationale doit encore être prise en grande considération. Cette excellente institution ne produira le bien qu'on peut attendre qu'après avoir été soumise à des restrictions. Elle ne devroit être composée à l'avenir que de citoyens assez riches pour servir l'état sans paie. Il s'en trouve en France plus d'un million, & c'est plus qu'il n'en faut pour la mettre à l'abri des commotions intérieures, & des invasions étrangères. L'état ne sera plus obéré par les frais d'un armement défensif. Les citoyens obligés de travailler pour leur subsistance, pourront exercer tranquillement leur métier ou leur profession; l'agriculture, le commerce & l'industrie conserveront leur activité dans tous les temps. La suppression de la solde facilitera cette innovation; la classe indigente renoncera volontairement au métier des armes, & un million d'hommes disciplinés dispenseront l'état d'entretenir une armée.

On m'observera sans doute que ce système détruit l'égalité. Je répondrai qu'il est impossible de détruire une égalité qui n'existe point & qui n'existera jamais tandis qu'il y aura en France des citoyens riches & des citoyens indigens. J'ajouterai que les riches étant les plus intéressés à la sûreté de l'état, doivent y faire les plus grands sacrifices; & qu'un système qui assure dans tous les temps l'activité des cultures, du commerce & de l'industrie; qui laisse aux pauvres la liberté de suivre dans tous les temps, les travaux nécessaires à la subsistance de leurs familles; qui dispense l'état d'entretenir une armée, & de tous les frais des armemens défensifs, mérite quelques considérations. Indépendamment des avantages que j'ai détaillés, j'en pourrois indiquer d'autres relatifs à la sûreté & à la tranquillité de la république, qui sera toujours précaire tandis qu'on laissera des armes entre les mains d'une classe indigente & vénale, toujours disposée à seconder les factions, & très-capable de se servir contre l'état des armes qu'on lui a confiées pour le défendre.

Tel fut lc systême militaire des Romains; & l'histoire nous apprend à quel degré de gloire & de prospérité ce systême les a conduits. Marius fut le premier qui dérogea à ces principes. Il composa son armée de la classe indigente, de tous les bandits de Rome & des environs. Mais Marius vouloit opprimer sa patrie, piller & égorger ses concitoyens. L'histoire nous a fidélement transmis les effrayantes atrocités des soldats de Marius; & nous avons eu chez nous, très-récemment, des échantillons de ces odieux massacres. Par-tout, les massacreurs étoient vêtus de l'uniforme national; & cette tache ne lui auroit pas été imprimée si le système que je présente eût été en vigueur. Ce système peut seul faire cesser les troubles de l'anarchie & ramener l'ordre, la sûreté & la tranquillité publiques, qu'il sera toujours impossible de maintenir tandis que tous les individus seront armés; car dans un état très-vaste il y aura toujours une nombreuse classe d'indigens qui, espérant gagner au tumulte, aux désordres, & surtout au pillage, tâchera de prolonger ou de renouveller les commotions & les insurrections, dont la durée entraîne toujours la dissolution des états, ou la tyrannie du gouvernement militaire dans toute sa barbarie. Je sais que de grandes fautes ont rendu cette mesure difficile; mais il faut vaincre ces obstacles, ou voir périr la république sous les coups de factieux, qui, pour parvenir plus facilement à la déchirer, se couvriront tour-à-tour du masque trompeur de la popularité.*

Depuis trois ans notre expérience à cet égard est douloureuse & plus que suffisante. Parmi ceux qui ont figuré sur la scène, & passe long-temps pour des patriotes ardens & désintéressés, en est-il un seul qui n'ait été reconnu pour un hypocrite ambitieux ou avide? Et n'auroit-on pas dû le prévoir chez un peuple où le patriotisme est le masque du moment, & où l'egoïsme est depuis trop long-temps le seul trait constant & prononcé du caractère national? Réfléchissez, législateurs, à ce que vous allez faire. A quoi nous serviroit la meilleure de toutes les constitutions, si elle est incompatible

---

* Je recommande à nos législateurs l'examen du système politique & militaire de Tullius Servius, que les Romains suivirent invariablement & avec les plus grands succès jusqu'au temps de Marius, qui n'y dérogea que pour faciliter ses vengeances & commettre impunément tous les genres de forfaits. Avec le secours d'une armée de bandits, il commanda despotiquement dans Rome, & tous les citoyens riches furent ou égorgés ou dépouillés de leurs biens.

avec nos mœurs & nos vices? Rappellez-vous la réponse de Solon aux Athéniens: "Je ne vous ai point donné les meilleures loix possibles, mais les meilleures qui puissent vous convenir." Un architecte chargé de construire un édifice, ne doit-il pas mesurer & calculer d'abord le terrein qu'on lui confie? & le plan le plus magnifique ne seroit-il pas une absurdité si la disposition du terrein en rendoit l'exécution impossible? Il ne suffit pas de faire des loix, il faut en assurer l'exécution. Vous les offrirez, dites-vous, à la sanction du peuple; mais cette sanction empêchera-t-elle qu'elles ne soient impracticables? Ceux qui les auront approuvées les violeront le lendemain. Et si vous êtes de bonne foi, relativement au vœu libre du peuple, ne sentez-vous pas qu'il est presqu'impossible de le connoître dans un temps de factions, de violences & d'atrocités impunies, où la terreur ferme la bouche à tous les citoyens timides qui composent la grande majorité de la nation? Votre mission est dangereuse; mais vous deviez le savoir quand vous l'avez acceptée: & si vous aviez alors le dessein de sauver la France, il faut y réussir ou périr avec elle. Et n'espérez pas de vous sauver en sacrifiant l'honneur & la patrie: cette insigne lâcheté, dont je vous crois incapable, ne serviroit qu'à rendre votre perte plus assurée. Il ne vous reste qu'un seul moyen de salut, c'est un courage & une loyauté imperturbables.

FIN

CHAPTER X

Reflections and Conclusion of the Translator

The goal of the English author of the present work having been to offer his countrymen advice and reflections grounded on facts and long experience, I thought that these same reflections might be of some use in the circumstances in which France finds itself today. This is the motive which made me undertake this translation.

At the moment of founding, and of giving laws to, a republic which is perhaps too large, our legislators can draw solid guidance only from studying the different constitutions of all the ancient republics and from sustained scrutiny of the circular path they followed from their birth to their fall.

They will see that the most famous legislators of antiquity all preferred mixed governments, or governments made up of different powers which are in balance and which keep each other within the bounds fixed by the constitution.

They will see that liberty has never existed in states where there was only one sole power, because a single power is always absolute: they will be obliged to agree that exclusively popular governments have always been the least durable, the most liable to factiousness, the nearest to anarchy; that they can survive only among a people whose manners are still pure, and among whom the public virtues are still in their prime: but that a corrupted people is still enslaved under the freest of constitutions; because such people know of no other use for their liberty but to sell it.

All the republics of antiquity have in their turn demonstrated this sorrowful truth; and history presents us with only a single example of a people whose manners have been regenerated. It was by means of a mixed government that the great Lycurgus effected this unique miracle.

The Romans multiplied the wisest laws to no purpose; the corruption of their manners was always increasing until their empire collapsed. Perhaps it will be said that what Lycurgus did can be done again. I reply that, to have a hope of doing so, you would also have to reassemble the same circumstances. In Sparta, corruption had not established very deep roots; the Spartans were a military people who were almost always at war, who still retained all their energy and a fund of public virtue which was real and not affected. They all lived together within the walls of the same city.

Lycurgus abolished debts, divided up the territory into equal and inalienable portions, and made the Spartans strictly equal: but that *de facto* equality could exist only amidst a people who all enjoyed an equal and inalienable fortune without working. A Spartan was severely forbidden to engage in servile work. The Helots, their slaves, performed all vile or lucrative functions. The Spartans were acquainted with no trade but that of arms. They passed their time in public assemblies or in military exercises, they ate in public at common messes, and the employment of all their time was prescribed by the constitution. Lycurgus forbad commerce and the use of gold and silver coin. Only with difficulty were the Spartans given permission to leave their country, and they were forbidden to have dealings with foreigners. Such were Lycurgus's precautions to restore and preserve purity of manners among his countrymen. Today, I know of no people amongst whom these measures would be feasible, and yet I believe they are indispensable for restoring corrupted manners and establishing equality in its fullest sense.

I note also that Lycurgus, and all the legislators of antiquity whose genius we still admire, placed religion and public observance in the foundation of their institution, that religious teaching formed part of national education, and that the slightest disrespect for religious ceremonies was rigorously punished. The victorious Alcibiades, suspected of having defaced the statues of Mercury and profaned religious mysteries, was condemned to death by the Athenians. The Romans were for long distinguished by their inviolable respect for their gods, and for all their religious ceremonies. I will add that all attentive students of history must have noticed that, among all the nations which have successively disappeared from the surface of the globe, vice and corruption had their birth and pursued their fatal course in proportion to the scorn expressed for religious beliefs. When the Romans began to despise their gods and their oracles, they also lost a great deal of their military merit and were not long in losing respect for good faith in treaties and human conventions. Of all known religions, that of the Christians has undeniably the purest and most sublime moral teaching; but they all more or less tend to make men just and charitable. They all support the rule of law. How many have been deflected from worldly crimes by the terrifying alternative of rewards and punishments after death! How many wavering virtues has it not sustained, how many wicked men has it not horrified, how many unfortunate men of virtue has it not consoled! If this sublime idea were chimerical, one would have to try to preserve it. It is said that some philosophers have loved and practiced virtue for her own sake, without the hope and fear of an afterlife. I do not know if their virtues would have been able to resist a strong trial: but, however that may be, such men will always be very rare; and one must reason on the basis of the character of men in general.

The legislators of antiquity did not limit themselves to establishing religious teachings; they reinforced them with ceremonies and attached thc samc importance to the performance of these ceremonies as to the teachings. They did so because they appreciated that man must be led to reflection by means of his senses and that religious ceremonies are the firmest support of religious teachings.

Among the nations of modern Europe, where the mass of the people, forced to labor without remission in order to live, cannot attain a high level of moral education, religious teachings are indispensable, because they contain in few words all the duties of man toward his fellow man; because they command respect for and obedience to the law. Strip these peoples of their public religion and they will soon forget their religious teachings and the moral teachings they contain. Their passions will be unbridled, and the law will always be inadequate to calm them. The wisest and most complete legal code cannot reach all reprehensible actions, having no purchase on either feelings or the will. Fear of the laws may prevent a man from committing a crime in public, but it will never be enough to inspire in him the love of virtue. Belief in a god who knows our most secret thoughts tends to purify the soul; and if virtue is not useless in this world, then it cannot do without religious principles.

Legislators who are truly friends to men, and to their homeland, will give serious consideration to these subjects. They will take care to ensure the unity of the French republic, and they will not disguise from themselves the difficulty of this undertaking. They will appreciate that, when enthusiasm has passed along with danger, when the republic has no more enemies to fight, the struggle to reach a common goal will also cease; and that each *département* of this vast republic will begin to turn its attention to its local or particular advantages. When this happens it may bring in its wake fatal disturbances and ruptures. They can perhaps be prevented only by a wise and moderate system. Under the pretext of taking full advantage of their liberty and their natural advantages, some coastal towns will perhaps attempt to free themselves from the burden of debt and public contributions by declaring themselves independent. Once that example has been set, it would be blindly followed by the other *départements*, without examining whether that secession would be equally advantageous to them all.

The national militia must also be given great consideration. This excellent institution will yield the expected benefit only after being subjected to restrictions. In the future it should be made up of only citizens rich enough to serve the state without pay. In France there are more than a million such people, and that is more than necessary to protect the country from internal disturbances and foreign invasions. The state will no longer be burdened by the cost of its armed defence. Citizens who have to work for their living will be able to pursue their trade or their profession in peace; agriculture, trade, and industry will maintain their activity at all times. The suppression of military pay will make possible this innovation: the poor will voluntarily surrender their military calling, and a million disciplined men will release the state from the maintenance of an army.

No doubt it will be pointed out to me that this system destroys equality. I will reply that it is impossible to destroy an equality which does not exist and which will never exist while there are in France rich citizens and poor citizens. I will add that the rich, having a greater interest in the security of the state, must make the greatest sacrifices for it, and that a system which ensures at all times the activity of cultivation, of trade, and of industry, which allows the poor the freedom to pursue, at all times, the labours necessary for the livelihood of their families, which frees the state from the maintenance of an army and of all the costs of defense, deserves some consideration. In addition to the advantages I have specified, I could point out others relating to the security and peace of the republic, which will always be precarious while weapons are left in the hands of a poor and venal class, always ready to support factions and quite capable of turning against the state those weapons entrusted to it for its defense.

Such was the military system of the Romans, and history teaches us to what degree of glory and prosperity this system led them. Marius was the first to depart from these principles. He made up his army from the poor, from all the bandits of Rome and the surrounding region. But Marius wished to oppress the state, to loot and slit the throats of his fellow-citizens. History has faithfully handed down to us the terrifying atrocities of Marius's soldiery; and, very recently, we have had among ourselves a sampling of those hateful massacres. Everywhere the perpetrators of the massacres were dressed in the national uniform; and that stain would not have been printed upon it had the system I am putting forward been established. This system alone is able to halt the troubles of anarchy and restore the public order, security and peace, which it will always be impossible to maintain while all individuals are armed; for in a very large state there will always be a numerous impoverished class who, hoping to gain from tumult, from disorder, and above all from looting, will try to prolong or to renew disturbances and insurrections, which if they last bring always in their wake the dissolution of the state, or the tyranny of military government, in all its barbarity. I know that great mistakes have made this measure difficult; but these obstacles must be surmounted, or we will see the republic perish under the blows of the factious, who, in order to attain more easily their goal of tearing it down, will conceal themselves in turn behind the deceitful mask of popularity.*

For the past three years our experience on that score has been distressing and more than adequate. Among those who have stepped upon the stage, and who have long been taken for ardent and disinterested lovers of their country, is there even one who has not been recognized as either an ambitious or a greedy hypocrite? And ought one not to have foreseen this among a people where patriotism is the mask of the moment and where selfishness has been for too long the sole constant and emphatic feature in the national character? Legislators, think about what you are going to do. What use will be the best of all constitutions if it is incompatible with our manners and our vices? Remember the reply made by Solon to the Athenians: "I have not given you the best laws possible, but the best laws that will suit you." An architect charged with constructing a building, must he not first of all measure and survey the plot of land which has been entrusted to him? And would the most magnificent design not be an absurdity if the lie of the land made it impossible to realize it? It is

---

* I advise our legislators to study the political and military system of Tullius Servius, which the Romans followed without variation and with the greatest success until the time of Marius, who departed from it only to make it easier for him to pursue his vendettas and to commit all sorts of crimes without punishment. With the help of an army of bandits, he ruled as a despot in Rome, and all the rich citizens either had their throats cut or were stripped of their possessions.

not enough to pass laws; you have to make sure they are put into practice. You say that you will offer them to be ratified by the people, but will that ratification prevent them from being impracticable? Those who have approved them will break them tomorrow. And if you are in good faith when it comes to the free wishes of the people, do you not appreciate that it is almost impossible to know what those wishes are in a time of faction, of violence, and of unpunished atrocities, and when terror stops the mouths of all the intimidated citizens who make up the great majority of the nation? Your mission is dangerous, but you must have known that when you accepted it: and if you still plan to save France, you must either succeed or perish with her. And do not think to save yourselves by sacrificing honor and the homeland: that egregious cowardice, of which I do not think you are capable, would serve only to make your loss more certain. There remains to you only one course of safety—that of undaunted courage and loyalty.

THE END

Extracts from Reviews of the First Edition of Montagu's *Reflections*

The Gentleman's Magazine

Mr. *Montague* observes in his preface, that "the *points* which have lately exercised so many pens, *turn* upon the expediency or absolute insignificancy of a militia; or, what principles conduce most to the power, the happiness, and the duration of a free people," and that in this dispute, historical facts have been sometimes unfairly, and sometimes imperfectly quoted.

This observation, we are told, determined him to examine impartially the evidence arising from antient history, relative to the subject; and he has in this work offered to the publick the result of his enquiries; his design is to warn his countrymen, by the example of other states, of the fatal consequences which must proceed from intestine divisions at this critical juncture; and to show, that the resemblance between the manners of our own times, and the manners of the celebrated republicks of antiquity, in their most degenerate periods, is in many particulars very striking; that the causes which contributed to their ruin operate very strongly among us; and that as the same causes, either soon or late, always produce the same effects, we cannot hope to escape, unless we apply speedy and adequate remedies.

The Gentleman's Magazine, vol. 29 (March 1759), pp. 138–39.

As he supposes degeneracy of manners to be the immediate cause of the subversion of a state, he has endeavoured to shew the causes that have first produced a degeneracy of manners. It is not possible for us to trace this author through his accounts of the republics of *Sparta, Athens, Thebes, Carthage,* and *Rome;* to remark the difference between their constitutions and ours, in all their particulars; or shew what might be safely admitted among us, that was dangerous to them; that there is, however, such difference, appears from his account of *Sparta.* [Here the reviewer quotes from pp. 42–43.] It is not the opinion of this writer that *Lycurgus,* in all these particulars, is a pattern to a *British* minister, and that the happiness and duration of our state would be secured by prohibiting commerce and the arts, banishing gold and silver, and circulating iron money. He seems to have included his principal admonition to *Britain* in the causes which he has assigned for the rapid declension of the republic of *Rome,* which we shall therefore extract as the best view of his performance which the nature of this miscellany will admit. [The reviewer then quotes from pp. 192–209 (abridged).]

The Critical Review

We are not here to enquire how far the author of this work has been obliged for many of his observations to authors antient and modern, foreign and domestic, it is sufficient to say, that the performance is in itself elegant, and at this time seasonable. The stile is animated and perspicuous, and the applications he has made of antient history to the present state of his own country, which seems to be the chief scope of the work, are, in general, just, and sometimes happy.

In an introduction prefixed to the work, he observes very truly, "that what has happened to those free states (the Antient Republics) may at last prove the melancholy fate of our own country: especially when we reflect, that the same causes which contributed to their ruin, operate at

The Critical Review, vol. 7 (March 1759), pp. 249–54.

this time strongly amongst us." One of the favourite views of the author (and a most laudable one it is) is to inculcate strongly, from the examples of the Antient Republics, the doctrine of a national militia to be kept up in England.

The work before us begins with a view of the Spartan Republic, which is exhibited in a most concise and elegant manner. He then proceeds to that of Athens, all along pointing out the foundation, the principles, and the excellencies of their several generals, statesmen, and other patriots. Amongst other striking resemblances between the old Athenians and the modern English, the author takes notice of the passion of both for theatrical exhibitions. As a specimen of our author's way of writing and reasoning, on this and other heads, the reader will please to accept of the following. [The reviewer then quotes from pp. 83–87.]

Our author next reviews the History of the Republic of Thebes, and draws a most beautiful character of those two great Theban heroes and patriots Pelopidas and Epaminondas.

He then proceeds to review the History of Carthage, which is the most entertaining as well as instructive part of his performance, because of the near resemblance, as he rightly observes, which Carthage bore to Britain, both in her commerce, opulence, sovereignty of the sea, and her method of carrying on her land-wars by foreign mercenaries. All our author's remarks under this head of his work are just, many of them are uncommon, and some of them new: he has with great force and propriety, established the parallel between the state of England and that of Carthage, and unanswerably shewn, that the ruin of the former was owing to her being unprovided of a national militia. He then vindicates the general character of the Carthaginians, against the misrepresentations of historians, both antient and modern. [The reviewer then quotes from pp. 117–19.]

Our author next proceeds to point out the defects of the plausible policy practised by the Carthaginians, of reserving their own natives for the purposes of commerce, agriculture, and manufacture, and employing foreign mercenaries in their wars.

The author then revives a comparison (which, if we rightly remember, was formerly made use of by Mr. Addison) between Hannibal the

Carthaginian general, and the great Duke of Marlborough, and shews how similar the histories of Carthage and England, in many periods, have been to one another.[1]

The review of the Roman republic, and the parallels he draws between the histories of Rome and England, are striking and just. His sixth chapter treats of the real cause of the rapid declension of the Roman republic, which he very properly observes has never satisfactorily been accounted for, either by Salust or any other historian; and which our author attributes to the introduction of atheistical notions to the doctrine of Epicurus, which he takes from Lucretius: but had he consulted a much better authority, that of Cicero in his treatise De Finibus, he would have seen how very little difference there is between the genuine docrines of Epicurus and those of Christianity.

Had he mentioned Stoicism as the root of Atheism, it had perhaps been more proper, because a true Stoic was a profest Atheist. We are not likewise sure, from some of our author's quotations from Cicero, and his manner of applying them, whether he has not fallen into the mistake which has been common with many great names in literature, that of confounding Cicero's sentiments with those of his interlocutors.

Our author's seventh chapter contains a comparison between the Carthaginians and the Romans.

His eighth treats of revolutions in mixed governments: and his ninth and last chapter treats of the British constitution; all full of curious remarks, all tending to inculcate the necessity of a national militia, and of public virtue, if we are careful to avoid the fates of the Republics he has reviewed.

1. See *The Tatler*, no. 187 (20 June 1710).

APPENDIX C

Thomas Hollis's Copy of Montagu's *Reflections*

Thomas Hollis's copy of the first edition of Montagu's *Reflections* is in the Houghton Library, Harvard.[1] It is bound in Hollis's characteristic manner, with symbols of liberty embossed in the panels of the spine and front board.

Unusually, however, the book was not presented to Harvard by Hollis himself. It found its way into the possession of Charles Eliot Norton, who gave it to Harvard on 3 December 1908. On the verso of a front free endpaper, Norton has written:

> This is one of the volumes bound for Thomas Hollis, with emblematic tooling. It was in this handsome, substantial style that he had the numerous books bound with which he enriched the library of Harvard College.
>
> *Charles Eliot Norton.*
> Shady Hill

On the recto of the next front free endpaper, Hollis transcribed the final lines of Mark Akenside's "On Leaving Holland":

> O FAIR BRITANNIA HAIL! . . . With partial love
> The tribes of men their native seats approve,
> Unjust and hostile to a foreign fame;
> But when from gen'rous minds & manly laws

---

1. Press mark HOU GEN *EC75 H7267 Zz759m2 Lobby IV.3.2.

A Nation holds her prime applause,
There public zeal defies the test of blame.
AKENSIDE.[2]

On the recto of the next front free endpaper, Hollis copied out a passage from Sandys's *Travailes* (in fact, the opening paragraph of Book IV, despite the reference Hollis supplies):

> Now shape we our course for England. *Beloved soil,* as in site . . . wholly from all the World disjoin'd, so in thy felicities. The summer burns thee not, nor does the winter benumb thee: Defended by the sea from wastful incursions, and by the valour of thy Sons from hostile invasions. All other Countries are in some things defective; when thou a provident parent dost minister unto thine whatsoever is usefull: foreign additions but only tending to vanity and luxury. Virtue in thee at the least is praised, and vices are branded with their names, if not pursued with punishments. That Ulysses Who knew many men's manners, and saw many Cities If as sound in judgment as ripe in experience, will confess thee to be the land that floweth with milk and honey.   Sandys's travells, book 3.[3]

On the half title, Hollis has written "virtue" beneath the word "RISE," and "corruption" beneath the word "FALL," linking each word to its sibling by dotted brackets.

There are no annotations in the text itself, but on the rectos of two rear free endpapers, Hollis has transcribed a passage from Conyers Middleton's *Life of Cicero:*

> From their railleries of this kind on the barbarity and misery of our island, one cannot help reflecting on the surprising fate and revolutions of kingdoms: Howe Rome, once the mistress of the World, the seat of arts, empire and glory now lies sunk in sloth, ignorance, and poverty; enslaved to the most cruel, as well as to the most contemptible of Tyrants, superstition and religious imposture: While this remote country, anciently the jest and contempt of the polite Romans, is become the happy seat of Liberty, plenty, and letters, florishing in all the Arts and refinements of civil life;

2. Mark Akenside, Ode VIII, "On Leaving Holland," in *Odes on Several Subjects* (1745), p. 35.

3. [George Sandys], *Sandys Travailes* (1652), p. 170.

yet running perhaps the same course which Rome itself had run before it; from virtuous industry to wealth; from wealth to luxury; from luxury to impatience of discipline and corruption of morals; till by a total degeneracy, and loss of virtue, being grown ripe for destruction, it falls a prey at last to some hardy oppressor, *and with the loss of Liberty, losing every thing else that is valuable,* sinks gradually again into its original barbarity.

> Middleton, Conyers Dr. the excellent in his life of Cicero, edit. 6, vol. I, p. 494, 495[4]

4. Conyers Middleton, *The History of the Life of Marcus Tullius Cicero,* second edition, 3 vols. (1741), vol. 2:102–3.

APPENDIX D

Emendations to the Copy Text

page.line	*error*	*correct reading*
2.25	destruction.	destruction."
10.16	people	peoples
12.11	endered	endeared
16.8	resolution,	resolution.
19.7	to latest	to the latest
21.3	eqally	equally
21.9	givos	gives
29.24	harangued.	harangued,
34.9	gerosity	generosity
36.35	[correct turned "e" in "friendship"]	
37.12	Union	Union.
37.20	Achidamus	Archidamus
39.11	runs	ruins
40.16	conntry,	country,
41.9	Philopater	Philopator
44.12	nationel	national
50, note a	Plut. 85.	Plut. p. 85.
53.11	fafety	safety
63.3	Audocides	Andocides
70, note a	ibid. p. 67.	ibid. 67.
71.2	opon	upon

page.line	error	correct reading
77.25	island,	island.
82.2	justed	justest
85.12	pantomine	pantomime
93.4	luxury!	luxury;
125.13	Speudius	Spendius
133.6	reconcilation	reconciliation
134.13	twen-two	twenty-two
140.8	Maherbal	Maharbal
140.13	Maherbal	Maharbal
144.9	fnndamental	fundamental
163.15	ambassadors.	ambassadors,
164.16	essentialty	essentially
183.17	poulous	populous
187.9	threatres	theatres
204, note b, line 2	ha	he
205.10	Goverument	Government
242, chapter number	IX.	VIII
249, note b	ἀνακύκλωσϛϛ	ἀνακύκλωσις
253.17	consequeutly	consequently
257.3	iufluenced	influenced
262.9	inneffectual	ineffectual

Index

Hortensius, Quintus, 165–66, 168
Hottentots, 202
Houghton Library (Thomas Hollis
 Library), vii–viii, 282–84
human society: causal regularity as
 operating in, 80*n*133; draconian penal
 laws repugnant to, 48; implications
 of leading fashion for, 79–83
Hume, David, xxvi, 43*n*68, 80*n*133
Hylas, 187

Ilotes (or Helots, slave underclass),
 15*n*9, 272
impersonal causes doctrine, 214*n*3
India: British governance of, 227*n*34;
 French and English ambitions in, xi
Interregnum (1649–60), 207
Iphicrates, 78
Ismenias, 104, 108
Isocrates, 108*n*15
Italy: opera of, 86; theatrical forms
 censured, 85*n*147

Jacobite rebellion (1715), 127
Jacobite rebellion (1745–46), xxvi*n*42,
 126*n*28, 260–61
James I (king of England), 255
James II (king of England, and James
 VII of Scotland), 248, 254, 257,
 257*n*14, 260*n*24
Jenkins, Robert, 143*n*79
Jenyns, Soame, 253*n*6
Johnson, Samuel, xiv, xv–xvi, 134*n*51,
 138*n*66, 247*n*9
Jugurtha, 171–72, 172*n*27, 215, 221*n*20
Justin, 77–78, 83, 110–11, 213

Kloster-Zeven, Convention of (1757), xiv
Kolin, battle at, xiv, 131*n*44

Lacedemonians and Laconia, 67,
 83–84, 104, 107, 266–67

Lamachus, 59–60
La Mettrie, Julien Offroy de, 203–4n26
La Rochefoucauld, François, duc de,
 176*n*39
Lartius, Titus, 156, 159
Lasthenes, 90
Latines (Latini), 155, 156, 158, 162, 167
Law, William, 190*n*77
Lawrence, John, 209
Leonidas: crime and defense of,
 30–31; death, 35–36; reign of, 25–26;
 revolution in favor of, 33; vindictive
 rage of, 34–35; women's appeal to,
 29
Leontidas, 104, 105
Lepidus. *See* Aemilius Lepidus,
 Marcus
Leuctra, battle of (371 B.C.), 107, 212
libertinism, 200–201
liberty: civil dissent in, 3–4;
 constitutional protection of, 253;
 degeneration of Roman, 168–70,
 172–73, 183–84; desire for wealth
 as replacing, 172–80; draconian
 penal laws incompatible with,
 48; opposition based in, 180–81;
 oppression's effect on, 98–99;
 origins of English idea of, 99*n*181;
 origins of European idea of,
 245*n*4; power of, 258–59; Roman
 Tribunes and, 163–64; subverted in
 democracy, 54–55
liberum veto principle, 218*n*14
literature: Greek enthusiasm for
 Belles Lettres, 117–18. *See also*
 poetry
Livy: Dionysius's writing compared
 with, 157*n*c; prejudice against
 Carthage, 115; WRITINGS ON:
 aristocracy in Rome, 163–64;
 battle of Cannae, 234–35*n*a, 236;
 Hannibal's victory, 137–39, 140;

This book is set in Adobe Caslon Pro, a modern adaptation by Carol Twombly of faces cut by William Caslon, London, in the 1730s. Caslon's types were based on seventeenth-century Dutch old-style designs and became very popular throughout Europe and the American colonies.

Printed on paper that is acid-free and meets the requirements of the American National Standard for Permanence of Paper for Printed Library Materials, z39.48-1992. ⊗

Book design by Louise OFarrell
Gainesville, Florida
Typography by Apex CoVantage
Madison, Wisconsin
Printed and bound by Worzalla Publishing Company
Stevens Point, Wisconsin

state in, 57–58. *See also specific battles and wars*

Washington, George, xvii

wealth: call to return to equality of, 29–30; equal division in Sparta, 13–15; focus on plundering for, 170–71; increased British, 254; landed versus moneyed interests in, 45n71; provincial governance and accrual of, 74, 168–69, 171–72, 184, 225–27; public virtue replaced with desire for, 172–81; reappearance in Sparta, 24–26, 33–36, 44–45. *See also* corruption; luxury

West Indies: French and English ambitions in, xi

Westminster, Convention of (1756), 210n43

Whig Party: divisions in, xix–xx; factional warfare of, 257n15; history interpreted by, 98n178; "Liberty and Property" slogan of, 253n6; Patriot circle of, xix–xx, 96n176; persistence of opinions based in, xxvi; popular sovereignty doctrine of, 146n4; on

roots of liberty, 99n181; on War of the Spanish Succession, 142n77

William III (king of England), 87n150, 99n182, 257

William III (king of Holland), 249, 254

William IV (king of Holland), 249n13

William V (king of Holland), 249n13

Wolfe, James, xiv

women: lesson of ambition for, 151–52; praise for Carthaginian, 228; praise for Roman, 259; praise for Spartan, 28–29, 33–34, 35, 43–44

Wood, Gordon, xxiv

Xanthus (king), 102

Xenares, 36–37

Xenophon, 14, 17na, 20, 75, 251–52

Xerxes, 64n66

York, Duke of. *See* James II

youth. *See* children and youth

Zama, battle of (202 B.C.), 120n18, 221